Lecture Notes in Computer Scie

Edited by G. Goos, J. Hartmanis and J. van]

T0237809

Springer
Berlin
Heidelberg
New York
Barcelona
Hong Kong
London
Milan
Paris
Singapore
Tokyo

Július Štuller   Jaroslav Pokorný
Bernhard Thalheim   Yoshifumi Masunaga (Eds.)

Current Issues in Databases and Information Systems

East-European Conference on Advances in Databases
and Information Systems Held Jointly with
International Conference on Database Systems
for Advanced Applications, ADBIS-DASFAA 2000
Prague, Czech Republic, September 5-9, 2000
Proceedings

 Springer

Series Editors

Gerhard Goos, Karlsruhe University, Germany
Juris Hartmanis, Cornell University, NY, USA
Jan van Leeuwen, Utrecht University, The Netherlands

Volume Editors

Július Štuller
Academy of Sciences of the Czech Republic, Institute of Computer Science
Pod Vodárenskou věží 2, 182 07 Prague 8, Czech Republic
E-mail: stuller@cs.cas.cz

Jaroslav Pokorný
Charles University, Faculty of Mathematics and Physics
Malostranské nám. 25, 118 00 Prague 1, Czech Republic
E-mail: pokorny@ksi.ms.mff.cuni.cz

Bernhard Thalheim
Brandenburg University of Technology, Computer Science Institute
P.O. Box 101344, 03013 Cottbus, Germany
E-mail: thalheim@informatik.tu-cottbus.de

Yoshifumi Masunaga
Ochanomizu University, Faculty of Science, Department of Information Science
2-1-1 Otsuka, Bunkyo-ku, Tokyo 112-8610, Japan
E-mail: masunaga@is.ocha.ac.jp

Cataloging-in-Publication Data applied for

Die Deutsche Bibliothek - CIP-Einheitsaufnahme

Current issues in databases and information systems : proceedings /
East European Conference on Advances in Databases and Information
Systems held jointly with International Conference on Database Systems
for Advanced Applications, ADBIS-DASFAA 2000, Prague, Czech Republic,
September 5 - 9, 2000. Július Stuller ... (ed.). - Berlin ; Heidelberg ; New York ;
Barcelona ; Hong Kong ; London ; Milan ; Paris ; Singapore ; Tokyo : Springer, 2000
    (Lecture notes in computer science ; Vol. 1884
    ISBN 3-540-67977-4

CR Subject Classification (1998): H.2, H.3, H.4, H.5

ISSN 0302-9743
ISBN 3-540-67977-4 Springer-Verlag Berlin Heidelberg New York

Springer-Verlag Berlin Heidelberg New York
a member of BertelsmannSpringer Science+Business Media GmbH
© Springer-Verlag Berlin Heidelberg 2000
Printed in Germany

Typesetting: Camera-ready by author, data conversion by PTP-Berlin, Stefan Sossna
Printed on acid-free paper   SPIN: 10722450   06/3142   5 4 3 2 1 0

Preface

The East European Conference on Advances in Databases and Information Systems (ADBIS) is the successor of the annual International Workshops with the same title that during 1993–1996 were organized in Russia by the Moscow ACM SIGMOD Chapter. Initiated in St. Petersburg, Russia, in 1997, it continued in Poznan, Poland, in 1998 and in Maribor, Slovenia, in 1999. The ADBIS Conference became the premier database and information systems conference in Eastern Europe. It intended to increase interaction and collaboration between researchers from the East and the West, and to provide an internationally recognized tribune for the presentation of research results.

The International Conference on Database Systems for Advanced Applications (DASFAA) was first held in Seoul, Korea, in 1989 to promote database research and development activities in Asian and Australasian countries. The Special Interest Group of Database Systems (SIGDBS) of the Information Processing Society of Japan (IPSJ) and the Special Interest Group of Data Base (SIGDB) of Korea Information Science Society (KISS) had important roles in the organization of DASFAA. Since that time the DASFAA has been held every two years: Tokyo in 1991, Daejon in 1993, Singapore in 1995, Melbourne in 1997, and Taiwan in 1999. The DASFAA became one of the most prestigious international conferences ever held in Asia or Australasia.

The decision to organize the 2000 ADBIS-DASFAA Symposium was made just before the ADBIS'98. The organizers of the DASFAA Conference nominated Professor Yoshifumi Masunaga as the co-chair from DASFAA for this joint event in 2000. The goal of the symposium was to promote interaction and collaboration between researchers from Eastern Europe and Asia and Australasia, and to provide an international forum for the presentation of research on database theory, the development of advanced data base management systems technologies, and their advanced applications. It is planned that this symposium will be held bi-annually in the years when DASFAA conferences are not organized. In addition, the 2000 ADBIS-DASFAA Symposium is considered to be the regular, Fourth ADBIS annual Conference.

The 2000 ADBIS-DASFAA Symposium took place on 5–8 September 2000, in Prague, Czech Republic. In addition to the usual program, a special session on mobile database technology was organized in collaboration with Sanjay Kumar Madria. Its main objective was to bring together researchers and developers interested in this topic and to enrich classical database themes.

This year the 42 members of the 2000 ADBIS-DASFAA Symposium Program Committee, from 22 countries, evaluated 115 submissions. After a careful review process, followed by a very long discussion at the PC meeting held on 4–5 May 2000 in Cottbus, Germany, 51 papers were selected for presentation at the 2000 ADBIS-DASFAA Symposium: 18 regular papers (14 pages long) and 9 short papers (8 pages) were accepted to be published by Springer-Verlag and

24 papers (10 pages) to be published in the "Proceedings of Challenges". The paper selection for the mobile database technology session was done by its own program committee which accepted 6 papers (3 regular and 3 short) for this volume and 1 paper for the local proceedings.

We obtained 17 submissions from Asia and Australasia from which 12 were either accepted for this volume (6) or for the "Proceedings of Challenges" (6). Thus, we consider the merge of the ADBIS and DASFAA conferences this year a good beginning.

The selected contributions are completed by 3 invited lectures. They are on spatio-temporal databases, database systems as middleware, and advanced processing environment for managing the continuous and semistructured features of multimedia content.

The staging of the 2000 ADBIS-DASFAA Symposium was made possible by the cooperation of many different organizations and people. We would like to express our thanks to all the institutions who actively supported this event, namely:

- Charles University, Faculty of Mathematics and Physics
- Institute of Computer Science (ICS), Academy of Sciences of the Czech Republic
- Brandenburg University of Technology at Cottbus, Computer Science Institute (CSI BUT)

We would also like to thank all members of the Program Committee and the Organizing Committee as well as the Action M Agency for their professional work. Special thanks go to Alfred Hofmann of Springer-Verlag for accepting these proceedings to the LNCS series, to Hana Bílková from ICS who did an excellent job in the completion of the proceedings, to the staff of Bernard Thalheim at CSI BUT for realizing a submission and review system that worked perfectly and for organizing a smooth PC session at Cottbus, and, particularly, to Leonid Kalinichenko for his kind help and advice during the symposium preparation.

July 2000

Yoshifumi Masunaga
Bernhard Thalheim
Jaroslav Pokorný
Július Štuller

2000 ADBIS-DASFAA Organization

The 2000 ADBIS-DASFAA Symposium on Advances in Databases and Information Systems was organized by the Charles University, Faculty of Mathematics and Physics, and the Institute of Computer Science of the Academy of Sciences of the Czech Republic, in cooperation with the Moscow ACM SIGMOD Chapter.

Executive Commitee

Conference Chair:	*Jaroslav Pokorný* (Charles University, Prague, Czech Republic)
Program Co-chairs:	*Yoshifumi Masunaga* (Department of Information Science, Ochanomizu University, Tokyo, Japan)
	Bernhard Thalheim (Computer Science Institute, Brandenburg University of Technology at Cottbus, Germany)
	Július Štuller (Institute of Computer Science, Academy of Sciences of the Czech Republic, Prague, Czech Republic)

Program Committee

Leopoldo Bertossi (Chile)
Yuri Breitbart (USA)
Omran Bukhres (USA)
Albertas Caplinskas (Lithuania)
Wojciech Cellary (Poland)
Arbee Chen (Taiwan)
Jan Chomicki (USA)
Bogdan Czejdo (USA)
Johann Eder (Austria)
Remigijus Gustas (Sweden)
Tomáš Hruška (Czech Republic)
Hannu Jaakkola (Finland)
Leonid Kalinichenko (Russia)
Michal Kopecký (Czech Republic)
Wolfgang Klas (Germany)
Dik-Lum Lee (Hong Kong)
Tok Wang Ling (Singapore)
Yannis Manolopoulos (Greece)
Yoshifumi Masunaga (Japan)
Tomaz Mohoric (Slovenia)
Tadeusz Morzy (Poland)

Pavol Návrat (Slovakia)
Dennis Ng (USA)
Nikolay Nikitchenko (Ukraine)
Boris Novikov (Russia)
Maria Orlowska (Australia)
Seog Park (Korea)
Oscar Pastor (Spain)
Antonín Říha (Czech Republic)
Colette Rolland (France)
Ivan Rozman (Slovenia)
Nand Lal Sarda (India)
Klaus-Dieter Schewe (Germany)
Július Štuller (Czech Republic)
Kazimierz Subieta (Poland)
Bernhard Thalheim (Germany)
Gottfried Vossen (Germany)
Benkt Wangler (Sweden)
Tatjana Welzer (Slovenia)
Viacheslav Wolfengagen (Russia)
Vladimir Zadorozhny (USA)
Alexander Zamulin (Russia)

Program Committee for Mobile Database Technology

Bharat Bhargava (USA)
Panos Chrysanthis (USA)
Margaret H. Dunham (USA)
Sumi Halal (USA)
Abdelkader Hameurlain (France)
Vijay Kumar (USA)
Mikhail Kogalovsky (Russia)
Sergei Kuznetsov (Russia)
Wang-Chien Lee (USA)

Wee-Keong Ng Nanyang (Singapore)
Evaggelia Pitoura (Greece)
George Samara (Cyprus)
Nand Lal Sarda (India)
Krishnamurthy Vidyasankar (Canada)
Radek Vingralek (USA)
Gottfried Vossen (Germany)
Ouri Wolfson (USA)
Arkady Zaslavsky (Australia)

ADBIS Steering Commitee

Chair:	Leonid Kalinichenko (Russian Academy of Sciences, Russia)
Members:	Andras Benczur (Hungary)
	Radu Bercaru (Romania)
	Albertas Caplinskas (Lithuania)
	Johann Eder (Austria)
	Janis Eiduks (Latvia)
	Hele-Mai Haav (Estonia)
	Mirjana Ivanovic (Yugoslavia)
	Mikhail Kogalovsky (Russia)
	Yannis Manopoulos (Greece)
	Rainer Manthey (Germany)
	Tadeusz Morzy (Poland)
	Pavol Návrat (Slovakia)
	Boris Novikov (Russia)
	Jaroslav Pokorný (Czech Republic)
	Anatoly Stogny (Ukraine)
	Tatjana Welzer (Slovenia)
	Viacheslav Wolfengagen (Russia)

DASFAA Steering Commitee

Chair:	Yahiko Kambayashi (Kyoto University, Japan)
Members:	Arbee L.P. Chen (Taiwan)
	Tok Wang Ling (Singapore)
	Fred Lochovsky (Hong Kong)
	Yoshifumi Masunaga (Japan)
	Seog Park (Korea)
	Ron Sacks-Davis (Australia)
	Kunitoshi Tsuruoka (Japan)
	Kyhun Um (Korea)
	Kyu-Young Whang (Korea)

Organizing Commitee

Chair:	Jaroslav Pokorný (Charles University, Prague, Czech Republic)
Members:	Martin Beran (Charles University, Prague)
	Hana Bílková (ICS, Prague)
	Andrea Kutnarová (Action M Agency, Prague)
	Günter Millahn (CSI BUT, Cottbus)
	Július Štuller (ICS, Prague)
	Lucie Vachová (Action M Agency, Prague)
	Milena Zeithamlová (Action M Agency, Prague)

Sponsoring Institutions

INTAX, s.r.o.
Hewlett Packard, s.r.o.
KOMIX, s.r.o.
Smart4U Ltd.
DCIT, s.r.o.

Table of Contents

An Advanced Processing Environment for Managing the Continuous and Semistructured Features of Multimedia Content

Shojiro Nishio[1,4], Katsumi Tanaka[2], Yasuo Ariki[3], Shinji Shimojo[4], Masahiko Tsukamoto[1], Masatoshi Arikawa[5], Keishi Tajima[2], and Kaname Harumoto[4]

[1] Department of Information Systems Engineering, Osaka University
2-1 Yamadaoka, Suita, Osaka 565-0871, Japan
[2] Department of Computer and Systems Engineering, Kobe University
Rokkodai, Nada, Kobe 657-8501, Japan
[3] Department of Electronics and Informatics, Ryukoku University
1-5 Yokotani, Ohe-cho, Seta, Otsu 520-2194, Japan
[4] Cybermedia Center, Osaka University
5-1 Mihogaoka, Ibaraki, Osaka 567-0047, Japan
[5] Center for Spatial Information Science (CSIS), The University of Tokyo
4-6-1 Komaba, Meguro-ku, Tokyo 153-8904, Japan

Abstract. The remarkable advances made in computer and communication hardware/software system technologies have made it possible for us to use multimedia data for many purposes in various service areas. Considering the importance of developing an advanced processing environment for the acquisition, management, retrieval, creation, and utilization of large amounts of multimedia content, the "Advanced Multimedia Content Processing (AMCP)" research project has been started in Japan, focussing on the management of the continuous and semistructured features of multimedia content. In this paper, we will present a part of research results achieved by this project, along with the process from the first time the multimedia content is acquired/organized until it is delivered to and presented at the client side.

1 Introduction

With the remarkable advances made in computer and communication hardware/software system technologies, we can now easily obtain large volume of multimedia data through advanced computer networks, store and handle them in our own personal disk devices. Sophisticated and integrated *multimedia content processing technologies*, which are essential to building a highly advanced information-based society, are attracting ever-increasing attention in various service areas, including broadcasting, publishing, medical treatment, entertainment, and communications. The prime concerns of these technologies are how to acquire multimedia data from the real world, how to automatically organize and

J. Štuller et al. (Eds.): ADBIS-DASFAA 2000, LNCS 1884, pp. 1–20, 2000.

store these obtained data in databases for sharing and reuse, and how to generate and create new, attractive multimedia content using the stored data.

Considering the importance of developing an advanced processing environment for the acquisition, management, retrieval, creation, and utilization of large amounts of multimedia content, we started in 1997 the five years research project titled "Advanced Multimedia Content Processing (AMCP)" under the support of a new farsighted program entitled "Research for the Future (RFTF)." This RFTF program, launched in 1996, is funded through a capital investment made by the Japanese government to promote and expand the frontiers of scientific research. Currently, our AMCP project is composed of fourteen members who are from four different universities.

The AMCP project aims at covering the following particular areas:

(1) Dynamic multimedia data modeling and intelligent structuring of content based on active, bottom-up, and self-organized strategies.
(2) Access architecture, querying facilities, and distribution mechanisms for multimedia content.
(3) Synthesis of virtual and augmented real environments using large amounts of multimedia data for the creation of multimedia content and the applications of such technology to mobile computing environments.

Artistic and innovative applications through the active use of multimedia content are also subjects of the project. In this paper, we will present some major results of research obtained by this project.

The rest of this paper will be organized as follows. In section 2, important properties of multimedia content are discussed, where its continuous and semistructured features are taken up, and then we briefly explain how research in this project manages these features. In section 3, we discuss the multimedia data organization by means of media integration. After that, in section 4, we discuss our approach in the organization and retrieval of Web data in WWW (World Wide Web) systems. Discussion on the algebraic filtering framework for continuous media will be given in section 5 followed by the discussion on access control for inline objects in Web data in section 6. After discussing our spatial querying and browsing environment in section 7, we give the conclusion of this paper in section 8.

2   Important Properties of Multimedia Content

When we think about storing, sharing, and retrieving multimedia content, "continuous" and "semistructured" are two key features that should get more serious consideration. This is because, without appropriate handling, these features could prohibit us from getting valuable information from the content. However, if we could manage them in an appropriate way, it is possible for us to perform more advanced operations including query and search on the multimedia content.

2.1 Continuity Feature

James Monaco (1981)[1] said that "There are no basic units of meaning in film". Although the above quote is describing his view as a film and media critic, the quote is exactly pointing at the continuity feature of film, and thus fit into our discussion here. For examples, in (digitized) video data, any video interval could become a result of searching. Therefore, any interval could become an information unit, thus it could be considered as one-dimensional (1-D) *continuous media*. Similar case also applies to audio data. However, the principle of continuity in multimedia is broader and not limited only to this obvious fact. In general, the continuity feature of multimedia data could be found at least in three aspects, i.e., *spatial continuity*, *time continuity* and *quality continuity*.

In spatial data like two-dimensional (2-D) map or three-dimensional (3-D) virtual space, any space could become a result of searching. Any space, therefore, could become an information unit, thus it could be considered as 2-D or 3-D continuous media. Including that of video and audio data, we call this continuity as spatial continuity. Later in this paper, we will introduce the *algebraic retrieval* method of fragmentarily indexed video which can handle efficiently the spatial continuity feature in providing answers to queries on video data. Furthermore, we will also introduce our spatial querying and browsing environment proposed for presenting multimedia data, including video data, in 3-D context.

Time continuity is closely related to the timeliness needed in presenting the content to the user. Timeliness and synchronization are imposed in order to ensure smooth and meaningful flow of contents to the user. In this paper, we will discuss *WebQoS* that exploits the feature of composite objects in Web data in the *Quality of Service* (QoS) control in order to ensure the time continuity (timeliness requirement) of Web data presented to the user.

Quality continuity is related to the access management regarding the presentation quality of multimedia content. So far, research in access management assumes that users have knowledge about the schema of database, and the types of data involved are of simple text or numerical data. Since handling such data types costs almost nothing and it could be done both in the client and server, the access performance and security have been the main problems. Accordingly, the approaches of existing access management methods are based on *all-or-nothing* principle.

However, the case is different when we are dealing with multimedia content. Besides the high cost of processing multimedia data, in general, users will determine if they want to access the multimedia data after viewing it at least once in any quality. When we are considering the commercialization of multimedia content, it is necessary to provide price based *Level of Detail* (LoD) management. Furthermore, when we are dealing with multimedia object in 3-D context,

---

[1] James Monaco is author or editor of more than a dozen books on film and media, published in more than 35 editions, including *American Film Now*, *The New Wave*, and *The Film Encyclopedia*. He is the founder of Baseline, the worldwide information source for the entertainment business. He is also well-known as a pioneer of the electronic publishing industry.

it is important to provide a smooth change in LoD according to the distance from the object, especially, if we want to support walk-through in virtual space. Accordingly, in handling multimedia content, quality continuity is among the important aspects to consider. Later, we will discuss our approach in controlling LoD in our spatial querying and browsing environment.

2.2   Semistructured Feature

In this paper, we mean the semistructured feature of data as the fact that the data do not have a unified schema like *tables* in a database, but elements that can be used in realizing schema-like organization exist in the data. By exploiting such an organization, to some degree, we can perform operations such as query and search which originally depend on the existence of schema. Below, we will explain this feature in more detail by using video and Web data as examples of semistructured data.

Video is composed of *frames* or *shots*. For the purpose of editing or authoring, frames or *video intervals* (an interval is composed of one or more consecutive frames or shots) are assigned with *keywords*. In this point, each frame or interval already has a kind of structure (for example, *grouping* is possible by using keywords). Though any frame or interval could be assigned with multiple keywords, in general there is no particular rule in assigning keywords. Considering this fact, we could classify video as semistructured data.

On the other hand, with some elaboration, it is possible to use these keywords in organizing frames and intervals in video data, and later use this organization in the structure (schema) dependent processing such as query and search. Considering this fact, we can see the video data with keywords as semistructured data.

The case is also similar with Web pages. Web pages usually consist of text and graphics. In general, each page is written following a structure determined by the author. However, it is a rare case that all pages are designed following a specific structure (this is because the original goal of providing information in Web pages is generally to disseminate information on the *Internet*. Therefore, the clarity of information and the artistic aspect are the most important motivation behind the author work, and for that goal the structure of pages is not the necessary condition). Considering this fact, we could classify Web pages as semistructured data.

On the other hand, Web pages generally contain also *links* to other pages for navigating the viewer to the related pages. Considering the existence of links in Web pages, we thus can see the Web data as a huge graph containing Web pages connected by links. By traversing nodes in this graph, we could perform search or query to find the information of our interest. According to this fact, we can see Web pages also as semistructured data.

As we can see in the above mentioned examples, data which are involved in the multimedia content presentation are generally semistructured and we need to do some operations on these data before they can be used in processing queries or search requests. Related to the semistructured aspect of multimedia content, in this paper, we will discuss our approaches in indexing multimedia content by using speech recognition technique, the organization and retrieval of Web and video data, and the visualization of multimedia data in 3-D context.

3   Multimedia Data Organization by Media Integration

3.1   Organization of Continuous Media

Contents stored in digital libraries or museums can be accessed quickly using their manually constructed table of contents or indices. On the other hand, broadcast news, animation, drama and movies usually have no table of contents or indices, so that data have to be accessed sequentially. To deal with such a problem in handling continuous media, a content based access architecture is required.

In video images, an index corresponds to an event that occurs in the video image. On the other hand, a table of contents corresponds to a hierarchical structure of topics, like chapters and sections of books. In order to access the continuous media, these indices and tables of contents have to be produced via automatic analysis on video and audio data. This is called *organization of continuous media* which mainly includes functions of indexing and topic segmentation.

A typical example of such organization of continuous media is a *news on demand* (NOD) system. Since TV news programs are broadcast to all over the world through the digitization, TV viewers are required to select and watch the most interesting news in a short time. In order to satisfy this requirement, we are now developing an NOD system with functions such as automatic topic segmentation, retrieval of related topics and summarization. These functions can be realized based on the organization of continuous media.

3.2   Approach to the Organization

In order to realize the indexing and topic segmentation in an NOD system, indices such as words, objects and shots have to be extracted automatically from audio and video data at first. Then they will be meaningfully integrated into topics. By these indexing and topic segmentation, new functions, such as cross media retrieval which can retrieve the content across the different media, could be prepared.

Fig. 1 shows the organization process of continuous media. Signal data are organized into contents through the processes of "Segmentation & classification", "Recognition & indexing", "Association in time and space", and finally "Construction of topic thesaurus" as shown in the left hand side. According to these organization processes, the signal data are converted into concept through pattern, symbol and topic as shown in the right hand side.

At each level of data presentation, the corresponding retrieval is available. For example, at the signal level, specific images, music or noises can be retrieved based on *signal processing*. At the pattern level, human faces and speech are retrieved using *pattern extraction techniques*. An example at the symbol level is a retrieval of the president's face and speech based on *pattern recognition techniques*. At the topic level, the president's speech concerning his/her economic policy or highlight scenes in TV sports program can be retrieved.

Finally at the concept level, the upper or lower topics as well as similar or opposite topics will be retrieved. Here the upper topics mean not only the summaries but also the topics at abstract level such as "economy" to "bankruptcy". In the same way, the lower topics mean not only the details but also the topics at concrete level. These retrieval of opposite, upper and lower topics based on automatic construction of topic thesaurus rather than summaries or detail is unique approach as compared to *Informedia-II* being developed at CMU. Informedia-II focuses on the distillation of information across multiple video paragraphs and visualization over time and space to understand how events evolve and are correlated over time and geographically [23].

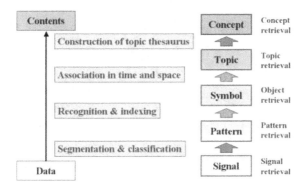

Fig. 1. Organization process of continuous media.

3.3   Media Integration

(a) Integration of Speaker Indexing and Speech Transcription

We have developed a system which can automatically index and classify TV news stories into 10 topics based on a speech transcribing technique [3]. After transcribing the spoken news stories, pre-defined keywords are searched and the news stories are classified based on the keywords.

In general, news speech includes reporter speech as well as announcer speech. The announcer speech is clear but the reporter speech is sometimes noisy due to wind or environmental noises so that the transcription accuracy for the reporter speech is lower than that for the announcer speech. Therefore, if the speech transcribing process is limited only to the announcer speech, the processing time can be reduced without decreasing the news classification accuracy.

From this point of view, our system can automatically divide the TV news speech into speaker sections at first and then perform indexing in real time who is speaking. This can be realized by using a technique of speaker verification. However, the speaker verification technique is sensitive to the time lapse. To solve this problem, speaker models are not prepared in advance but are constructed in a course of indexing in self-organization mode.

We verified the effectiveness of our proposed methods by carrying out an experiment of extracting and transcribing only the announcer speech and then classifying the news stories into 10 topics. At present, 75% accuracy of news story classification is obtained. This system is applicable to meeting documents as shown in Fig. 2.

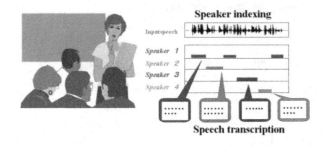

Fig. 2. Integration of speaker indexing and speech transcribing.

(b) Integration of Video OCR and Speech Transcription

We have also developed a system of cross media retrieval for TV news as shown in Fig. 3. At first, the video caption is recognized through video OCR (Optical Character Recognition). Then a vector is constructed for a video caption using the recognized nouns. Next, speech transcription of a news story (called *spoken document* hereafter) is converted into a vector using extracted important words.

The widely used *vector space model* counts only the number of common words between documents, but it does not take into consideration the similarity between non-common words. This causes a decrease of the retrieval performance in a case where the number of words included in video captions is small. To solve this problem, *word distance* has to be computed based on similarity between words.

Though mutual information and co-occurrence are usually used as the similarity measure, they show the similarity between words in only 1-D space. On the other hand, word distance is defined as the distance between words in a 3-D space of mutual information, TF (Term Frequency) and IDF (Inverse Document Frequency). We call such a 3-D space as a *word space*.

The method to compute the inner product of two vectors, a vector for video caption and a vector for spoken document, is formalized by incorporating this word distance into vector space model. Our experiments to retrieve the spoken documents by the video caption demonstrated 80% recall and 80% precision. This is extremely higher than the original vector space model.

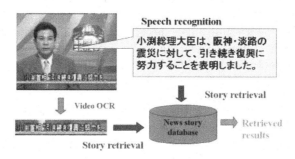

Fig. 3. Integration of video OCR and speech transcribing.

4   Web Data Organization and Retrieval

One of the most popular and the most important example of multimedia content is Web data. Currently, a huge amount of information resources are stored as Web data, and in some sense, Web is the largest database that we have ever had. The Web data, however, have a property which makes them very different from data in traditional databases. In traditional databases, data are created in a *well-organized* form in the first place so that they can easily be retrieved by using queries. On the other hand, the Web data are usually organized mainly for good presentation in the browsers, and the creators of the Web data are not necessarily very conscious of the retrieval by queries. As a result, the structure of the Web data does not necessarily reflect the intended logical structure, and sometimes the necessary information for queries is not described as explicitly as in the traditional databases.

The lack of explicit logical structure causes difficulty in retrieving Web data by using queries. We first need to extract the necessary logical structures from the given structures in the Web data, such as HTML (HyperText Markup Language) tags or link structures. Those structures are, however, very heterogeneous, and thus, Web data are semistructured data. This heterogeneity also causes difficulty in extracting necessary information. We need techniques to extract logical structure which is described only implicitly and heterogeneously.

In this section, we discuss the techniques of extracting three kinds of logical structures: (1) hierarchical standard routes in Web sites, (2) logical data units in Web graphs, and (3) components correspondence within Web pages.

4.1   Hierarchical Standard Routes in Web Sites

Web data consist of pages and only one kind of links connecting them. Links are, however, used in various meanings. Some links jump to pages including related information (*jump links*) and some are meant to be the standard routes going through pages in a Web site (*route links*). Links go from a page back to some previous pages on the route to the page (the links are often assigned with anchor strings such as "back" or "top") are also often used (*back links*).

If we extract only route links, the graph structure of most Web sites are reduced to one or multiple hierarchies. We designed an algorithm that identifies hierarchical route links within a Web site [9]. Identifying such a hierarchical structure is useful for helping users when browsing, and furthermore for identifying logical data units as will be discussed later.

Here, we explain only the outline of the algorithm. For each page, the algorithm selects, based on heuristics, one incoming link that is the most likely to be the route link to the page (or it selects no link if the page is recognized as one of the roots of the hierarchies). The concatenation of all selected links corresponds to the hierarchical structure of the Web site. We determine, incoming links in a page are likely to be the route link in the following priority order:

1. downward links (links from pages in ancestor directories),
2. intradirectory links (links from pages in the same directory), and
3. sibling links (links from pages in incomparable directories).

We determine, neither upward links (links from pages in subdirectories) nor intersite links (links from pages on different Web sites) can be route links.

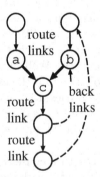

Fig. 4. Finding Route Links

When there are multiple candidates of the same priority, we select one of them so that there would be the largest number of links going back from the children pages to the ancestor pages of the selected link. For example, if the links denoted by bold arrows in Fig. 4 are candidates for the route link of the page c, we select the link from the page **b**. This decision is taken based on the fact that the existence of many back links over a link, in many cases, suggests that the link is certainly a route link.

4.2   Logical Data Units in Web

In most existing search engines for Web data, the data units for retrieval are individual pages. As mentioned before, however, Web pages are often organized not for expressing logical structure. As a result, one logical document discussing one topic is often organized into a hierarchy of pages connected via route links. In this way, a logical data unit in Web data is not a page but is a connected subgraph corresponding to one logical document. When we use individual pages as the data units, conjunctive queries with multiple keywords sometimes fail to retrieve an appropriate document if those keywords happen to appear in different pages of that document.

To solve this problem, we developed a method to identify connected subgraphs corresponding to logical data units in Web data [16,17]. By using those subgraphs as the querying data units, we can avoid the problem of conjunctive queries above. Our method identifies such subgraphs in two steps. First, we extract hierarchical structure of Web sites by using the method explained above. After that, we divide those hierarchies into connected subgraphs based on the similarity of appearing words in neighboring pages. In the partitioning, our algorithm allows overlapping among subgraphs because logical data units in real Web data are often not disjoint.

The approach mentioned above statically divides Web graph into logical data units. Another approach is to dynamically find minimal subgraphs that include all query keywords [5,8,18]. The advantage of this approach is that we can always get "best N results" [8]. Some of minimal subgraphs, however, may not be part of one logical data unit. To give priority to subgraphs that are more likely to be part of a single document, we proposed ranking methods based on the *localities* of query keywords [5,18]. If the localities of query keywords in a subgraph greatly overlap, this subgraph is estimated to have a higher rank. We examine both the locality of words across the pages and the locality of words within each page.

4.3   Components Correspondence within Web Pages

The Web browsing operation is easy for experienced computer users, but it is still difficult for inexperienced users and ordinary TV audience. Current Web browsers enforce users to have *activeness* and knowledge about computers. In order to acquire necessary information from Web data, users must read pages and navigate themselves through hyperlinks by clicking anchors. We call such a browsing interface a *read and click interface*. On the other hand, TV audience just need to watch and listen to the TV programs, and acquire necessary information in a passive manner. Our idea is to introduce a new *passive* Web browsing interface called a *watch and listen interface*.

We have implemented a prototype system of such an interface for Web pages [19]. Given an URL, this system analyzes the tag structures of the Web page of the URL, and transforms the page into a TVML (TV Program Making Language) script describing a TV-program, which is then executed by a TVML player [6,22]. In that TV program, CG (Computer Graphics) characters in 3-D space spell out the text portion of the page, and images appearing in that page are shown one by one on the panel in the same space. The appearance of images is synchronized with the characters' speech, and CG characters explain the images by playing several performances (e.g., pointing out to the panel).

In order to transform the data of ordinary HTML pages into TV-programs in TVML, we need the following techniques:

- text summarization,
- text conversion into speech with behaviors of animation characters,
- discovery of *components correspondence* between images and text explaining them,
- synchronized presentation of images and characters' speech/behaviors, and
- several presentation techniques such as camera movements.

Even if the technologies mentioned above have been developed, the automatic transformation of HTML pages into TV-like programs could not be done completely. This is due to the fact that HTML and its successor XML (eXtensible Markup Language) are not invented to describe data that will be shown to the users in TV-program-like presentation. Therefore, in addition to the full-automatic translation approach, we also consider a semi-automatic approach, where the page authors are provided with an authoring mechanism where the authors can partially use automatic translation, and can also explicitly specify necessary information [11]. We also proposed a new markup language called Scripting-XML (S-XML) which extends the XML to facilitate the description of Web data which are appropriate for passive browsing.

5 Algebraic Filtering Framework for Continuous Media

In this section, an *algebraic framework* for filtering fragmentarily indexed video data is discussed. We have been focussing on how to compute semantically meaningful video intervals dynamically from the fragmentarily indexed shots, when queries are issued. Our goal is to develop a new framework for logical query optimizations of video queries, which retrieve meaningful intervals from such fragmentarily indexed video data. We proposed algebraic operations, what we call *glue join* operations, to compose longer intervals from short indexed shots [13,14]. These operations compose as many *answer intervals* (i.e., the intervals that become the query results) as possible. However, answer intervals may be of very long ones, thus they may contain too many irrelevant shots as well. Therefore, we propose *selection* operations with several *filter* functions which can be applied to discard irrelevant intervals from the answer set. Both glue join and selection operations possess certain algebraic properties that are useful for logical query oprimization. Especially, we obtained a necessary and sufficient condition under which a class of selection operations can be *pushed down* in a given query.

For I, a set of subintervals of a given video data, and for F, a predicate which maps a video interval into *true* or *false*, a selection from I by the predicate F is defined as a subset I' of I such that I' includes all and only intervals satisfying F. That is, the selection from I by F, denoted by $\sigma_F(I)$, is defined below:

$$\sigma_F(I) = \{i | i \in I, F(i) = true\}$$

Hereafter, the predicate F is also called a filter of the selection σ_F. There are several kinds of practically useful filters. Among them, we show some basic filters in Table 1. By using the interval logic filters shown below, it is possible to represent *Allen's interval logic* [1].

Table 1. Primitive Filters

name	notation	meaning
keyword selection	keyword $= k$	the interval has a keyword k
maximum length	length $\leq c$	the interval length $\leq c$
maximum noise length	maxnoise$(K) \leq c$ for a set K of keywords	the length of the longest noise $\leq c$
interval logic	$S(k_a) \leq S(k_b)$ for keywords k_a, k_b etc.	each interval with k_a start earlier than all intervals with k_b

The *interval glue join* is an operation to connect two intervals (together with an interval exists in between). Let x and y be subintervals of a given video v. Intuitively, the interval glue join of x and y, denoted by $x \bowtie y$, is a minimum subinterval of v that contains x and y.

Given two sets X and Y of subintervals of a video v, *pairwise glue join* of X and Y, denoted by $X \bowtie Y$, is defined as a set of video intervals yielded by taking glue joins of every combination of an element of X and an element of Y in a pairwise manner. That is,

$$X \bowtie Y = \{x \bowtie y | x \in X, y \in Y\}$$

Given two sets X and Y of subintervals of a video v, *powerset glue join* of X and Y, denoted by $X \bowtie^* Y$, is defined as a set of video intervals that are yielded by applying glue join operation to an arbitrary number (but not 0) of elements in X and Y. More formally, it is defined as follows:

$$X \bowtie^* Y = \{\bowtie (X' \cup Y') | X' \subseteq X, Y' \subseteq Y,$$
$$X' \neq \phi \text{ and } Y' \neq \phi\}$$

where $\bowtie \{i_1, i_2, \ldots, i_n\} = i_1 \bowtie \ldots \bowtie i_n$. Fig. 5 illustrates an example of powerset glue join operation.

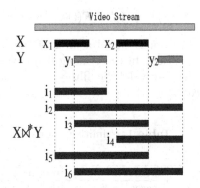

Fig. 5. Powerset Glue Join between X and Y

For arbitrary interval sets X, Y, Z, the powerset glue join satisfies the following algebraic properties [20]:

- Commutativity: $X \bowtie^* Y = Y \bowtie^* X$
- Associativity: $(X \bowtie^* Y) \bowtie^* Z = X \bowtie^* (Y \bowtie^* Z)$
- $X \bowtie^* X = X \bowtie X$
- Pairwise glue reduction: $X \bowtie^* Y = (X \bowtie Y) \bowtie (X \bowtie Y)$

If a filter F satisfies the following condition for any intervals sets X and Y, then we call F an *optimizable filter:*

$$\sigma_F(X \bowtie Y) = \sigma_F(\sigma_F(X) \bowtie \sigma_F(Y))$$

Then if F is optimizable, by the *pairwise glue reduction* property, we can process the following selection and powerset glue join expression more efficiently by using the following transformation:

$$\sigma_F(X \bowtie^* Y) = \sigma_F(\sigma_F(\sigma_F(X) \bowtie \sigma_F(X))$$
$$\bowtie \sigma_F(\sigma_F(Y) \bowtie \sigma_F(Y)))$$
$$= \sigma_F(\sigma_F(\sigma_F(X) \bowtie \sigma_F(Y))$$
$$\bowtie \sigma_F(\sigma_F(X) \bowtie \sigma_F(Y)))$$

Since optimizable filter we defined can be incorporated with the glue join operations as the expression above, at the initial stage of query processing, we can discard intervals that will eventually become useless for computing relevant answer intervals. As for the optimizable filters. We have the following: A filter F is an optimizable filter if and only if the following holds:

$$(\forall i, i' \text{ s.t. } F(i) = true \text{ and } i' \subseteq i)(F(i') = true)$$

The three filters – *maximum length, maximum noise length,* and *interval logic* filters are easily shown to be optimizable filters. Furthermore, the class of optimizable filters is closed under *conjunction* and *disjunction*. On the other hand, the class of optimizable filters is not closed under negation.

6   Controlling QoS of Web Pages

For managing the multimedia content, the content delivering system is one of the important system components. Since the volume of multimedia content is usually very large and the network bandwidth is limited, a QoS control mechanism is required to meet the users' requests under the available network resource. In this section, we discuss such a control mechanism for Web pages.

In the WWW, impressive information can be provided by embedding a large number of *inline objects* such as still images, animated images, and background sounds in a Web page. However, if the available network bandwidth between the client and the Web server is insufficient, it takes a long time for a client to get all inline objects in a Web page. Users often terminate the downloading of the Web page before it is completed.

To solve this problem, *total page transmission time* should be controlled so that users are not irritated. Controlling *transmission order* of inline objects is also important because inline objects in a Web page generally appear on Web browsers in the order of transmission. Therefore, we define a language to specify the total transmission time and transmission order of inline objects, and propose a new transfer protocol, HTSP (Hypertext Streaming Protocol), which is an extension of HTTP (Hypertext Transfer Protocol). In the proposed language, content providers can describe the *total transmission time threshold* and the transmission order of inline objects in the head section of the HTML document. More detailed specifications on how the quality of inline objects should be controlled can be described within the inline objects themselves [4]. HTSP is used to realize the transmission order control of inline objects [12]. The new method, MGET, is introduced in HTSP to retrieve multiple objects with specified order by a single request.

Fig. 6 presents an example of the proposed specification. We show how the inline objects are transmitted based on the description. This WWW page contains one important image and one picture consisting of three interlaced images and one animated image. Moreover, a background sound and many other images are embedded. Based on the description, the important image is transferred first. Next, four partial images are transferred in parallel so that it gives the users a quick preview of the full picture. After that, the background sound, the rest of the frames of the animated image and other images whose transmission order is

```html
<html>
  <meta name="TransmissionTime" content="30">
  <meta name="AllowAll" content="ToJpegIfLowQuality">
  <dto rest="par" cache="ordered">
    <seq>
      <xfer object="B"/>
      <par slice="10">
        <xfer object="C" volume="1f"/>
        <xfer object="D"/>
        <xfer object="E"/>
        <xfer object="F"/>
      </par>
      <xfer object="A"/>
      <xfer object="C" volume="rest"/>
    </seq>
  </dto>
  <bgsound src="bgm.midi" id="A">
</head>
<body>
  ......
  <img src="important.jpg" id="B" priority="High">
  <img src="animation.gif" id="C">
  <img src="interlace1.gif" id="D">
  <img src="interlace2.gif" id="E">
  <img src="interlace3.gif" id="F">
  ......
</body>
</html>
```

Fig. 6. Example of the specification of transmission time and order.

not specified are transferred sequentially. Note that the quality of these inline objects may be reduced if they cannot be delivered in the specified transmission time threshold, i.e., within 30 seconds. In such a case, however, the quality of the important image tend to be preserved or slightly reduced, regardless of quality of other objects.

7 Spatial Querying and Browsing Environment

In this section, we discuss querying and browsing environments for multimedia data by using spatial data representations.

7.1 Problems in Media Fusion

As mentioned earlier, multimedia data consist of various kinds of data such as texts, images, videos, and 3-D polygons. As a result, it is difficult to represent such data in a uniform manner while keeping the support for users to easily recognize their continuous and semistructured features. We consider that spatial representation is a solution for such a problem because of the following reasons:

- Human vision is the most dominant sense organ of human beings. Spatial visualization of multimedia data can improve users' capability in recognizing the data in a vision-based manner.
- It is easy for human beings to remember something by associating it with a location of the space in the real world.
- 3-D space provides three dimensions of continuous axes which are suitable for representing continuous features of multimedia data.

In the viewpoint of retrieval and browsing, the main problems that should be solved in our project are the following two points:

- How to display multimedia data in a compact manner. It is not appropriate for users to see huge amount of data at a time in a single space. It causes a lot of burden to users to explore the space and choose the meaningful data.
- How to display multimedia data in 3-D context. For example, video data are constructed from 2-D images and the time dimension is generally incompatible with 3-D space.

The first problem could be solved by the scale change. Virtual space can be displayed in any scale and, according to the scale, any object in the virtual space can change its LoD, i.e., how precisely it is described. For the second problem, there are several possible answers. One is the use of geographical information. That is, each video frame is pasted on the virtual space which models the real space at the corresponding place where it is taken. The problem is more difficult in the case where data are fragmentary and fine-grained. In the following subsections, we show our approaches in dealing with these two problems.

7.2   Approaches to Spatial Level of Detail Control

The notion of LoD is the basic form of information. It is applied not only to image data such as photographs and computer graphics but also to text. The attribute data for spatial object may be a set of text, keywords with varying importance, or a feature vector composed of weighted numerical values derived from *tf-idf method* [15] corresponding to keywords characteristic of the object. Some objects may have detailed data and some may have only coarse data. The data are visualized in a 3-D space with the extent determined by an algorithm we developed in the *InfoLOD* system. While *spatial glue operation*, i.e., an extended glue operation, specifies the regions where the objects which the user wishes to view could be found, the algorithm controls the visualization of the attribute information of individual objects existing in the retrieved regions. In this algorithm, we mainly use two parameters, the orientation of a view and the distance to the object. By combining these parameters, users can change the

LoD of the objects according to their movement in the virtual space as shown in Fig. 7.

We also applied a similar mechanism to a real-time video. The system is called *Name-at*. The video camera parameters, such as *pan* and *tilt* values, are controlled by remote users through the network. Semistructured information, such as text, is associated with the objects shown in the video (camera parameters in a practical sense). The video whose LoD is controlled according to the zoom parameter of the camera is overlaid with the associated information. Fig. 8 is an example of this system. The method can also be applied to a stored video. In that case, it is impossible to directly control camera parameters by users' requests, and therefore, it should be simulated based on the analysis and the calculation of the stored video data.

Fig. 7. InfoLOD System

Fig. 8. Name-at System

7.3 Approaches to Fine-Grained Spatial Data

A virtual space becomes scalable when it is divided into fine-grained scenes, i.e., it can be represented by a set of small descriptions of spaces that are tractable by a computer. In this case, the following three points should be considered:

– How to express data in a simple manner.
– How to simplify the topological association of each scene.
– How to make the management of each scene independent.

A typical approach to the first problem is using the box shape of a subspace. If the users' activities in the space are essentially of 2-D actions only, a rectangular or square shape of the floor can be used. Since we can easily put such boxes (or rectangles) side by side to construct larger regions of space, this approach can provide answer also to the second problem. In this case, the topological association will be defined by side-sharing. Many associated regions may form a grid topology, which means each region can be identified by the row and the column numbers. Although the grid topology is easy to manage, it does not solve the last problem. The global coordinate of the region arrangement should be defined beforehand. The division and merging of regions cannot be done locally. Furthermore, two different spaces cannot be easily combined.

(a)   (b)

Fig. 9. IBNR System

A possible solution to the last problem is the scene-based approach. That is, each region can be independently constructed without assuming any global view, and multiple regions are linked together to construct the local association, or topology. We call such a unit of region a *scene*. If the scene shape is rectangle, four links are typically defined where each link corresponds to each edge of a rectangle. Note that this is different from the grid approach because it does not have any global constraints.

When we visualize a scene in the scene-based approach, we may take several other scenes into consideration since we can see distant places if there is no obstacle. Unfortunately, this fact worsens the scene independence. In order to maintain independence, we should put restriction in the visualization. In our method, called *Image-Based Non-Rendering* (IBNR), we apply a fixed viewpoint constraint into scene visualization. In IBNR, we first prepare a scenic image and eight human images. Each human image represents a person with a specific movement direction, i.e., to the front, back, right, left, and the intermediate of all those directions. Next, we give the trapezoid of the scenic image to specify the floor region where a user can move on by using an *avatar*. Based on this configuration, we can construct the scenic and an avatar image as shown in Fig. 9 (a). A persons' picture could be enlarged and shrunk by the users' input to give an effect of the depth in the pseudo 3-D space. In a scene, if a user repeats the act of forwarding and the avatar comes out from a predefined floor region, i.e., one of the sides of the trapezoid, the scene automatically changes to another one, as shown in Fig. 9 (b). The scene is constructed in a similar manner to the previous one, but with different background image, trapezoid region, and linkage information. In this way, from pictures taken in the real space, the IBNR system could construct a virtual space with high reality. The use of pictures makes it easy for a creator to construct a virtual space that contains many objects in the real world without any modeling.

8   Conclusion

We have presented the activities and the motivation behind our AMCP project. The main challenge in our project is the realization of efficient management of two important features of multimedia content, i.e., *continuous* and *semistructured* features.

We have presented a part of important research results achieved by our project and how they are contributing in the management of continuity and semistructured features in the processing of multimedia content. We have shown that both features appears in every aspect, spanning from the first time when the content is acquired/organized until it is delivered to and presented at the client side. Appropriate methods of managing these features are needed in order to achieve a meaningful and satisfactory multimedia content service. We believe that the research results presented here could give suggestions about the processing of multimedia content.

This project will be completed in March 2002, and now we are developing attractive application systems based on the technologies we have developed so far, such as TEKIJUKU[2] Digital Museum.

Acknowledgement. We would like to thank Professors Fumio Kishino, Yoshifumi Kitamura, Toshihiro Masaki and Mr. Takahiro Hara of Osaka University, and Professors Kuniaki Uehara and Kazutoshi Sumiya of Kobe University for the intensive discussion during the preparation of this paper. Special thanks go to Dr. Budiarto of Osaka University for his invaluable comments on this paper.

This work is supported by Research for the Future Program of Japan Society for the Promotion of Science under the Project "Research on Advanced Multimedia Content Processing" (JSPS-RFTF97P00501).

References

1. Allen, J. F.: Maintaining Knowledge about Temporal Intervals. Communications of the ACM **26(11)** (1983) 832–843
2. Arikawa, M., Maesako, T., Sueda, T.: Time Extension to LoD for Browsing Spatio-Temporal Databases. Proc. Intl. Workshop on Urban Multi-Media/3-D Mapping (UM3'99) (1999) 57–62
3. Ariki, Y., Ogata, J.,Nishida, M.: News Dictation and Article Classification Using Automatically Extracted Announcer Utterance. Proc. 1st Intl. Conf. on AMCP (1998) 78–89
4. Harumoto, K., Nakano, T., Shimojo, S., Nishio, S.: A WWW Server with Media Scaling Mechanism based on Page Transmission Latency. IEEE Pacific Rim Conference on Communications, Computers and Signal Processing (1999) 444–447
5. Hatano, K., Sano, R., Duan, Y., Tanaka, K.: An Interactive Classification of Web Documents by Self-Organizing Maps and Search Engine. Proc. 6th Intl. Conf. on Database Systems for Advanced Applications (1999) 35–42

---

[2] TEKIJUKU is a medical school which is one of the origins of Osaka University.

6. Hayashi, M., Ueda, H., Kurihara, T.: TVML (TV program Making Language) -Automatic TV Program Generation from Text-based Script-. Proc. Imagina'99 (http://www.strl.nhk.or.jp/TVML/Japanese/J09.html) (1998)

7. Koiso, K., Matsumoto, T., Mori, T., Kawagishi, H., Tanaka, K.: InfoLOD and Landmark: Spatial Presentation of Attribute Information and Computing Representative Objects for Spatial Data. Intl. Journal of Cooperative Information Systems (to appear)

8. Li, W.-S., Wu, Y.-L.: Query Relaxation by Structure for Web Document Retrieval with Progressive Processing (Extended Abstract). Proc. IPSJ Advanced Database Symposium (1998) 19–25

9. Mizuuchi, Y., Tajima, K.: Finding Context Paths for Web Pages. Proc. ACM Hypertext (1999) 13–22

10. Murao, M., Arikawa, M., Okamura, K.: Augmented/Reduced Spatial Hypermedia Systems for Networked Live Videos on Internet. Proc. Intl. Workshop on Urban Multi-Media/3-D Mapping (UM3'99) (199) 15–20

11. Nadamoto, A., Hattori, T., Kondo, H., Sawanaka, I., Tanaka, K.: Passive Web-Browsing by TV-Program Metaphor. A draft submitted to Intl. Conf. (2000)

12. Nakano, T., Harumoto, K., Shimojo, S., Nishio, S.: Controlling Transmission Order of Inline Objects for Effective Web Page Publishing. Proc. ACM Symposium on Applied Computing **2** (2000) 942–947

13. Pradhan, S., Tajima, K., Tanaka, K.: A Query Model for Retrieving Relevant Intervals within a Video Stream. Proc. IEEE Multimedia Systems **II** (1999) 788–792

14. Pradhan, S., Tajima, K., Tanaka, K.: A Query Model to Synthesize Answer Intervals from Indexed Video Units. IEEE Trans. Knowledge and Data Eng. (to appear)

15. Salton, G., Yang, C. S.: On the Specification of Term Values in Automatic Indexing. J. Documentation, **29(4)** (1973) 351–372

16. Tajima, K., Mizuuchi, Y., Kitagawa, M., Tanaka, K.: Cut as a Querying Unit for WWW, Netnews, and E-mail. Proc. ACM Hypertext (1998) 235–244

17. Tajima, K., Tanaka, K.: New Techniques for the Discovery of Logical Documents in Web. Proc. Intl. Symposium on Database Applications in Non-Traditional Environments (1999)

18. Tajima, K., Hatano, K., Matsukura, T., Sano, R., Tanaka, K.: Discovery and Retrieval of Logical Information Units in Web (invited). Proc. Workshop of Organizing Web Space (in conjunction with ACM Conference on Digital Libraries (1999) 13–23

19. Tanaka, K., Nadamoto, A., Kusahara, M., Hattori, T., Kondo, H., Sumiya, K.: Back to the TV: Information Visualization Interfaces Based on TV-Program Metaphors. Proc. IEEE Intl. Conf. on Multimedia and Expo (ICME'2000) (to appear)

20. Tanaka, K., Tajima, K., Sogo, T., Pradhan, S.: Algebraic Retrieval of Fragmentarily Indexed Video. Next Generation Computing (to appear)

21. Tsukamoto, M.: Image-based Pseudo-3D Visualization of Real Space on WWW. Digital Cities: Experiences, Technologies and Future Perspectives. Lecture Notes in Computer Science **1765** (2000) 288-302

22. TVML (TV Program Making Language). http://www.strl.nhk.or.jp/TVML

23. http://www.informedia.cs.cmu.edu/dli2

Database Systems as Middleware – Events, Notifications, Messages

H. Schweppe, A. Hinze, D. Faensen

Freie Universität Berlin Institut für Informatik

Database systems have been traditionally used as integration tools. Data integration was the primary goal of first generation systems. After relational technology had become a mature base for application development, new architectures where developed for the tight integration of data, procedures and all kinds of processing. This phase of DBS research and development was dominated by object-oriented database management and specific architectures like Starburst [HaCH 1990], which had a strong impact on current object-relational technology. The ubiquitous computer network has added another facet to the usage of DBS as an integration tool.

In distributed environment, middleware aims at making distribution transparent. Corba or RMI are well-known examples. The call-oriented style of communication has been complemented by message-oriented, event-driven interaction of independent programs. System processes use this type of communication for decades. However, it is not well known as a mechanism on the application level – despite the fact that it has been employed for quite some time, e.g. in workflow systems [LeRo 2000]. The event-driven message passing paradigm becomes more and more important for highly distributed applications. Many kinds of interactions between applications follow a common pattern: n inde-pendent providers submit their output as messages, which in turn will be consumed asynchronously by m consumer applications. As opposed to call-level interaction, providers and consumers may or may not know each others identity. In a stock ticker application for example, there is no reason why providers should know the identity of consumers. In most cases, consumers need to know only a subset of the messages produced by the providers. This is one reason why database systems play an important role in message based systems: filtering is one of the primary strength of DBS. They furthermore guarantee failsafe execution environments, and at least more advanced DBS allow to define triggers. This last point seems to be an excellent mechanism for event-based interaction of loosely coupled systems. Triggers allow to define conditions and actions in a declarative way. In an information publish / subscribe application database systems provide an excellent technological basis: Publishing will activate the system by means of triggers, messages which announce the advent of new information will be filtered according to profiles specified by the individual clients, and the delivery will be guaranteed with transactional support.

Unfortunately, the situation is not as easy: DBS are too slow at least for high traffic applications. The persistence mechanism of DBS is time consuming, the trigger mechanism does not scale. We discuss different technologies for event-based messaging, among them core database technology, discuss functional requirements of

J. Štuller et al. (Eds.): ADBIS-DASFAA 2000, LNCS 1884, pp. 21–22, 2000.

different applications and report on performance studies and compare the base technologies.

Database systems play a twofold role in application oriented message communication. As mentioned they provide the technology for lightweight and reliable communication between independent and even heterogeneous systems. On the other hand, DBS technology and DBS applications may benefit from event-based message passing themselves. We will discuss how to employ this technology in order to keep widely replicated data coherent. Furthermore, we will investigate the message passing technology for dissemination of information in large scale distributed systems [YaGr 1999].

Finally, we will argue that DBS can be successfully used as a reliable middleware for the integration of distributed, independent applications using event-based messaging.

References

[HaCh 1990] L. Haas, W. Chang et al.: Starburst Mid-Flight: As the Dust Clears, TKDE 2(1), 1990

[LeRo 2000] F. Leymann, D. Roller: Production Workflow Concepts and Techniques, Prentice Hall, 2000

[YaGr1999] T. Yan, H. Garcia-Molina: The SIFT Information Dissemination System, ACM TODS 24(4) 1999

Managing Schemata for Semistructured Databases Using Constraints

André Bergholz* and Johann Christoph Freytag

[1] Stanford University, Stanford, CA 94305, U.S.A.,
bergholz@db.stanford.edu
[2] Humboldt-Universität zu Berlin, Unter den Linden 6, 10099 Berlin, Germany,
freytag@dbis.informatik.hu-berlin.de

Abstract. Managing semistructured data requires more flexibility than traditional database systems provide. Recently we proposed a query language for semistructured data represented as labeled directed graphs. This language is based on matching a partial schema into the database. In this paper we describe how we achieve this matching using constraints. We show how to match a schema into a database without using any additional information. In order to match schemata more efficiently, we are able to incorporate results of previously matched schemata. To this end, we formulate a sufficient condition for schema containment and describe how to test this condition, again, using constraints. We show how the knowledge of schema containment can be used for optimization. As a theoretical contribution we prove that, under some circumstances, schema matches can be found without any backtracking and in polynomial time.

1 Introduction

Semistructured data is one of the recent challanges in database research. In contrast to traditional database management, where design ensures declarativity, a more flexible approach is needed. Typically, semistructured data, "data that is neither raw data nor strictly typed" [Abi97], lacks a fixed and rigid schema. Often their structure is irregular and implicit. Examples for semistructured data include HTML files, BibTEX files or genome data stored in ASCII files.

We propose a query language for semistructured data [BF99]. We interpret the three layers in databases as the operation layer, the description layer and the instance layer. In semistructured data the descriptions have to be handled in a more flexible manner. To this extent, we define a semantically rich notion of (partial) schemata and use the matching of these schemata as a base for querying. Thus, we get the benefit that descriptions do not rely on the presence

---

* This research was done while André Bergholz was at Humboldt-University Berlin. It was supported by the German Research Society, Berlin-Brandenburg Graduate School in Distributed Information Systems (DFG grant no. GRK 316). André Bergholz is now supported by the German Academic Exchange Service (DAAD program HSP III).

of a database designer. They can also be defined gradually or even be extracted from user queries instead. Of course, such generated (partial) schemata may not always be "meaningful" for a user but they can be useful for query optimization. Additionally they can at least give users a hint about the database content. In summary, our approach shall be guided by the principle that answering a query *works without*, *benefits from* and *induces new* schema information.

This paper is organized as follows. Section 2 gives an overview of our proposed query language. Section 3 demonstrates how a schema can be matched into a database directly, i. e., without any additional information, by transforming the problem into a Constraint Satisfaction Problem. Section 4 proves that matches of a tree-shaped schema without variables can be found without backtracking and in polynomial time if the requirement of injectivity of the match function is ignored. In Section 5 we present a sufficient condition for schema containment and show how to test it again using constraints. In Section 6 we describe how the knowledge of schema containment in either direction can be used for optimization. We conclude with related work and a discussion.

2   The Query Language

We briefly revisit our query language as presented in [BF99]. We use labeled graphs, "the unifying idea in semi-structured data" [Bun97], as the underlying syntax. Let $\mathcal{L}$ be an arbitrary set of *labels*. A tuple $G = (V, A, s, t, l)$ is a *($\mathcal{L}$-) labeled directed graph* if (V, A, s, t) is a total directed graph with a set of vertices V, a set of arcs A and two total functions s and t assigning each arc its source and target vertex, respectively. Furthermore, $l : V \cup A \longrightarrow \mathcal{L}$ is a total *label function* assigning a label from $\mathcal{L}$ to each vertex and arc. We talk about *elements* of a graph when we do not distinguish between the vertices and arcs. We also use the term *node* as a synonym for vertex, but stick to the term arc to emphasize that we use directed graphs. An *object* is simply a labeled directed graph. We use the term *database* referring to "large" objects that we want to query.

In Figure 1 we present an example that we use throughout the paper. The example shows a semistructured database of persons having names, surnames, a year of birth, a profession etc. Furthermore, we include a sibling relationship between persons.

As outlined in the introduction, we distinguish the description layer and the operation layer. On the description layer we introduce the notion of (partial) schemata. These schemata are linked to objects by the notion of conformity. We describe these schemata in some detail and then move on to the operation layer, i. e., the queries, towards the end of the section.

The schemata. We start with a simple notion of schema. Informally, a schema is an object that describes a set of objects. This concept exists in many areas. For example, when looking at the world of labels one label can describe a set of other labels. Examples are data types, predicates and regular expressions. In our first step we use these label world schemata and assign them to the elements

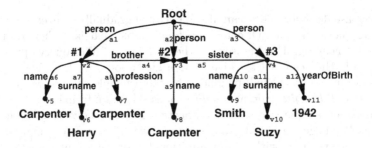

Fig. 1. A labeled directed graph

of a graph. We choose predicates to be the label world schemata and define a *predicate schema* to be an object labeled with unary predicates.

In order to establish a relationship between the schema and the objects described by it we have to establish the notion of *conformity* between schemata and objects. In the simple case of predicate schemata we say that an object *o* conforms to a schema *s* if there is an isomorphic embedding from *s* into *o* respecting the predicates. In Figure 2 we show a predicate schema together with its minimal matches (the minimal conforming objects) from the database shown in Figure 1. They are minimal in the sense that any of their supergraphs but none of their subgraphs is a match of the schema.

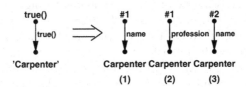

Fig. 2. The predicate schema and its minimal matches

We now add a little more semantics to the schemata in order to use them as a base for querying. We add the notions of variables and quantifiers to describe paths. Adding variables is in the flavor of the join operation in the relational world. The example schema in Figure 3 matches every object with the name being the same as the profession.

Paths are an important concept in semistructured data. This is due to the observation that sometimes information is represented at different levels of granularity. We demonstrate the idea by presenting an example in Figure 4. The schema matches every object that has a path of arbitrary positive length (indicated by the + in the label of the first arc) emanating from the root node and ending with an arc labeled *'name'*. Without the path notion we are not able to get all the five results so easily.

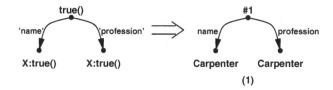

Fig. 3. Adding variables

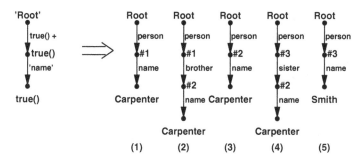

Fig. 4. Adding paths

The queries. We move on to the operation layer and discuss the queries that we introduce. A schema in itself already forms the most simple kind of query: It queries all subobjects (i. e., subgraphs) of a database that conform to it. A *schema query* is a tuple $q = (s)$ where s is a schema. The *answer* to q with respect to a database o is the set of minimal matches of s in o. As an example you can imagine any of the schemata from the previous sections.

With a schema we are able to formulate conditions. This ability roughly corresponds to the selection operator in the relational world. Additionally we present an operation that corresponds to the projection operator in the relational world. A *focus query* is a tuple $q = (s_1, s_2)$ where s_1 is a schema and s_2 is a subobject of s_1. The *answer* to q with respect to a database o is the union of the minimal matches of s_2 over all minimal matches of s_1 in o. As an example you can imagine a query that asks for the surnames of all persons with the name 'Carpenter'.

Our approach also allows to restructure the answer to a query completely. We introduce the *transformation query*, which allows us to give a graph structure and compute new labels by using terms over the old ones. A *transformation query* is a tuple $q = (s, t)$ with s being a schema and t being an object labeled with terms over the elements in s. The *answer* to q is built by creating for every match of s in o a new object isomorphic to t. The elements are labeled with the evaluated terms of t instantiating them by using the match of s. The example in Figure 5 queries for the age of Suzy Smith. The age is computed from the year of birth. Note, that schema and focus queries can be expressed as transformation queries.

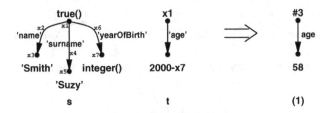

Fig. 5. A transformation query

Our query language is rich in that it allows to give the structure of the answer in advance, but limited in that we always produce one answer per schema match. That is, we cannot express aggregation queries with our current formalism.

3   Matching Schemata Using Constraints

In this and the following sections we present how query processing is performed using constraints. We focus on finding the matches for a given schema since this is the computationally challenging part. In this section we describe how to match schemata *without* any additional schema information given. We achieve this by transforming our problem into a Constraint Satisfaction Problem. How we make use of previously matched schemata will be discussed in the following two sections.

We base our query processing on constraint satisfaction techniques because there are many techniques and heuristics for solving Constraint Satisfaction Problems (CSPs) available. Furthermore, CSPs form a reasonably general class of search problems. Thus, we get a good framework for specifying our needs, for adapting our algorithms for richer kinds of schemata and most importantly for formulating our query processing based on previously matched schemata.

Constraint satisfaction deals with solving problems by stating properties or constraints that any solution must fulfill. A *Constraint Satisfaction Problem (CSP)* is a tuple (X, D, C) where X is a set of *variables* $\{x_1, \ldots, x_m\}$, D is a set of finite *domains* D_i for each variable $x_i \in X$ and C is a set of *constraints* $\{C_{S_1}, \ldots, C_{S_n}\}$ restricting the values that the variables can simultaneously take. Here each $S_i = (x_{S_{i_1}}, \ldots, x_{S_{i_k}})$ is an arbitrary tuple of variables from X and each C_{S_i} is a relation over the cross product of the domains of these variables $(C_{S_i} \subseteq D_{S_{i_1}} \times \cdots \times D_{S_{i_k}})$. Solving a CSP is finding assignments of values from the respective domains to the variables so that all constraints are satisfied. In database applications we are usually interested in finding all solutions of a CSP.

General idea. Our problem is related to the SUBGRAPH-ISOMORPHISM problem, which is known to be NP-complete [Coo71]. However, our problem gets exponentially harder in the size of the schema, but only linearly harder in the size of the database. Furthermore, the labels in the graphs greatly reduce the average complexity. The basic idea of the transformation into a CSP as shown in Figure 6 works as follows. The database graph is transformed into suitable domains, and variables are introduced for the elements in the schema. Furthermore, constraints reflecting the match semantics are introduced. They can be categorized into the ones that represent the label part and the ones that represent the structure part of the match semantics.

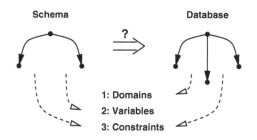

Schema   **Database**

?

1: Domains
2: Variables
3: Constraints

Fig. 6. Schema matching by Constraint Satisfaction

First, we derive the domains of vertices and arcs from the database graph in Figure 1.

$$D_V = \{v_1, v_2, v_3, \ldots, v_{11}\}$$
$$D_A = \{a_1, a_2, a_3, \ldots, a_{12}\}$$

Second, we derive the variables and the domain assignments from the example schema in Figure 7 (same as Figure 2). Finally, we derive two kinds of constraints.

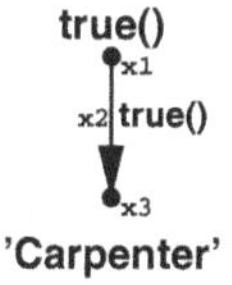

true()
x1
x2 **true()**

x3
'Carpenter'

$$X = \{x_1, x_2, x_3\}$$
$$D_1 = D_3 = D_V$$
$$D_2 = D_A$$

Fig. 7. A simple predicate schema

The first kind is derived from the predicates in the schema. For each variable we define a constraint that consists of all nodes or arcs whose label satisfies the predicate associated with the variable, i. e., a constraint $C^{lab}_{(x_i)} = \{(d_j) \in D_i | l^{(s)}(x_i)(l^{(o)}(d_j)) = true\}$ where $l^{(s)}$ and $l^{(o)}$ indicate the label functions of the schema s and the object o. In our example this leads to:

$$C^{lab}_{(x_1)} = \{(v_1), (v_2), (v_3), \ldots, (v_{11})\}$$
$$C^{lab}_{(x_2)} = \{(a_1), (a_2), (a_3), \ldots, (a_{12})\}$$
$$C^{lab}_{(x_3)} = \{(v_5), (v_7), (v_8)\}$$

The second kind of constraints is derived from the graph structure of the schema. We have to respect the properties of graph morphisms: The mapping between arcs implies the mapping between their source and target nodes. Thus, we introduce constraints $C^{src}_{(x_i,x_s)} = \{(d_j, d_v) \in D_i \times D_s | s^{(o)}(d_j) = d_v\}$ and $C^{tar}_{(x_i,x_t)} = \{(d_j, d_v) \in D_i \times D_t | t^{(o)}(d_j) = d_v\}$. In the example we get:

$$C^{src}_{(x_2,x_1)} = \{(a_1, v_1), (a_2, v_1), (a_3, v_1), \ldots, (a_{11}, v_4), (a_{12}, v_4)\}$$
$$C^{tar}_{(x_2,x_3)} = \{(a_1, v_2), (a_2, v_3), (a_3, v_4), \ldots, (a_{11}, v_{10}), (a_{12}, v_{11})\}$$

Our sample CSP has the solutions (v_2, a_6, v_5), (v_2, a_8, v_7) and (v_3, a_9, v_8) for the variables (x_1, x_2, x_3). They correspond to the matches of the schema as shown in Figure 2. Please note that if you want to ensure injectivity of the match, additional constraints must be introduced.

Variables and paths. If a schema contains variables, we must introduce additional constraints. The example in Figure 8 (same as Figure 3) has the variable X defined at x_3 and x_5. We link both nodes by introducing a constraint $C^{var}_{(x_3,x_5)}$. In the general case, we must link all variables pairwise to each other by introducing constraints $C^{var}_{(x_i,x_j)} = \{(d_u, d_v) \in D_i \times D_j | l^{(o)}(d_u) = l^{(o)}(d_v)\}$.

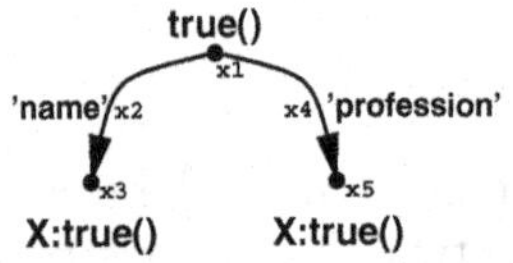

$$C^{var}_{(x_3,x_5)} = \{(v_1, v_1), (v_2, v_2), \ldots, (v_5, v_5),$$
$$(v_5, v_7), (v_5, v_8), \ldots, (v_{11}, v_{11})\}$$

Fig. 8. Adding variables

Paths are represented by introducing an additional domain. We ensure that this domain is always finite by requiring all arcs of a path to be distinct. (This concept is called a *trail* in graph theory.) For the database in Figure 1 we get:

$$D_P = \{\varepsilon, (a_1), (a_2), \ldots, (a_{12}), (a_1, a_4), (a_1, a_6), \ldots, (a_3, a_5, a_9)\}$$

where ε denotes the empty path. Of course, the constraints have to be adapted. The label constraints must represent the fact that a path is in the constraint if and only if the predicate associated with the respective variable is true for the labels of all arcs in the path. Source and target of nonempty paths can naturally be defined as the source of the first and the target of the last arc. For the empty path we only require that the source and the target node are the same. Thus, we represent the structural requirements in one ternary constraint rather than in two binary ones. In addition, we introduce constraints on the length of the path if this is indicated in the schema.

4   A Theoretical Observation on Our Approach

This section proves an important property of our approach. We give a condition under which a CSP in our approach can be solved without search and in polynomial time. Our theorem is based on the following well-known theorem by Freuder [Fre82].

Theorem 1. *If a constraint graph is strongly k-consistent, and $k > w$ where w is the width of the constraint graph, then there exists a search order that is backtrack-free.*

In the *constraint graph* of a CSP nodes represent variables and arcs represent constraints. An *ordered constraint graph* is a constraint graph whose vertices are ordered linearly. The *width of an ordered constraint graph* is defined as the maximum number of arcs leading from an arbitrary vertex to previous vertices. The *width of a constraint graph* is the minimum width over all its ordered constraint graphs. A constraint graph is *k-consistent* if the following is true: Choose values of any $k - 1$ variables that satisfy all the constraints among these variables. Then choose any kth variable. There exists a value in the current domain of this variable that satisfies all the constraints among all the K variables. A constraint graph is *strongly k-consistent* if it is j-consistent for all $j \leq k$.

We are ready to formulate our theorem.

Theorem 2. *Let s be a tree-structured schema with an empty variable mapping. Using the previously described transformation into a CSP and ignoring the requirement of injectivity, the matches of s in an arbitrary database can be found without any search and in polynomial time.*

Proof. The key to the proof is that if the schema is a tree the resulting constraint graph for the constructed CSP is a tree as well. We see that the CSP has only label and structure constraints but no variable or injectivity constraints. The label constraints are unary so they can be incorporated into the domains and ignored for this proof. Hence, we only must care about the structure constraints. When constructing the constraint graph we simply replace every arc in the schema by a vertex that represents the variable introduced for the arc. The only constraints that are introduced, are the source and the target constraints for these arcs. In the constraint graph two edges are added between every newly introduced vertex and the vertices representing the source and target of the respective arc. Figure 9 illustrates this construction by showing a tree-structured schema on the left side and the resulting constraint graph on the right side. During the construction of the constraint graph the properties connectivity and acyclicity remain untouched. Hence, if the schema is a tree the constraint graph is a tree as well.

A tree-structured constraint graph always has width one [Fre82]. Because of the above theorem it is clear that after making our CSP node and arc consistent (i. e., strongly 2-consistent), there exists a search order that is backtrack-free. This search order can be found by using breath-first traversal of the constraint

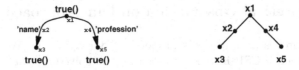

Fig. 9. A tree-structured schema and the corresponding constraint graph

graph [Fre82]. Making a CSP node and arc consistent can be achieved in poly-nomial time [Mac77].

It is important to notice that the injectivity constraints heavily blow up the constraint graph. Since every pair of vertices and every pair of arcs in the schema is linked by an injectivity constraint the constraint graph then contains two cliques of sizes $|V^{(s)}|$ and $|A^{(s)}|$. This immediatley implies that the constraint graph then has a width of at least $max(\{|V^{(s)}| - 1, |A^{(s)}| - 1\})$. Hence, no polynomial algorithm can ensure the necessary level of consistency. Thus, it might be preferable to postpone the injectivity check and reduce a possibly larger set of CSP solutions in a seperate postprocessing step.

5   Schema Containment

In this section we formulate a sufficient condition for schema containment and show how this condition can be formulated as a CSP. The techniques used are somewhat similar to those in the previous section.

First, we define the meaning of *schema containment*. A schema s_1 *contains* a schema s_2 if for all databases o all matches of s_2 are also matches of s_1. This definition is related to the more traditional notion of query containment as defined in [ASU79]. How to make use of a detected schema containment is the subject of the next section.

A sufficient condition for schema containment. The following condition assu-mes the notion of *predicate containment*. p_1 contains p_2 if for all labels x the implication $p_2(x) \longrightarrow p_1(x)$ holds. A schema s_1 contains another schema s_2 if

1. the graph of s_1 is a subgraph of the graph of s_2, and
2. for all nodes and arcs in s_1 the predicate of the node or arc contains the predicate of the respective node or arc in s_2, and
3. for all arcs in s_1 the path descriptions, if present, indicate that paths in s_1 are at least as long as the respective ones in s_2.

The reverse direction of this implication does not hold.

Testing schema containment. We describe the testing of this condition again as a CSP. This problem is, like the one in the previous section, related to the SUBGRAPH-ISOMORPHISM problem. Similar to the principles shown in Fi-gure 6, we transform schema s_2, into domains, and schema s_1 into variables. We again derive constraints representing the label part and constraints representing the structure part of the containment. Let us call the mapping that we are searching a *containment embedding* from s_1 into s_2. We must keep in mind that it is s_2 that is contained in s_1 once we find this mapping.

The simple example in Figure 10 shows two schemata s_1 and s_2 where s_2 is contained in s_1. Thus, we are looking for a containment embedding of s_1 into s_2 to verify this schema containment. Variables, domains, and structure constraint are introduced as in the previous section.

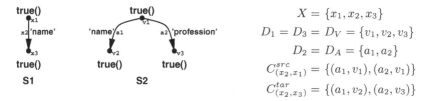

$$X = \{x_1, x_2, x_3\}$$
$$D_1 = D_3 = D_V = \{v_1, v_2, v_3\}$$
$$D_2 = D_A = \{a_1, a_2\}$$
$$C^{src}_{(x_2, x_1)} = \{(a_1, v_1), (a_2, v_1)\}$$
$$C^{tar}_{(x_2, x_3)} = \{(a_1, v_2), (a_2, v_3)\}$$

Fig. 10. Schema containment

For the label part we ensure that the predicates in s_1 contain the respective ones in s_2 using the definition of predicate containment. In the example, this condition is rather easy to achieve. The predicate $true()$ contains every predicate and a constant predicate $X = c$ is contained by a predicate p if $p(c)$ holds.

$$C^{pred}_{(x_1)} = \{(v_1), (v_2), (v_3)\}$$
$$C^{pred}_{(x_2)} = \{(a_1)\}$$
$$C^{pred}_{(x_3)} = \{(v_1), (v_2), (v_3)\}$$

In the general case, we assume that information on predicate containment is given. We are currently working on a prototype and support predicates such as $lessthan(num)$ with the obvious meaning and $sgrep(str)$ which is true iff str is a substring of the label in question. For those predicates we explicitly give sufficient conditions for predicate containment. $lessthan(num_1)$ contains $lessthan(num_2)$ if $num_1 \geq num_2$. $sgrep(str_1)$ contains $sgrep(str_2)$ if str_1 is a substring of str_2.

The CSP for the example has the solution (v_1, a_1, v_2) which corresponds to the containment embedding that we already were aware of. We rewrite this embedding as $\{(x_1, v_1), (x_2, a_1), (x_3, v_2)\}$, store it, and see how we can make use of it in the next section.

Variables and paths are also treated in a similar manner as before. If s_1 contains elements that are linked via a variable, we must make sure that the respective elements in s_2 are also linked via a variable or have the same constant predicate as their label. Constraints on the path length ensure that paths in s_1 are not shorter than the respective ones in s_2.

6   Using Schema Containment for Optimization

This section describes how we make use of schema containment once we detect it using the methods described in the previous section. We show that we can make use of the containment information in both directions. If a schema s_1 contains another schema s_2 then

1. matches of s_2 can only be found among the matches of s_1. If we want to find the matches of s_2 and have the ones for s_1 we can *reduce the search space*.
2. all matches of s_2 are also matches of s_1. If we want to find the matches of s_1 and have the ones for s_2 we can present the *first few matches immediately*.

We show how to reduce the search space if we have a schema s_1 together with its matches in a database and another schema s_2 that is contained in s_1 and whose matches we are looking for. Consider the example in Figure 11. The schema s_2 on top is contained in the schema s_1 on the left. The containment is the same as in Figure 10 in the previous section. We have renamed the elements a little, the containment embedding is now $\{(y_1, x_1), (y_2, x_2), (y_3, x_3)\}$. We are

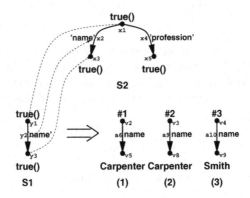

Fig. 11. Reducing the search space

interested in the matches of s_2 in the database shown in Figure 1 in Section 2. The variables x_1, x_2 and x_3 can only be matched to the matches of their partners in the containment embedding. Thus, we get the following variables and domains:

$$X = \{x_1, x_2, x_3, x_4, x_5\}$$

$$D_1 = \{v_2, v_3, v_4\}$$
$$D_2 = \{a_6, a_9, a_{10}\}$$
$$D_3 = \{v_5, v_8, v_9\}$$

D_4 and D_5 cannot be reduced, they are equal to D_A and D_V, respectively. In order to fully exploit the containment information we introduce an additional constraint.

$$C^{sol}_{(x_1, x_2, x_3)} = \{(v_2, a_6, v_5), (v_3, a_9, v_8), (v_4, a_{10}, v_9)\}$$

Vice versa, consider the case that we have a schema s_2 together with its matches and an s_2 containing schema s_1, whose matches should be computed. We are able to derive some matches of s_1 immediately. Consider the example in Figure 12. The schemata are the same as in the previous example, but we are now interested in the matches of s_2 and have the ones for s_1. The containment embedding of s_1 into s_2 is $\{(y_1, x_1), (y_2, x_2), (y_3, x_3)\}$, just as before.

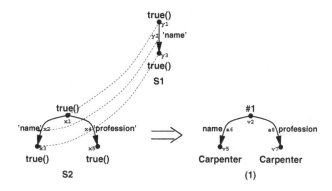

Fig. 12. First few matches

The matches of x_1, x_2 and x_3 are immediately also matches of y_1, y_2 and y_3. Thus, (v_2, a_6, v_5) is one solution to the CSP constructed for s_1. There may exist more solutions though (see Figure 11).

7   Related Work

Core issues and basic characterizations concerning semistructured data are discussed in [Abi97] and [Bun97]. Query languages for semistructured data (and XML) include Lorel [AQM+97], StruQL [FFK+98] and UnQL [BDHS96]. The whole area has been influenced by query languages for the World Wide Web, such as the languages of the ARANEUS project [AMM97].

Graph pattern matching plays an important role in the area of graph transformations. [Rud98] discusses graph pattern matching based on constraints whereas [Zue93] uses an approach that is more in the flavor of traditional database optimization. Techniques and heuristics for solving constraint satisfaction problems are discussed in a variety of papers, see for instance [Bar99].

Query containment in the context semistructured data is discussed in [FLS98]. They show that query containment for a union-free, negation-free subset of their StruQL language is decidable. For a further subset of this language restricting the allowed kinds of path expressions query containment is even NP-complete. The usefulness of the "first few" answers to a query has been observed in [CK97].

8   Conclusion

This paper describes the query processing in our query language for semistructured data. The query language seperates the "what"-part of a query (a partial schema) and the "how"-part (additional operations). We have introduced schemata covering predicates, variables and paths and used them from schema, focus and transformation queries. The matching of the schemata forms the foundation for query processing. In this work we have described how the matches for such a schema can be found in a database either directly or by making use of previously matched schemata. Both of these algorithms are based on constraints. For the latter, the notion of schema containment plays an important role. We have formulated a sufficient condition for schema containment and described how to test this condition. Schema containment can be used to reduce the search space or to produce the first few matches of a schema immediately.

On the theoretical side we have shown that schema matches for a tree-shaped schema without variables can be found in polynomial time and without backtracking when the requirement of injectivity of a match is ignored.

We have implemented our ideas in a Prolog-based system and are currently working on an implementation using the Constraint Logic Programming system ECLiPSe [Ecl]. ECLiPSe provides a Finite Domain Library that is well-suited for our purposes. We have implemented a chronological backtracking algorithm and choose the variable to be instantiated dynamically. The choice criterion is the current size of the domain. ECLiPSe uses so called delayed goals to perform a full look-ahead in order to reduce domain sizes. First results indicate that schema matches can indeed be found without backtracking. We believe that this uniform constraint framework can be an alternative to the many different database traversal strategies discussed e. g. in [MW99]. On the other hand, constraint systems need to be improved with respect to physical aspects of query optimization. Additional future work for us lies in assessing schemata in order to determine "good" schemata for optimization.

Acknowledgment. The authors wish to thank all members of the Berlin-Brandenburg Graduate School in Distributed Information Systems for providing an inspiring environment and for many interesting discussions and useful comments. In particular, we thank Felix Naumann for critically reviewing our manuscript.

References

Abi97.   S. Abiteboul. Querying semi-structured data. In *Proceedings of the International Conference on Database Theory (ICDT)*, pages 1–18, Delphi, Greece, January 1997.

AMM97.   P. Atzeni, G. Mecca, and P. Merialdo. To weave the web. In *Proceedings of the International Conference on Very Large Databases (VLDB)*, pages 206–215, Athens, Greece, August 1997.

AQM⁺97.   S. Abiteboul, D. Quass, J. McHugh, J. Widom, and J. Wiener. The Lorel query language for semistructured data. *Journal of Digital Libraries*, 1(1):68–88, 1997.

ASU79.   A. Aho, Y. Sagiv, and J. D. Ullman. Equivalence of relational expressions. *SIAM Journal on Computing*, 8(2):218–246, 1979.

Bar99.   R. Bartak. Constraint programming: In pursuit of the holy grail. In *Proceedings of the Week of Doctoral Students (WDS)*, Prague, Czech Republic, June 1999.

BDHS96.   P. Buneman, S. Davidson, G. Hillebrand, and D. Suciu. A query language and optimization techniques for unstructured data. In *Proceedings of the ACM SIGMOD International Conference on Management of Data*, pages 505–516, Montreal, Canada, June 1996.

BF99.   A. Bergholz and J. C. Freytag. Querying semistructured data based on schema matching. In *Proceedings of the International Workshop on Database Programming Languages (DBPL)*, Kinloch Rannoch, Scotland, UK, September 1999.

Bun97.   P. Buneman. Semistructured data. In *Proceedings of the Symposium on Principles of Database Systems (PODS)*, pages 117–121, Tucson, AZ, USA, May 1997.

CK97.   M. J. Carey and D. Kossmann. On saying "Enough Already!" in SQL. In *Proceedings of the ACM SIGMOD International Conference on Management of Data*, pages 219–230, Tucson, AZ, USA, May 1997.

Coo71.   S. A. Cook. The complexity of theorem-proving procedures. In *Proceedings of the ACM Symposium on Theory of Computing*, pages 151–158, Shaker Heights, OH, USA, May 1971.

Ecl.   ECLiPSe - The ECRC Constraint Logic Parallel System, http://www.ecrc.de/eclipse/.

FFK⁺98.   M. Fernandez, D. Florescu, J. Kang, A. Levy, and D. Suciu. Catching the boat with Strudel: Experiences with a web-site management system. In *Proceedings of the ACM SIGMOD International Conference on Management of Data*, pages 414–425, Seattle, WA, USA, June 1998.

FLS98.   D. Florescu, A. Levy, and D. Suciu. Query containment for conjunctive queries with regular expressions. In *Proceedings of the Symposium on Principles of Database Systems (PODS)*, pages 139–148, Seattle, WA, USA, June 1998.

Fre82.   E. Freuder. A sufficient condition for backtrack-free search. *Journal of the ACM*, 29(1):24–32, 1982.

Mac77.   A. K. Mackworth. Consistency in networks of relations. *Artificial Intelligence*, 8(1):99–118, 1977.

MW99.   J. McHugh, , and J. Widom. Query optimization for XML. In *Proceedings of the International Conference on Very Large Databases (VLDB)*, pages 315–326, Edinburgh, Scotland, UK, September 1999.

Rud98.   M. Rudolf. Utilizing constraint satisfaction techniques for efficient graph pattern matching. In *Proceedings of the International Workshop on Theory and Application of Graph Transformations (TAGT)*, Paderborn, Germany, November 1998.

Zue93.   A. Zuendorf. A heuristic for the subgraph isomorphism problem in executing PROGRES. Technical Report AIB 93-5, RWTH Aachen, Aachen, Germany, 1993.

Caching for Mobile Communication

Tamra Carpenter, Robert Carter, Munir Cochinwala, and Martin Eiger

Telcordia Technologies, 445 South Street, Morristown, NJ 07960 USA

Abstract. We study caching as a means to reduce the message traffic and database accesses required for locating called subscribers in a Personal Communication Services (PCS) network. The challenge of caching routing information for mobile clients lies in the uncertainty of the length of time that the information remains valid. We use expiration timestamps to safeguard against using stale cached data. We study a variety of caching algorithms and a variety of methods for setting timestamps based on client mobility. We report results from simulation studies.

1 Introduction

The growing popularity of wireless communication systems is well-known. Recent measurements show that wireless accounts for 10.7% of global telecommunications traffic. This figure is predicted to rise to 17.7% by 2002 [16]. Meanwhile, the market for wireless handsets is expected to grow from the current 24 million to 32 million in the next 2 years [17].

One of the critical elements of wireless systems is the call delivery problem: how are the locations of mobile devices identified so that calls can be routed to them? Each mobile device has a logical address which must be translated to a physical routing address every time it is called. However, the physical routing address of a mobile endpoint changes as the device moves. In a typical PCS system, this translation is determined for each call by a 2-level lookup utilizing both the Home Location Register (HLR) and the Visiting Location Register (VLR). As the number of subscribers increases so does the rate of queries to the HLR. In this paper we study caching as a means of alleviating this increasing load on the HLR and VLR while also reducing the traffic load on the signalling network. In particular, we study how expiration timestamps on translations, which model the mobility patterns of the subscribers, can be used to support consistency of the cached data.

Caching data together with an expiration timestamp or a time-to-live is a mechanism for promoting, but not necessarily guaranteeing, the consistency of cached data. A timestamp provides an estimate of how long a cached item is likely to remain valid. Prior to the expiration time the cached copy is used, but after the expiration time the database is consulted for fresh data. In practice, an item may change before its expiration time or may remain unchanged beyond it. In the former case stale data is returned to the user; in the latter the client makes an unnecessary query for fresh information. In a client-server setting, expiration timestamps are attractive at least partly because of their simplicity: there are

J. Štuller et al. (Eds.): ADBIS-DASFAA 2000, LNCS 1884, pp. 37–50, 2000.

no complicated consistency protocols that require centralized control, so caches can be managed independently by the clients. Thus, there is distributed control at the possible price of occasional data inconsistency.

There are several well-known examples where expiration timestamps are used in Internet applications. Expiration timestamps are used by the Domain Name System (DNS) to promote consistency of name resolution [13,14], and they have been successful in this application because the name-to-address translations change infrequently and consistency is defined as "eventual" consistency. Expiration timestamps are also a current topic of research in web caching [4,9].

In previous work [5], we studied caching with expiration timestamps for traditional telephony applications like 800-number service. In this paper we focus on caching with expiration timestamps for mobile telephony applications. The challenge of caching data associated with mobile clients lies in the uncertainty associated with the time a client remains within a given area and thus the duration for which a translation remains valid. To study the impact of client mobility on system performance, we classify mobile users into two categories: tortoises and hares. The tortoises move slowly so their routing addresses change infrequently, while the hares move quickly so their routing addresses change often. Ideally, these differences can be captured by expiration timestamps associated with routing addresses. In turn, the caching scheme should adapt and adjust the timestamp duration appropriately, as the rate at which a user moves between cells changes.

We follow the traditional HLR and VLR model to translate and route addresses. (For an introduction to PCS architectures see [2,12].) We propose the addition of caches at the originating endpoint and/or HLR to reduce signalling network traffic and database query load. We explain a protocol to access the cache and we describe how the caches are updated. To study system performance we simulate the system with caches at the HLR and/or at the originating endpoints. The timestamp duration in the caches adapts to the changing behavior of the destinations. We measure the improvement in system performance in terms of the hit rates achieved at the caches, since each request satisfied by a cache reduces signalling network traffic, database query load and user-perceived response time.

2   Model

In our model for a Personal Communication System (PCS), illustrated in Figure 1, mobile users roam about in a network of cells. In a particular cell, an endpoint device (e.g. wireless handset) communicates with the base station for that cell. At all times, the endpoint is associated with a routing address that is used as the destination for incoming calls. The mobile user (and any ongoing call) is handed from one base station to the next as it moves among the cells. Groups of cells are organized into Registration Areas (RAs). Each RA is served by one end-office switch, or Service Switching Point (SSP), which handles call set-up between local endpoints and other endpoints or wireline devices. Co-located with each SSP is a Visiting Location Register (VLR) that keeps track of which mobile units are currently resident in the RA and their routing addresses within the RA. The Home Location Register (HLR) is a database with an entry for each mobile user containing the address of the VLR currently handling calls on that user's behalf. Thus, the HLR is used as the starting point in any attempt to locate a particular mobile endpoint.

As a user moves between RAs, its routing address and its VLR will change, so its HLR record must be updated to reflect the change in VLR. When a mobile endpoint moves between cells, its local routing address changes, and the VLR is notified, but there is no notification to the HLR. Our proposal is to track these local routing address changes in caches at the HLR and/or at the originating endpoints.

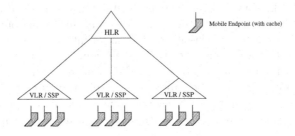

Fig. 1. Reference PCS network architecture.

Given this architecture, how are incoming calls routed to mobile endpoints? The basic location algorithm involves following a series of pointers from the HLR to a VLR and then to the endpoint itself. Specifically, call set-up involves these steps:

1. The call to a PCS user is directed to the switch (SSP) nearest the originating endpoint.
2. Assuming the destination is not in the local RA, the switch queries the HLR for routing information.
3. The HLR looks up the VLR associated with the destination endpoint and queries that VLR.
4. The VLR determines if the endpoint is available (i.e. not busy) and, if so, returns a routing address to the HLR.
5. The HLR relays the routing address back to the originating switch.

At this point the originating switch can route the call to the destination endpoint. The basic algorithm takes four messages: ($VLR_{orig} \rightarrow HLR$, $HLR \rightarrow VLR_{dest}$, $VLR_{dest} \rightarrow HLR$ and $HLR \rightarrow VLR_{orig}$) to complete the routing address translation.

This two-level lookup algorithm always involves the HLR. Clearly, if a particular endpoint tends to move slowly, its routing address will remain unchanged for extended periods of time. If that endpoint is also called frequently, many

VLR lookups can be avoided through caching. In other words, we propose to exploit the spatial and temporal locality in the system by introducing caches. Previous work [10] has suggested the idea of caching for mobile PCS users. This work extends those ideas by introducing expiration timestamps to model fast- and slow-moving users and by studying cache placement at the endpoints, the HLR and the combination of both locations.

Firstly, we propose that the originating endpoints each maintain a small cache mapping numbers dialed from that endpoint into routing addresses. Secondly, we add a cache at the HLR. The HLR cache could serve to enhance the effect of small endpoint caches by simply providing more cache space and would also be beneficial when a common destination is called by several endpoints. In this preliminary study we limit ourselves to this two-level hierarchy, leaving more complex topologies for future work.

With the introduction of endpoint caches, the location algorithm changes to allow the initial request to the SSP to include a cached routing address. If a cached routing address is present in the request, the SSP can forgo the initial query to the HLR and contact the destination endpoint directly. This will save the four-message query through the HLR that is required in the absence of caching thus increasing system throughput and reducing call setup times.

In the new caching architecture, when a routing address is supplied with the request the new location algorithm becomes:

1. The call to a PCS user is directed to the switch nearest the originating endpoint. Included in the call-request message is the cached routing address information, if available.
2. The originating switch connects the call to the destination endpoint.

However, there are now two new penalties that we may incur. Firstly, there may be no routing address in the originating endpoint cache for a particular destination. In this case, the SSP queries the HLR as before, incurring the usual four-message overhead in addition to a small latency penalty for the cache query. Secondly, the cache may return stale data. That is, the destination endpoint may no longer be associated with the routing address returned from the cache—it may have moved since we last communicated with it. As previously stated the most profitably cached translations are those for destination endpoints that are relatively motionless. But, in our model, endpoints can and will move at times. As in the first case, this second case must be recognized (the attempt to route to the cached address will fail) and handled. A fresh query to the HLR will be necessary at the cost of 4 messages. There is an additional latency penalty in this case due to the failed initial connection attempt.

The proposed caching scheme avoids unnecessary messages between the originating switch and the HLR and between the HLR and the VLR for relatively stationary destinations. However, as with any caching application, the efficacy depends on the hit rate that can be achieved. Intuition suggests that routing addresses for tortoises can be effectively cached, while caching for hares will be less beneficial.

So far we have concentrated on classifying the destination points of calls, all of which are mobile. While some of the callers will be mobile, there will also be a class of stationary callers. Stationary users are assumed to have bigger caches and should therefore see greater hit rates. In addition to the endpoint caches, a cache at the HLR can exploit the shared popularity of destination endpoints by providing extra cache space to augment the small caches at the endpoints.

Regardless of the location of the cache (endpoint, HLR, or both) consistency of the cache is addressed using expiration timestamps. Each cache entry has an associated timestamp after which the data is no longer used. These timestamps are an attempt to capture the speed of movement of the destination endpoints: fast-moving endpoints have smaller timestamps and slower-moving endpoints have larger timestamps.

3 Caching Details

We now describe our proposed caching algorithms.

3.1 Query Sequence

Since all routing information is obtained through the HLR, we can assume that the callers interact directly with the HLR, and that when the HLR maintains its own cache, client requests are filtered through that cache. Figure 2 provides a basic illustration. Here, we have a set of customers that independently query the HLR to obtain routing addresses.[1] Each customer has its own personal request profile and a private cache. The HLR has a database associating dialed numbers with their current VLR locations, and may also have a cache containing routing addresses for a subset of the numbers.

At each query, the HLR consults the called VLR for the current routing address and a new estimate of the time-to-live of the queried number translation. The time-to-live or expiration timestamp is computed from past expirations known to the VLR. This history of prior expirations is passed from one VLR to another as mobile users move.

Since this timestamp is a prediction of expiration, a cached address may in fact remain valid after its timestamp expires, or it may become stale before the prescribed time. Table 1 illustrates the four possible outcomes for a cache lookup (assuming the item is in the cache). If the expiration timestamp correctly identifies a valid cache entry then we have a *cache hit*. If the expiration timestamp correctly identifies an expired cache entry then we have a *cache miss*. In the case where the timestamp optimistically indicates an expired entry is still valid we have a *stale hit*. Finally, in the case when the timestamp pessimistically indicates that a valid entry has expired, we have a *false miss*.

Whenever a client initiates a request, that client's local cache is consulted. If the requested item is found and its expiration timestamp is valid, the query

---

[1] In fact, the queries are made by switches on behalf of customers during call set-up. To simplify the discussion we assume that customers query the HLR directly.

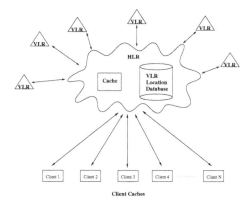

Fig. 2. A schematic view of caching at the endpoints and the HLR.

Table 1. Definition of query outcomes.

		actual expiration	
		Valid	Expired
predicted	Valid	Cache Hit	Stale Hit
expiration	Expired	False Miss	Cache Miss

results in an endpoint hit. In this case, the cached translation is used to place the call and no HLR query is immediately required. If the cache lookup is unsuccessful, either because the requested item is not in the cache or because the timestamp has expired, a miss occurs. On a miss, the client queries the HLR and caches the routing address provided by the HLR.

When the HLR receives a request, it checks its own cache, with outcomes that are analogous to those at the endpoint cache. When a miss occurs, the HLR reverts to the usual protocol wherein it looks up the VLR for the called number and then queries the VLR for the routing address.

3.2   Online Algorithms

Upon any miss—either at an endpoint cache or the HLR cache—the item causing the miss is inserted into the cache once the correct data is obtained. If the cache is full, some item must be evicted in order to accommodate the new address. The algorithm used to determine which item to evict is called a *caching algorithm*. Examples of well-known caching algorithms are:

LRU : Evict the item in the cache that was *least recently used*;
LRU-K : If all items have been accessed at least K times since insertion into the cache, evict the item that was least recently used. Otherwise evict the item accessed fewer than K times that was least recently used. (See [15].)

The problem of determining which items to keep in cache, when data has no associated expiration time, is a classic problem in online computation. An excellent discussion of important theoretical results is provided in [3]. We focus on LRU and LRU-2 in this paper because they are known to perform well in practice [15].

If we operate under the assumption that expired data should be removed from the cache at the first opportunity, then 2-tiered variants of the basic algorithms emerge [5]. The idea is to partition the cache into expired and fresh data at the time that an eviction is to occur. If there are expired data, we select an expired item to evict (and are indifferent as to which one). If there are no expired data, we apply the standard algorithm. We call this a *2-tiered algorithm* because we consider the expired items separately from the fresh items in the cache. In the simulations that follow, we observe the relative benefit of 2-tiered caching when expiration timestamps are predictions that may be somewhat inaccurate. As before, the first tier contains items whose timestamp has expired, but now this may not accurately characterize the validity of the associated data.

3.3 Offline Algorithms

All of the caching algorithms we have described so far are called online algorithms because they process each request in sequence without knowledge of future requests. In assessing caching algorithms, it is sometimes useful to compare the performance of online algorithms to the performance of an offline algorithm that optimizes its eviction decisions using complete knowledge of future requests. *The optimal offline algorithm provides the best-possible performance by a caching algorithm for any given request sequence.* If we had caches only at one level in the hierarchy—either at the endpoints or at the HLR, but not both—and the expiration timestamps were accurate, then the following algorithm is the optimal offline algorithm (see [5], for a proof):

OPT : If there are items in the cache that are expired at their next use, choose one of them to evict from the cache. Otherwise, evict the item whose next use is *farthest in the future*. (See also [3].)

Unlike the previous caching algorithms, OPT uses knowledge of the entire future sequence of requests to make its eviction selection. This makes OPT an impractical algorithm, but it serves as a useful benchmark against which to measure more practical algorithms.

4 Simulation Setup

We simulate the distributed caching schemes described in the previous sections. This provides an empirical gauge of system performance and allows us to vary key parameters to understand the impact of both subscriber behavior and system design variables.

For each of the studies presented in Section 5, we vary some parameters and hold others fixed. The variable parameters and their default settings (those used when the parameter itself is not being studied) include:

- The percentage breakdown of tortoises and hares: We study cases ranging from all tortoises to all hares. As a default, we assume that half of the subscribers are tortoises and half are hares.
- The definitions of tortoises and hares: Each category is defined by the frequency with which their routing address changes. As defaults, we assume that tortoises move once per hour and hares move 10 times per hour. In all cases, the precise movement times are random and independent.
- The cached expiration formula: The expiration timestamp of a cached item is an estimate of its next expiration. We study several approaches. In the "last" approach, a data item has a remaining life equal to the amount of time elapsed since its last expiration, multiplied by a scale factor. The "average" approach is similar, using a running average based on all previous expirations. For both approaches, we study scale factors of $1/8$, $1/4$, $1/2$, 1, 2, 4, and 8. As a benchmark, we study an omniscient approach in which predicted and actual times are the same. The default is the "last" approach with a scale factor of 1.
- The percentage breakdown of stationary and mobile callers: We study all stationary callers, all mobile callers, and several cases in between. The default is half stationary and half mobile.
- The definitions of stationary and mobile callers and cache sizes: Stationary callers are defined as having large endpoint caches (default size is 20), while mobile callers have small caches (default size is 5). We study cases where the size of callers' caches are halved, and where endpoint caches do not exist. We also study cases where the HLR's cache (default size is 100) is doubled, and where the HLR's cache does not exist.
- Eviction algorithm: We study LRU and LRU-2 in both the 1-tiered and 2-tiered versions. With no HLR cache, we also study the optimal offline algorithm.

In addition to these parameters which vary, several parameter values are fixed.

- The number of callers is 100, and the number of mobile destinations is 10,000.
- The inter-request time at each endpoint is exponentially distributed with a mean of 2 minutes.
- The requested items from each endpoint follow a Zipf probability distribution [11][2]. The Zipf distributions at the various endpoints are independent. A value of 1.0 is used for α.

---

[2] The Zipf distribution is a skewed distribution characterized by a parameter $\alpha \geq 0$. Higher values of α indicate more skewed distributions, or a stronger locality of reference. Recent studies [8,7] have shown that the Zipf distribution provides a good fit of observed web access data. Based on our limited observation of proprietary data, we believe that the same is probably true for telephone calling patterns.

– Cache lookups take 20 microseconds, and disk accesses take 7 milliseconds. Caches can process 1 request at a time, and the HLR can process up to 10 requests concurrently; messages requiring resources that are occupied are queued. All messages between endpoints and the HLR take 1 ms in transit, and 100 ms (in addition to any appropriate network transit delays) elapse between a stale hit and the time the request continues through the system.
– Each run of the simulation takes two hours (of simulation time), and 10 trials for each testcase are run, using different random number seeds. Requests generated in the first hour of the simulation are ignored, to eliminate start-up effects. The simulation runs until all pending requests are completed, but no new requests are generated after two hours.

5 Simulation Results

In this section we discuss the results of several simulations. We use cache hit rate as the measure of system performance. Each valid translation in our proposed endpoint cache eliminates signalling network messages and HLR database accesses. Each translation satisfied by the HLR cache eliminates an HLR database access. Cache hits also reduce call setup time. Thus, cache hit rate serves as a measure of improved system performance compared to the typical PCS architecture which does not employ caches.

Table 2 examines the impact of cache size and cache placement . The rows of the table give the HLR cache size . In the first column no endpoints have caches. In the second column the mobile callers have caches of size 3 and the stationary callers have caches of size 10. In the last column mobile callers have caches of 5 entries while stationary callers can store up to 20 cache entries. In this table 50% of the destinations are hares and 50% are tortoises.

Table 2. Cache hit rates for LRU 2-tiered experiments.

		Endpoint cache size (mobile/stationary)		
		0/0	3/10	5/20
HLR	0		4.5%/0.0%	5.2%/0.0%
cache	100	0.0%/2.5%	4.5%/0.9%	5.2%/0.8%
size	200	0.0%/4.5%	4.5%/1.7%	5.2%/1.5%

(Endpoint Cache Hit Rate / HLR Cache Hit Rate)

We find that system performance is better with caches at both locations, followed by caches at the endpoints alone. The presence or size of the HLR cache has no effect on endpoint cache hit rates because the endpoint query precedes the HLR query. Total cache hits drop off precipitously when there is a single shared cache at the HLR and no caches at the endpoints. This underscores the

value of endpoint caching, which not only allows cached data to be customized
to each endpoint, but also reduces query-related traffic in the network.

HLR cache hit rate is impacted by several factors. Larger endpoint caches
imply fewer HLR cache hits, because more frequently requested data will be
found in the endpoint caches. As expected, larger HLR caches imply more HLR
cache hits.

Table 3 examines the impact of 1-tiered vs 2-tiered caching and compares
caching algorithms (LRU, LRU-2 and offline). For the offline algorithm we show
the endpoint cache hit rate of 10.2%. For the LRU and LRU-2 algorithms we show
both the endpoint cache hit rate and the number of false misses. Recall that a
false miss occurs when the timestamp associated with the cache entry indicates
that the entry has expired when in fact it is still valid.

Table 3. Cache Placement Experiments

	1-tiered	2-tiered
offline		10.2% cache hits
LRU	4.7% cache hits	5.1% cache hits
	2.4% false misses	2.1% false misses
LRU-2	4.9% cache hits	5.2% cache hits
	2.7% false misses	2.2% false misses

We see that 2-tiered is slightly better than 1-tiered for both LRU and LRU-2.
This suggests that cache eviction schemes should preferentially evict expired data
before unexpired data even though the expiration timestamps are just estimates.
Second, a comparison of the LRU and LRU-2 approaches shows a very slight
advantage (more cache hits) for LRU-2, suggesting that it may be worthwhile for
caching architectures to track cache hits and incorporate them in their eviction
policies. Third, the 2-tiered strategies yield fewer false misses because these
strategies preferentially evict data with expired timestamps. Thus, there is less
expired data to yield false misses.

Figure 3 and Figure 4 show the endpoint cache hit rate and the number of
stale hits for out alternative timestamp estimation techniques.

Figure 3 plots endpoint cache hit rates for two estimation methods as the
scale factor is varied as well as an optimal method when predicted and actual
times are the same. Figure 4 plots the number of stale hits at both the endpoint
and database caches for both the average and last methods of estimation as the
scale factor is varied. The omniscient approach does not generate stale hits since
it knows precisely when caches entries will become invalid. At low scale factors
the number of cache hits is significantly diminished, but the number of times that
caches return stale data is relatively modest. At high scale factors, the number of
cache hits comes closer to the theoretical maximum, but only with a significant
number of instances of caches returning stale data. At intermediate scale factors,
the two trade off. These results suggest that there may be a significant system

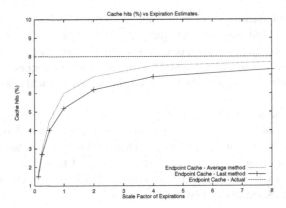

Fig. 3. Cache hits as scale factor on expiration estimation is varied.

performance penalty resulting from the uncertainty of future data expirations. However, if mobile users exhibit regular patterns, more efficient methods to predict data expirations may be possible. Further study of mobility patterns is suggested.

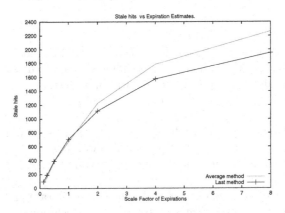

Fig. 4. Stale hits as scale factor on expiration estimation is varied.

Figure 5 shows system performance as the speed of movement varies among the tortoises and hares. By *move* we mean that a destination user's movement causes a routing address change. In this graph, each bar shows the cache hit rate at the endpoint cache and the HLR cache. The bars are grouped by frequency of hare movement: starting from the left we have the slowest hares who move 5 times per hour, then hares that move 10 times per hour and finally those that move 20 times per hour. Within each group of bars the left-most bar represents tortoises moving once in two hours, the middle bar those tortoises moving once an hour and the rightmost bar those tortoises that move twice per hour. In all cases the HLR cache handled about 0.8% of the requests and the rest were handled by the HLR itself. As one would expect, the faster either category of user moves, the more frequently their data expires, and the more times the HLR must be consulted. It is interesting to note, however, that doubling the expiration rate of tortoises has a greater impact than doubling the expiration rate of hares. Since the tortoises tend to have longer timestamps than hares, they remain in the cache longer and therefore, subsequent requests are more likely to be satisfied by the cache.

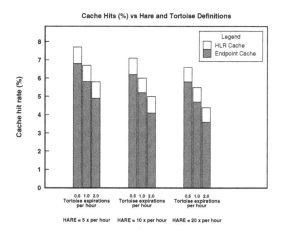

Fig. 5. Cache Hits as Frequency of hare and tortoise expiration is varied.

Figure 6 measures a similar effect, this time varying the proportions of tortoises and hares. This has a more profound impact on system performance, because the number of times that destinations' translations change in this study spans a greater range than in Figure 5. We see that the cache hit rate at the endpoint caches increases with the proportion of tortoises in the population while the hit rate at the HLR cache is almost constant at approximately 0.8%.

Our last experiment reveals the impact of callers' mobility on system performance. This is similar to varying the cache size, since stationary callers have caches of size 20 and mobile callers have caches of size 5. We found that with smaller caches at the endpoints, cache hits can diminish significantly, although the decreased cache performance (about 20% in this case) is significantly less than the decreased cache size (75%). See [5,6] for a more thorough treatment of the tradeoffs between cache size and system performance.

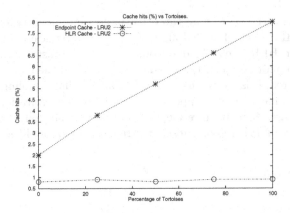

Fig. 6. Cache hits as proportion of hares and tortoises is varied.

6   Conclusion and Future Work

Uncertainty in the expiration timestamps yields two types of caching errors. In the first type, overestimating the lifetime of a cached item results in attempting to use a stale routing address to place a call. The second stems from underestimating lifetimes and results in unnecessary queries to the HLR and the VLR. Both errors incur relatively well-defined costs: overestimation may cost us the time associated with a failed call attempt and underestimation may cost us the time to ask for and receive a routing address from the VLR. Intuitively, the timestamp should weigh the tradeoff between these two costs. When the cost of a failed call is relatively high (as in this study), timestamps should be set conservatively, sacrificing true cache hits to avoid stale hits. Alternatively, when the cost of communicating with the HLR and VLR is relatively high (as during overload events) timestamp estimates should be more optimistic, allowing stale cache hits to avoid queries to the HLR and VLR.

The cases studied here explored the tradeoff between these two types of caching errors, but absent knowledge of the future, they could not reduce errors of one type without increasing errors of the other type. An area for future study is to see if it might be possible to reduce both types of error simultaneously. A caching algorithm that integrates recency and/or frequency of use with time-to-live may improve system performance.

The problem of stale hits might also be addressed using an *invalidation* protocol. As mobile endpoints move between RAs (and hence VLRs) their translations become invalid. When an invalid translation is used for call routing, a stale hit occurs. In our simulations we have imposed a stiff penalty for stale hits of 100ms. In an invalidation scheme, as an endpoint moves between RAs the HLR would be notified and would invalidate cached translations for the endpoint. The overhead of storage and signalling would depend on the exact architecture of the system but could be relatively small compared to the large stale hit penalty.

Other areas for future work include the issue of the real-time constraints of call setup, fault-tolerance of HLR and VLRs and a cost-benefit analysis of network traffic and database load.

References

1. C. Aggarwal, J. Wolf and P. Yu, "Caching on the World Wide Web", *IEEE Transactions on Knowledge and Data Engineering*, Jan/Feb 1999, Vol. 11, No. 1, pp 94–107.
2. I. Akyildiz and J. Ho, "On Location Management for Personal Communications Networks", *IEEE Communications Magazine*, September 1996, Vol. 34, No. 9, pp 138–145.
3. A. Borodin and R. El-Yaniv, *Online Computation and Competitive Analysis*, Cambridge University Press, 1998.
4. P. Cao and C. Liu, "Maintaining Strong Cache Consistency in the World Wide Web", *IEEE Transactions on Computers*, 47:445–457, 1998.
5. T. Carpenter, R. Carter, M. Cochinwala, M. Eiger, and M. Mihail, "Competitive Analysis of Client-Server Caching with Expiration Timestamps", Working Paper, 1998.
6. T. Carpenter, R. Carter, M. Cochinwala, and M. Eiger, "Data Caching for Telephony Services", to appear in Proceedings of the International Database Engineering and Application Symposium, September, 2000.
7. C. R. Cunha, A. Bestavros, and M. E. Crovella, "Characteristics of WWW Client-based Traces", Technical Report TR-95-010, Boston University Computer Science Department, June 1995.
8. S. Glassman, "A Caching Relay for the World Wide Web", in *Proceedings of the First International Conference on the World Wide Web*, 1994.
9. J. Gwertzman and M. Seltzer, "World-Wide Web Cache Consistency", in *Proceedings of the 1996 USENIX Technical Conference*, San Diego, California, April, 1996.
10. R. Jain, Y. Lin, C. Lo, and S. Mohan, "A Caching Strategy to Reduce Network Impacts of PCS", in *IEEE Journal on Selected Areas in Communications*, Vol. 12, No. 8, October, 1994.
11. D. Knuth, *The Art of Computer Programming, Volume 3: Sorting and Searching*, Addison Wesley, 1973.
12. Y-B. Lin and I. Chlamtac, "Heterogeneous Personal Communications Services: Integration of PCS Systems", *IEEE Communications Magazine*, September 1996, Vol. 34, No. 9, pp 106–113.
13. P. Mockapetris, "Domain Names - Concepts and Facilities", Internet Engineering Task Force RFC-1034, November, 1987.
14. P. Mockapetris, "Domain Names - Implementation and Specification", Internet Engineering Task Force RFC-1035, November, 1987.
15. E. O'Neil, P. O'Neil, and G. Weikum, "The LRU-K Page Replacement Algorithm for Database Disk Buffering" *Proceedings of the ACM SIGMOD Conference*, 297-306, May, 1993.
16. Wireless Review, http://www.wirelessreview.com/facts17.htm
17. Philips Consumer Communications, http://www2.wca.org/WCA/dgibson/sld004.htm, June 1998

Efficient Cache Management Protocol Based on Data Locality in Mobile DBMSs

IlYoung Chung, JeHyok Ryu, and Chong-Sun Hwang

Dept. of Computer Science and Engineering, Korea University
5-1, Anam-dong, Seongbuk-Ku, Seoul 136-701, Korea
{jiy, jhryu, hwang}@disys.korea.ac.kr

Abstract. In mobile client-server database systems, caching of frequent-ly accessed data is an important technique that will reduce the contention on the narrow bandwidth wireless channel. As the server in mobile en-vironments may not have any information about the state of its clients' cache(stateless server), using *broadcasting approach* to transmit the list of updated data to numerous concurrent mobile clients is an attractive approach. In this paper, a new caching method is proposed to support transaction semantics at mobile clients. The proposed protocol adopts *adaptive broadcasting* as the way of sending invalidation reports, in order to dynamically adapt to system workload(update pattern, data locality). We study the performance of the proposed protocol by means of simu-lation experiments.

1   Introduction

Data caching is an important technique for improving data availability and ac-cess latency[10]. It is especially important for mobile computing environments which are characterized by narrow bandwidth wireless links and frequent dis-connection from the server[2]. Those features of a mobile environment coupled with the need to support seamless mobility of clients distinguish its cache inva-lidation strategy unique and different from those used for wired network, since the strategy must try to optimize conflicting requirements under the constraints of limited bandwidth and frequent disconnection from the server[3].

Several proposals have appeared in the literature regarding the support of transactions in mobile systems[1]. And *broadcasting* approach is widely accep-ted to maintain cache consistency, and to control the concurrent transactions in mobile environments. With the broadcasting approach, a mobile client sends the commit request of a transaction after executing all operations, to install the updates in the central database. Then the server decides commit or abort of the requested transaction, and notifies this information to all clients in its cell with broadcasting invalidation reports. The broadcasting strategy does not require high communication costs, nor require the server to maintain additional infor-mation about mobile clients in its cell, thus is attractive in mobile databases[5,6].

Most approaches using broadcasting strategy adopt *synchronous(periodic)* manner as the way of broadcasting invalidation reports[3,4]. In these approaches,

J. Štuller et al. (Eds.): ADBIS-DASFAA 2000, LNCS 1884, pp. 51–64, 2000.

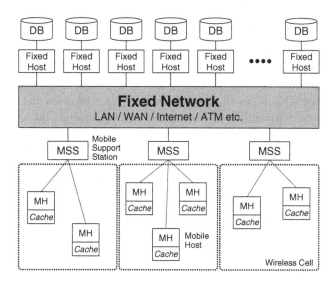

Fig. 1. The mobile database system architecture

server broadcasts the list of updated data items and the list of transactions that will be committed among those which have requested commit during the last period. These approaches present some problems due to the synchronous manner of broadcasting approach.

Considering these problems, we previously proposed and studied *asynchronous broadcasting protocol*. With asynchronous broadcasting approach, invalidation reports are broadcasted *immediately after* a commit request arrives. Thus, this protocol can reduce broadcasting occurrence and abort rate, at the expense of frequent broadcasting costs. However, for data items which show high degree of locality, this frequent broadcasting can be an unnecessary communication overhead.

In this paper, considering the tradeoffs of such existing protocols, we present an adaptive protocol which is a hybrid of the synchronous and asynchronous algorithm. With this approach, the proposed protocol can dynamically adjust the broadcasting method according to the system workload.

Figure 1 presents a general mobile database system model. Users of the mobile computers may frequently query databases by invoking a series of operations, generally referred to as a transaction. *Serializability* is widely accepted as a correctness criterion for execution of transactions[12]. This correctness criterion is also adopted in this paper. Database server is intended to support basic transaction operations such as resource allocation, commit, and abort[9].

The remainder of the paper is organized as follows. In section 2, we discuss synchronous and asynchronous broadcasting protocols, and in section 3, we describe and discuss the proposed protocol, adaptive broadcasting protocol. Section 4 presents experiments and results, and finally we state our concluding remarks in section 5.

2   Related Works

Some proposals have appeared in the literature regarding the use of the broadcasting for the control of the concurrent transactions, and all of these approaches adopted *synchronous(periodic)* manner as the way of sending broadcasting invalidation reports[4,6,8]. In these schemes, the server broadcasts the list of data items that should be invalidated and the list of transactions that will be committed among those which have requested commit during the last period[4]. These schemes present some problems due to the synchronous manner of broadcasting approach.

- if two or more conflicting transactions have requested commit during the same period, only one of them can commit and others have to abort.
- the mobile client is blocked on the average for the half of the broadcasting period until it decides commit or abort of the transaction.

Thus, existing proposals which adopted synchronous broadcasting cannot dynamically adapt to system workload(e.g. update pattern and data locality), since they broadcast invalidation reports by fixed period.

In previous work, we proposed and studied *asynchronous broadcasting protocol*[7]. It may resolve those problems of synchronous broadcasting by sending invalidation reports immediately after receiving commit requests. Thus, asynchronous broadcasting protocol can dynamically adjust the frequency of the broadcasting occurrence according to the update pattern of transactions. However, for data items that are used by a specific mobile client exclusively, applying asynchronous approach is quite wasteful. In this case, it is sufficient to send the updated data items periodically, along with the list of data items updated during the last period.

Thus the synchronous protocol can be advantageous, when high degree of locality is shown on accessed data by mobile clients. When a data item is updated by a transaction, and if there is no other mobile clients caching this data, synchronous broadcasting strategy is advantageous, because delayed invalidation report of data items does not cause aborts of other transactions, and it dose not degrades the throughput of transaction processing seriously. So, it is unnecessary to send invalidation reports separately, wasting the broadcasting bandwidth of wireless channel.

On the other hand, when mobile clients do not show such locality pattern on data items that are accessed, asynchronous broadcasting approach is more attractive, since the immediate invalidation of the updated data items can prevent large portion of aborts of other transactions which access local copies of these data items.

3   Proposed Protocol

In order to dynamically adjust the broadcasting method according to the system workload, we present a new cache management protocol, which can adapt to locality of data items.

3.1 Adaptive Broadcasting

Considering the tradeoffs discussed in section 2, integrating two broadcasting strategies (synchronous and asynchronous broadcasting) yields an adaptive algorithm, which we call *adaptive broadcasting protocol*. In this protocol, the server dynamically adopts appropriate broadcasting strategy between synchronous broadcasting and asynchronous broadcasting according to the locality pattern of data items which have been updated. With adaptive broadcasting, when the server receives commit request from a mobile client, it checks if any data item which has been updated by the transaction is widely shared by many clients' cache or not.

If all updated data items are cached by few mobile clients, the server just put these items to the invalidating list. Immediate broadcasting of data items which are cached by few clients or no other client except the updating one is quite wasteful. Thus, in this case, the protocol just adds those data items to the invalidating list that will be broadcast periodically. On the other hand, when the server receives a commit request of a transaction which has updated widely shared data items, the protocol applies asynchronous approach as the way of sending the invalidation reports. So, in this case, the server immediately sends data items which have been updated, along with the invalidating list produced after the last broadcasting. Thus, with adaptive broadcasting, invalidation reports are broadcasted in one of the following two situations.

− when a commit request contains widely shared data items in its write_set.

− when it is time to send periodic invalidation reports.(unless the invalidating list is empty)

3.2 The Protocol

Now, we need to explain how to apply appropriate broadcasting approach according to data items which have been updated by transactions. Because asynchronous broadcasting itself is adaptive to the change of update frequency, the proposed protocol should control the broadcasting mechanism based on the *locality* pattern of cached copies that should be invalidated. For this, we define the *sharing state* for each data item, in order to classify them. Checking this sharing state, the server adopts appropriate broadcasting approach for each updated data item.

Based on this criteria, all data items are assigned one of the following two classes by the server. The sharing state should be managed dynamically as the access pattern or locality of data changes.

− *shared* : data items that are cached by many clients

− *exclusive* : data items that are cached by no or few clients

Now, we need to summarize algorithms of the proposed protocol, which utilizes the sharing state of data items. Our protocol uses a modified version of optimistic control, in order to reduce the communication costs on the wireless network. With optimistic approach, all operations of a transaction can be processed locally using cached data, and at the end of the transaction, the mobile client sends the commit request message to the server[11]. Receiving invalidation report, the invalidating action *preempts* the ongoing transaction, thus transactions which are concurrently processed locally and show conflicts with the committing transaction, should be aborted. With this approach, the mobile client can early detect the conflicts of a transaction without interaction with the server[4].

All data items in the system are tagged with a sequence number which uniquely identifies the state of the data. The sequence number of data item is increased by the server, when the data item is updated. The mobile client includes the sequence number of its cached copy of data(if the data item is cache resident) along with the commit request message.

We now summarize our protocol for both the mobile client and the server.

Mobile Client Protocol:

- Whenever a transaction becomes active, the mobile client opens two sets, read_set and write_set. Initially, the state of a transaction is marked as *reading*. Data item is added to these sets with the sequence numbers, when the transaction requests read or write operation on that data item. The state of the transaction is changed into *updating* state, when the transaction requests write operation.
- Whenever the mobile client receives an invalidation report, it removes copies of the data items that are found in the invalidating list. And, if any of the following equations becomes true, the transaction of *reading* state is changed into *read-only* state, and the transaction of *updating* state is aborted.

$$\text{read\_set} \cap \text{invalidatinglist} \neq \emptyset$$
$$\text{write\_set} \cap \text{invalidatinglist} \neq \emptyset$$

- When a transaction of *read-only* state requests any write operation, the mobile client aborts the transaction.
- When a transaction is ready to commit, the mobile client commits the transaction locally, if the state of the transaction is *reading* or *read-only*. If the state of the transaction is *updating*, the mobile client sends a commit request message along with the read_set, write_set and the identification number of the transaction.
- After that, the mobile client listens to the broadcasting invalidation report which satisfies any of the following equation.

$$\text{read\_set} \cap \text{invalidatinglist} \neq \emptyset$$
$$\text{write\_set} \cap \text{invalidatinglist} \neq \emptyset$$

If the invalidation report, satisfying above equations, is attached with the identification number of its own transaction, the mobile client commits the transaction. Otherwise, the mobile client aborts the transaction, and removes copies of the data items that are found in invalidating list.

When T_i requests no write operation, the decision of commit or abort of T_i is done locally by the mobile client, using the invalidation reports broadcasted asynchronously by the server. In this case, the state of T_i is changed into *read-only*, if the mobile client is informed about the commit of a conflicting transaction T_j by a invalidation report, and T_i follows T_j in serialization order. The mobile client aborts the T_i, if T_i requests any write operation during *read-only* state, because such write operations can produce conflict relation T_i to T_j, which is unacceptable for serializable execution.

These remarks can be made more formally as follows.

Lemma 1 *Let T_i be a transaction of reading or read-only state executed in mobile client i (MC_i), and let T_j be a transaction of updating state in MC_j, which conflicts with T_i. If MC_i receives the invalidation report which includes T_j before it starts T_i, then T_i follows T_j in serialization order.*

Proof: Since T_i conflicts with T_j, for some data item x there exist conflicting operations $r_i(x)$ and $w_j(x)$. $r_i(x)$ reads the value of x which has been updated by the committed transaction T_j, since MC_i receives the invalidation reports which notifies commit of T_j before it starts T_i. Thus, for all $p_i(x)$ which conflicts with $q_j(x)$, $q_j(x) < p_i(x)$, therefore $T_j \to T_i$.   □

Lemma 2 *Let T_i be a transaction of reading or read-only state executed in mobile client i (MC_i), and let T_j be a transaction of updating state in MC_j, which conflicts with T_i. If MC_i receives the invalidation report which includes T_j after it starts T_i, then T_i precedes T_j in serialization order.*

Proof: Since T_i conflicts with T_j, for some data item x there exist conflicting operations $r_i(x)$ and $w_j(x)$. With OCC-ASB, if MC_i receives the invalidation report which invalidates x after it starts T_i, MC_i does nothing as the state of T_i is *reading* or *read-only*, and delays the invalidation of x until T_i commits. Thus, for all $p_i(x)$ which conflicts with $q_j(x)$, $p_i(x) < q_j(x)$, therefore $T_i \to T_j$.   □

Lemma 3 *Let T_i and T_j be transactions of reading or read-only state which are executed in MC_i and MC_j respectively. Then, there exists no serialization order between T_i and T_j.*

Proof: Since T_i and T_j request no write operation, there exists no conflicting operations $p_i(x)$ and $q_j(x)$.   □

Theorem 1 *Every transaction T_i that is committed autonomously by MC_i, does not produce a cycle with any other transaction in serialization graph.*

Proof : Suppose that the serialization graph contains $T_j \to T_i \to T_k$. By Lemma 1, 2 and 3, the state of T_j and T_k are *updating*, and MC_i received the invalidation report of T_j before T_i started, and the invalidation report of T_k after T_i started. As we assumed that invalidation reports are received as the order that they are broadcasted, T_j has committed earlier than T_k, in the server, therefore $T_k \rightarrow T_j$ is impossible. □

Unlike transactions of *reading* or *read-only* state, the decision of committing a transaction of *updating* state is done by the server, as the mobile client cannot determine the serialization order of the transaction autonomously, if the transaction has executed any write operation. Thus, when an *updating* transaction is ready to commit, the mobile client sends a commit request message to the server, as shown in mobile client protocol.

Now, we summarize the protocol which is performed continuously by the server.

Server Protocol:

- Whenever the server receives a commit request from a mobile client, it checks the sequence numbers of all data items in read_set and write_set.

  - If they are identical with the server's, and if all data items in write_set are marked as *exclusive* state, the server just adds these data items to invalidating list. The identification of the transaction is also attached to the invalidation report.
  - If they are identical with the server's, and if there is any data item in write_set which is marked as *shared* state, the server adds the updated data items to the invalidating list, and attaches the identification of the transaction. Then the server sends the invalidation report containing invalidating list and transaction identifiers immediately.
  - If sequence numbers have fallen behind the server's number, the server just ignores the commit request.

- When it is time to broadcast periodic invalidation report, the server checks if the invalidating list is empty. If the list is not empty, the server broadcasts invalidation report.

Lemma 4 *Let T_i be a transaction of updating state which requests commit to the server. When a server receives a commit request of $T_i(CR_i)$, T_i will be checked against every conflicting transaction whose CR has arrived earlier in the server.*

Proof : The server checks the sequence numbers in CR_i with those in the server, which have been updated by transactions whose CR have been arrived earlier. □

Lemma 5 *Let T_i and T_j be conflicting transactions of updating state in MC_i and MC_j respectively. If the server receives CR_j earlier than CR_i, T_i cannot precede T_j in serialization order.*

Proof : There are three cases.

- MC_i gets the invalidation report of T_j while T_i executes. In this case, MC_i aborts T_i autonomously.
- MC_i gets the invalidation report of T_j after sending CR_i to the server. Suppose T_i and T_j conflict on data item x. In this case, MC_i aborts T_i, when it receives the invalidation report of T_j which invalidates x.
- MC_i gets the invalidation report of T_j before starting T_i. In this case, $T_j \rightarrow T_i$, by Lemma 1.

$\square$

Theorem 2 *Every updating transaction T_i that is committed in the server, does not produce a cycle with any other updating transaction in serialization graph.*

Proof : Suppose that the serialization graph contains $T_j \rightarrow T_i \rightarrow T_k$. By Lemma 4, the server receives CR_j earlier than CR_k. Thus, T_k cannot precede TR_j in serialization order, by Lemma 5. $\square$

Theorem 3 *The OCC-ASB produces serializable hostories.*

Proof : By Theorem 1 and 2. $\square$

3.3   Examples

Example execution under the protocol is shown in Figure 2. This example uses two mobile clients and a server. In this example, a, b and x denote data items that are cached by each mobile client, and we assume that data item x is classified as *shared* state, and data item a and b are classified as *exclusive* state. And, r(x) and w(x) denote a read and write operation performed by a transaction on data item x.

In (a), both mobile client 1 and mobile client 2 should send commit request message to the server, as the state of both transactions are *updating* when they are ready to commit. Receiving these commit requests, the server find that sequence numbers of data items in read_set and write_set are identical with the server's. Since data items in write_sets, a and b in this example, are maintained as *exclusive* state, the server just appends these items to invalidating list. When it is time to broadcast invalidation report, the server checks if the invalidating list is empty or not. Since there exist data items, a and b, in invalidating list, the server sends invalidation reports which notifies commit of both transactions, and update of data items.

In (b), when the server receives commit request of the second transaction from mobile client 1, it broadcasts invalidation reports immediately, as the write_set includes data item of *shared* state. The transaction initiated in mobile client 2 can be committed by the server, as it has read the current value of data item x which has been updated by the transaction in mobile client 1. Unless the server

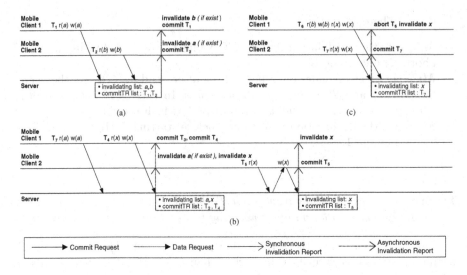

Fig. 2. Example execution of the proposed protocol

applies asynchronous approach to data item x, the transaction in mobile client 2 cannot read the up-to-date value of data item x, and it has to abort.

In (c), the transaction in mobile client 2 cannot commit in spite of immediate broadcasting, since mobile client 2 sends commit request message slightly before it receives invalidation report which indicates updates of data item x. In this case, the server does not have to notify mobile client 2 that the transaction cannot be committed, as mobile client 2 can abort the transaction when it receives invalidation report including data item x with identification of other transaction.

4   Performance

In this section, we present results from several performance experiments involving the proposed protocol, and the protocols with synchronous[4] and asynchronous[7] broadcasting scheme. While the main performance metric presented is system *throughput*, we also present other performance measures, *the number of aborts* and *the number of broadcasting occurrences*, to provide additional insights into the fundamental tradeoff between protocols. Table 1 shows the values of the simulation parameters used for these experiments.

We performed experiments under the following conditions: (1)when low portion of entire data items are shared by mobile clients, (2)when high portion of them are shared. In order to provide such experimental environments, we set the system parameter *SharedDegree* as 10% and 40%, as shown in Table 1. It implies that 10% or 40% of entire data items are classified as *shared* state, and the rest of them is classified as *exclusive* state.

We ran a number of simulations to compare the behavior of the proposed protocol and the protocols with synchronous and asynchronous broadcasting

Table 1. Simulation parameter settings

Parameter	Meaning	Value
NObject	Number of objects	500
CachePercent	Percentage of cache size	5%
TRSize(Max)	Maximum number of operations in a transaction	15
TRSize(Min)	Minimum number of operations in a transaction	3
ProWrite	Probability of write operations	0 - 25 %
ReadDelay	Average delay of a read operation	10 ms
WriteDelay	Average delay of a write operation	40 ms
NClient	Number of mobile clients	50
NetDelay	Average communication delay	20 ms
DBAcessDelay	Average delay to access DB	50 ms
CacheAccessDelay	Average delay to access cache	10 ms
ReadHitProb	Probability of read hit	0.5
IRPeriod	Interval of synchronous broadcasting	1000 ms
SharedDegree	Percentage of *shared* data	10, 40%

scheme. In this section, we present the results from these performance experiments. At first, Figure 3 and Figure 4 show the average number of transactions that should be aborted with proposed protocols and the synchronous protocol. As can be seen, more transactions are aborted with increasing write operations, in both cases of Figure 3 and Figure 4, when *SharedDegree* is low and high, respectively. In case of Figure 3(*SharedDegree*=10%), increased write operations don't cause frequent conflicts between updating transactions, because most of data items are accessed exclusively by each mobile client. Thus, in this case, the protocol with synchronous broadcasting does not suffer with high ratio of aborts. On the other hand, in Figure 4(*SharedDegree*=40%), the number of aborts is more dependent on the probability of write operations. Thus, as the probability of write operations gets higher, aborts increase significantly with all three protocols. This is because updates on shared data make copies cached by large number of mobile clients out-of-date. In case of the protocol with synchronous broadcasting, aborts increase more rapidly, because more conflicting transactions request commit during the same broadcasting period. In this case, the synchronous protocol permits only one transaction to commit, thus all other transactions that show conflicts with the committing one should abort. It shows the primary drawback of the synchronous protocol. For the protocol with asynchronous broadcasting, the number of aborts increases relatively slowly, as the server sends broadcasting message immediately after receiving commit requests. The immediate broadcasting avoids most aborts of the synchronous protocol, as it reduces transactions' chance to access stale copies of updated data items. The proposed protocol shows satisfying results, which are similar to those of asynchronous broadcasting protocol, as it applies immediate broadcasting scheme to updated data items which are likely to be accessed by lots of clients.

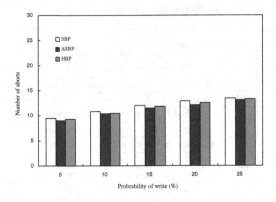

Fig. 3. Average number of aborts with 10% *SharedDegree*

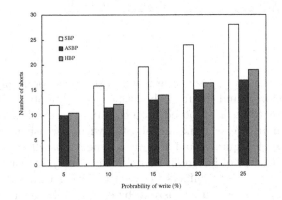

Fig. 4. Average number of aborts with 40% *SharedDegree*

Figure 5 and Figure 6 show the number of broadcasting occurrence with three protocols. This performance measure clearly presents the characteristics of the broadcasting strategy of each protocol. In case of the protocol with synchronous broadcasting, the server issues uniform number of broadcastings independent of the write probability or *SharedDegree*, as shown in the Figure 5 and Figure 6. On the contrary, asynchronous broadcasting protocol shows very sensitive results to the probability of writes, since the server issues broadcasting once for every commit of an updating transaction. With the proposed protocol, as shown in the figure, the number of broadcasting occurrences shows an intermediate form between other two protocols. When *SharedDegree* is low, the server applies synchronous broadcasting approach to updates on most of data items, thus our protocol arises similar number of broadcastings with the synchronous protocol. On the other hand, as shown in Figure 5, the number of broadcastings of the proposed protocol is close to that of asynchronous broadcasting protocol, when

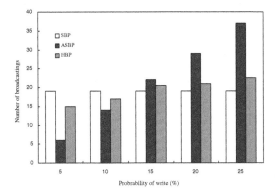

Fig. 5. Average number of broadcastings with 10% *SharedDegree*

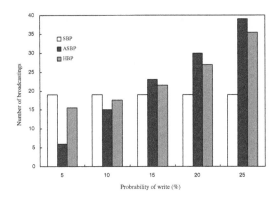

Fig. 6. Average number of broadcastings with 40% *SharedDegree*

SharedDegree is high, and as a result, our protocol arises almost as low aborts as asynchronous broadcasting protocol, as shown in Figure 4. Thus the proposed protocol can adapt not only to update probability but also to locality pattern of cached data.

Figure 7 and Figure 8 show the throughput results for three protocols. As shown in this figure, the throughput degrades with increasing write operations, because of aborts and delay for updating transactions. When only 10% of data items are widely shared by mobile clients, the protocol with synchronous broadcasting shows stable throughput as can be seen in Figure 7. When the write probability is low, our protocol and asynchronous broadcasting protocol show better performance than the synchronous protocol, because of autonomous commit of read-only transactions. However, the throughput of asynchronous protocol degrades rapidly with increasing write operations, mainly due to the frequent transmission of broadcasting messages. The immediate broadcasting strategy

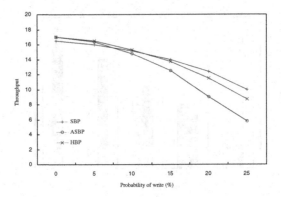

Fig. 7. Throughput with 10% *SharedDegree*

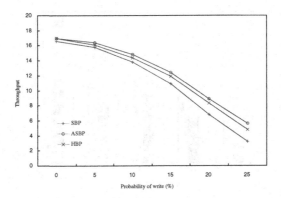

Fig. 8. Throughput with 40% *SharedDegree*

of asynchronous protocol is an communication overhead which cannot reduce aborts of transactions, when *SharedDegree* is low(see Figure 3). Thus, in this case, the synchronous protocol is more satisfying, because it does not suffer from serious ratio of aborts without high communication costs(see Figure 5). The proposed protocol shows intermediate result between the asynchronous protocol and the synchronous protocol, as it applies immediate broadcasting to 10% of entire data items. On the other hand, when 40% of data items are widely shared by mobile clients, proposed protocols show better performance in whole range of update probability, because our protocol and asynchronous protocol can avoid a number of aborts with asynchronous broadcasting(see Figure 4).

5   Conclusions

Caching of data items in mobile clients is an effective model that may reduce contention on the narrow bandwidth wireless channel. In this paper, we propose a new cache management protocol, supporting transaction semantics. The proposed protocol dynamically adopts appropriate broadcasting strategy between synchronous and asynchronous strategy, according to the locality pattern of cached copies of updated data. Thus the protocol can dynamically adapt not only to update probability, but also to locality of data copies. Simulations were conducted to evaluate the performance of the proposed protocol. Our performance experiments show that the proposed protocol performs well independent on the degree of locality of data items by achieving satisfying balance between abort probability and broadcasting costs.

References

1. A.Elmagarmid, J.Jing and O.Bukhres, "An Efficient and Reliable Reservation Algorithm for Mobile Transactions," *Proc. of International Conference on Information and Knowledge Management*, 1995.
2. A.Elmagarmid, J.Jing and T.Furukawa, "Wireless Client/Server Computing for Personal Information Services and Applications," *Proc. of ACM SIGMOD International Conference on Management of Data*, 1997.
3. B.Y.Chan, A.Si and H.V.Leong, "Cache Management for Mobile Databases: Design and Evaludation," *Proc. of the International Conference on Data Engineering*, 1998.
4. D.Barbara, "Certification Reports: Supporting Transactions in Wireless Systems," *Proc. of IEEE International Conference on Distributed Computing*, 1997.
5. D.Barbara and T.Imielinsky, "Sleepers and Workaholics: Caching in Mobile Environments," *Proc. of ACM SIGMOD International Conference on Management of Data*, 1994.
6. E.Pitoura and P.K.Chrysanthis, "Scalable Processing of Read-Only Transactions in Broadcast Push," *Proc. of International Conference on Distributed Computing Systems*, 1999.
7. I.Chung and C.-S. Hwang, "Transactional Cache Management with Aperiodic Invalidation Scheme in Mobile Environments," *Proc. of Asian Conputing Science Conference*, LNCS 1742, Springer Verlag, 1999.
8. J.Shanmugasundaram, A.Nithrakashyap and R.Sivasankaran, "Efficient Concurrency Control for Broadcast Environments," *Proc. of ACM SIGMOD International Conference on Management of Data*, 1999.
9. K.Voruganti, M.T.Ozsu and R.C.Unrau, "An Adaptive Hybrid Server Archtecture for Client Caching Object DBMSs," *Proc. of the International Conference on Very Large Data Bases*, 1999.
10. M.J.Franklin, "Caching and Memory Management in Client-Server Database Systems," Ph.d. Thesis, Dept. of Computer Science, University of Wisconsin, 1993.
11. M.T.Ozsu, K.Voruganti and R.C.Unrau RC, "An Asynchronous Avoidance-Based Cache Consistency Algorithm for Client Caching DBMSs," *Proc. of the International Conference on Very Large Data Bases*, 1998.
12. P.A.Berstein, V.Hadzilacos and N.Goodman, *Concurrency Control and Recovery in Database Systems*, Addison-Wesley, 1987.

Algorithms for Rewriting Aggregate Queries Using Views

Sara Cohen[1], Werner Nutt[2], and Alexander Serebrenik[3]

[1] Computer Science Dept., The Hebrew University, Jerusalem, Israel
sarina@cs.huji.ac.il
[2] German Research Center for Artificial Intelligence
(DFKI GmbH), 66123 Saarbrücken, Germany
Werner.Nutt@dfki.de
[3] Computer Science Dept., K. U. Leuven, Heverlee, Belgium
Alexander.Serebrenik@cs.kuleuven.ac.be

Abstract. Queries involving aggregation are typical in database applications. One of the main ideas to optimize the execution of an aggregate
query is to reuse results of previously answered queries. This leads to
the problem of rewriting aggregate queries using views. Due to a lack
of theory, algorithms for this problem were rather ad-hoc. They were
sound, but were not proven to be complete.

Recently we have given syntactic characterizations for the equivalence of
aggregate queries and applied them to decide when there exist rewritings.
However, these decision procedures do not lend themselves immediately
to an implementation. In this paper, we present practical algorithms
for rewriting queries with *count* and *sum*. Our algorithms are sound.
They are also complete for important cases. Our techniques can be used
to improve well-known procedures for rewriting non-aggregate queries.
These procedures can then be adapted to obtain algorithms for rewriting
queries with *min* and *max*. The algorithms presented are a basis for
realizing optimizers that rewrite queries using views.

1   Introduction

Aggregate queries occur in many applications, such as data warehousing and
global information systems. The size of the database in these applications is
generally very large. Aggregation is often used in queries against such sources as
a means of reducing the granularity of data. The execution of aggregate queries
tends to be time consuming and costly. Computing one aggregate value often
requires scanning many data items. This makes query optimization a necessity.
A promising technique to speed up the execution of aggregate queries is to reuse
the answers to previous queries to answer new queries. If the previous queries
involved aggregation, the answers to them will tend to be much smaller than the
size of the database. Thus, using their answers will be much more efficient.

We call a reformulation of a query that uses other queries a *rewriting*. Finding
such rewritings is known as the problem of *rewriting queries using views*. In

J. Štuller et al. (Eds.): ADBIS-DASFAA 2000, LNCS 1884, pp. 65–78, 2000.

this phrasing of the problem, it is assumed that there is a set of *views*, whose answers have been stored, or *materialized*. Given a query, the problem is to find a rewriting, which is formulated in terms of the views and some database relations, such that evaluating the original query yields the same answers as evaluating first the views and then the rewriting.

Rewriting queries using views has been studied for non-aggregate queries [LMSS95]. Rewriting aggregate queries has been investigated mainly in the special case of datacubes [HRU96]. However, there is little theory for general aggregate queries, and the rewriting algorithms that appear in the literature are by and large ad hoc. These algorithms are sound, that is, the reformulated queries they produce are in fact rewritings, but there is neither a guarantee that they output a rewriting whenever one exists, nor that they generate all existing rewritings [SDJL96,GHQ95].

Syntactic characterizations for the equivalence of SQL queries with the aggregate operators *min*, *max*, *count*, and *sum* have been given [NSS98]. They have been applied to decide, given an aggregate query and a set of views, whether there exists a rewriting, and whether a query over views and base relations is a rewriting [CNS99]. Using these characterizations, one can "guess" candidates for rewritings and verify if they are equivalent to the original query. This process is highly nondeterministic. It is more efficient to gradually build a candidate for rewriting in a way that will ensure its being a rewriting. The characterizations do not immediately yield practical algorithms of this sort. There are several subtle problems that must be dealt with in order to yield complete algorithms.

In this paper, we show how to derive practical algorithms for rewriting aggregate queries. The algorithms are sound, i.e., they output rewritings. We can also show that they are complete for important cases, which are relevant in practice. In Section 2 we present a motivating example. A formal framework for rewritings of aggregate queries is presented in Section 3. In Section 4 we give algorithms for rewriting aggregate queries and in Section 5 we conclude. Additional explanations and examples can be found in the full paper [CNS00].

2   Motivation

We discuss an example that illustrates the rewriting problem for aggregate queries. All the examples in this paper are written using an extended Datalog syntax. This syntax is more abstract and concise than SQL. In Section 3 we present a formal definition of the Datalog syntax. In [CNS00] we describe how queries written in SQL can be translated to our Datalog syntax and vice versa.

The following example models exactly the payment policy for teaching assistants at the Hebrew University in Jerusalem. There are two tables with relations pertaining to salaries of teaching assistants (TAs):

ta(name,course_name,job_type) and
salaries(job_type,sponsorship,amount).

At the Hebrew University, there may be many teaching assistants in a course. Each TA has at least one job_type in the course he assists. For example, he may give lectures or grade exercises. Teaching assistants are financed by different sources, like science foundations and the university itself. For each job type, each sponsor gives a fixed amount. Thus, a lab instructor may receive \$600 per month from the university and \$400 from a government science foundation.

We suppose that there are two materialized views. In v_positions, we compute the number of positions of each type held in the university. In v_salary we compute the total salary for each type of position. In the query q_salary_per_job we calculate the total amount of money spent on each job position. We express aggregate queries with an extended Datalog notation, where in the head we separate grouping variables and aggregate terms by a semicolon:

$$\text{v\_positions}(j; count) \leftarrow \text{ta}(n, c, j)$$
$$\text{v\_salary}(j; sum(a)) \leftarrow \text{salaries}(j, s, a)$$
$$\text{q\_salary\_per\_job}(j; sum(a)) \leftarrow \text{ta}(n, c, j) \,\&\, \text{salaries}(j, s, a).$$

An intelligent query optimizer could now reason that for each type of job we can calculate the total amount of money spent on it if we multiply the salary that one TA receives for such a job by the number of positions of that type. The two materialized views contain information that can be combined to yield an answer to our query. The optimizer can formulate a new query that only accesses the views and does not touch the tables in the database:

$$r(j'; a' * cnt) \leftarrow \text{v\_positions}(j'; cnt) \,\&\, \text{v\_salary}(j'; a')$$

Using the new query, we no longer need to look up the teaching assistants nor the financing sources. Thus, the new query can be executed more efficiently.

In this example, we used our common sense in two occasions. First, we gave an argument why evaluating the original query yields the same result as evaluating the new query that uses the views. Second, because we understood the semantics of the original query and the views, we were able find a reformulation of the query over the views. Thus, we will only be able to build an optimizer that can rewrite aggregate queries, if we can provide answers to the following two questions.

- **Rewriting Verification:** How can we prove that a new query, which uses views, produces the same results as the original query?
- **Rewriting Computation:** How can we devise an algorithm that systematically and efficiently finds all rewritings?

If efficiency and completeness cannot be achieved at the same time, we may have to find a good trade-off between the two requirements.

3 A Formal Framework

We extend the well-known Datalog syntax for non-aggregate queries [Ull89] to cover aggregates. These queries express nonnested SQL queries without a HAVING clause and with the aggregate operators *min*, *max*, *count*, and *sum*. A generalization to queries with the constructor UNION is possible, but beyond the scope of this paper. For queries with arbitrary nesting and negation no rewriting algorithms are feasible, since equivalence of such queries is undecidable.

3.1 Non-aggregate Queries

We recall the Datalog notation for conjunctive queries and extend it to aggregate queries. A *term* (denoted as s, t) is either a variable (denoted as x, y, z) or a constant. A *comparison* has the form $s_1 \, \rho \, s_2$, where ρ is either $<$ or $\leq$. If C and C' are conjunctions of comparisons, we write $C \models C'$ if C' is a consequence of C. We assume all comparisons range over the rationals.

We denote predicates as p, q and r. A *relational atom* has the form $p(\bar{s})$ or $p(s_1, \ldots, s_k)$ where $\bar{s}$ denotes the tuple of terms $s_1, \ldots, s_k$. An *atom* (denoted as a, b) is either a relational atom or a comparison.

A *conjunctive query* has the form $q(x_1, \ldots, x_k) \leftarrow a_1 \, \& \, \cdots \, \& \, a_n$. The atom $q(x_1, \ldots, x_k)$ is the *head* of the query. The atoms $a_1, \ldots, a_n$ form the query *body*. They can be relational or comparisons. If the body contains no comparisons, then the query is *relational*. A query is *linear* if it does not contain two relational atoms with the same predicate symbol. We abbreviate a query as $q(\bar{x}) \leftarrow B(\bar{s})$, where $B(\bar{s})$ stands for the body and $\bar{s}$ for the terms occurring in the body. Similarly, we may write a conjunctive query as $q(\bar{x}) \leftarrow R(\bar{s}) \, \& \, C(\bar{t})$, in case we want to distinguish between the relational atoms and the comparisons in the body, or, shortly, as $q(\bar{x}) \leftarrow R \, \& \, C$. The variables appearing in the head are *distinguished variables*, while those appearing only in the body are *nondistinguished variables*. Atoms containing at least one nondistinguished variable are *nondistinguished atoms*. By abuse of notation, we will often refer to a query by its head $q(\bar{x})$ or simply by the predicate of its head q.

A database $\mathcal{D}$ contains for every predicate symbol p a relation $p^{\mathcal{D}}$, that is, a set of tuples. Under *set semantics,* a conjunctive query q defines a new relation $q^{\mathcal{D}}$, which consists of all the answers that q produces over $\mathcal{D}$. Under *bag-set semantics,* q defines a multiset or *bag* $\{\!\{q\}\!\}^{\mathcal{D}}$ of tuples. The bag $\{\!\{q\}\!\}^{\mathcal{D}}$ contains the same tuples as the relation $q^{\mathcal{D}}$, but each tuple occurs as many times as it can be derived over $\mathcal{D}$ with q [CV93]. Under set-semantics (bag-set semantics), two queries q and q' are *equivalent* if for every database, they return the same set (bag) as a result.

3.2 Aggregate Queries

We now extend the Datalog syntax so as to capture also queries with GROUP BY and aggregation. We assume that queries have only one aggregate term. The general case can easily be reduced to this one [CNS99]. We are interested in queries with the aggregation functions *count, sum, min* and *max*. Since results for *min* are analogous to those for *max*, we do not consider *min*. Our function *count* is analogous to the function COUNT(*) of SQL.

An *aggregate term* is an expression built up using variables, the operations addition and multiplication, and aggregation functions.[1] For example, *count* and

---

[1] This definition blurs the distinction between the function as a mathematical object and the symbol denoting the function. However, a notation that takes this difference into account would be cumbersome.

$sum(z_1 * z_2)$, are aggregate terms. We use κ as abstract notations for aggregate terms. If we want to refer to the variables occurring in an aggregate term, we write $\kappa(\bar{y})$, where $\bar{y}$ is a tuple of distinct variables. Note that $\bar{y}$ is empty if κ is the *count* aggregation function. Terms of the form *count*, $sum(y)$ and $max(y)$ are *elementary aggregate terms*. Abstractly, elementary aggregate terms are denoted as $\alpha(y)$, where α is an aggregation function.

An aggregate term $\kappa(\bar{y})$ naturally gives rise to a function $f_{\kappa(\bar{y})}$ that maps multisets of tuples of numbers to numbers. For instance, $sum(z_1 * z_2)$ describes the aggregation function $f_{sum(z_1*z_2)}$ that maps any multiset M of pairs of numbers (m_1, m_2) to $\sum_{(m_1,m_2)\in M} m_1 * m_2$.

An *aggregate query* is a conjunctive query augmented by an aggregate term in its head. Thus, it has the form $q(\bar{x}; \kappa(\bar{y})) \leftarrow B(\bar{s})$. We call $\bar{x}$ the *grouping variables* of the query. Queries with elementary aggregate terms are *elementary queries*. If the aggregation term in the head of a query has the form $\alpha(y)$, we call the query an α-*query* (e.g., a max-query). In this paper we are interested in rewriting elementary queries using elementary views. However, as the example in Section 2 shows, even under this restriction the rewritings may not be elementary.

We now give a formal definition of the semantics of aggregate queries. Consider the query $q(\bar{x}; \kappa(\bar{y})) \leftarrow B(\bar{s})$. For a database $\mathcal{D}$, the query yields a new relation $q^{\mathcal{D}}$. To define the relation $q^{\mathcal{D}}$, we proceed in two steps. We associate to q a non-aggregate query, $\breve{q}$, called the *core* of q, which is defined as $\breve{q}(\bar{x}, \bar{y}) \leftarrow B(\bar{s})$. The core is the query that returns all the values that are amalgamated in the aggregate. Recall that under bag-set-semantics, the core returns over $\mathcal{D}$ a bag $\{\!\{\breve{q}\}\!\}^{\mathcal{D}}$ of tuples $(\bar{d}, \bar{e})$. For a tuple of constants $\bar{d}$ of the same length as $\bar{x}$, let

$$\Gamma_{\bar{d}} := \left\{\!\!\left\{ \bar{e} \;\middle|\; (\bar{d}, \bar{e}) \in \{\!\{\breve{q}\}\!\}^{\mathcal{D}} \right\}\!\!\right\}.$$

That is, the bag $\Gamma_{\bar{d}}$ is obtained by first grouping together those answers to $\breve{q}$ that return $\bar{d}$ for the grouping terms, and then stripping off from those answers the prefix $\bar{d}$. In other words, $\Gamma_{\bar{d}}$ is the multiset of $\bar{y}$-values that $\breve{q}$ returns for $\bar{d}$. The result of evaluating q over $\mathcal{D}$ is

$$q^{\mathcal{D}} := \{(\bar{d}, e) \mid \Gamma_{\bar{d}} \neq \emptyset \text{ and } e = f_{\kappa(\bar{y})}(\Gamma_{\bar{d}})\}.$$

Intuitively, whenever there is a nonempty group of answers with index $\bar{d}$, then we apply the aggregation function $f_{\kappa(\bar{y})}$ to the multiset of $\bar{y}$-values of that group.

Aggregate queries q and q' are *equivalent* if $q^{\mathcal{D}} = q'^{\mathcal{D}}$ for all databases $\mathcal{D}$.

3.3   Equivalence Modulo a Set of Views

Up until now, we have defined equivalence of aggregate queries and equivalence of non-aggregate queries under set and bag-set-semantics. However, the relationship between a query q and a rewriting r of q is not equivalence of queries, because the view predicates occurring in r are not regular database relations, but are determined by the base relations indirectly. In order to take this relationship into account, we define equivalence of queries modulo a set of views.

We consider aggregate queries that use predicates both from $\mathcal{R}$, a set of base relations, and $\mathcal{V}$, a set of view definitions. For a database $\mathcal{D}$, let $\mathcal{D}_\mathcal{V}$ be the database that extends $\mathcal{D}$ by interpreting every view predicate $v \in \mathcal{V}$ as the relation $v^\mathcal{D}$. If q is a query that contains also predicates from $\mathcal{V}$, then $q^{\mathcal{D}_\mathcal{V}}$ is the relation that results from evaluating q over the extended database $\mathcal{D}_\mathcal{V}$. If q, q' are two aggregate queries using predicates from $\mathcal{R} \cup \mathcal{V}$, we define that q and q' are *equivalent modulo* $\mathcal{V}$, written $q \equiv_\mathcal{V} q'$, if $q^{\mathcal{D}_\mathcal{V}} = q'^{\mathcal{D}_\mathcal{V}}$ for all databases $\mathcal{D}$.

3.4   General Definition of Rewriting

Let q be a query, $\mathcal{V}$ be a set of views over the set of relations $\mathcal{R}$, and r be a query over $\mathcal{V} \cup \mathcal{R}$. All of q, r, and the views in $\mathcal{V}$ may be aggregate queries or not. Then r is a *rewriting* of q using $\mathcal{V}$ if $q \equiv_\mathcal{V} r$ and r contains only atoms with predicates from $\mathcal{V}$. If $q \equiv_\mathcal{V} r$ and r contains at least one atom with a predicate from $\mathcal{V}$ we say that r is a *partial rewriting of* q *using* $\mathcal{V}$.

We reformulate the intuitive questions we asked in the end of the Section 2.

- **Rewriting Verification:** Given queries q and r, and a set of views $\mathcal{V}$, check whether $q \equiv_\mathcal{V} r$.
- **Rewriting Computation:** Given a query q and a set of views $\mathcal{V}$, find all (some) rewritings or partial rewritings of q.

4   Rewritings of Aggregate Queries

We now present techniques for rewriting aggregate queries. Our approach will be to generalize the known techniques for conjunctive queries. Therefore, we first give a short review of the conjunctive case and then discuss in how far aggregates give rise to more complications.

4.1   Reminder: Rewritings of Relational Conjunctive Queries

Recall the questions related to rewriting relational conjunctive queries. Suppose, we are given a set of conjunctive queries $\mathcal{V}$, the views, and another conjunctive query q. We want to know if there is a rewriting of q using the views in $\mathcal{V}$.

The *first question* that arises is, what is the *language* for expressing rewritings? Do we consider arbitrary first order formulas over the view predicates as candidates, or recursive queries, or do we restrict ourselves to conjunctive queries over the views? Since reasoning about queries in the first two languages is undecidable, researchers have only considered conjunctive rewritings.[2] Thus, a candidate for rewriting $q(\bar{x})$ has the form $r(\bar{x}) \leftarrow v_1(\theta_1 \bar{x}_1) \mathbin{\&} \ldots \mathbin{\&} v_n(\theta_n \bar{x}_n)$, where the θ_i's are substitutions that instantiate the view predicates $v_i(\bar{x}_i)$.

---

[2] It is an interesting theoretical question, which as yet has not been resolved, whether more expressive languages give more possibilities for rewritings. It is easy to show, at least, that in the case at hand allowing also disjunctions of conjunctive queries as candidates does not give more possibilities than allowing only conjunctive queries.

The *second question* is whether we can *reduce reasoning* about the query r, which contains view predicates, to reasoning about a query that has only base predicates. To this end, we *unfold* r. That is, we replace each view atom $v_i(\theta_i \bar{x}_i)$, with the instantiation $\theta_i B_i$ of the body of v_i, where v_i is defined as $v_i(\bar{x}_i) \leftarrow B_i$. We assume that the nondistinguished variables in different occurrences of the bodies are distinct. We thus obtain the unfolding r^u of r, for which the Unfolding Theorem holds, $r^u(\bar{x}) \leftarrow \theta_1 B_1 \, \& \, \ldots \, \& \, \theta_n B_n$.

Theorem 1 (Unfolding Theorem). *Let $\mathcal{V}$ be a set of views, r a query over $\mathcal{V}$, and r^u be the unfolding of r. Then r and r^u are equivalent modulo $\mathcal{V}$, that is,*

$$r \equiv_{\mathcal{V}} r^u.$$

The *third question* is how to check whether r is a rewriting of q, that is, whether r and q are *equivalent modulo $\mathcal{V}$*. This can be achieved by checking whether r^u and q are set-equivalent: if $r^u \equiv q$, then the Unfolding Theorem implies $r \equiv_{\mathcal{V}} q$. Set-equivalence of conjunctive queries can be decided syntactically by checking whether there are homomorphisms in both directions [Ull89].

4.2   Rewritings of Count-Queries

When rewriting *count*-queries, we must deal with the questions that arose when rewriting conjunctive queries. Thus, we first define the language for expressing rewritings. Even if we restrict the language to conjunctive aggregate queries over the views, we still must decide on two additional issues. First, which types of aggregate views are useful for a rewriting? Second, what will be the aggregation term in the head of the rewriting? A *count*-query is sensitive to multiplicities, and *count*-views are the only type of aggregate views that do not lose multiplicities.[3] Thus, the natural answer to the first question is to use only *count*-views when rewriting *count*-queries. The following example shows that there are an infinite number of aggregate terms that can be usable in rewriting a *count*-query.

Example 1. Consider the query q_positions and the queries r_1 and r_2 that use the view v_positions defined in Section 2.

$$\text{q\_positions}(j; count) \leftarrow \text{ta}(n, c, j)$$
$$r_1(j'; z) \leftarrow \text{v\_positions}(j'; z)$$
$$r_2(j'; \sqrt{z_1 * z_2}) \leftarrow \text{v\_positions}(j'; z_1) \, \& \, \text{v\_positions}(j'; z_2).$$

The query q_positions computes the number of positions of each type held in the university. It is easy to see that r_1 and r_2 are rewritings of q_positions. By adding additional view atoms and adjusting the power of the root we can create infinitely many different rewritings of q_positions. It is natural to create only r_1 as a rewriting of q. In fact, only for r_1 will the Unfolding Theorem hold.

---

[3] Although *sum*-views are sensitive to multiplicities, they lose these values. For example, *sum*-views ignore occurrences of zero values.

A *candidate* for a rewriting of $q(\bar{x}; count) \leftarrow R \ \& \ C$ is a query of the form

$$r(\bar{x}; sum(\prod_{i=1}^{n} z_i)) \leftarrow v_1^c(\theta_1 \bar{x}_1; z_1) \ \& \ \ldots \ \& \ v_n^c(\theta_n \bar{x}_n; z_n) \ \& \ C',$$

where v_i^c are *count*-views, possibly with comparisons, defined as $v_i^c(\bar{x}_i; count) \leftarrow B_i$ and z_i are variables not appearing elsewhere in the body of r. We call r a *count*-rewriting candidate.

Note that it is possible to omit the summation if the values of z_i are functionally dependent on the value of the grouping variables $\bar{x}$. This is the case, if only grouping variables appear as $\theta_i x_i$ in the heads of the instantiated views. Then the summation is always over a singleton group.

After presenting our rewriting candidates we now show how we can reduce reasoning about rewriting candidates, to reasoning about conjunctive aggregate queries. We use a similar technique to that shown in Subsection 4.1. In the unfolding, we replace the view atoms of the rewriting with the appropriate instantiations of their bodies, and we replace the aggregate term in the rewriting with the term *count*. Thus, we obtain as the unfolding r^u of r the query

$$r^u(\bar{x}; count) \leftarrow \theta_1 B_1 \ \& \ \ldots \ \& \ \theta_n B_n \ \& \ C'.$$

In [CNS99], it has been proven that for r^u the Unfolding Theorem holds, i.e., $r \equiv_\mathcal{V} r^u$. Moreover, it has been shown that this definition of unfolding uniquely determines the aggregation function in the head of our candidates. That is, summation over products of counts is the only aggregation function for which the Unfolding Theorem holds if r^u is defined as above. Now, in order to verify that r is a rewriting of q, we can check that r^u is equivalent to r, without taking into account the views any more.

We now present an algorithm that finds a rewriting for a *count*-query using views. Our approach can be thought of as reverse engineering. We have characterized the "product" that we must create, i.e., a rewriting, and we now present an automatic technique for producing it.

In [NSS98], a sound and complete characterization of equivalence of conjunctive *count*-queries with comparisons has been given. The only known algorithm that checks equivalence of conjunctive *count*-queries creates an exponential blowup of the queries. Thus, it is difficult to present a tractable algorithm for computing rewritings. However, it has been shown [CV93,NSS98] that two relational *count*-queries are equivalent if and only if they are isomorphic. In addition, equivalence of linear *count*-queries with comparisons is isomorphism of the queries [NSS98]. Thus, we will give a sound, complete, and tractable algorithm for computing rewritings of relational *count*-queries and of linear *count*-queries. This algorithm is sound and tractable for the general case, but is not complete.

We discuss when a view $v(\bar{u}; count) \leftarrow R_v \ \& \ C_v$, instantiated by θ, is usable in order to rewrite a query $q(\bar{x}; count) \leftarrow R \ \& \ C$, that is, when the instantiated view can occur in a partial rewriting. By the characterization of equivalence for relational and linear queries, a rewriting of q is a query r that when unfolded yields a query isomorphic to q. Thus, in order for θv, to be usable, θR_v must "cover" some part of R. Therefore, θv is usable for rewriting q only if there exists an isomorphism, φ, from θR_v to $R' \subseteq R$. Note that we can assume, w.l.o.g. that φ is the identity mapping on the distinguished variables of v. We would like to replace R' with θv in the body of q in order to derive a partial rewriting of q. This cannot always be done. After replacing R' with θv, variables that appeared in R' and do not appear in $\theta \bar{u}$ (i.e., the nondistinguished variables in v) are inaccessible. Thus, we can only perform the replacement if these variables do not appear anywhere else in q, in q's head or body. We define that $v(\bar{u}; count) \leftarrow R_v \,\&\, C_v$ is R-usable under θ w.r.t. φ, denoted R-usable(v, θ, φ), if

1. $\varphi \theta R_v$ is isomorphic to a subset R' of R, and
2. every variable that occurs both in R' and in $R \setminus R'$ must occur in $\theta \bar{u}$.

There is a partial rewriting of q using v only if v R-usable(v, θ, φ) for some φ.

Example 2. Consider the query q_db_ta_sponsors that computes the number of sponsors for each assistant in the database course. The view v_jobs_per_ta computes the number of jobs that each TA has in each course that he assists.

q_db_ta_sponsors$(n; count) \leftarrow$ ta$(n, \text{Database}, j) \,\&\,$ salaries(j, s, a)

v_jobs_per_ta$(n', c'; count) \leftarrow$ ta(n', c', j')

In order to use v_jobs_per_ta in rewriting q_db_ta_sponsors we must find an instantiation θ such that θta(n', c', j') covers some part of the body of q_db_ta_sponsors. Clearly, θta(n', c', j') can cover only ta$(n, \text{Database}, j)$. We take, $\theta = \{n'/n, c'/\text{Database}\}$ and thus, $\varphi = \{n/n, j'/j\}$. However, j appears in ta$(n, \text{Database}, j)$ and not in the head of θv_jobs_per_ta and therefore, j is not accessible after replacement. Note that j appears in salaries and thus, v_jobs_per_ta is not R-usable in rewriting q_db_ta_sponsors.

For our algorithm to be complete for linear queries, the set of comparisons in the query to be rewritten has to be deductively closed (see [CNS00]). The deductive closure of a set of comparisons can be computed in polynomial time [Klu88]. In addition, it must hold that $C \models \varphi(\theta C_v)$, thus, the comparisons inherited from v are weaker than those in q. For a rewriting using θv to exist it must be possible to strengthen $\varphi(\theta C_v)$ by additional comparisons C' so that $\varphi(\theta C_v) \,\&\, C'$ is equivalent to C. We have seen that when replacing R' with θv we lose access to the nondistinguished variables in v. Therefore, it is necessary for the comparisons in $\varphi(\theta C_v)$ to imply all the comparisons in q that contain an image of a nondistinguished variable in v. Formally, let $ndv(v)$ be the set of nondistinguished variables in v. Let $C^{\varphi(\theta ndv(v))}$ consist of those comparisons in C that contain variables in $\varphi(\theta ndv(v))$. Then, in order for θv to be usable in a partial rewriting, $C_v \models C^{\varphi(\theta ndv(v))}$ must hold. If this condition and $C \models \varphi(\theta C_v)$ hold, then v is C-usable under θ w.r.t. φ and write C-usable(v, θ, φ).

Theorem 2. *Let* $q(\bar{x}; count) \leftarrow R \,\&\, C$ *be a count-query whose set of comparisons* C *is deductively closed, and let* $v(\bar{u}; count) \leftarrow R_v \,\&\, C_v$ *be a count-view. There exists a partial rewriting of* q *using* v *if and only if there is a* φ *such that* R-usable(v, θ, φ) *and* C-usable(v, θ, φ).

We present an algorithm for computing rewritings of conjunctive *count*-queries in Figure 1. The underlying idea is to incrementally cover the body of the query by views until no atom is left to be covered. The algorithm non-deterministically chooses a view v and an instantiation θ, such that v is both R-usable and C-usable under θ. If the choice fails, backtracking is performed.

When the while-loop is completed, the algorithm returns a rewriting. By backtracking we can find additional rewritings. Of course, the nondeterminism in choosing the views can be further reduced, for instance, by imposing an ordering on the atoms in the body of the query and by trying to cover the atoms according to that ordering. Note, that the same algorithm may be used to produce partial rewritings if we relax the termination condition of the while-loop. This will similarly hold for subsequent algorithms presented.

Algorithm   Count_Rewriting
Input   A query $q(\bar{x}; count) \leftarrow R \& C$ and a set of views $\mathcal{V}$
Output   A rewriting r of q.

(1) $Not\_Covered := R$.
(2) $Rewriting := \emptyset$.
(3) $n := 0$.
(4)   **While** $Not\_Covered \neq \emptyset$ **do:**
(5)   **Choose** a view $v(\bar{x}'; count) \leftarrow R' \& C'$ in $\mathcal{V}$.
(6)   **Choose** an instantiation, θ, and an isomorphism φ,
              such that R-usable(v, θ, φ) and C-usable(v, θ, φ).
(7)   **For each** atom $a \in R'$ **do:**
(8)   **If** a is a nondistinguished atom, **then**
(9)   **Remove** $\varphi(\theta a)$ from R.
(10)   **If** $\varphi(\theta a) \notin Not\_Covered$ **then fail.**
(11)   **Remove** $\varphi(\theta a)$ from $Not\_Covered$.
(12)   **Remove from** C comparisons containing a variable in $\varphi(\theta R')$,
              but not in $\theta\bar{x}'$
(13)   **Increment** n.
(14)   **Add** $v(\theta\bar{x}'; z_n)$ to $Rewriting$, where z_n is a fresh variable.
(15) **Return** $r(\bar{x}; sum(\prod_{i=1}^{n} z_i)) \leftarrow Rewriting \& C$.

Fig. 1. Count Query Rewriting Algorithm

We note the following. In Line 9, R is changed and thus, q is also changed. Therefore, at the next iteration of the while-loop we check whether v is R-usable under θ to rewrite the updated version of q (Line 6). Thus, in each iteration of the loop, additional atoms are covered. In Line 10, the algorithm checks if a nondistinguished atom is already covered. If so, then the algorithm must fail, i.e., backtrack, as explained above. Observe that we modify C in Line 12. We remove from C comparisons containing a variable that is inaccessible after replacing the appropriate subset of R by the appropriate instantiation of v. These comparisons are not lost because v is C-usable. The comparisons remaining in C are needed to strengthen those inherited from the views so as to be equivalent to the comparisons in the query to be rewritten.

Count_Rewriting is both sound and complete for linear queries and relational queries and is sound, but not complete, for arbitrary queries. Our algorithm runs in nondeterministic polynomial time by guessing views and instantiations and verifying in polynomial time that the obtained result is a rewriting. For relational queries this is optimal, since checking whether there exists a θ such that v is R-usable under θ is NP-hard, which can be shown by a reduction of the graph matching problem. Since for linear queries q and views v the existence of θ and φ such that R-usable(v, θ, φ) and C-usable(v, θ, φ) can be decided in polynomial time, one can obtain a polynomial time variant of the algorithm that computes partial rewritings in the linear case.

Theorem 3. (Soundness and Completeness of Count Rewriting) *Let q be a count-query and $\mathcal{V}$ be a set of views. If r is returned by* Count_Rewriting$(q, \mathcal{V})$, *then r is a count-rewriting candidate of q and $r \equiv_\mathcal{V} q$. If q is either linear or relational, then the opposite holds by making the appropriate choices.*

4.3   Rewritings of Sum-Queries

Rewriting *sum*-queries is similar to rewriting *count*-queries. When rewriting *sum*-queries we must also take the summation variable into consideration. We present an algorithm for rewriting *sum*-queries that is based on the algorithm for *count*-queries.

We define the form of rewriting candidates for *sum*-queries. Since *sum* and *count*-views are the only views that are sensitive to multiplicities, they are useful for rewritings. However, *sum*-views may lose multiplicities and make the aggregation variable inaccessible. Thus, at most one *sum*-view should be used in the rewriting of a query. The following are rewriting candidates for *sum*-queries:

$$r_1(\bar{x}; sum(y * \prod_{i=1}^{n} z_i)) \leftarrow v_1^c(\theta_1\bar{x}_1; z_1) \;\&\; \ldots \;\&\; v_n^c(\theta_n\bar{x}_n; z_n) \;\&\; C'$$

$$r_2(\bar{x}; sum(y * \prod_{i=1}^{n} z_i)) \leftarrow v^s(\theta_s\bar{x}_s; y) \;\&\; v_1^c(\theta_1\bar{x}_1; z_1) \;\&\; \ldots \;\&\; v_n^c(\theta_n\bar{x}_n; z_n) \;\&\; C'$$

where v_i^c is a *count*-view of the form $v_i^c(\bar{x}_i; count) \leftarrow B_i$ and v^s is a *sum*-view of the form $v^s(\bar{x}_s; sum(y)) \leftarrow B_s$. Note that the variable y in the head of the query r_1 must appear among $\theta_i\bar{x}_i$ for some i. In [CNS99], it has been shown that if a rewriting candidate is equivalent modulo the views to its unfolding then it must be one of the above forms. As in the case of *count*-query rewritings, in some cases the rewriting may be optimized by dropping the summation.

Once again, we reduce reasoning about rewriting candidates to reasoning about conjunctive aggregate queries. For this purpose we extend the unfolding technique introduced in Subsection 4.2. Thus, the unfoldings of the candidates presented are:

$$r_1^u(\bar{x}; sum(y)) \leftarrow \theta_1 B_1 \,\& \,\ldots\, \& \,\theta_n B_n \,\& \,C'.$$
$$r_2^u(\bar{x}; sum(y)) \leftarrow \theta_s B_s \,\& \,\theta_1 B_1 \,\& \,\ldots\, \& \,\theta_n B_n \,\& \,C'.$$

Now, instead of checking whether r is a rewriting of q we can verify whether r^u is equivalent to r. The only known algorithm for checking equivalence of sum-queries, presented in [NSS98], requires an exponential blowup of the queries. However, relational sum-queries and linear sum-queries are equivalent if and only if they are isomorphic. Thus, we can extend the algorithm presented in the Figure 1 for sum-queries.

We first extend the algorithm in Figure 1, such that in Line 5 sum-views may be chosen as well. We call this algorithm Compute_Rewriting. We derive an algorithm for rewriting sum-queries, presented in Figure 2. The algorithm runs in nondeterministic polynomial time.

Algorithm   Sum_Rewriting
Input   A query $q(\bar{x}; sum(y)) \leftarrow B$ and a set of views $\mathcal{V}$
Output   A rewriting r of q.

(1)   **Let** q' be the query $q'(\bar{x}; count) \leftarrow B$.
(2)   **Let** $r'=$Compute_Rewriting$(q', \mathcal{V})$.
(3)   **If** r' is of the form
$$r'(\bar{x}; sum(y * \textstyle\prod_{i=1}^n z_i)) \leftarrow v^s(\theta_s \bar{x}_s; y) \,\&$$
$$v_1^c(\theta_1 \bar{x}_1; z_1) \,\& \,\ldots\, \& \,v_n^c(\theta_n \bar{x}_n; z_n) \,\& \,C'$$
(4)   **Then return** r'
(5)   **If** r' is of the form
$$r'(\bar{x}; sum(\textstyle\prod_{i=1}^n z_i)) \leftarrow v_1^c(\theta_1 \bar{x}_1; z_1) \,\& \,\ldots\, \& \,v_n^c(\theta_n \bar{x}_n; z_n) \,\& \,C'$$
      and y appears among $\theta_i \bar{x}_i$
(6)   **Then return**
$$r(\bar{x}; sum(y * \textstyle\prod_{i=1}^n z_i)) \leftarrow v_1^c(\theta_1 \bar{x}_1, z_1) \,\& \,\ldots\, \& \,v_n^c(\theta_n \bar{x}_n, z_n) \,\& \,C'.$$

Fig. 2. Sum Query Rewriting Algorithm

Theorem 4. (Soundness and Completeness of Sum Rewriting) *Let q be a sum-query and $\mathcal{V}$ be a set of views. If r is returned by* Sum_Rewriting$(q, \mathcal{V})$, *then r is a sum-rewriting candidate of q and $r \equiv_{\mathcal{V}} q$. If q is linear or relational, then the opposite holds by making the appropriate choices.*

4.4   Rewritings of Max-Queries

We consider the problem of rewriting max-queries. Note that max-queries are insensitive to multiplicities. Thus, we use nonaggregate views and max-views when rewriting a *max*-query. When using a *max*-view the aggregation variable becomes inaccessible. Thus, we use at most one *max*-view. The following are rewriting candidates of the query q:

$$r_1(\bar{x}; max(y)) \leftarrow v_1(\theta_1\bar{x}_1) \& \ldots \& v_n(\theta_n\bar{x}_n) \& C'$$
$$r_2(\bar{x}; max(y)) \leftarrow v^m(\theta_m\bar{x}_m; y) \& v_1(\theta_1\bar{x}_1) \& \ldots \& v_n(\theta_n\bar{x}_n) \& C'$$

where the v_i's are nonaggregate views and v^m is a *max*-view. The variable y in the head of the query r_1 must appear among $\theta_i\bar{x}_i$ for some i. In [CNS99] it has been shown that if a rewriting candidate is equivalent to its unfolding then it must have one of the above forms.

Reasoning about rewriting candidates can be reduced to reasoning about *max*-queries, by extending the unfolding technique. It has been shown [NSS98] that equivalence of relational *max*-queries is equivalence of their cores. There is a similar reduction for the general case. Algorithms for checking set-equivalence of queries can easily be converted to algorithms for checking equivalence of *max*-queries. Thus, algorithms that find rewritings of nonaggregate queries can be modified to find rewritings of *max*-queries.

Rewriting nonaggregate queries is a well known problem [LMSS95]. One well-known algorithm for computing rewritings of queries is the *buckets algorithm* [LRO96]. Consider a query $q(\bar{x}) \leftarrow R \& C$. The algorithm creates a "bucket" for each atom $p(\bar{z})$ in R. Intuitively, this bucket contains all the views whose bodies can cover $p(\bar{z})$. The algorithm places into this bucket all the views $v(\bar{y}) \leftarrow R_v \& C_v$ such that R_v contains an atom $p(\bar{w})$ that can be mapped by some mapping φ to $p(\bar{z})$ such that $C \& \varphi C'$ is consistent. Next, all combinations of taking a view from each bucket are considered in the attempt to form a rewriting.

Note that by reasoning similarly as in the case of *count* and *sum*-queries, we can reduce the number of views put into each bucket, thus improving on the performance of the algorithm. Suppose there is a nondistinguished variable $w \in \bar{w}$ mapped to $z \in \bar{z}$ and there is an atom containing z in q that is not covered by φR_v. In such a case, if v is used in a rewriting candidate there will not exist a homomorphism from the unfolded rewriting to q such that the body of v covers $p(\bar{z})$. However, a rewriting candidate r is equivalent to a query q if and only if there exist homomorphisms from r^u to q and from q to r^u. Thus, v should not be put in the bucket of $p(\bar{z})$.

Observe that this condition is a relaxed version of the R-usability requirement that ensures the existence of an isomorphism. Clearly this restriction filters out the possible rewritings of q, thereby improving the performance of the buckets algorithm. Thus, our methods for finding rewritings of aggregate queries may be relaxed and used to improve the performance of algorithms for rewriting relational queries. These, in turn, may be modified to rewrite *max*-queries.

5   Conclusion

Aggregate queries are increasingly prevalent due to the widespread use of data warehousing and related applications. They are generally computationally expensive since they scan many data items, while returning few results. Thus, the computation time of aggregate queries is generally orders of magnitude larger than the result size of the query. This makes query optimization a necessity.

Optimizing aggregate queries using views has been studied for the special case of datacubes [HRU96]. However, there was little theory for general aggregate queries. In this paper, based on previous results in [NSS98,CNS99], we presented algorithms that enable reuse of precomputed queries in answering new ones. The algorithms presented have been implemented in SICStus Prolog.

References

CNS99.   S. Cohen, W. Nutt, and A. Serebrenik. Rewriting aggregate queries using views. In Ch. Papadimitriou, editor, *Proc. 18th Symposium on Principles of Database Systems*, Philadelphia (Pennsylvania, USA), May 1999. ACM Press.

CNS00.   S. Cohen, W. Nutt, and A. Serebrenik. Algorithms for rewriting aggregate queries using views. Technical Report CW292, Departement Computerwetenschappen, K.U.Leuven, Leuven, Belgium, 2000. Available at http://www.cs.kuleuven.ac.be/publicaties/rapporten/CW2000.html.

CV93.   S. Chaudhuri and M. Vardi. Optimization of real conjunctive queries. In *Proc. 12th Symposium on Principles of Database Systems*, Washington (D.C., USA), May 1993. ACM Press.

GHQ95.   A. Gupta, V. Harinarayan, and D. Quass. Aggregate query processing in data warehouses. In *Proc. 21st International Conference on Very Large Data Bases*. Morgan Kaufmann Publishers, August 1995.

HRU96.   V. Harinarayan, A. Rajaraman, and J. Ullman. Implementing data cubes efficiently. In *Proc. 1996 ACM SIGMOD International Conference on Management of Data*, pages 205–227, Montreal (Canada), June 1996.

Klu88.   A. Klug. On conjunctive queries containing inequalities. *J. ACM*, 35(1):146–160, 1988.

LMSS95.   A.Y. Levy, A.O. Mendelzon, Y. Sagiv, and D. Srivastava. Answering queries using views. In *Proc. 14th Symposium on Principles of Database Systems*, pages 95–104, San Jose (California, USA), May 1995. ACM Press.

LRO96.   A.Y. Levy, A. Rajaraman, and J. Ordille. Querying heterogeneous information sources using source description. In *Proc. 22nd International Conference on Very Large Data Bases*, Bombay (India), September 1996. Morgan Kaufmann Publishers.

NSS98.   W. Nutt, Y. Sagiv, and S. Shurin. Deciding equivalences among aggregate queries. In J. Paredaens, editor, *Proc. 17th Symposium on Principles of Database Systems*, pages 214–223, Seattle (Washington, USA), June 1998. ACM Press. Long version as Report of Esprit LTR DWQ.

SDJL96.   D. Srivastava, Sh. Dar, H.V. Jagadish, and A.Y. Levy. Answering queries with aggregation using views. In *Proc. 22nd International Conference on Very Large Data Bases*, Bombay (India), September 1996. Morgan Kaufmann Publishers.

Ull89.   J. Ullman. *Principles of Database and Knowledge-Base Systems, Vol. II: The New Technologies*. Computer Science Press, New York (New York, USA), 1989.

A New High-Dimensional Index Structure Using a Cell-Based Filtering Technique

Sung-Geun Han and Jae-Woo Chang

Dept. of Computer Engineering, Chonbuk National University
Chonju, Chonbuk 560-756, South Korea
{sghan,jwchang}@dblab.chonbuk.ac.kr

Abstract. In general, multimedia database applications require to support similarity search for content-based retrieval on multimedia data, i.e., image, animation, video, and audio. Since the similarity of two multimedia objects is measured as the distance between their feature vectors, the similarity search corresponds to a search for the nearest neighbors in the feature vector space. In this paper, we propose a new high-dimensional indexing scheme using a cell-based filtering technique which supports the nearest neighbor search efficiently. Our Cell-Based Filtering (CBF) scheme divides a high-dimensional feature vector space into cells, like VA-file. However, in order to make a better effect on filtering, our CBF scheme performs additional filtering based on a distance between an object feature vector and the center of a cell including it, in addition to filtering based on cell signatures before accessing a data file. From our experiment using high-dimensional feature vectors, we show that our CBF scheme achieves better performance on the nearest neighbor search than its competitors, such as VA-File and X-tree.

1 Introduction

Multimedia database applications generally require to support similarity search for content-based retrieval on multimedia data, i.e., image, animation, video, and audio. The similarity search is briefly defined as finding the k objects 'most similar' to a given object. Mostly, similarity is not measured based on objects in the database directly, but rather based on the abstraction of objects, called feature vectors. Thus the similarity of two multimedia objects is assumed to be proportional to the similarity of their feature vectors, being measured as a distance between their feature vectors in an n-dimensional (n>1) space. As such, the similarity search corresponds to a search for the k nearest neighbors in the space. When a user provides an n-dimensional query vector for k nearest neighbor (k-NN) search, we can measure Euclidean distances between the given query vector and all object feature vectors and obtain the most similar multimedia objects corresponding to the k nearest neighbors in the database.

There are many studies on indexing schemes which support the nearest neighbor search efficiently. However, most of the conventional indexing schemes work well at low dimensionality, but they may perform poorly as dimensionality increases. To overcome the difficulties of high dimensionality, we propose a new high-dimensional indexing scheme using a cell-based filtering technique which supports the nearest

J. Štuller et al. (Eds.): ADBIS-DASFAA 2000, LNCS 1884, pp. 79–92, 2000.
© Springer-Verlag Berlin Heidelberg 2000

neighbor search efficiently. Our Cell-Based Filtering (CBF) scheme divides a high-dimensional vector space into cells, like VA-file. However, in order to make a better effect on filtering, our CBF scheme performs additional filtering based on a distance between an object feature vector and the center of a cell including it, in addition to filtering by first scanning all of cell signatures and finding candidate cells before accessing a data file. For this, we define new upper and lower bounds for pruning cells which need not to be visited. Finally we compare the performance of our CBF scheme with those of its competitors, such as VA-file and X-tree, which are well known as high-dimensional indexing schemes.

The remainder of this paper is organized as follows. Section 2 investigates the conventional high-dimensional indexing schemes and the concept of nearest neighbor search in these schemes. Section 3 describes the overall structure of our CBF scheme and presents its nearest neighbor search algorithm based on newly defined upper and lower bounds for cell pruning. Section 4 provides experimental performance results in terms of insertion time, nearest neighbor search time, storage overhead. Finally, we conclude Section 5 by summarizing our contributions and giving future research.

2 Related Work

There are many studies on indexing schemes to support nearest neighbor search efficiently. However, most of indexing schemes work well at low dimensionality, but they may perform poorly as dimensionality increases. To overcome the difficulties of high dimensionality, some high-dimensional indexing schemes have been proposed [1,2,3,4,5,6,7,]. In this section, we introduce X-tree and VA-File which are well known as high-dimensional indexing schemes. The X-tree was proposed to improve retrieval efficiency by avoiding the overlap of data areas in a high-dimensional data space [8]. To avoid the overlap, the X-tree makes use of an overlap free algorithm as well as a new concept of super nodes. Based on the super node concept, the X-tee uses a hierarchical directory structure for low-dimensional vectors and a linear directory structure for high-dimensional vectors, leading to fast accesses to object feature vectors. Figure 1 shows the directory structure of the X-tree. The nodes of the X-tree are composed of directory nodes with Minimum Bounding Region (MBR) information and data nodes with object feature vectors. However, the X-tree degrades on retrieval performance as dimensionality increases and bring about worse

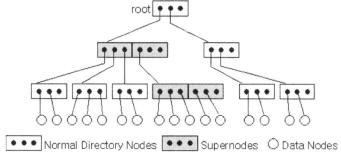

Fig. 1. Directory structure of X-tree

performance than sequential scan when the number of dimensions is greater than 16 [9].

The VA-File was proposed to improve the deterioration of retrieval performance against the sequential scan [10]. It can reduce the number of disk I/O accesses for the sequential scan by using vector approximations. Therefore, the VA-File divides a high-dimensional vector space into a set of cells, generates an approximation from each cell, and stores the approximation into a sequential file. Figure 2 describes vector approximations in a two-dimensional vector space. When a user query is given, the VA-File is first scanned to select candidate cells before accessing the data file. Then feature vectors within candidate cells are searched to obtain the k nearest neighbors in the data file.

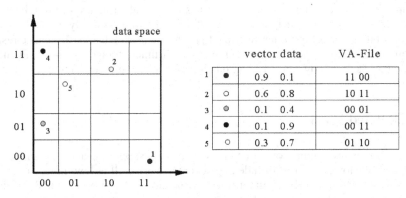

Fig. 2. Vector Approximation

Meanwhile, the nearest neighbor search algorithm proposed by Roussopoulos [11] makes use of MINDIST and MINMAXDIST as lower and upper bounds for pruning MBRs, respectively, where MINDIST is a minimum distance from a query point to a given MBR and MINMAXDIST is a maximum distance from a query point to at least an object within a given MBR. Using MINDIST and MINMAXDIST, the algorithm can reduce the number of nodes to be visited in a tree. Figure 3 shows MINDIST(Q,R) and MINMAXDIST(Q,R) between a query point Q and an MBR R. The nearest neighbor search algorithm uses three strategies to prune MBRs as follows.

- **STEP 1.** An MBR R with MINDIST(Q,R) greater than the MINMAXDIST(Q,R') of another MBR R' can be discarded because it does not contain the nearest neighbor.
- **STEP 2.** An actual distance from a query Q to a given object O which is greater than MINMAXDIST(Q,R) for an MBR R can be discarded because R contains a object O' nearer to Q.
- **STEP 3.** An MBR R with MINDIST(Q,R) greater than the actual distance from Q to a given object O can be discarded because it does not enclose another object nearer than the object O.

Fig. 3. MINDIST and MINMAXDIST

3   Cell-Based Filtering Scheme

3.1   Overall Structure

As a new high-dimensional indexing scheme, we propose a Cell-Based Filtering (CBF) scheme using signatures. A signature is an abstraction of a feature vector [12]. To map object feature vectors into signatures, we divide the space of high-dimensional feature vectors into cells in the similar way to the VA-file and assign each cell to its own signature. In our CBF scheme, we, however, use only equivalent intervals for space partitioning since we make cells to be hyper-cubes. Therefore, the number of bits for each dimension is used to determine how many partitions each dimension space is divided into. When using b-bit cell signatures, there are 2^b partitions for each dimension. Figure 4 shows how to get cell signatures in a two-dimensional feature vector space. Since two bits are used for each dimension, there are four partitions and sixteen cells for the two-dimensional space. Since the points of the partitions in the example are 0.25, 0.50, 0.75, and 1.0, object feature vectors in the range of 0 to 0.25, 0.25 to 0.50, 0.50 to 0.75, and 0.75 to 1 can be mapped to partition signatures '00', '01', '10', and '11', respectively. Thus, a cell signature for the object feature vector A <0.28, 0.53> is represented as the concatenation of '01' with '10' (i.e., '0110') because 0.28 in the X-axis is mapped to '01' and 0.53 in the Y-axis to '10'. In the same way, cell signatures for the object feature vectors B and C are represented as '1000' and '1111', respectively.

Meanwhile, our CBF scheme is made up of two files; a signature file and a data file. All of object feature vectors are stored in the data file. The signature file includes

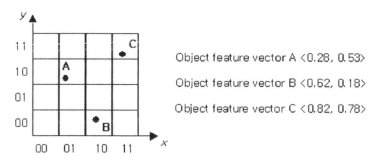

Fig. 4. Example for generating cell signatures

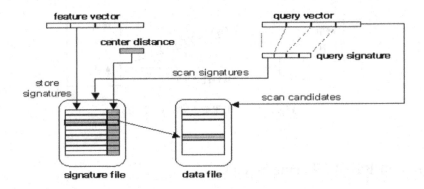

Fig. 5. Overall structure of our CBF scheme

cell signatures for the object feature vectors as well as distances between object feature vectors and the center of cells surrounding them. When inserting an object feature vector into our CBF file, we not only get a cell signature for it, but also compute the distance. After storing both the cell signature and the distance into the signature file, we finally store the object feature vector into the data file. In order to eliminate an additional file for mapping a cell signature into a feature vector, we keep the positions of the feature vector and its cell signature to be same in each file. For answering a user query in our CBF scheme, we first map its query vector into a query signature and then find candidate cells to contain the nearest neighbors by scanning all of cell signatures in the signature file, before accessing the data file. We finally visit real feature vectors within the candidate cells and obtain a final set of object feature vectors to answer the query. As dimensionality is increased, the data size of an object feature vector is larger, leading to the larger number of disk I/O accesses. However, when we use a signature instead of a real object feature vector, we require only the small number of disk I/O accesses because we can store the large number of cell signatures into a block (i.e., page). By doing additional filtering based on a distance between an object feature vector and the center of a cell surrounding it, our CBF scheme can achieve a better effect on filtering than the VA-File. Figure 5 shows the overall architecture of our CBF scheme.

3.2   New Definition of MINDIST and MAXDIST

A minimum distance (MINDIST) and a maximum distance (MAXDIST) are generally used as lower and upper bounds for selecting candidate cells. That is, before calculating the actual distance from a query vector to an object feature vector in the data file, we can decide whether a cell surrounding the object feature vector is a candidate or not. When we assume that an object feature vector (O) is surrounded by a cell, both $MINDIST_{VA}$ and $MAXDIST_{VA}$ in the VA-File are defined as the minimum distance and the maximum distance between a query vector (Q) and a cell surrounding the object feature vector, respectively. The position of an object feature vector within a cell is not important, but which cell surrounds the object feature vector is important. Figure 6 shows the $MINDIST_{VA}$ and the $MAXDIST_{VA}$ of the VA-File.

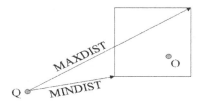

Fig. 6. $MINDIST_{VA}$ and $MAXDIST_{VA}$

Our CBF scheme make use of new definitions of MINDIST and MAXDIST in order to do good filtering based on an Euclidean distance between a query vector (Q) and the center of a cell surrounding an object feature vector, i.e., CENTER_DIST. Let RADIUS be an Euclidean distance between an object feature vector and the center of a cell surrounding it. Therefore, the lower bound of our CBF scheme ($MINDIST_{CBF}$) is defined as the subtraction of RADIUS from CENTER_DIST and the upper bound ($MINDIST_{CBF}$) as the addition of CENTER_DIST with RADIUS. Since the $MINDIST_{CBF}$ is greater than the $MINDIST_{VA}$ and the $MAXDIST_{CBF}$ is less than the $MAXDIST_{VA}$ in most cases, our CBF scheme can achieve a better effect on filtering than the VA-File. Figure 7 shows the new $MINDIST_{CBF}$ and $MAXDIST_{CBF}$.

- $$MINDIST_{CBF} = CENTER\_DIST - RADIUS$$
$$= \overline{QC} - r$$
$$= \overline{Qm}$$

- $$MAXDIST_{CBF} = CENTER\_DIST + RADIUS$$
$$= \overline{QC} + r$$
$$= \overline{QM}$$

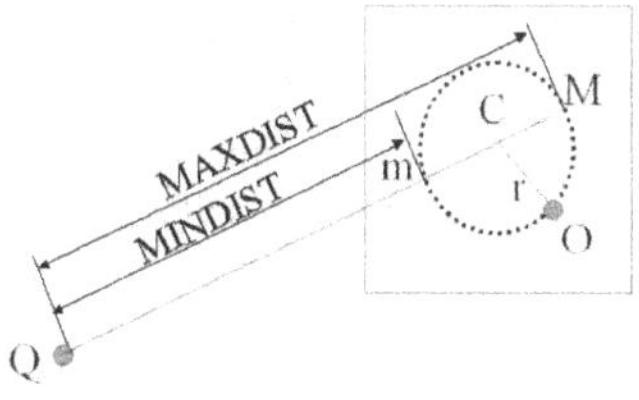

Fig. 7. $MINDIST_{CBF}$ and $MAXDIST_{CBF}$

Because it is possible to filter out a cell whose $MINDIST_{CBF}$ is grater than a current k-th $MAXDIST_{CBF}$, the k-th $MAXDIST_{CBF}$ is used to select candidate cells by scanning all of cell signatures. Figure 8 shows the filtering areas of the VA-File and our CBF scheme for the nearest neighbor search. In the figure, the first $MAXDIST_{CBF}$ is assumed to be the maximum distance of the cell A. To decide whether the cell B is a candidate or not, the $MAXDIST_{CBF}$ is compared with the $MINDIST_{CBF}$ of the cell B. Since the $MINDIST_{VA}$ of cell B is less than the $MAXDIST_{VA}$, the cell B is selected as a candidate in the VA-File. However, the cell B is pruned out in our CBF scheme because the MINDIST$_{CBF}$ is greater than the MAXDIST$_{CBF}$. Therefore, our CBF scheme can achieve a better effect on filtering than the VA-File, by using the newly defined MINDIST$_{CBF}$ and MAXDIDST$_{CBF}$.

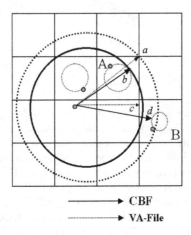

$$\longrightarrow \text{CBF}$$
$$\cdots\cdots\cdots\cdots\cdots\blacktriangleright \text{VA-File}$$

Fig. 8. Filtering area of VA-File and our CBF scheme

3.3 k-Nearest Neighbor Search Algorithm

For our CBF scheme, we provide a k-nearest neighbor (k-NN) search algorithm based on the newly defined MINDIST$_{CBF}$ and MAXDIST$_{CBF}$. Our algorithm is composed of three filtering steps. In the first step, for a given query, it filters out cells which need not to be visited by scanning all of cell signatures in the signature file and by using MINDIST$_{CBF}$ and MAXDIST$_{CBF}$. In the second step, our algorithm prunes the candidate cells selected in the first step which have a greater distance than the k-th MAXDIST$_{CBF}$. In the last step, our algorithm scans all feature vectors within the candidate cells from the data file and obtains the k nearest neighbors for a query vector. Figure 9 shows the k-nearest neighbor search algorithm of our CBF scheme. Here PHASE_ONE, PHASE_TWO, and PHASE_THREE describe the three filtering steps, respectively.

In the PHASE_ONE, all of cell signatures are fully loaded from the signature file into main memory and sequentially scanned, instead of accessing a partial part of the signature file, which results in reducing the number of disk I/O accesses. Figure 10 describes PHASE_ONE for the first filtering step. In order to decide whether a given cell (sig_vector) is a candidate or not, we calculate MINDIST$_{CBF}$ (c_mindist) based on CENTER_DIST from a query vector (q_vector) as well as RADIUS (r_dist). Then the MINDIST$_{CBF}$ is compared with a current k-th MAXDIST$_{CBF}$. If the MINDIST$_{CBF}$ is less than the k-th MAXDIST$_{CBF}$, the cell is selected as a candidate and otherwise it is pruned out. Finally, a list of candidate cells (list_mindist) being used in the next step is obtained.

```
int CBF_KNN(q_vector, k_value, nlist_result)
float       *q_vector,        // query vector
int         k_value,     // k
cNSDLL      *nlist_result      // results
{
    // Initialization
    k_maxdist = MAXREAL;
    // PHASE-1 : scan signatures
    for(sig_node=sigbuf_list->getHead();
            sig_node!=NULL; sig_node=sig_node->next) {
        // center distance (r)
        r_dist = sig_node->distance;
        // PHASE-1 Pruning
        PHASE_ONE(q_vector, sig_node->data, r_dist,
         nlist_maxdist, list_mindist, sig_node->index);
    }
    k_maxdist = nlist_maxdist->getLastValue()->mbrdist;
    // PHASE-2 Pruning
    PHASE_TWO(k_maxdist, list_mindist);
    // PHASE-3 Pruning
    PHASE_THREE(q_vector, list_mindist, nlist_result);
    return (nlist_result->num);
}
```

Fig. 9. our k-NN search algorithm

```
void PHASE_ONE(q_vector, sig_vector, r_dist,
            nlist_maxdist, list_mindist, int rec_index)
float       *q_vector,  // query vector
char        *sig_vector,        // signature
float       r_dist,        // center distance
cNSDLL      *nlist_maxdist,     // MAXDIST list
cUSDLL      *list_mindist,      // candidates list
int         rec_index      // record index
{
  k_maxdist=nlist_maxdist->getLastValue()->mbrdist;
  c_mindist=getMindist(q_vector,sig_vector,r_dist);
    // do filtering
  if (c_mindist <= k_maxdist)  {
        list_mindist->insert(mindist_data->mbrdist,
                                        mindist_data);
        // k-th MAXDIST
        c_maxdist=getMaxdist(q_vector,sig_vector,r_dist);
        if (c_maxdist < k_maxdist) {
         nlist_maxdist->insert(maxdist_data->mbrdist,
                                        maxdist_data);
         k_maxdist=nlist_maxdist->getLastValue()->mbrdist;
        }
  }
}
```

Fig. 10. PHASE_ONE filtering step

Figure 11 describes PHASE_TWO for the second filtering step. From the candidate cell list obtained in the first step, those whose MINDIST_{CBF} is greater than the k-th MAXDIST_{CBF} (k_maxdist) are pruned. Figure 12 describes PHASE_TREEE for the last filtering step. Because our algorithm visits all of candidate cells of the list in the increasing order of MINDIST_{CBF}, it is possible to scan cells near to a query vector in the early stage. For the filtering of candidate cells, MINDIST_{CBF} of a cell in the candidate cell list (sorted_mindist[idx].mindist) is compared with the k-th object feature vector distance (k_dist). If the MINDIST_{CBF} is greater than the k_dist, the cell is excluded from a result list. Otherwise, a distance (obj_dist) between a query vector and a feature vector within a candidate cell is computed. If the object_dist is less then the k_dist, the feature vector is inserted into a result list to answer the query.

```
void PHASE_TWO(k_maxdist, list_mindist)
float       k_maxdist,  // k-th MAXDIST
cUSDLL      *list_mindist     // candidates list
{
    for (pos = list_mindist->getHead();
                    pos != NULL; pos = next_pos){
        next_pos = pos->next;
        // pruning cells by k-th MAXDIST
        if (k_maxdist < pos->value->mindist)
            list_mindist->deleteNode(pos);
    }
}
```

Fig. 11. PHASE_TWO filtering step

Figure 13 shows an example for k-NN (k=1) search in our CBF scheme. We use two-bit signatures for each dimension. When we insert an object feature vector A<0.2, 0.3> into our CBF scheme, we first transform the feature vector into a signature ('0001') for the cell surrounding it. Next, we compute the distance between the feature vector A and the center of the cell and map it to an 1-byte distance signature ('5') as well. Finally, we store the cell signature of '0001' and the distance signature of '5' into the signature file and store A<0.2, 0.3> into the data file. When a query vector Q<0.4, 0.2> is given for k nearest neighbor search, we first scan all of cell signatures in the signature file, i.e., S_A, S_B, S_C, S_D, and S_E. For selecting candidate cells, we compute MAXDIST_{CBF} and MINDIST_{CBF} for each cell. As candidate cells, we choose two cells surrounding feature vectors A and D because each MINDIST_{CBF} for A and D is less than MAXDIST_{CBF}. We finally scan all object feature vectors within the candidate cells from the data file and find D<0.6, 0.4> as the nearest neighbor to a query vector (Q).

```
void PHASE_THREE(q_vector, list_mindist,nlist_result)
float       *q_vector,  // query vector
cUSDLL      *list_mindist,    // candiates list
cNSDLL      *nlist_result     // results list
{
    // sorting the candidates by MINDIST
    qsort(sorted_mindist,list_mindist->getTotalNum(),
                    sizeof(sDATA_MBR), QS_Compare);
    for (idx=0;idx<list_mindist->getTotalNum();
                                        idx++){
        if (k_dist != MAXREAL) {
            // pruning cells by k-th object distance
            if (k_dist < sorted_mindist[idx].mindist)
                break;
        }
        // data file access
        index = sorted_mindist[idx].index;
        fseek(vec_fptr,index*vec_rec_size+sizeof(char),
                                        SEEK_SET);
        fread((char*)object_vector,
            sizeof(float)*header->dimension,1,vec_fptr);
        fread((char*)id, header->id_length, 1,
                                        vec_fptr);
        obj_dist=getObjectdist(q_vector,object_vector);
        k_dist=nlist_result->getLastValue()->distance;
        // select objects
        if (obj_dist < k_dist)
            nlist_result->insert(obj_dist,result_data);
    }
}
```

Fig. 12. PHASE_THREE filtering step

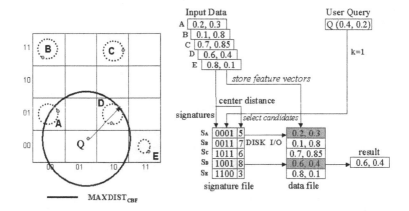

Fig. 13. Example for our k-NN search algorithm

4 Performance Evaluation

To evaluate the performance of our CBF scheme, we implement it using Visual C++ 6.0 under Windows NT 4.0 machine with 450 MHz CPU and 256 MB main memory. For our experiment, we make use of 10, 20, 50 and 80-dimensional synthetic data sets, each being obtained by randomly generating 100,0000 points in the data space, $[0,1]^{\#\_of\_dimensions}$. We also use 10, 20, 50 and 80-dimensional real data sets extracted from 100,000 paper instances by using the Hadamard algorithm of TV-tree[7]. For performance evaluation, we compare our CBF scheme with sequential scan (SeqScan), X-tree, and VA-File (VA-NOA: Near Optimal search Algorithm) in terms of insertion time, k-NN search time, and storage overhead.

4.1 Insertion Time

The insertion time is measured as a total time for inserting feature vectors. Figure 14 show the insertion time for 10, 20, 50, 80-dimensional synthetic data sets. In the X-tree, it takes longest time to insert a data set, i.e., 220 seconds for 10-dimensional data and 1,700 seconds for 80-dimensional data. While it takes about 2 seconds to insert a data set in the sequential scan because it only appends object feature vectors sequentially into a data file, it takes about 10 seconds in the VA-file because it needs time for storing vector approximations. In our CBF scheme, it takes about 13 seconds because it needs time for calculating a distance between a feature vector and the center of a cell surrounding it, in addition to the time for storing cell signatures for object feature vectors. The insertion times for the real data sets are similar to those for the synthetic data sets.

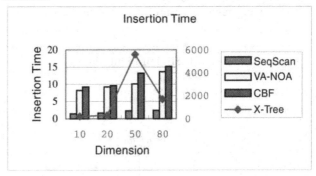

Fig. 14. Insertion Time

4.2 k-Nearest Neighbor Search Time

The k-NN search time is measured as a total time for searching for the k nearest neighbors to a given query vector. Figure 15 shows the number of disk I/O accesses required for the k-NN (k=100) search for the synthetic data sets. It is shown that the X-tree shows good performance at low dimensionality, but its performance become worse at high dimensionality, i.e., about 18,000 disk accesses when the number dimensions is 80. The performance of the X-tree is inferior to that of the sequential scan when the number of dimensions is greater than 20. Our CBF scheme requires less than 1,000 disk accesses even though dimensionality increases, leading to the best performance. Figure 16 shows the number of disk I/O accesses for 100-NN search for the real data sets. The X-tree shows the best performance for the 10- and 20-dimensional data sets, but its performance degrades as dimensionality increases. Our CBF scheme and the VA-File achieve very good performance for the 50- and the 80-dimensional data sets. Figure 17 and Figure 18 shows real time (or response time) for k-NN search (k=100) in the synthetic data sets and the real data sets, respectively. Our CBF scheme shows the best performance over the other schemes for all dimensions. That is, it takes about 0.2 second for the 10-dimensional real data set and about one second for the 80-dimensional real data set. When the number of dimensions is 80, our CBF scheme achieves about 30% better performance on k-NN search in the real data sets than the VA-File.

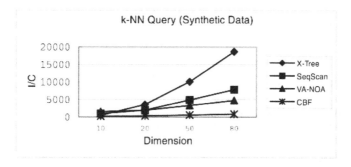

Fig. 15. Disk I/O accesses for k-NN search in synthetic data sets

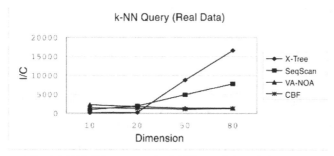

Fig. 16. Disk I/O accesses for k-NN search in real data sets

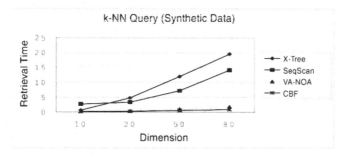

Fig. 17. Real time for k-NN search in synthetic data sets

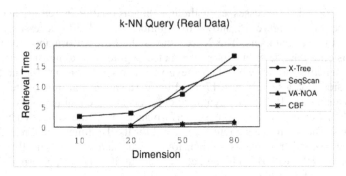

Fig. 18. Real time for k-NN search in real data sets

4.4 Storage Overhead

The storage overhead is computed as (index size / data size) * 100. Table 1 shows the storage overhead for the four index schemes. The storage overhead of the X-tree is 93% for the synthetic data sets and 84% for the real data sets, which results in the greatest storage overhead. While the VA-file requires only about 15-28% storage overhead because it stores only vector approximations, our CBF scheme requires about 15-31% storage overhead because it stores both cell signatures and distance information.

Table 1. Storage overhead

Indexing scheme	dimension	10	20	50	80
SeqScan	synthetic	0 %	0 %	0 %	0 %
	real				
X-Tree	synthetic	93 %	86 %	112 %	142 %
	real	84 %	78 %	102 %	119 %
VA-File	synthetic	28 %	20 %	16 %	15 %
	real				
CBF	synthetic	31 %	21 %	17 %	15 %
	real				

5 Conclusion

Many indexing schemes have been proposed to support k-NN search efficiently, but their performance degrades as dimensionality increases. So, we proposed a new indexing scheme which overcome the difficulties of high dimensionality, called CBF scheme. Our CBF scheme newly defined upper and lower bounds for cell filtering so that we might achieve good performance for the k-NN search. For performance evaluation, we implemented our CBF scheme under Windows NT and compare its performance with those of the X-tree, the VA-file, and the sequential scan. It is shown that the X-Tree requires the longest time (200 seconds) for insertion time while our CBF scheme requires only about 10 seconds. For the k-NN search, our CBF scheme requires only less than one second even though dimensionality increases, thus showing the best performance. As future work, we should study on its concurrency control and recovery mechanisms for multiple users as well as its parallel architectures for improving retrieval efficiency.

References

1. Robinson J. T., "The K-D-B-tree : A Search Structure for Large Multidimensional Dynamic Indexes", Proc. ACM SIGMOD Int. Conf. on Management of Data, pp. 10-18, 1981.
2. Henrich, A., "The LSDh-tree : An Access Structure for Feature Vectors", Proc. 14th Int. Conf. on Data Engineering, Orlando, 1998
3. D.A. White and R. Jain, "Similarity Indexing : Algorithms and Performance", InProc. Of the SPIE : Storage and Retrieval for Image and Video Databases IV, Vol. 2670, pp.62-75, 1996.
4. D. A. White and R. Jain, "Similarity Indexing with the SS-tree", In Proc. 12th Intl. Conf. On Data Engineering, New Orleans, pp.516-523, 1996.
5. Katayama N., Satoh S., "The SR-tree: An Index Structure for High-Dimensional Nearest Neighbor Queries", Proc. ACM SIGMOD Int. Conf. on Management of Data, pp. 369-380, 1997.
6. Berchtold S., Bohm C., Kriegel H.-P., "The Pyramid-Tree : Indexing Beyond the Curse of Dimensionality", Proc. ACM SIGMODE Int. Conf. on Management of Data, Seattle, 1998
7. H.I. Lin, H. Jagadish, and C. Faloutsos, "The TV-tree : An Index Structure for High Dimensional Data", VLDB Journal, Vol. 3, pp.517-542, 1995.
8. S. Berchtold, D. A. Keim, H-P. Kriegel, "The X-tree : An Index Structure for High-Dimensional Data, Proceedings of the 22nd VLDB Conference, pp.28-39, 1996.
9. Roger Weber, Hans-Jorg Schek, Stephen Blott: A Quantitative Analysis and Performance Study for Similarity-Search Methods in High-Dimensional Spaces. VLDB 1998: 194-205
10. Roger Weber, Stephen Blott, " An Approximation-Based Data Structure for Similarity Search", Technical report Nr. 24, ESPRIT project HERMES (no. 9141), October 1997.
11. Roussopoulos N., Kelley S., Vincent F., "Nearest Neighbor Queries", Proc. ACM SIGMOD Int. Conf. on Management of Data, pp. 71-79, 1995.
12. Faloutsos. C. "Design of a Signature File Method that Accounts for Non-Uniform Occurrence and Query Frequencies", ACM SIGMOD, 165-170, 1985.

Active System for Heterogeneous ODBMS Using Mobile Rule Codes[*]

K. C. Kim[1], S. B. Yoo[2], K. W. Ko[3], and S. K. Cha[4]

[1] Dept. of Computer Engineering
[2] Dept. of Automation Engineering
Inha University, Inchon, Korea
{kchang, syoo}@inha.ac.kr
[3,4] School of Electrical Engineering
Seoul National University, Seoul, Korea
{kwko, chask}@kdb.snu.ac.kr

Abstract. Throughout many research and development projects for active rule systems, active rules are implemented with different syntax and semantics. It becomes one of the stumbling blocks to apply active database systems especially in networked heterogeneous multidatabase environments. Utilizing the recent development of CORBA and ODMG standards, an active rule system is developed for heterogeneous ODBMS. Active rules represented in an ECA type are managed by a rule base. When events included in application database programs are detected, triggered rules by the events are retrieved from the rule base over network and interpreted dynamically. To ensure fast interpretations, the rules are stored in a bytecode format. Separation of rule-managing function will allow updating rules anytime without modifications in application programs or DBMS. The changes in rules will be reflected instantly in application programs via dynamic interpretation. The active rule system described is applied for integrity maintenance of spatial objects. With experimental results, overheads of byte code interpretation and runtime retrieval of triggered rules through network are discussed.

1 Introduction

As an effort to provide the users with the knowledge management features that are orthogonal to database programming, database community has conducted many research and development projects to utilize active rules for such applications as integrity constraint maintenance, view maintenance, and workflow management [9, 10]. However, because active database systems have been designed and implemented with different syntax and semantics of active rules, it is hard to build applications (such as e-commerce [5] and IDE [6]) with heterogeneous multiple database systems in distributed environments. The main idea of this paper is to provide active rules for heterogeneous ODBMS by taking advantage of the recent development of CORBA [7] and ODMG [1] standards.

---

[*] This work is supported by Inha University in 1999.

J. Štuller et al. (Eds.): ADBIS-DASFAA 2000, LNCS 1884, pp. 93–106, 2000.
© Springer-Verlag Berlin Heidelberg 2000

The active rule system described in this paper has been developed as a component of a larger middleware project called SDBC (Spatial Data Base Connectivity) [2], which give programmers a singe, object-oriented view of database and programming while relieving them from the burden of knowing the implementation-specific details of individual databases such as the physical location and the ODBMS process architecture. The key to such transparency is the extension of the ODMG object model [1] with a set of spatial data types and operators based on OpenGIS [8].

Commercial database systems provide only limited supports for data integrity checking because of the high computing cost. However, integrity maintenance becomes more important especially in distributed environments because the behavior of the whole system is not predictable unless the integrity of the shared data is maintained properly. When there is no applicable service for data integrity checking, the application programmer usually inserts his own code for checking constraints in his program. He has to do this whenever there is a database operation that need to check of constraints. As the number and complexity of integrity conditions increase, this will become unmanageable by the application programmers. It becomes almost impractical to demand every programmer to have the exact knowledge on the complex integrity constraints and to code them correctly.

The proper solution would be relieving the programmers of the responsibility of data integrity checking and letting a separate system to handle it. The integrity constraints can be collected by specialists who have the proper domain knowledge for the required constraints in detail and can be stored in a rule base as a set of rules. The active rule system, then, can monitor the database accessing activity of application programs and check whether the constraints are being satisfied when required. The integrity constraints can be expressed as ECA-rules (Event-Condition-Action rules).

Architectures for active database systems can be classified into layered, built-in, and compiled [9]. Because, in a built-in architecture, all active database components are included in the database system itself, the layered and compiled architectures are applicable for heterogeneous DBMS's. The compile approach has the advantage of fast running of precompiled triggered rules without the intervention of run-time event monitoring [11]. However, because all the triggering events must be detected in compile-time, the compile approach could not reflect runtime facts such as real time and memory allocation. The other drawback of the compile approach is that the compiled code should be recompiled when the corresponding rules are changed.

The active database system presented in this paper implements the layered architecture. Based on the uniform interface to heterogeneous ODBMS's, triggering events are detected and active rules are executed. Because the active rules are considered as global to distributed databases, a rule base is managed and interacts with event handlers through network in order to provide triggered rules for detected events. Once the triggered active rules are sent to a event handler, they are interpreted on the data from corresponding DBMS. In order to minimize the overhead of run-time interpretation of active rules, we save the active rules in terms of Lua byte code [4]. Like Java, Lua supports a stack-based virtual machine. We select Lua because it is portable embedded language (written in C) and its size is small (about 130 Kbytes).

2   Layered Architecture of Active Rule System for Spatial ODBMS

The overall architecture of SDBC and active rule system is depicted in Fig. 1. It employs the OMG Object Request Broker (ORB) for transparent network-level access. Right above this ORB layer lies the SDBC access layer, which implements the transparent access provider (TAP) library. An application program is linked to this TAP library and runs as a client process. The shaded ovals in the figure represent process boundaries.

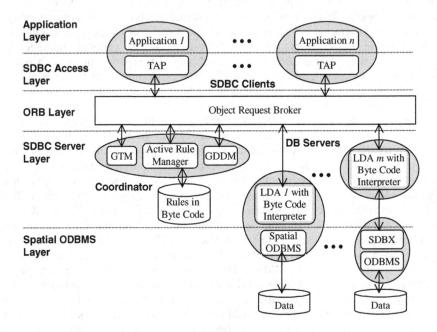

Fig. 1. Layered architecture of active rule system.

Below the ORB layer lies the SDBC server layer, which implements the LDA (Local DBMS Adapter) and the SDBC Coordinator consisting of GDDM (Global Data Dictionary manager), GTM (Global Transaction Manager), and Active Rule Manager. Active rules are compiled into byte codes and saved in the Rule Base. LDA is linked with Lua byte code interpreters and executes triggered rules. Either an LDA or an LDA with an ODBMS library runs as a process depending on the process architecture of a specific ODBMS. The SDBC coordinator exists as another process.

Four functional modules of the SDBC server layer, LDA, GDDM, GTM, and Global Rule Manager are implemented as CORBA objects and registered in the ORB. LDAs hide ODBMS-specific implementation details. The interfaces of these objects, called SDBC server layer interface (SLI), are described by the OMG interface definition language (IDL), and the ORB directs a client request to an appropriate object. The ORB itself supports the method shipping.

SDBC assumes that the underlying ODBMS conforms to the ODMG standard and supports a set of spatial data types and operators defined by SDBC. In case the ODBMS does not provide these spatial data management functions as in most commercial implementations, the SDBX (Spatial DataBase eXtension) layer is provided. SDBX implements SDBC-defined spatial data types, operators, and spatial indexes on top of commercial ODBMSs.

Although an application programmer can access SLI directly through the ORB, this approach has the following limitations. First, an application programmer has to know how to deal with CORBA. Second, because IDL does not support function overloading, runtime polymorphism, parameterized types, and so on, an application programmer cannot take advantage of the full expressive power of popular ODBMS programming languages like C++. Third, the performance of certain applications is bound to be limited only with the method shipping mechanism. The TAP in the SDBC access layer has been introduced to overcome these limitations.

Hiding the existence of ORB, the TAP shields an application programmer from the burden of knowing ORB programming. It solves the mismatch in the expressive power between SDBC C++ OML and OMG IDL. It provides facilities for managing the object cache in the client, and supports the object shipping mechanism. Applications that have frequent access to a set of objects can benefit from this mechanism.

3   Active Rules

The syntax of ECA rules consists of event, condition, and action as follows.

```
active_rule =
DEFINE rule_mode RULE rule_id
FOR '(' class_name_list ')' ';'
VAR var_list ':' [ARRAY OF | LIST OF | SET OF]
class_name ';'
EVENT trigger_event ';'
CONDITION cond_stmt ';'
ACTION action_stmt ';'
END_RULE ';'
```

The rule_mode specifies whether a rule is regarding multiple object instances or not (i.e., set-oriented or instance-oriented). Active rules in this work are defined for specific class(es) and can be referred as targeted rules. Targets for a rule are defined in FOR clause. The event in active rules can be one of transition operations (i.e., create, update, and delete) of persistent objects.

```
Rule_mode = "SET-ORIENTED" | "INSTANCE-ORIENTED"
trigger_event = INSERT '(' instance ')'
              | DELETE '(' instance ')'
              | UPDATE '(' instance [ '.' attribute ]')'
```

The condition statement in a rule should be evaluated true before the rule can be triggered. Conditional predicates can be connected by AND or OR operators recursively.

```
cond_stmt = [ '(' ] cond_pred [ ')' ]
{connector [ '(' ] cond_pred [ ')' ] }
            | [ '(' ] cond_stmt [ ')' ] connector [ '(' ]
               cond_pred [ ')' ]
            | [ '(' ] TRUE [ ')' ]
cond_pred = [ NOT ] logical_expression
            | [NOT] spatial_operation
            | [NOT] collection_expression
            | [NOT] user-defined_function
collection_expression = universal_quant
            | existential_quant
            | membership_expr
            | aggregate_opr
connector = AND | OR
```

Actions in rules can be general functions such as system functions or user defined functions. One of the frequent actions is ABORT, which cancels all the changes made by the current transaction.

```
action_stmt = action  action {AND action_stmt}
action = built-in_procedure | user-defined_procedure
built-in_procedure = create_procodure
                   | replace_procedure
                   | remove_procedure
                   | update_procedure
                   | INFORM_INTEGRITY_VIOLATION
                   | ABORT
```

Example 1. This example is an set-oriented rule defined for the classes *BulidingLayout* and *RoadLayout*. It states that apartments or tenements cannot constructed within 50 meters from any express way.

```
DEFINE SET-ORIENTED RULE R2 FOR (BuildingLayout,
RoadLayout);
VAR building: BuildingLayout; roads: SET OF RoadLayout;
roads := QUERY(temp FROM RoadLayout WHERE temp.type =
EXPRESS);
EVENT INSERT(building);
CONDITION (building.type = APARTMENT OR building.type =
    TENEMENT) AND EXISTS temp IN
    roads: Distance(building.area, temp.area) < 50;
ACTION INFORM_INTEGRITY_VIOLATION;
END_RULE;
```

We assume that the integrity of database is maintained at the beginning of a transaction and it should be assured before the transaction is committed. This means that the integrity of the database might be violated temporarily during a transaction. For example, during a pair of delete and paste operation of a design object, the disappearance of the object could violate design rules temporarily. We allow this kind of temporal violation of integrity rules by deferring the evaluation of integrity rules to the end of transactions.

4   Dynamic Rule Interpretation

The basic idea is twofold: rules are managed by a separate entity, the rule manager, and whenever a rule is required, it is fetched and interpreted dynamically. To ensure a fast interpretation, the rules are stored in a bytecode format. Separation of rule-managing function will allow updating rules anytime without modifications in application programs or DBMS. The change in rules will be reflected instantly in application programs via dynamic interpretation. Fig. 2 shows the overall picture of our rule interpretation system. In the left side, there is a rule manager which is reponsible for compiling rule programs (or rule definitions) into bytecodes and servicing them to application programs. On the right side, we see an application program linked with a rule and Lua library that help the application program in requesting and interpreting rules during the run-time.

4.1 Rule Manager

The rule manager accepts rule programs, converts them into bytecodes, and responds to outside requests for the rules. For the bytecode format, Lua bytecode is being used.[1] Conversion to Lua bytecodes is being done by the Lua compiler. To use the Lua compiler, the rule program is first transformed to Lua program.

4.1.1 Symbol Table
When changing rule programs into Lua programs, we need the attribute information for system-provided classes. Rule programmers can use system-provided classes without including their definitions, and the rule system should include them when changing the rule programs into Lua programs. The needed attribute information of the system-wide classes are extracted from the schema definitions written in ODL(Object Definition Language) by the ODL preprocessor (as shown in Fig. 2) and stored in the symbol table.

4.1.2 Rule Preprocessor
The rule preprocessor is responsible for transforming the rule programs into Lua programs. With the help of the symbol table, it first generates codes for loading all objects referred in the rule program in the interpreter stack. The condition and action part is transformed into an if-statement. If the action part updates the database, it is considered to be another event to be checked. The rule preprocessor inserts codes for requesting rule-checking in this case. Below we show an example to explain how a rule program is converted into a Lua program.

---

[1] Lua bytecode is chosen, because the Lua interpreter is small and fast. Also Lua programming language provides a convenient mechanism to communicate between the host language and Lua (Lua is an embedded language). Using this feature, we can implement time-consuming DB operations, especially spatial operations, in the host language, and call them from Lua programs.

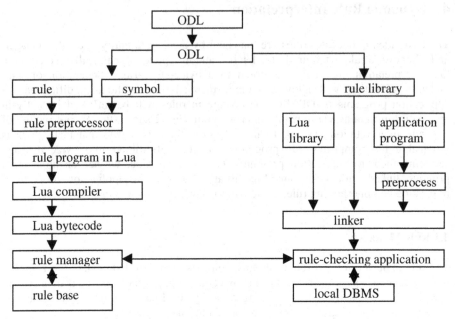

Fig. 2. Overview of the dynamic rule interpretation system

```
DEFINE INSTANCE-ORIENTED RULE R3 FOR(SewerPipe);
    VAR sp: SewerPipe;
    EVENT INSERT(sp);
    CONDITION (sp.type = Transport OR sp.material =
              "Steel") AND sp.diameter < 350;
    ACTION update(sp.diameter, 350);
    END_RULE;
```

The above is a rule program written in a rule language defined in Section 3. It defines an instance-oriented rule with name R3. The target class and event this rule is applied is "SewerPipe" and "INSERT" respectively; that is if an object of "SewerPipe" is inserted (or created), rule R3 should be applied. This program will be transformed into the following Lua program.

```
sp = {oid, type, material, diameter}
sp.oid, sp.type, sp.material, sp.diameter =
load_object("SewerPipe")
function Exec_R3(sp)
    if ((sp.type == Transport or sp.material ==
        "Steel")AND sp.diameter < 350
    then
      update("SewerPipe", sp.oid, "diameter", "350")
      raise_internal_event(1,"SewerPipe","UPDATE",
            "diameter")
    end
end
Exec_R3(sp)
```

In the first two lines above, an object of "SewerPipe" class is defined and loaded. Without loading this object, the access to the field of it as in the fourth line will have no meaning. In the fourth line, "type", "material", and "diameter" attributes are examined, and if the condition is satisfied, the "diameter" attribute is updated. Since this rule is updating the database, the preprocessor raises "UPDATE" event for class "SewerPipe" in the 8th line. This event will be collected in the event set and handed over to the rule manager when the above rule is executed.

Another example is shown below for a set-oriented rule.

```
DEFINE SET_ORIENTED RULE R1 FOR(SewerPipe, WaterPipe);
VAR sp: SewerPipe; Wps: SET OF WaterPipe;
    wps := QUERY(temp FROM WaterPipe)
EVENT INSERT(sp);
CONDITION EXISTS temp IN wps: Intersect(sp,temp);
ACTION INFORM_INTEGRITY_VIOLATION;
END_RULE;
```

The above rule is set-oriented because a set of "WaterPipe" objects are involved. A set-oriented rule is more complicated to transform than an instance-oriented rule. When it involves one or more spatial queries and spatial operations, spatial indexes are created and filtering operations are inserted. The resulting Lua program is as follows.

```
sp = {oid, type, material, diameter}
wp = {type, material, diameter}
sp.oid,sp.type,sp.material,sp.diameter =
load_object("SewerPipe")
function Exec_R1(queried_class)
   create_RTree_key("SewerPipe",0)
   local count = filter_objects("SewerPipe",
                        "s_RTree_WaterPipe")
   local objIndex = 0
   while objIndex < count do
      result = LineString_intersects_LineString
                   ("SewerPipe","WaterPipe",objIndex)
      if (result == 1) then
         violate_integrity(1,"R1")
         t_abort()
      else objIndex = objIndex + 1
      end
   end
end
Exec_R1(sp)
```

In set-oriented rules, the condition part is closely related to the query part. The rule preprocessor remembers the relationship between them during the parsing stage and generates codes accordingly.

4.2 Rule Execution

The application program should collect events that need to be checked for rules and initiate rule-checking processes for them. Rules are requested at the same time right before the "commit" statement. All events collected so far are sent to the rule manager, and a list of rules (in Lua bytecode) is received in return. The bytecodes are stored in "active rule list" and interpreted one by one by the Lua interpreter.

4.2.1 Rule Library

The functions called in Lua program (or Lua bytecode after compilation) but not defined should be provided in the rule library. The Lua compiler passes the string of the function name as part of arguments when converting function calls to bytecodes. The Lua interpreter, when processing a function call, retrieves this function name, finds the corresponding function pointer in the host language, and calls it. Therefore all functions in the host language that are to be called from the Lua code should be registered with the interpreter.

In the functions of the rule library, database object manipulation functions are used to modify database objects and are schema dependent. They are schema dependent because each manipulation function should treat each class differently when loading or updating them. The ODL preprocessor in Fig. 2 generates schema-dependent library functions automatically from the schema definitions (written in ODL). The rest of the library functions are schema independent. In the next section, we will show how these functions are used in application programs or in Lua programs.

4.2.2 Rule Interpretation

To check rules, the application program collects events and calls "validate_integrity()" just before the "commit" statement. "validate_integrity()" passes the event list over to the rule manager, receives rule codes in bytecode format, and calls the rule interpreter for each of them. An example of an application program with rule-checking codes is in Fig. 3. Rule-checking codes that are added by the preprocessor are in bold face.

```
#include "mylib.h"
  int main(){
    d_Database pipeDB;
    . . . . . . . . . . . . .
    pipeDB.open("pipeFD");
    . . . . . . . . . . . . .
    Point p[4];
    p[0] = Point(192235,254320);
    p[1] = Point(192245, 254350);
    . . . . . . . . . . . . .
    LineString pipe_geo(4,p);
    d_Ref<SewerPipe>sp = new(oovTopDB)
        SewerPipe(Transport,"Cast",200.0,pipe.geo);
    created_objs.push_back(sp);
    . . . . . . . . . . . . .
    validate_integrity(created_objs, deleted_objs,
                    modified_objs, violated_objs);
    . . . . . . . . . . .
  }
```

Fig. 3. An example of application program with rule-checking codes added

To see how rules are interpreted, assume rule R1 and R3 in Section 4.1.2 are the rules related to this event (creation event of "SewerPipe" object). When the application program runs, the validate_integrity function will send an event list which contains only one event: INSERT on "SewerPipe" class. Rule R1 and R3 will be returned (in bytecode format) in response. Assume R1 is first processed. The rule interpreter detects "CALLFUNC" bytecode which calls a host-language function that corresponds to Lua function "load_object()". Suppose the registered function for "load_object()" is "lua_load_object()". The interpreter calls "lua_load_object()" to load the current SewerPipe object just created. "lua_load_object()" should look like as follows.

```
static void lua_load_object(void){
    lua_Object t_class = lua_getparam(1);
    load_object(lua_getstring(t_class));
}
```

It first retrieves the name of the class this object belongs to from the interpreter stack, and calls "load_object()" with this class name as an argument. Note this "load_object()" is a host-language function, different from the Lua function with the same name. The "load_object()" is a big case statement; for each class it calls a class-specific loading function.

```
void load_object(char *t_class){
    if (!strcmp(t_class, "SewerPipe"))
        load_SewerPipe_object();
    else if (!strcmp(t_class, "WaterPipe"))
        load_WaterPipe_object();
. . . . . . . . .
}
```

Since t_class is "SewerPipe" in our case, "load_SewerPipe_object()" will be called, and this function will load the just-created SewerPipe object on the interpreter stack so that its members can be checked for the rule. The rest of the interpretation process is similar and straightforward. If a host-language function is called, find the corresponding function pointer and executes; otherwise interpret the given bytecode.

5   Experiments

The biggest advantage of our rule system is that it can handle constantly changing rules without recompilation of the application program or DBMS itself. The price for this flexibility is an increase in rule processing time. The processing time increases because of two reasons. One is interpretation; the other communication over network. In this section, we examine how much delay is caused by these two reasons, and suggest a couple of ways to improve it.

5.1 Interpretation Overheads

Lua code, when interpreted, is about 20 times slower than a native code. To see how this slowness affects our rule system, we picked the rule in Fig. 4, coded it in C++ and Lua respectively, and ran them 10 times.

```
DEFINE SET-ORIENTED RULE R7 FOR (BuildingLayout);

VAR building: BuildingLayout; buildings: SET OF BuildingLayout;

    buildings := QUERY(temp FROM BuildingLayout WHERE temp.type == KINDERGARTEN);

EVENT INSERT(building);

CONDITION building.type == GAS_STATION AND

            EXISTS temp IN buildings : Distance(building, temp) < 50;

ACTION INFORM_INTEGRITY_VIOLATION;

END_RULE;
```

Fig. 4. A set-oriented rule

Fig. 5 shows the average time taken by each code. Lua code only shows 2 to 3% increases in processing time. The reason is that the rule in Fig. 4 requires a number of spatial operations to be done, which consumes most of the processing time, but these spatial operations are already provided by the rule library in native code. Lua program just calls them, and the pre-compiled native code runs for it. This case, however, is not special. Most time-consuming rules are spending most of time in processing spatial operations. If the rule does not contain any spatial operation, it will be processed very quickly, and Lua code will not cause a significant delay over native code. On the other hand, if the rule contains spatial operations, it will take time because of the spatial operations, but again Lua code and native code will not show much difference in processing time since the spatial operations are run in native code in both cases anyway.

5.2 Communication Overheads

A more serious delay comes from the communication between the application program and the rule manager. Since the rules are fetched in run time, the application program should wait until the rules arrive. In our case, we are using CORBA mechanism for communication, and the communication overhead is as shown in Fig. 6. The time is measured inside our laboratory, and the network traffic delay is not counted; but the overhead already reaches about 1.5 seconds. However we can observe that the overhead stays relatively same regardless of the number of fetched rules (less than 1% increase for 100 rules compared to 1 rule). This means fetching a large rule set at once is better than fetching smaller rule sets several times, in terms of communication time. Also, since the overhead is relatively a constant, it becomes less significant as the rule processing time is increasing

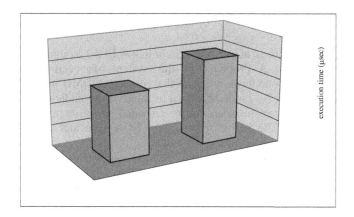

Fig. 5. Comparing Lua code to native code in rule execution time

Still the delay is not negligible, and it seems the communication overhead is unavoidable and is the price we have to pay for to get the flexibility in handling dynamically changing rules. However we can reduce the communication time in several ways. One is to use more improved communication mechanism than CORBA. The inefficiency of CORBA in communication overhead is well pointed out by researchers [3]. Other ways are caching or pushing. By caching some of the rules in the local system and by providing a local rule manager, we can improve the processing speed considerably. Pushing will be initiated by the rule manager: it can push changed or newly created rules to the local rule manager. The local manager will decide whether to cache these pushed rules depending on the relevance of them to the local DBMS.

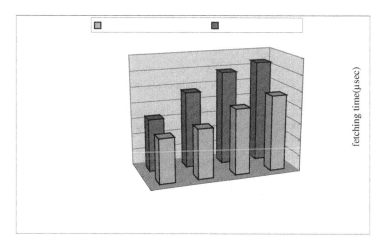

Fig. 6. Communication overheads of rule fetching

6   Conclusion

In this paper, we present an active rule system that is based on dynamic interpretation of mobile rule codes. A prototype of this system has been implemented as a component of a larger middleware system that provides ODMG interfaces and spatial extensions to ODBMS. By implementing it as a part of a middleware, heterogeneous ODBMS in distributed environment can be provided an active rule system in system independent manner. The active rules are in ECA type and used for validating integrity constraints in this prototype.

A global rule base manages the active rules and interacts with local event handlers to provide triggered rules for detected events. Active rules are saved in Lua byte codes and interpreted efficiently on the data from local database systems. Comparing to other architecture of active rule systems (i.e., tightly coupled built-in architecture or compiled architecture), this approach can separate the rule-managing function from local DBMS and enables the rules to be updated without any changes in application programs. Any changes in the rule base will be reflected instantly via dynamic interpretation while application programs run on a local DBMS. The overheads of transmitting triggered rules from the rule base turn out insignificant comparing to set-oriented spatial operations.

There are still rooms left for further improvements. Firstly, local DBMS can maintain the cache of triggered rules and reduce the overheads of network communcation. In this case, any changes in the global rule base should be pushed to the local cache. Secondly, rule conditions from different active rules often include common parts. Analysis using dependency graph can identify the shared parts and the optimal order of evaluation for the given rule conditions [12]. Thirdly, we can receive valuable information for optimization from the target ODBMS. We need to devise more general approaches to optimize spatial operations in various application contexts.

References

1. R. Cattell and D. Barry ed., The Object Database Standard: ODMG 2.0, Morgan Kaufmann Publishers, Inc., 1997.
2. S. K. Cha et al., "A middleware architecture for transparent access to multiple spatial object databases," Interoperating Geographic Information Systems, M. F Goodchild ed., Kluwer Academic Publishers, pp. 267 – 282, 1999.
3. Aniruddha S. Gokhale and Douglas C. Schmidt, "Evaluating Latency and Scalability of CORBA Over High-Speed ATM Networks," In *Proceedings of the International Conference on IEEE Distributed Computing Systems*, Baltimore, Maryland, May 1997.
4. Roberto Ierusalimschy, Luiz Henrique de Figueiredo, Waldemar Celes, "Lua – an extensible extension language," *John Wiley & Sons, Ltd.*, 1995.8.
5. Anant Jhingran et al., "Is E-Commerce a New Wave for Database Research? - Panel," Proceedings of the Sixteenth International Conference on Data Engineering, pp 473, San Diego, USA, February 2000.
6. R. Kidwell and J. Richman, "Preliminary IDE Framework Implementation Concept, and Rationale Report for the DoD CALS IDE Project," ManTech Advanced Technology Systems, 1996.
7. OMG, CORBA Services: Common Object Services Specification, 1996.

8. Open GIS, OpenGIS Simple Features Specification for CORBA, Revision 0, Open GIS Consortium, Inc., 1997.
9. J. Widom and S. Ceri, "Active Database Systems," Morgan Kaufmann Publishers, Inc., 1996.
10. S. Yang and S. Chakravarthy, "Formal Semantics of Composite Events for Distributed Environments," Proceedings of the Fifteenth International Conference on Data Engineering, pp 400 - 409, Sydney, Australia, March 1999
11. S. B. Yoo, K. C. Kim, S. K. Cha, "A Middleware Implementation of Active Rules for ODBMS," Proceedings of The Sixth International Conference on Database Systems for Advanced Applications, Hsinchu, Tiwan, pp. 347 – 354, April 1999.
12. S. B. Yoo and S. K. Cha, "Integrity maintenance in a heterogeneous engineering database environment," Data & Knowledge Engineering, Vol. 21, Elsevier Science, pp.347 – 363, 1997.

2-D Spatial Indexing Scheme in Optimal Time

Nectarios Kitsios[1], Christos Makris[1], Spyros Sioutas[1], Athanassios Tsakalidis[1,2], John Tsaknakis[1], and Bill Vassiliadis[1,2]

[1] Department of Computer Engineering and Informatics: Graphics, Multimedia and GIS Laboratory, University of Patras, 26500 Patras, Greece
{sioutas,tsaknaki}@ceid.upatras.gr
[2] Computer Technology Institute: Research Unit 5
P.O. Box 1122
26110 Patras, Greece
{tsak,bb}@cti.gr

Abstract. We consider the 2-dimensional space with integer coordinates in the range [1, N] x [1, N]. We present the MPST (Modified Priority Search Tree) index structure which reports the k points that lie inside the quadrant query range $(-\infty, b] \times (-\infty, c]$ in optimal O(k) time. Our Index Scheme is simple, fast and it can be used in various geometric or spatial applications such as: (1) 2 D dominance reporting on a grid (2) 2D maximal elements on a grid. Then, based on structures of Gabow et al. [6] and Beam and Fich [31] we describe an index scheme, which handles in an efficient way window queries in spatial database applications. In the general case in which the plane has real coordinates the above time results are slowed down by adding a logarithmic factor due to the normalization technique.

1 Introduction

The problem of range searching is one of the most extensively studied problems in computational geometry and spatial databases. In a general formulation of the problem we are given a set of n points in d-dimensional space and we are asked to preprocess them in a data structure so that for any query range the points inside the range can be found efficiently. Numerous solutions for the problem have appeared (see the survey papers of Matousek [10] and Agarwal [1]). In this paper we consider the 2-dimensional case in which the points lie on an integer grid and the query ranges are of the forms $(-\infty, b] \times (-\infty, c]$ or $[a, b] \times (-\infty, c]$ or $[a_1, b_1] \times [a_2, b_2]$. The significance of our results is obvious for 2D (GIS and spatial DB) applications. Our main memory structure relies on the priority search tree, which we modify appropriately. In our solution the query algorithm consists of two separate stages: searching and reporting. The searching part finds the nodes of the priority search tree that are roots of subtrees with points inside the query range. Then the reporting part simply traverses these subtrees in the same way as in an ordinary priority search tree. So apart from a small constant time in the search part the points in the query range can be found in a simple and efficient manner.

J. Štuller et al. (Eds.): ADBIS-DASFAA 2000, LNCS 1884, pp. 107–116, 2000.
© Springer-Verlag Berlin Heidelberg 2000

The majority of the related work makes use of spatial indexing schemes, most often R-trees and their variants [16, 17, 18], to answer a subset of spatial queries in 2D (usually topological or directional) [19, 20]. Lately R-trees have been also utilised for higher dimensionalities [21].

The wide adoption of secondary memory indexing schemes, especially the R-tree family, for this type of problems, is mainly attributed to their satisfactory average performance in terms of page accesses. However, this does not undermine approaches towards main memory structures, for several factors: i) the worst-case performance for the R-tree family can be very bad and the claimed theoretical average performance estimation has been particularly evasive (see [22] for some late results) ii) in spatial data management it is not always true (see [23, 24]) that most searches are I/O-bound than CPU-bound and iii) the availability of increasingly larger memories at lower costs justifies the use of main memory structures even for the processing of large datasets.

Nowadays, for up to three dimensions there are available secondary memory structures, that exhibit worst case performance analogous to that of main memory ones, i.e. query time of the form $O(\log_B n + t/B)$ and space usage close to linear $(O(n/B))$, for range queries (where n is the number of stored items, B the page size and t the output size) (see [2,4,25,27,28,29,30,32])

In main memory the three-sided range query [a, b] x $(-\infty, c]$ (and consequently the quadrant range query $(-\infty, b]$ x $(-\infty, c]$) has been studied from Gabow, Bentley and Tarjan [6] they solved the problem in O(N+n) space and O(k) time. Their structure relies on the Cartesian tree of Vullemin [14] which in essence is a predecessor of the priority search tree. They make use of the machinery developed in [8] for answering lowest common ancestor (lca) queries for two nodes of an arbitrary tree in O(1) time. Their algorithm finds each point in the range by forming and answering a lca query. It incurs also a time overhead for each reported point and the algorithm for lowest common ancestors on arbitrary trees is also somewhat complicated.

In the following section we review the basic component of our solution that is the priority search tree. In section 3 we propose a more simple and concrete index scheme for the case in which the query ranges are half-infinite in the x- and y-directions. This case is known as quadrant range search or dominance search. In section 4 we discuss some geometric or spatial applications of our structure. In section 5 we present a new index scheme based on structures of both Gabow et al. [6] and Beam and Fich [31] which handles window queries in spatial database applications in $O(\sqrt{\log n}/\log\log n + k)$ time. In section 6 we consider the general case in which the plane has real coordinates and we show that the above time results are slowed down by an added logarithmic factor due to the normalization technique. Finally in section 7 we conclude.

2   The Priority Search Tree

We will briefly review the priority search tree of McCreight [11]. Let S be a set of n points on the plane. We want to store them in a data structure so that the points that lie inside a half infinite strip of the form $(-\infty, b]$ x $(-\infty, c]$ can be found efficiently.

The priority search tree is a binary search tree of depth $O(\log n)$ for the x-coordinates of the points. The root of the tree contains the point p with smallest y-coordinate. The left (resp. right) subtree is recursively defined for the set of points in S-{p} with x-coordinates in the left (resp. right) subtree. From this definition it is easily seen that a point is stored in a node on the search path from the root to the leaf containing its x-coordinate.

To answer a range query with a quadrant $(-\infty, b] \times (-\infty, c]$ we find the $O(\log n)$ nodes in the search path P_b for b. Let L_b be the left children of these nodes, that don't lie on the path. For the points of the nodes of $P_b \cup L_b$ we can determine in $O(\log n)$ time which lie in the query-range. Then for each node of L_b whose point is inside the range we visit its two children and check whether their points lie in the range. We continue recursively as long as we find points in the query-range.

For the correctness of the query algorithm first observe that nodes on the right of the search path have points with x-coordinate larger than b and therefore lie outside the query-range. The points of P_b may have x-coordinate larger than b or they may have y-coordinate larger than c. If any of these is true then they are not reported. The nodes of L_b and their descendants have points with x-coordinate smaller than b so only their y-coordinates need to be tested. For the nodes of L_b whose points lie inside the query-range we need to look further at their descendants. The search proceeds as long as we find points inside the query-range. If a point of a node u does not lie inside the query-range then this point has y-coordinate larger than c. Therefore all points in the subtree rooted at u lie outside the query-range and need not to be searched. From the above discussion we can easily bound the query time by $O(\log n + k)$, since we need $O(\log n)$ time to visit the nodes in $P_b \cup L_b$ and $O(k)$ time for searching in their subtrees.

3 Quadrant Range Search on a Grid

Let S be a set of n points on the plane with integer coordinates in the range $[1, N] \times [1, N]$. Without loss of generality we assume that no two points have the same value for some coordinate. We will show how to store the points in a data structure so that the k points in a query range of the form $(-\infty, b] \times (-\infty, c]$ can be found in $O(k)$ time. Our structure relies on the priority search tree, which we augment with list-structures similar to those in [12].

We store the points in a priority search tree T of size $O(n)$ as described in the previous section. For convenience we will assume that the tree T is a complete binary tree (i.e. all its leaves have depth $\log n$). Note that if n is not a power of 2 we may add some dummy leaves to the right so that T becomes complete.

We also use an array A of size N which stores pointers to the leaves of T. Specifically A[i] contains a pointer to the leaf of T with maximum x-coordinate smaller or equal to i. With this array we can determine in $O(1)$ time the leaf of the search path P_b for b.

In each leaf u of the tree with x-coordinate i we store the following lists L(u), $P_L(u)$: The list L(u) stores the points of the nodes of L_i. The list $P_L(u)$ stores the points of the nodes of P_i which have x-coordinate smaller or equal to i. Both lists also contain pointers to the nodes of T that contain these points. Each list L(u), $P_L(u)$, stores its nodes in increasing y-coordinate of their points.

To answer a query with a range $(-\infty, b] \times (-\infty, c]$ we find in $O(1)$ time the leaf u of the search path P_b for b. Then we traverse the list $P_L(u)$ and report its points until we find a point with y-coordinate greater than c. We traverse the list L(u) in the same manner and find the nodes of L_b whose points have y-coordinate less than or equal to c. For each such node we report its point and then we continue searching further in its subtree as long as we find points inside the range.

The following theorem bounds the size and query time of our structure.

Theorem 3.1 Given a set of n points on the plane with integer coordinates in the range [1, N] x [1, N] we can store them in a data structure with O(N+nlogn) space that allows quadrant range queries to be answered in O(k) time, where k is the number of answers.

Proof. The query algorithm finds the k' points of nodes of $P_b \cup L_b$ that lie inside the query-range in O(k') time by simple traversals of the lists $P_L(u)$, L(u). The search in subtrees takes O(k) additional time for reporting k points in total. Therefore the query algorithm takes O(k) time.

Each list $P_L(u)$, L(u) stores respectively points in the nodes of a path, and points in the left children of nodes of a path. So the size of each list is O(logn) and the space of T is O(nlogn). The space of the whole structure is O(N+nlogn) because of the size of the array A.

The nlogn term in the space bound is due to the size of the lists $P_L(u)$ and L(u). We can reduce the total space of these lists to O(n) by making them persistent. Ordinary structures are ephemeral in the sense that update operations make permanent changes to the structures. Therefore in ordinary structures it is impossible to access their old versions (before the updates). According to the terminology of Driscoll et al. [3] a structure is persistent if it allows access to older versions of the structure. There are two types of persistent data structures: partially and fully persistent. A partially persistent data structure allows updates of its latest version only while a fully persistent one allows updates of any of its versions. In [3] a general methodology is proposed for making data structures of bounded in-degree persistent. With their method such a structure can be made partially persistent with O(1) amortized space cost per change in the structure. In our case a list can be made partially persistent with a O(1) amortized increase in space per insertion/deletion.

We show how to implement the lists $P_L(u)$ using a partially persistent list. Let u be a leaf in T and let w be its predecessor (the leaf on the left of u). We denote by x_u the x-coordinate of u and by x_w, the x-coordinate of w. The two root-to-leaf paths Px_u, Px_w, share the nodes from the root of T to the nearest common ancestor of u, w. So we can create $P_L(u)$ by updating $P_L(w)$ in the following way: First we delete from list $P_L(w)$ the points that don't lie on Px_u. Then we insert the points of Px_u which have x-coordinate smaller or equal to x_u. In this way we can construct all lists as versions of a persistent list: we begin from the leftmost leaf and construct the list $P_L(u)$ of each leaf u by updating the one of its predecessor. The total number of insertions and deletions is O(n) because each point is inserted and deleted only once. Therefore the space of all the lists is O(n). In the same way we can construct the lists L(u) for all leaves in O(n) space. Therefore:

Theorem 3.2 Given, a set of n points on the plane with integer coordinates in the range [1, N] x [1, N] we can store them in a data structure with O(N+n) space that allows quadrant range queries to be answered in O(k) time, where k is the number of answers.

The preprocessing time is $O(N+n\log n)$ but with a more careful implementation we can reduce the $\log n$ factor to a smaller one. A different way to reduce the space and preprocessing time is to use pruning as in [5], [12]. To handle query ranges of the form $[a, b]$ x $(-\infty, c]$ we use the structure of Gabow et al [6] .

4   Applications

We present some applications of our structure for known geometric problems and spatial database query problems.

2D dominance reporting on a grid. A point p_1 is said to dominate p_2 if all coordinates of p_2 are smaller than the respective coordinates of p_1. In the dominance reporting problem we are given a set S of n d-dimensional points and we want to report all dominance pairs (p_1,p_2). For d = 2, d = 3 the problem can be solved in time $O(n\log n+k)$ using a priority search tree and a space sweeping technique. For d = 4 the problem can be solved in time $O(n\log^2 n+k)$ [13] or $O(n\log n\log\log n+k\log\log n)$ [7]. For the planar case we can achieve $O(N+n+k)$ time if the points lie on a grid. This can be done by building the structure of theorem 3.2 for the n points and querying it with the range $(-\infty, x_p)$ x $(-\infty, y_p]$ for each point $p(x_p, y_p)$. Since the structure can be built in $O(N+n)$ time and each query takes time $O(k')$ to report k' pairs, we have the following:

Theorem 4.1 The planar dominance reporting problem for a set of n points with integer coordinates in the range [1, N] x [1, N] can be solved in O(N+n+k) time and O(N+n) space.

2D maximal elements on a grid. Let S be a set of d-dimensional points. The maximal elements are the points of S that are not dominated by another point of S. The case in which the points lie on a three dimensional grid has been studied by Karlsson and Overmars [9]. Their solution runs in $O(N+n\log\log N)$ time and $O(N+n)$ space. Using the structure of theorem 3.2 can solve the planar problem more efficiently. In fact we store the n points on a similar structure that answers queries of the form $[x, +\infty)$ x $[y, +\infty)$. For each point $p(x_p, y_p)$ we query the structure with $[x_p, +\infty)$ x $[y_p, +\infty)$ and if no answer is found then the point (x_p, y_p) is maximal. Clearly the time and space bound are as stated in the following:

Theorem 4.2 The planar maximal elements problem for a set of n points with integer coordinates in the range [1, N] x [1, N] can be solved in O(N+n) time and space.

5   Window Queries in Spatial Database Applications

Let S be a set of n 2-dimensional rectangles. We want to store them in a data structure so that the rectangles whose at least one endpoint lies in a window query can be found efficiently (see figure 1).

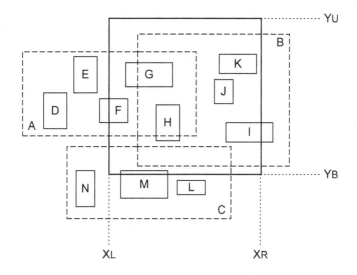

Fig. 1: An example of window query with x-coordinates between X_L and X_R and y-coordinates between Y_B and Y_U ($X_L \leq x \leq X_R$, $Y_B \leq y \leq Y_U$)

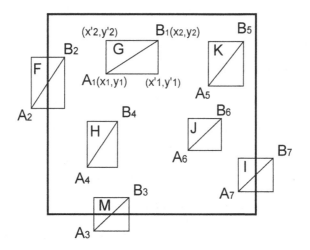

Fig. 2. The enclosed or intersected rectangles

It's obvious that we have to do with a 2-dimensional range searching. We use a balanced binary tree T, which stores in its leave nodes the points according to their y-coordinate. To each interval node u we associate two sets of points S_1, S_2. S_1 contains the points of the left subtree of u while the set S_2 contains the points of the right subtree. Each set S_1 is stored in a secondary structure D_1 while each set S_2 is stored in a secondary structure D_2. We use D_1 to answer queries of the form $[a_1,b_1] \times [a_2, +\infty]$ and D_2 to answer queries of the form $[a_1,b_1] \times [-\infty, b_2]$.

$D_1(u)$ and $D_2(u)$ are implemented according to [6]. Moreover the sets S_i are stored in two instance of the [31] structure that permits 1-dimensional searching in $O(\sqrt{(}logn/loglogn))$ time and linear space. Since each point is stored in $O(logn)$ secondary structures the space is $O(nlogn)$.

To answer a window query of the form $[a_1, b_1]$ x $[a_2, b_2]$ we find in T the node u where the search paths for a_2 and b_2 split. With other words we find the nearest common ancestor of a_2 and b_2 in constant time $O(1)$ [8]. Then we locate in S_1 and S_2 (using the [31] structures) the a_1, b_1 values and query the structure $D_1(u)$ with $[a_1,b_1]$ x $[a_2, +\infty]$ and $D_2(u)$ with $[a_1,b_1]$ x $[-\infty, b_2]$. This takes time $O(\sqrt{l}ogn/loglogn+ k)$.

Note that since the search paths for a_2 and b_2 split in u it follows that the points in $S_1(u)$ have their y-coordinates smaller than b_2 and the points in $S_2(u)$ have their y-coordinate greater than a_2. Furthermore, all points with y-coordinates with ranges in the interval $[a_2, b_2]$ belong to $S_1(u) \cup S_2(u)$, so the query algorithm is correct.

Application: We want to report all the rectangles enclosed from or intersected (with at least one endpoint in the query range) by the window query of figure 2 (the answer is enclosed={G, H, K, J}, intersected={ F, M, I}.

In order to use as less space as possible we could use the "diagonal" representation, for example in Figure 2 the down-top diagonal. The diagonal belongs entirely inside the window, only if the respective rectangle is enclosed inside the window. If the diagonal intersects to the bounds of the window then the same goes for the respective rectangle. The inverse assumption is not true. So, this kind of 2-points (the points of diagonal) representation is insufficient. For this reason we store in structure T all the points of rectangle, totally four, associating to each of them a flag that describes the rectangle to which the point belongs. For a rectangle R_i the flag is a 4-tuple with bounds x_{il} ,x_{ir}, y_{ib} and, y_{iu} respectively. In figure 2 the flag for point $A_1(x_1,y_1)$ is the tuple (x_1,x_2,y_1,y_2) or for reducing the worthless information the tuple (x_2,y_2). In structure T, we associate the query $[x_0, x_1]$ x $[y_0, y_1]$ to report the subset of rectangles that lie inside or intersect with a given axis-parallel window (x_0, x_1, y_0, y_1). More precisely, we count the number of the same flags. If we count the same flag exactly four times we say that the respective rectangle belongs entirely to the window or else that it intersect by it. This takes time $O(\sqrt{(}logn/loglogn)+ k)$.

If we use R-trees then we have the representation of figure 3 and the time for reporting all rectangles enclosed from or intersected by the window query is $O(nlog_Bn+|k|)$ since in the worst case, on every node of R-tree we should visit all its childs. In the example of figure 3, B = 4, n = 11, k=7.

Comparing to this method, we can see that we succeeded in handling these kinds of queries efficiently.

6 Plane with Real Coordinates

We consider the general 2-dimensional range query of the form $[a_1, b_1]$ x $[a_2, b_2]$. We store for each coordinate its rank in the tree which is an integer between 1 and n. Then we replace the coordinates of the points with their respective ranks. We call the new set of points the normalized set, and denote it by S'.

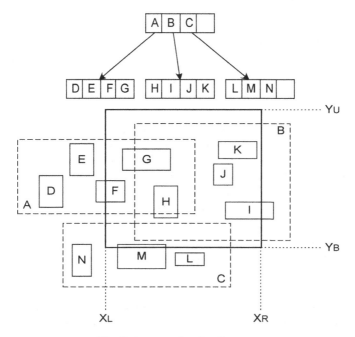

Fig. 3. An example of an R-tree

Given a query $[a_1, b_1] \times [a_2, b_2]$ we will normalize it in the following way. We search for a_1 and b_1 in the tree storing the first coordinates of the points. Let p_1 be the largest coordinate, which is less than a_1 and let q_1 be the smallest coordinate greater than b_1. We denote by a_1', b_1' the ranks of p_1, q_1. Similarly we find the values a_2', b_2'. This step takes $O(logn)$ time. The points of S' that lie in $[a_1', b_1'] \times [a_2', b_2']$ are the normalized versions of points of S that lie in $[a_1, b_1] \times [a_2, b_2]$. So we need only solve the normalized problem on the integer grid $[1, N] \times [1, N]$.

7 Conclusions

In this work we have focused on mechanisms for the efficient processing of spatial selection queries (especially planar selection queries). On these grounds we have proposed new main memory structures that answer 2-dimensional queries in either optimal or the best known asymptotic time. Unless explicitly stated otherwise, the time and space complexities refer to problems for continuous space.

Overall, the techniques proposed in this work are significant for GIS, temporal databases, spatial databases and other disciplines for which the handling and efficient querying of 2-dimensional data is of primary importance.

Some of the proposed structures are currently being implemented and the results so far are promising. Our next step for future continuation of this work is an extensive experimental evaluation of various structures for several classes of selection queries.

References

1. Agarwal, P. K.: Range searching, Technical Report CS-1996-05, Dept. of Computer Science, Duke University (1996)
2. Arge, L., Vitter, J.S.: Optimal dynamic interval management in external memory, Proceedings of the IEEE Symposium on Foundations of Computer Science (1996)
3. Driscoll, J. R., Sarnak, N., Sleator, D. D., Tarjan, R. E.: Making data structures persistent, J. Comp. Syst. Sci. 38 pp. 86-124 (1989)
4. Comer, D.: The ubiquitous B-tree, ACM Computing Surveys, 11(2) (1979)
5. Fries, O., Mehlhorn, K., Naher, S. and Tsakalidis, A.: A loglogn data structure for three sided rane queries, Inform. Process. Lett. 25, pp. 269-273 (1987)
6. Gabow, H. N., Bentley, J. L., and Tarjan, R. E.: Scaling and related techniques for geometry problems, in Proceedings, 16th Annual ACM Symp. on Theory of Computing, pp. 135-143 (1984)
7. Gupta, P., Janardan, R., Smid, M. and Dasgupta, B.: The rectangle enclosure and point dominance problem revisited, in, Proceedings, 11th Annual ACM Symp. on Comp. Geometry, pp. 162-171 (1995)
8. Harel, D., Tarjan, R. E.: Fast algorithms for finding nearest common ancestor, SIAM J. Comput.13, pp. 338-355 (1994)
9. Karlsson, R. G. and Overmars, M. H.: Scanline algorithms on a grid, Technical Rep. RUU-CS-86-18, Dept. of Computer Science, University of Utrecht (1986)
10. Matousek, J.: Geometric range searching, ACM Computing Surveys 26, pp. 421-561 (1994)
11. McCreight, E. M.: Priority search trees, SIAM J. Comput. 14, pp. 257-276 (1985)
12. Overmars, M. H.: Efficient data structures for range searching on a grid, J. Algorithms 9, pp. 254-275 (1988)
13. Preparata, F. P. and Shamos, M. I.: Computational Geometry, Springer- Verlag, New York, (1985)
14. Vuillemin, J.: A unifying look at data structures, C. ACM 23 pp. 229-239 (1980)
15. Grossi, R., Italiano, G., F.: Efficient cross-trees for external memory, In J.Abello and J.S. Vitter, editors, External Algorithms and Visualization (1998)
16. Guttman, A.: R-trees: A Dynamic Index Structure for Spatial Searching, ACM SIGMOD, (1984)
17. Sellis, T., Roussopoulos, N., Faloutsos, C.,: The R$^+$-tree: A Dynamic Index for Multidimensional Objects, VLDB (1987)
18. Beckmann, N., Kriegel, H.P., Schneider, R., Seeger, B.: The R*-tree: an Efficient and Robust Access Method for Points and Rectangles, ACM SIGMOD (1990)
19. Papadias, D., Theodoridis, Y.: Spatial Relations, Minimum Bounding Rectangles, and Spatial Data Structures, International Journal of Geographic Information Science, Vol. 11(2) (1997)
20. Theodoridis, Y., Papadias, D., Stefanakis, E., Sellis, T.: Direction Relations and Two-Dimensional Range Queries: Optimization Techniques, Data & Knowledge Engineering, vol. 27(3) (1998)
21. Theodoridis, Y., Vazirgiannis, M., Sellis, T.: Spatio-Temporal Indexing for Large Multimedia Applications, 3rd IEEE Conference on Multimedia Computing and Systems, (1996)
22. Theodoridis, Y., Sellis, T.: A Model for The Prediction of R-Tree Performance, ACM PODS (1996)
23. Gaede, V.: Optimal Redundancy in Spatial Database Systems, International Symposium on Spatial Databases (SSD) (1995)
24. Hoel, E., Samet, H.: Benchmarking Spatial Join Operations with Spatial Output, VLDB Conference (1995)
25. Kanellakis, P.C., Ramaswamy, S., Vengroff, D.E., Vitter, J.S.: Indexing for data models with constraints and classes, Journal of Computer and System Sciences, 52(3) (1996)

26. Mehlhorn.,K., Data Structures and Algorithms 3-Multidimensional Searching and Computational Geometry, Springer Verlag (1984)
27. Ramaswamy, S., Subramanian, S.: Path Caching: a technique for optimal external searching in Proceedings of the 13th ACM Conference on Principles of Database Systems (1994)
28. Subramanian, S., Ramaswamy, S.: The P-range tree: a new data structure for range searching in secondary memeory, ACM-SIAM Symposium on Discrete Algorithms (1995)
29. Vengroff, D.,E., Vitter, J.,S., Efficient 3-d range searching in external memory, ACM Symposium on Theory of Computation (1996)
30. Vitter, J.S.: External Memory Algorithms invited paper in European Symposium on Algorithms (1998)
31. Beam, P., Fich, F.: Optimal Bounds for the Predecessor Problem, In Proceedings of the Thirty First Annual ACM Symposium on Theory of Computing, Atlanta, GA (1999)
32. Arge, L., Samoladas, V., Vitter, J.S.: Two dimensional indexability and optimal range search indexing, in Proceedings of the ACM Symposium on Principles of Database Systems, (1999)

Mining around Association and Representative Rules

Marzena Kryszkiewicz

Institute of Computer Science, Warsaw University of Technology,
Nowowiejska 15/19, 00-665 Warsaw, Poland
mkr@ii.pw.edu.pl

Abstract. Discovering association rules among items in large databases is a recognized database mining problem. In the paper, we address the issue of association rules generation in the context of changing user requirements. The data mining system user is frequently interested in results of mining around rules that consists in examining how change of attribute values or addition of new attributes influences the discovered dependencies. The set of association rules is often huge. However it is possible to represent it with usually much smaller set of representative rules. If needed, the user can derive all association rules from the set of representative rules syntactically by means of a cover operator. Incremental solutions of mining around representative rules are discussed in the paper as well.

1 The Origin of the Problem

Recently, the researches from Warsaw University of Technology have collaborated with the Network Planning and Maintenance Department of a Polish cellular telecom provider within a data mining project. The project was devoted to knowledge discovery from the technology area data. The objective of one of the experiments was to discover the influence of neighboring cells on parameters of other cells, in particular on *misbehaving* cells. A cell is called *misbehaving* if anomalies such as channel congestion, blocking, call drops etc. occur for it on levels higher than acceptable for well designed GSM network. Each cell in the network is described by a set of different attributes. There are available configuration attributes as well as measured attributes that describe the behavior of certain network elements assigned to cells. Two cells are called *neighbors* if it is possible to make a handover of a call between them. The experiment objective was to find association rules of the following form:

$(CellId_1, Alarm\_or\_<attribute, valueRange>) \land \ldots \land$
$(CellId_n, Alarm\_or\_<attribute, valueRange>) \Rightarrow$
$(CellId_{n+1}, Alarm\_or\_<attribute, valueRange>) \land \ldots \land$
$(CellId_m, Alarm\_or\_<attribute, valueRange>)$

where:
- *CellId_1*, *CellId_2*,..., *CellId_n* are identification numbers of cells in the network that are neighbors of some cells identified by *CellId_{n+1}*,..., *CellId_m*;

J. Štuller et al. (Eds.): ADBIS-DASFAA 2000, LNCS 1884, pp. 117–127, 2000.
© Springer-Verlag Berlin Heidelberg 2000

- *Alarm* is a Boolean formula defined by a telecom expert;
- *<attribute,valueRange>* - a cell attribute and a value range to which the attribute value of a respective cell belongs.

To be more precise, an alarm was defined as a Boolean formula comparing some expression built from original attributes with the expert specified threshold value. Looking at the discovered dependencies, the telecom expert was often interested in how the dependencies would change if the definition of alarms was changed by increasing or decreasing the threshold values.

In the paper, we formalize the original problem of mining around the discovered set of rules and propose an incremental algorithm for rules mining, which is a modification of the *Apriori* algorithm [2]. Then we remind the notion of representative rules that constitute a least set of rules from which all other can be derived syntactically. Finally, we discuss incremental solutions of how to update representative rules in correspondence with user mining requests.

2   Basic Notions of Association Rules and Algorithms

2.1   Association Rules

The notion of association rules and the problem of their discovering were introduced in [1] for a sales transaction database. However, the dependencies we presented in Section 1 are examples of *association rules* discovered in a relational database. In the sequel, we will discuss generation of association rules in the context of a relational database.

Let us consider a table $D = (O, AT)$, where O is a non-empty finite set of *tuples* and AT is a non-empty finite set of *attributes*, such that $a: O \to V_a$ for any $a \in AT$, where V_a denotes the domain of a. Any *attribute-value pair* (a,v), where $a \in AT$ and $v \in V_a$ will be called an *item*. A set of items will be called *itemset*. An itemset consisting from k items will be called k-itemset.

An *association rule* is an implication:

$$X \Rightarrow Y, \tag{1}$$

where X and Y are non-empty itemsets and $X \cap Y = \varnothing$.

Statistical significance of an itemset X is called *support* and is denoted by $sup(X)$. $sup(X)$ is defined as the percentage (or the number) of tuples in D that contain X. Statistical significance (*support*) of a rule $X \Rightarrow Y$ is denoted by $sup(X \Rightarrow Y)$ and is defined as follows:

$$sup(X \Rightarrow Y) = sup(X \cup Y). \tag{2}$$

Additionally, an association rule is characterized by *confidence*, which expresses its strength. The confidence of an association rule $X \Rightarrow Y$ is denoted by $conf(X \Rightarrow Y)$ and is defined in the following way:

$$conf(X \Rightarrow Y) = sup(X \Rightarrow Y) / sup(X). \tag{3}$$

2.2 Mining Association Rules with the Apriori Algorithm

The problem of mining association rules is to generate all rules that have support greater than the user specified minimum support s and confidence not less than the user specified minimum confidence c. The set of such rules will be denoted by $AR(s,c)$, i.e.:

$$AR(s,c) = \{r|\ sup(r) > s \text{ and } conf(r) \geq c\}. \tag{4}$$

If s and c are fixed we will write briefly AR.

Several efficient solutions applicable for large databases were proposed to solve the problem of generating association rules with sufficient support and confidence (see e.g. [2,7]). The problem is usually decomposed into two subproblems:

1. Generate all itemsets whose support exceeds the minimum support s. The itemsets of this property are called *frequent* (*large*).
2. Generate all association rules from frequent itemsets. Let Z be a frequent itemset and $\emptyset \neq Y \subset Z$. Then any candidate rule $Z \setminus Y \Rightarrow Y$ is an association rule if $(sup(Z) / sup(Z \setminus Y)) \geq c$.

The second subproblem is relatively straightforward therefore we will describe only the solution of the first subproblem known as the *Apriori* algorithm [2].

Computing Frequent Itemsets. The *Apriori* algorithm (see Fig. 1) exploits the following properties of frequent and infrequent itemsets: All subsets of a frequent itemset are frequent and all supersets of an infrequent itemset are infrequent.

The following notation is used in the *Apriori* algorithm:

- C_k - set of candidate k-itemsets;
- F_k - set of frequent k-itemsets;
- $c[1] \bullet c[2] \bullet ... \bullet c[k]$ is a k-itemset consisting from items $c[1]$, $c[2]$,..., $c[k]$.

The items in itemsets are assumed to be ordered totally. Associated with each itemset is a *count* field to store the support for this itemset.

```
Algorithm Apriori (table D);
  F₁ = {frequent 1-itemsets in D};
  for (k = 2; Fₖ₋₁ ≠ ∅; k++) do begin
    Cₖ = AprioriGen(Fₖ₋₁);
    forall transactions t∈D do
      forall candidates c∈Cₖ do
        if c ⊆ t then
          c.count++;
    Fₖ = {c∈Cₖ | c.count > minSup};
  endfor;
return ∪ₖ Fₖ;
```

Fig. 1. The *Apriori* algorithm

At the beginning the supports of all 1-itemsets are determined during one pass over the database D. All infrequent 1-itemsets are discarded. Frequent 1-itemsets are used to generate candidate 2-itemsets by the *AprioriGen* function (see Fig. 2). Their supports are determined by scanning the database. Infrequent 2-itemsets are discarded and new candidate 3-itemsets are computed by *AprioriGen* from frequent 2-itemsets. The procedure repeats in a similar way in next iterations. In general, some k-th iteration consists of the following operations:

1. *AprioriGen* is called to generate the candidate k-itemsets C_k from the frequent $(k\text{-}1)$-itemsets F_{k-1}.
2. Supports for the candidate k-itemsets are determined by a pass over the database.
3. The candidate k-itemsets that do not exceed the minimum support are discarded; the remaining k-itemsets in F_k are found frequent.

```
function AprioriGen(F_{k-1});
  C_k ={f[1]•f[2]•...•f[k]•c[k] | f,c∈F_k and
      f[1]=c[1] ∧ ... ∧ f[k-2]=c[k-2] ∧ f[k-1]<c[k-1]};
  delete all itemsets c∈C_k such that
    some (k-1)-subset of c is not in F_{k-1};
return C_k;
```

Fig. 2. The *AprioriGen* function

The *AprioriGen* function constructs candidate k-itemsets as supersets of frequent $(k\text{-}1)$-itemsets. This restriction of extending only frequent $(k\text{-}1)$-itemsets is justified since any k-itemset, which would be created as a result of extending an infrequent $(k\text{-}1)$-itemset, would not be frequent either. Before returning newly created candidates, the function *AprioriGen* prunes such candidates from C_k that do not have all their $(k\text{-}1)$-subsets in the frequent $(k\text{-}1)$-itemsets F_{k-1}. If k-itemset c does not have all its $(k\text{-}1)$-subsets in F_{k-1} then there is some infrequent $(k\text{-}1)$-itemset $c' \notin F_{k-1}$ which is a subset of c. This means that c is infrequent as a superset of an infrequent itemset.

Let us illustrate the *AprioriGen* function with an example. Let {{A,B}, {A,C}, {A,D}, {B,C}, {B,D}} be a family of frequent 2-itemsets F_2. Then the subsequent candidate 3-itemsets would be generated: {A,B,C}, {A,B,D}, {A,C,D}, {B,C,D}. Nevertheless, the final set of candidates is smaller. In the pruning process the candidates {A,C,D} and {B,C,D} will be discarded because there is not their subset {C,D} among 2-itemsets in F_2.

3   Formalization of Mining around Association Rules Problem

Given a table (or a view) D we divide its attributes into two categories: attributes the values of which do not change during the knowledge discovery process and attributes whose values are subject to changes (e.g. because the attribute is derivable and its formula can be modified according to user requests). The *attributes* of the former type will be called *constant*, whereas the attributes of the latter type will be called *modifi-*

able. Similarly, an *item* that refers to a constant attribute will be called *constant*, otherwise it will be called *modifiable*. Furthermore, an *itemset* (*association rule*) will be called *modifiable* if it contains at least one modifiable item, otherwise it will be called *constant*.

Let F be the set of frequent itemsets discovered in D for a given minimum support s. Let AR be the set of association rules created from F for a given minimum confidence c. Our task is to update F and AR incrementally instead of computing them from scratch.

Let $Const(F)$ denote the subset of all constant itemsets in F and $Const(AR)$ denote the subset of those rules in AR that contain only constant items. Clearly, if changes are restricted to the modifiable attributes only, then the frequent itemsets discovered in the modified D will contain $Const(F)$ (and new frequent modifiable itemsets) and newly derived association rules will contain $Const(AR)$ (and association rules built from new frequent modifiable itemsets).

Now, we can restate our goal as looking for new frequent itemsets and new association rules without redundant computing of $Const(F)$ and $Const(AR)$, i.e. we want to compute only new frequent modifiable itemsets and new modifiable association rules.

4   Computing Frequent Modifiable Itemsets and Modifiable Association Rules

In this section we consider two ways of generating frequent modifiable itemsets and modifiable association rules. First we consider the case when the information on constant frequent itemsets is maintained. Then, we will discuss the case when this information is not available.

4.1   Mining with Constant Frequent Itemsets

Computing Frequent Modifiable Itemsets. In order to compute frequent modifiable itemsets we propose the *ModApriori* algorithm, which is a modification of *Apriori*. The following notation is used in the *ModApriori* algorithm (see Fig. 3):

- F – frequent itemsets found prior modification of the contents of the table D;
- F_k - set of frequent k-itemsets in F;
- ΔF - set of frequent modifiable itemsets discovered in the updated table D;
- ΔF_k - set of frequent modifiable k-itemsets in ΔF;
- C_k - set of candidate modifiable k-itemsets.

The items in itemsets are assumed to be ordered totally. Additionally, we assume that modifiable items precede constant items.

The outline of *ModApriori* is similar to that of *Apriori*, however it differs in the way the candidate itemsets are created. The assumption that modifiable items precede constant items allows to restrict the generation of candidates to modifiable itemsets easily. Actually, each 2-itemset candidate is constructed from a pair of frequent 1-itemsets such that the first itemset is modifiable and the second one is of any type.

```
Algorithm ModApriori (updated table D; frequent constant
1-itemsets Const(F₁));
  ΔF₁ = {frequent modifiable 1-itemsets in D};
  C₂ = {f • c | f∈ΔF₁, c∈ΔF₁ ∪ Const(F₁) and f < c};
  for (k = 2; Cₖ ≠ ∅; k++) do begin
    forall tuples t∈D do
      forall candidates c∈Cₖ do
        if c ⊆ t then
          c.count++;
    ΔFₖ = {c∈Cₖ | c.count > minSup};
    Cₖ₊₁ = ModAprioriGen(ΔFₖ);
  endfor;

  ΔF = ∪ₖ ΔFₖ ;
return ΔF;
```

Fig. 3. The *ModApriori* algorithm

The generation of longer candidates (see *ModAprioriGen* in Fig. 4) does not require the knowledge on frequent constant itemsets. Each modifiable candidate $(k+1)$-itemset, $k \geq 2$, can be created from a pair of two frequent modifiable k-itemsets. One can also easily observe that a modifiable candidate $(k+1)$-itemset can have at most one subset being a constant k-itemset. This happens only in the case, when the $(k+1)$-itemset has exactly one modifiable item. Therefore, a $(k+1)$-itemset with one modifiable item can have at most k subsets being modifiable frequent k-itemsets and at most one subset being a constant k-itemset. To the contrary, a $(k+1)$-itemset with more than one modifiable item can have at most $k+1$ subsets being modifiable frequent k-itemsets and no subset being a constant k-itemset. These properties are used by the *ModAprioriGen* function.

```
function ModAprioriGen(ΔFₖ);
  Cₖ₊₁ = {f[1]•f[2]•...•f[k]•c[k] | f,c∈ΔFₖ and
         f[1]=c[1] ∧ ... ∧ f[k-1]=c[k-1] ∧ f[k]<c[k]};
  /* Pruning */
  forall c∈Cₖ₊₁ do
    if c contains more than 1 modifiable item and
    |{f∈ΔFₖ| f⊂c}| < k+1 then
      delete c from Cₖ₊₁
    elseif |{f∈ΔFₖ|f⊂c}|<k or |{f∈Const(Fₖ)|f⊂c}|=0 then
      delete c from Cₖ₊₁;
return Cₖ₊₁;
```

Fig. 4. The *ModAprioriGen* function

Computing Modifiable Association Rules. All modifiable association rules will be generated by applying any algorithm of rules generation (e.g. described in [2]) to new modifiable itemsets ΔF. Though new modifiable association rules can be created only from ΔF, the knowledge on $Const(F)$ may turn out necessary:

Let Z be a frequent modifiable itemset, $\varnothing \neq Y \subset Z$ and $Z \setminus Y \Rightarrow Y$ be a candidate rule. It may happen that the antecedent of the candidate rule is a constant itemset, say X, so in order to compute its confidence, it is necessary to know the support of this constant itemset. Obviously, X belongs to $Const(F)$, hence its support is already known.

4.2 Mining without Constant Frequent Itemsets

Computing Modifiable Frequent Itemsets. One may note that storing information on constant frequent itemsets is not crucial for discovery of modifiable candidate itemsets in the updated database. It is applied only in two cases:

- when creating candidate 2-itemsets (see *ModApriori*),
- for pruning candidates (see *ModAprioriGen*).

In the former case, we used the knowledge on $Const(F_1)$. These itemsets can be discovered easily when looking for ΔF_1. In the latter case, $Const(F_k)$ can be used for pruning new candidates that contain exactly one modifiable item - the validity of other candidates does not depend on the knowledge of $Const(F)$ at all. Additionally, candidates containing one modifiable item still are likely to be pruned by checking subsets in ΔF_k.

Computing Modifiable Association Rules. As we observed previously, candidate modifiable association rules are created only from frequent modifiable itemsets, but we may need to know $Const(F)$ in order to evaluate their confidence. More precisely, we may need to know support of constant antecedents of candidate modifiable rules. If $Const(F)$ is not materialized then it is necessary to compute support for all *potential constant antecedents* of new rules, which we will denote by PCA in the sequel. Clearly, PCA is the family of all constant itemsets that are proper subsets of new frequent modifiable itemsets in ΔF. PCA can be computed either by applying the knowledge on maximal itemsets in ΔF or by applying the knowledge on the itemsets in ΔF that contain at most one modifiable item. Both methods are provided below:

Supports of itemsets in PCA can be determined by a pass over the database.

```
input: new frequent modifiable itemsets ΔF;
output: potential constant rules antecedents PCA;
X = {maximal itemsets in ΔF};
delete modifiable items from itemsets in X;
remove non-maximal itemsets from X;
PCA = {all subsets of itemsets in X};
```

Fig. 5. Deriving *PCA* from maximal itemsets

```
input: new frequent modifiable itemsets ΔF;
output: potential constant rules antecedents PCA;
X = {itemsets in ΔF that contain at most one modifiable
item};
{* Make itemsets in X constant by removing first item,
which is modifiable *}
remove first item from each itemset in X;
remove duplicates from X;
PCA = X;
```

Fig. 6. Deriving *PCA* from itemsets with one modifiable item

5   Representative Rules

The notion of representative association rules was introduced in [4]. Informally speaking, the set of representative association rules is a least set of rules that covers all association rules by means of a *cover operator*.

The *cover C* of the rule $X \Rightarrow Y$, $Y \neq \emptyset$, is defined as follows:

$$C(X \Rightarrow Y) = \{X \cup Z \Rightarrow V | Z, V \subseteq Y \text{ and } Z \cap V = \emptyset \text{ and } V \neq \emptyset\}. \tag{5}$$

Each rule in $C(X \Rightarrow Y)$ consists of a subset of items occurring in the rule $X \Rightarrow Y$. The antecedent of any rule r covered by $X \Rightarrow Y$ contains X and perhaps some items from Y, whereas r's consequent is a non-empty subset of the remaining items in Y. Below, we remind a simple property of the cover operator that will be used further in the paper:

Property 1. Let $r: (X \Rightarrow Y)$ and $r': (X' \Rightarrow Y')$ be association rules. Then:

$$r \in C(r') \text{ iff } X \cup Y \subseteq X' \cup Y' \text{ and } X \supseteq X'. \tag{6}$$

It was proved in [4] that each rule r in the cover $C(r')$, where r' is an association rule having support s and confidence c, has support not less than s and confidence not less than c. Hence, if $r \in AR(s,c)$ and $r' \in C(r)$ then $r' \in AR(s,c)$. The number of different rules in the cover of the association rule $X \Rightarrow Y$ is equal to $3^m - 2^m$, where $m = |Y|$ (see [4]).

Now, we can recall the notion of representative rules:

A set of *representative association rules* wrt. minimum support s and minimum confidence c is denoted by $RR(s,c)$ and is defined as follows:

$$RR(s,c) = \{r \in AR(s,c) | \neg \exists r' \in AR(s,c), r' \neq r \text{ and } r \in C(r')\}. \tag{7}$$

Each rule in *RR* is called a *representative association rule*. No representative association rule belongs to the cover of another association rule. Clearly, $AR(s,c) =$

$\bigcup_{r \in RR(s,c)} C(r)$, i.e. all association rules can be derived by means of the cover operator from the set of representative rules.

Example 1. Let us consider the relational database D from Fig. 7. Fig. 8 contains some association rules induced from D.

O	a	b	c	d	e	f
1	1	0	0	1	1	1
2	1	0	0	1	1	1
3	1	1	1	1	2	1
4	0	1	1	0	3	1
5	0	1	1	0	3	1
6	0	1	1	0	3	2
7	0	1	1	2	2	2
8	0	1	1	2	2	2
9	0	1	1	2	2	2
10	1	1	0	2	2	2
11	1	1	0	2	2	3
12	1	1	0	3	2	3
13	1	0	0	3	2	3
14	1	0	0	3	2	3
15	1	0	0	3	2	3

Fig. 7. Example relational database D

rule #	$X \Rightarrow Y$	$sup(X \Rightarrow Y)$	$conf(X \Rightarrow Y)$
1.	$\{(c,1)\} \Rightarrow \{(a,0),(b,1)\}$	40%	86%
2.	$\{(c,1),(e,2)\} \Rightarrow \{(b,1)\}$	27%	100%
3.	$\{(c,1),(f,2)\} \Rightarrow \{(a,0),(b,1)\}$	27%	100%
4.	$\{(c,1),(e,2),(f,2)\} \Rightarrow \{(b,1),(d,2)\}$	20%	100%
5.	$\{(c,1),(e,2),(f,2)\} \Rightarrow \{(a,0),(b,1),(d,2)\}$	20%	100%

Fig. 8. Example association rules found in D from Fig. 7

Given minimum support $s = 1\%$ and minimum confidence $c = 80\%$, one can discover 1730 association rules and 59 representative rules, which is 3.41% of AR (actually, we used the *Miner* system described in [5] in order to compute AR and RR).

One may observe that all rules from Fig. 8 belong to $AR(1\%,80\%)$. One can also note that the rule #4 does not belong to $RR(1\%,80\%)$ since it belongs to the cover of the association rule #5.

As verified in [9], the ratio between the number of representative RR and association rules AR being in the cover of RR is high in the case when frequent itemsets are long. For example, a test in [9] on synthetic data indicated that for frequent itemsets with expected number of items equal to 8 the ratio reached 100. This feature seems to be promising for the rules generated from databases with taxonomies [6,8], where frequent itemsets are usually long.

Representative rules can be obtained by extracting them from association rules according to the definition or can be generated directly from frequent itemsets (see [4,5] for the algorithms for direct generation of representative rules).

6 Updating Representative Rules

Let *Const(RR)* denote constant rules in *RR*. Unfortunately, unlike in the case of frequent constant itemsets (*Const(F)*) and constant association rules (*Const(AR)*) we
cannot hope that *Const(RR)* is this part of representative rules which does not depend
on changes of modifiable attributes. As follows from the definition (7), no representative association rule belongs to the cover of another association rule. Additionally, it
follows from Property 1 that a rule *r* can belong to the cover of another rule *r'* if *r* is
built from a subset of items present in *r'*. Hence, if *r*∈*Const(RR)* is built from an itemset in *PCA*, which is a (proper) subset of some frequent itemset in *ΔF*, then *r* can become non-representative in the updated database. Otherwise, it is still representative.
Let *ΔF-Const(RR)* denote rules in *Const(RR)* that are built from itemsets for which
there is no superset in *ΔF*. As follows from our discussion *ΔF-Const(RR)* contains
rules that are representative before and after the update of the database.

Fig. 9 and 10 show how to find representative rules directly from frequent itemsets
and how to find representative rules indirectly by extraction from association rules,
respectively.

```
input: new frequent modifiable itemsets ΔF,
       potential constant rules antecedents PCA;
output: updated representative rules RR';
ΔRR = {representative rules created from ΔF ∪ PCA};
RR' = ΔRR ∪ ΔF-Const(RR);
```

Fig. 9. Direct incremental computation of representative rules

```
input: new frequent modifiable itemsets ΔF,
       potential constant rules antecedents PCA;
output: updated representative rules RR';
W = {X ⇒ Y ∈ AR| X∪Y ∈ PCA};
ΔAR = {association rules created from ΔF};
ΔRR = {representative rules extracted from ΔAR ∪ W};
RR' = ΔRR ∪ ΔF-Const(RR);
```

Fig. 10. Indirect incremental computation of representative rules

7 Conclusions

The paper was devoted to the specific mining around rules that consists in checking
how attribute modifications influence the discovered knowledge. Incremental solutions were proposed for discovery of up-to-date association and representative rules.

In the paper we did not address more classical mining around rules problem that consists in changing minimum required support and confidence of rules. We find useful continuation of the research in order to work out a common solutions to both subproblems.

Acknowledgements

I would like to thank to Micha• Gondzik for stimulating discussions on needs and expectations of a data mining system user and in particular for indicating the title-problem. I wish to thank to Tomasz Gerszberg for his support for data mining research in the telecommunication area.

References

1. Agrawal, R., Imielinski, T., Swami, A.: Mining Associations Rules between Sets of Items in Large Databases. In: Proc. of the ACM SIGMOD Conference on Management of Data. Washington, D.C. (1993) 207-216
2. Agrawal, R., Mannila, H., Srikant, R., Toivonen, H., Verkamo, A.I.: Fast Discovery of Association Rules. In: Fayyad, U.M., Piatetsky-Shapiro, G., Smyth, P., Uthurusamy, R. (eds.): Advances in Knowledge Discovery and Data Mining. AAAI, Menlo Park, California (1996) 307-328
3. Gajek, M.: Comparative Analysis of Selected Association Rules Types. To appear in Proc. of the Ninth International Symposium on Intelligent Information Systems (2000)
4. Kryszkiewicz, M.: Representative Association Rules. In: Proc. of PAKDD '98. Melbourne, Australia. Lecture Notes in Artificial Intelligence 1394. Research and Development in Knowledge Discovery and Data Mining. Springer-Verlag (1998) 198-209
5. Kryszkiewicz, M.: Fast Discovery of Representative Association Rules. In: Proc. of RSCTC '98. Warsaw, Poland. Lecture Notes in Artificial Intelligence 1424. Rough Sets and Current Trends in Computing. Springer-Verlag (1998) 214-221
6. Meo, R., Psaila, G., Ceri, S.: A New SQL-like Operator for Mining Association Rules. In: Proc. of the 22nd VLDB Conference. Mumbai (Bombay), India (1996)
7. Savasere, A, Omiecinski, E., Navathe, S.: An Efficient Algorithm for Mining Association Rules in Large Databases. In: Proc. of the 21st VLDB Conference. Zurich, Swizerland (1995) 432-444
8. Srikant, R., Agrawal, R.: Mining Generalized Association Rules. In: Proc. of the 21st VLDB Conference. Zurich, Swizerland (1995) 407-419
9. Walczak, Z.: Selected Problems and Algorithms of Data Mining. M.Sc. Thesis. Warsaw University of Technology (in Polish) (1998)

A New Algorithm for Page Access Sequencing in Join Processing

Andrew Lim, Oon Wee Chong, and Chi-Hung Chi

Department of Computer Science
National University of Singapore
Lower Kent Ridge Road, Singapore 119260
{alim,oonwc,chich}@comp.nus.edu.sg

Abstract. One of the fundamental problems in relational database management is the handling of the join operation. Two of the problems are: 1) finding a page access sequence which requires the minimum number of buffer pages if there are no page reaccesses, and 2) finding a page access sequence which requires the minimum number of page reaccesses given a fixed buffer size. In general, a heuristic for the first problem can be converted to a corresponding heuristic to the second problem.
In this paper, a new heuristic is proposed. The experimental results show that the new heuristic performs significantly better than existing heuristics for data which is modelled with geometric graphs, and no worse in others, for the first problem. It performs similarly better for the second problem if the fixed buffer size is not much less than the maximum buffer size generated in the first problem.

1 Introduction

One of the fundamental operations in database management is the join operation. It is not uncommon to find databases today with millions of entries, and inefficient memory use when performing the join operation on large numbers of tuples would rapidly swamp the available memory. There is hence a definite need to minimise the amount of memory space that is used for these operations.

The task of join processing involves the reading of tuple information into the main memory, such that information on two tuples to be joined must be in memory at the same time at some point, so that the join can be processed. Several approaches to this problem have previously been tried ([1,2,7]).

One strategy to minimise memory usage is to first scan the indices of the relevant relations to obtain a set of data page pairs *(x, y)*, where page x contains some tuple which is joined with some tuple in page y. This set of data page pairs can then be used to find an efficient *page access sequence* to minimise the amount of memory required.

Since this problem is believed to be NP-complete, this project focuses on the creation of a heuristic which would find such an efficient page access sequence. In particular, we wish to find the solutions to the following problems:

J. Štuller et al. (Eds.): ADBIS-DASFAA 2000, LNCS 1884, pp. 128–141, 2000.

1. Given that there are no page reaccesses, what page access sequence will require the minimum number of buffer pages?
2. Given a fixed buffer size, what page access sequence will require the minimum number of page reaccesses?

Using the terms first coined in [4], the above problems shall be referred to as OPAS1 and OPAS2 respectively, for *optimal page access sequence problems*.

In Section 2, the problem will be examined in detail. The symbols and terminology which are used in this report are explained, and we describe the types of graphs which we feel are representative of the problem domain. In Section 3, we examine the existing heuristics for this problem. After providing a general overview, we describe Omiecinski's Heuristic (OH) [3], and Chan & Ooi's Heuristic (COH) [4].In Section 4, we present the new heuristic (LOCH). The effectiveness of LOCH for the two problems OPAS1 and OPAS2 will be compared to the existing heuristics in Section 5. Finally, in Section 6 and 7, we conclude our findings, as well as detail some potentially fruitful new directions of research.

2 Terminology and Notation

Existing work has focused on the creation of a heuristic to produce a good solution to OPAS1, and then adapting it to OPAS2. This is a reasonable approach, as a page access sequence that requires a minimum number of buffer pages could be applied with a fixed buffer size, given an appropriate page replacement rule. In fact, a solution to OPAS1 is the same as that for OPAS2 if the fixed buffer size in OPAS2 is greater or equal to the maximum buffer size found in OPAS1. A generic algorithm for this conversion is given in the next section. For this reason, **we shall concentrate on OPAS1 solutions**.

We can represent the page-pair information of a join by an undirected join graph $G = (V, E)$, where the set of vertices V represents the pages in the join, and the set of edges $E \subseteq V \times V$ represents the set of page-pairs which contains tuples to be joined with each other. As pages are fetched into the buffer, the join graph is updated as follows: An edge (x, y) is removed from the graph if the pages x and y have been fetched and joined. A vertex x is removed from the graph if the degree of x becomes zero. Such a page is said to be *released*.

Definition 1. *Let $G = (V, E)$ be a join graph. A* **page access sequence** *$S =< p_1, p_2, \cdots, p_{|v|} >$ is a sequence of distinct pages from V where p_i denotes the ith page fetched into the buffer.*

A page access sequence (PAS) specifies the order of fetching the pages of the join graph into the buffer.

Definition 2. *Let $S =< p_1, p_2, \cdots, p_{|v|} >$ be a page access sequence. The* **upper bound of S**, *denoted by $MAX(S)$, is defined to be the upper bound on the buffer size of S. S is an* **optimal page access sequence** *iff $MAX(S) \leq MAX(S')$ for all page access sequences S'.*

A join graph may have a number of distinct optimal page access sequences. A heuristic to produce such an optimal PAS for a given join graph is the target of this paper.

Definition 3. *Let* $S = <p_1, p_2, \cdots, p_{|v|}>$ *be a page access sequence.* $S' = <p_i, p_{i+1}, \cdots, p_{i+k}>, 1 \leq i \leq (|V| - k)$ *is a* **segment of page access sequence** **S** *iff* S' *is a nonempty subsequence of* S *such that*

1. *No page is released by the entry of* p_j *for* $i \leq j < i + k$,
2. *One or more pages are released by the entry of* p_{i+k}, *and*
3. *One or more pages are released by the entry of* p_{i-1} *if* $i > 1$.

Thus, each PAS can be uniquely expressed as a sequence of m segments.

Theorem 1. *Let* $S = S_1 \circ S_2 \circ \cdots \circ S_m$ *be a page access sequence with m segments. Let* B_{last_i} *be the buffer size when the last page of segment i is fetched, for* $1 \leq i \leq m$. *Then,* $MAX(S) = max\{B_{last_1}, B_{last_2}, \cdots, B_{last_m}\}$.

The proof for this theorem is provided in [4].

2.1   Types of Graphs

As previously shown, the OPAS problems can be dynamically represented by join graphs. Given that the domain of our problem is database systems, it would be desirable for us to focus on only the types of graphs which would more closely represent typical database systems. As such, we restrict our investigation to the following 3 types of graphs:

General Graph If G is a general graph with v vertices and *degree n%*, then
$\forall v_i, v_j \in V, \text{Prob}[(v_i, v_j) \in E] = \frac{n}{100}$.
All vertices in a general graph has the same probably of having an edge with any other vertex in the graph. A general graph simulates a join operation for a set of pages with no well-defined relational structure. This type of graph is also known as a **random graph**.

Bipartite Graph If G is a bipartite graph such that $V = V_1 \cup V_2$ and $V_1 \cap V_2 = \emptyset$, and *degree n%*, then $\text{Prob}[(v_i, v_j) \in E] =$
1. $\frac{n}{100}$ if $v_i \in V_1$ and $v_j \in V_2$,
2. 0 otherwise.
Therefore, a bipartite graph is partitioned into 2 sets of vertices, where the vertices within a set cannot be connected to each other. This is a model for a join of 2 relations, with each relation's pages contained in one partition.

Previous papers have focused on the application of heuristics on the above two types of graphs. However, we feel that this is not enough, and examine a third type of graph:

Geometric Graph If G is a geometric graph with v vertices and the expected degree of each vertex $E(\theta) = k$, then G is generated as follows:

1. Compute d $= \sqrt{\frac{k}{v\pi}}$.
2. Generate v points randomly in a unit square, i.e. assign a pair of coordinates $(x_k,\ y_k)$, $x_k,\ y_k \in [0,\ 1]$ to each vertex v_k.
3. Add $(v_i,\ v_j)$ into E iff the distance between v_i and $v_j < d$,
   i.e. if $\sqrt{(x_i - x_j)^2 + (y_i - y_j)^2} < d$.

Thus in a geometric graph, there is only an edge if 2 points are "close enough", and therefore the points tend to form clusters. It is our opinion that a geometric graph is a good approximation of multi-relation joins. Each cluster would approximate a relation, which would have most pages joined with each other within it. The number of joins between clusters would be smaller, giving rise to the structure of the geometric graph. *See Figure 1*

We feel that these 3 graph types sufficiently capture the qualities of the likely database system relationships.

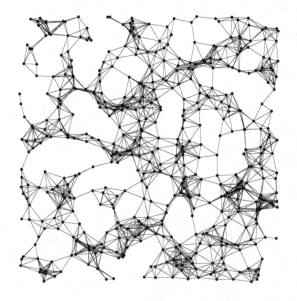

Fig. 1. A geometric graph with $|V| = 500$, $E(\theta) = 10$

3   Existing Heuristics

3.1   Converting from OPAS1 to OPAS2

The general heuristic for converting a solution from OPAS1 to OPAS2 is given as follows:

General Heuristic to convert from OPAS1 to OPAS2

while there are pages to be read **do**
1. $p := $ **SelectPage**
2. **if** buffer is full
    a) $v := $ **SelectVictim**
    b) remove v from the buffer
3. put p into the buffer
4. remove all edges which connects two pages in the buffer
5. remove all pages with no edges from the buffer

The **SelectPage** function is the main distinction between the different heuristics. This selects the next page in the PAS. The **SelectVictim** function selects the page to be replaced when the buffer is full and another page is brought in. In general, the **SelectVictim** function finds the page in the buffer with the highest non-resident degree that is not connected to the current page/segment. The reason behind this is that if a page has a high non-resident degree, then it is unlikely to be released in the near future, and hence should be replaced and fetched later. Another possible premise for the **SelectVictim** function is to find the page with the lowest resident degree, so that it contributes to the release of as few pages in the memory as possible. It is not clear which approach is better, so we arbitrarily chose the former.

Due to this ready conversion from OPAS1 to OPAS2, this paper focuses first on devising a good heuristic for the OPAS1 problem, and then converting it to the OPAS2 problem.

3.2   Omiecinski's Heuristic (OH)

Omiecinski's Heuristic (OH) attempts at every step of the heuristic to find the smallest number of fetches which would remove one page from the memory. The heuristic was initially formulated for use on bipartite graphs only, but it is easily converted to cater for any graph. The following is the slightly modified heuristic OH:

OH heuristic for the OPAS1 problem

1. Choose a page p_i in the join graph G such that the degree of p_i is minimal to bring into the buffer.
2. Choose a page p_j to bring into the buffer such that
    a) an edge exists in G between p_j and a page p'_j in the buffer, and
    b) the number of edges connecting p'_j to a node outside the buffer is minimal, i.e. p'_j has the lowest non-resident degree.
3. Delete all edges (p, q) from G where p and q are contained in the buffer. If the degree of a page becomes zero, then remove the page from the buffer and delete the vertex from G.
4. If G is empty, then quit; if the buffer is empty, goto Step 1; else goto Step 2.

As noted in [4], this algorithm is generally outperformed by COH for the OPAS1 problem. Importantly, however, it outperforms COH for the OPAS2 problem when the fixed buffer size is lower than a certain threshold.

The run-time complexity of this heuristic is $O(|V|^2 \times |E|^2)$. For full details of this heuristic, refer to [3].

3.3   Chan & Ooi's Heuristic (COH)

Chan and Ooi's Heuristic (COH) does not restrict itself to removing pages from the buffer, but rather examines all the pages to be fetched collectively. At each step, it looks for the smallest number of pages to be read in order to release a page, or the *smallest minimal segment*, and puts it into the buffer.

The COH algorithm, modified to reflect the *page* that is brought in at each step rather than the *segment*, is as follows:

COH heuristic for the OPAS1 problem

1. Choose a page p_i in the join graph G such that the value of **Priority**(p_i) is minimal, where **Priority**(p_i) = non-resident degree of p_i, plus one if p_i is not in the buffer.
2. **while** Degree$(p_i) > 0$ **do**

   Choose a page p_j to bring into the buffer such that
   a) an edge exists in G between p_j and a page in the buffer, and
   b) the number of edges connecting p_j to a node inside the buffer is maximal, i.e. p_j has the largest resident degree.
3. Delete all edges *(p, q)* from G where p and q are contained in the buffer. If the degree of a page becomes zero, then remove the page from the buffer (the page is released) and the vertex is deleted from G.
4. If G is empty, then quit; else goto Step 1.

Priority(p_i) gives the number of pages that must be brought into the buffer in order to release p_i, which is its non-resident degree, plus itself if it is not already in the buffer. Thus the minimal segment is the page with the smallest **Priority**() value and all the pages connected to it.

The order of fetching the pages in the minimal buffer is unimportant for OPAS1, but matters in OPAS2. Hence the above algorithm fetches the page with the largest resident degree in the segment. The runtime complexity for this heuristic is $O(|V|^2)$. The full details can be found in [4].

4   The New Heuristic (LOCH)

4.1   Premise

The best existing heuristic for the OPAS1 problem is COH, which seeks to find the smallest minimal segment during each iteration. However, there are cases when it is not optimal to fetch the *smallest* minimal segment. One obvious case of this is when the smallest minimal segment is made up of several pages with very high non-resident degrees. These pages would then be left in the buffer for a long time since they require many pages to be brought in before they are released.

We use the the notation *N-Release-M* to denote that N pages are brought into the buffer to release M pages. We also define $BufSize_i(S)$ as the buffer size after fetching page i in page access sequence S.

COH looks for the smallest minimal segment by finding the smallest number of pages to be fetched in order to release *one or more* pages, i.e. N-Release-(≥ 1). In graphs containing several heavily-connected clusters, COH tends to fetch the pages with the lowest degrees from several clusters. In fact, COH performs arbitrarily badly in the graph type shown in Figure 2.

Assume here that p_1 is identified to be the page released in the smallest minimal segment. Hence p_{1a} and p_{2a} will be brought into the buffer. According to the COH heuristic, the next page to be brought in should be p_2, since it requires only 2 pages to release. Thus p_{3a} is pulled in, whereupon p_3 is identified as the smallest minimal segment, and so on. Thus, depending on the length of the chain, the p_{ka} pages will accumulate in the memory buffer.

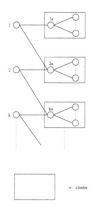

Fig. 2. Constructed graph on which COH performs poorly

One class of graph which contains several clusters is the geometric graph and it is found that COH does not perform well on them.

4.2   The Matching Algorithm

We noted that the increase in net buffer size as a result of fetching N pages is the difference between N and the number of pages released, i.e. for N-Release-M, the increase is N-M. Obviously, if the number of pages released is greater than the number of pages fetched (N-Release-($>N$)), then the net buffer size will decrease. Instinctively, it is better to fetch an N-Release-($>N$) sequence before an N-Release-($\leq N$) sequence, since the net buffer size will decrease after the former but increase or remain the same after the latter. This is provided that the former sequence does not involve bringing in too many pages, so that the maximum buffer size is raised.

In order to detect some of the cases of N-Release-($>N$), we employed the *maximum matching algorithm* [6], which is a solution to the *maximum matching problem.* We restrict our definitions to *bipartite* graphs, since the algorithm pertains to only this class of graphs.

matching Given a bipartite graph with partitions X and Y, a matching in the graph corresponds to a set of edges no two of which meet at the same vertex.
complete matching A matching where all vertices in X are matched.
maximum matching The matching with the maximum number of edges.

There is an existing algorithm which makes use of the concept of *alternating paths* to construct the maximum matching of any bipartite graph.

alternating path If G is a bipartite graph with partitions X and Y, and M is the matching set of G, then a series of vertices $A = < v_1, v_{1a}, v_2, v_{2a}, \cdots, v_k, v_{ka} >$ is an alternating path of G iff $(v_i, v_{ia}) \notin M$ for all $1 \leq i < k$, and $(v_{(j-1)a}, v_j) \in M$ for all $1 < j \leq k$. Furthermore, v_1 and v_{ka} must not be matched.

We shall depict this maximum matching algorithm as **DoMatching**(X, Y), where X and Y are the two partitions to be matched. The maximum matching algorithm can be found in [5].

At the point where page p_i is fetched in the PAS S, if we consider pages currently in the memory as one partition X, and all the pages connected to the in-memory pages but not yet fetched into the memory as the other partition Y, we have a bipartite sub-graph $G_S(i)$ of the original join graph G. We can then make use of the maximum matching algorithm to detect instances of N-Release-($>N$) subsequences.

Theorem 2. *If there is no complete matching of $G_S(i)$, then there exists a subsequence after the fetching of page p_i which is N-Release-($>$N).*

Proof. Let $G_S(i)$ be a bipartite graph with two partitions *IM* and *OM*, and a maximum matching M. We choose a page p_1 in X which is not matched, and construct an alternating path tree, which graphically depicts all alternating paths emanating from p_1, with p_1 as the root, as shown in Figure 3. Every page on an odd level of the tree is composed of pages in *IM*, each connected to its parent (if any) by an edge **in** M. Every page on an even level is composed of pages in *OM*, each connected to its parent by an edge **not in** M. Since all alternating paths start and end with a matched edge, the height of the tree must be odd.

From Figure 3, it is clear that every page $p_{(k-1)a}$ in *OM* is paired with the page p_k in *IM*. Thus if every *OM* page in the tree is fetched into the buffer, the *IM* page which it is paired with will be released, plus page p_1. Hence, there exists a subsequence, consisting of all the pages in *OM* in the tree, which is N-Release($>N$).

Consequently, given a maximum matching on $G_S(i)$, the following algorithm finds a N-Release-($>N$) subsequence:

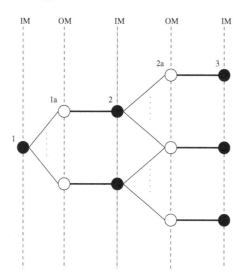

Fig. 3. An alternating path tree

Algorithm to find *N*-Release-(>*N*) subsequence

1. Let IM[ ] be an array of in-memory pages, initially empty, and p_i be an unmatched page in a maximum matching on $G_S(i)$. Set *Curr* as 0, and *NumSeq* as 1. Assign IM[*Curr*]:= p_i.
2. **while** *Curr* < *NumSeq* **do**
   a) Set Mark(IM[*Curr*]):= TRUE;
   b) For all non-memory pages connected to page IM[*Curr*], call it p_j with Mark = FALSE,
      i. Set Mark(p_j):= TRUE;
      ii. Assign IM[*NumSeq*] as the page matched to p_j, and increment *NumSeq*.
   c) Increment *Curr*
3. Set S as the set of all out-memory pages connected to the pages in IM[ ]. This is the *N*-Release-(>*N*) subsequence.

We shall denote the above algorithm as **FindSeq()**. The *N*-Release-(>*N*) subsequence found is the one which contains the smallest number of pages, so as to reduce the risk of raising the maximum buffer size.

4.3   The LOCH Algorithm

One problem with the *N*-Release-(>*N*) approach is that there is a possibility that such a subsequence is detected close to the point of MAX(S), so that the greater number of pages read in brings the maximum buffer size higher than it would be if the smallest minimal segment is read in instead.

In order to somewhat reduce this problem, we made the COH algorithm the basis of the new heuristic. One run of COH will be made to find the value of MAX(S) under COH. This value is used as a threshold to judge whether the N-Release-$(>N)$ subsequence is detected as too close to the point of MAX(S) to be used. Furthermore, if a N-Release-$(>N)$ subsequence is *not* detected, then the smallest minimal segment will be used instead.

After a complete run, the resultant MAX(S) is compared to the Threshold value. If it is better, the Threshold value is assigned the value of MAX(S), and the algorithm is run once again with the new threshold value.

Preliminary testing discovered that it is often the case that although a N-Release$(>N)$ subsequence is found, it is rejected because the size of the subsequence plus the current buffer size is greater than the threshold. However, it is actually possible to make use of the subsequence as the threshold is not breached if the subsequence is brought in by order of smallest minimal segments.

We discovered that the average performance of the algorithm improves if, at the times when an N-Release$(>N)$ subsequence is found, we simply bring in the smallest minimal segment in the subsequence if its size does not bring the current buffer size over the Threshold. We call this algorithm, simply the LOCH heuristic:

The LOCH Heuristic for the OPAS1 problem

1. Run COH Algorithm *(see Section 3.3)*. Let Threshold:= MAX(S) under the COH Algorithm. Let *Seg* be a set of pages, initially empty.
2. Choose a page p_i in the join graph G such that the value of **Priority**(p_i) is minimal, where **Priority**$(p_i) =$
   non-resident degree of p_i, plus one if p_i is not in the buffer.
3. Find IM, the set of pages in the buffer, and OM, the set of pages that are not in the buffer and are connected to one or more pages in IM.
4. Assign as *MinPage* the single page p_i found in Step 2.
5. **if DoMatching**(IM, OM) = FALSE, **then**
   a) Use **FindSeq()** to find S_{min}, the N-Release-$(>N)$ subsequence with the smallest value of N.
   b) Find the page p_{min}, which is the page with the smallest degree in S_{min}. If the degree of $p_{min}+$ the current buffer size < Threshold, then assign MinPage = p_{min}.
6. If *MinPage* is not in the buffer, bring it into the buffer.
7. Bring all pages connected to *MinPage* into the buffer.
8. Delete all edges *(p, q)* from G where p and q are in the buffer. If the degree of a page becomes zero, remove it from the buffer and delete it from G. If the page is in *Seg*, remove it from *Seg*.
9. If G not empty goto Step 2.
10. If G is empty, then
    - If MAX(S) < Threshold then set Threshold:= MAX(S), reload the graph G and goto Step 2.
    - else, QUIT.

To speed up the heuristic, Step 3 can be modified so that the in-memory and out-memory sets IM and OM are updated as the pages are fetched and released. This can be done at the same time as the detection of the smallest minimal segment in Step 2. With practical testing, it was found that the number of runs it takes for the heuristic to find the final solution is usually 4 or less. $O(|V| \times |V||E|)$ as bipartite matching can be performed easily in $O(|V||E|)$ time. If incremental matching is done at each iteration, the runtime complexity can be reduced to between $O(|V||E|)$ and $O(|V|^2|E|)$.

The conversion to the OPAS2 problem is not as straightforward for LOCH. There is a possibility that too many pages that are in the buffer are connected to pages in the N-Release-($>N$) subsequence, and hence there is no good candidate for replacement when the fixed buffer size is reached. To overcome this problem, we only fetch the N-Release-($>N$) subsequence if it is possible to fetch it into the buffer without the need for replacements. Further, the Threshold value to decide if another run is required is now the number of replacements of the previous run.

5   Performance Analysis

5.1   OPAS1 Heuristics

According to the results given in [4], COH generally outperforms both OH and FPH for the OPAS1 problem. Therefore, for the OPAS1 problem, we only provide the comparison between COH and LOCH. However, due to the nature of the LOCH heuristic, in that it always takes the COH result if it cannot find a better one, LOCH will never generate an answer which is worse than COH.

The performance experiments are characterized by the following parameters: type of join graphs, parameters of join graphs, size of join relations and type of heuristic. For each class, 20 join graphs are randomly generated, and the optimal buffer size obtained by COH and LOCH are reflected.

The results for geometric graphs are shown in Table 1. As a representative result, all 20 test graphs with 500 vertices and $E(\theta) = 50$ are shown, ranked in terms of best percentage improvement of the LOCH heuristic over the COH heuristic. For the other distributions, the best 5 results are shown.

For certain examples of geometric graphs, the LOCH heuristic clearly outperforms the COH heuristic by a significant margin. The percentage improvement is generally less when the density of the graph is higher. This is instinctively correct, as the denser graphs have fewer clear-cut clusters, and hence there are fewer opportunities to detect N-Release-($>N$) subsequences. Nevertheless, the amount of improvement over COH for some geometric graphs is substantial.

The amount of improvement by the LOCH heuristic over the COH heuristic for general graphs is minimal, seldom going over 3 or 4 pages better. By tracing the program during the running of these tests, it was found that for general graphs, the N-Release-($>N$) subsequences that are detected tended to be very large. This is due to the fact that the nodes in general graphs are equally likely to be connected to any node, and hence there are few clear-cut clusters. As a

Table 1. Results of COH and LOCH on geometric graphs for OPAS1

Filename	$|V|$ (pages)	$E(\theta)$ (edges)	B(COH) (a)	B(LOCH) (b)	Improvement (%)
Geo500_50_16			130	89	31.54
Geo500_50_20			108	85	21.30
Geo500_50_15			122	99	18.85
Geo500_50_9			116	96	17.24
Geo500_50_1			119	105	11.76
Geo500_50_4			102	93	8.82
Geo500_50_2			106	97	8.49
Geo500_50_14			104	98	5.77
Geo500_50_18			102	97	4.90
Geo500_50_10	500	50	114	110	3.51
Geo500_50_17			95	92	3.16
Geo500_50_13			100	97	3.00
Geo500_50_19			106	103	2.83
Geo500_50_3			112	110	1.79
Geo500_50_8			113	113	
Geo500_50_11			113	113	
Geo500_50_12			109	109	
Geo500_50_6			95	95	
Geo500_50_7			90	90	
Geo500_50_5			89	89	
Geo500_25_6			84	63	25.00
Geo500_25_14			82	63	23.17
Geo500_25_18	500	25	82	67	18.29
Geo500_25_12			79	67	15.19
Geo500_25_16			69	59	14.49
Geo500_75_20			136	121	11.03
Geo500_75_16			129	120	6.98
Geo500_75_9	500	75	130	121	6.92
Geo500_75_12			152	142	6.58
Geo500_75_8			142	133	6.34
Geo1000_50_3			156	130	16.67
Geo1000_50_15			193	162	16.06
Geo1000_50_4	1000	50	186	166	10.75
Geo1000_50_18			148	134	9.46
Geo1000_50_14			131	122	6.87

result of the large subsequences, it often turned out that fetching the subsequence would bring the maximum buffer size above the threshold.

It is interesting to note that the LOCH heuristic derives *no* improvement at all compared to the COH heuristic when performed on bipartite graphs. It is the nature of bipartite graphs to have almost no clusters to speak of, and hence the special case of an N-Release-($>N$) subsequence is almost never found.

5.2 OPAS2 Heuristics

As an indication of the performance of LOCH in OPAS2, we present the comparison of the results betwen COH and LOCH for 20 geometric graphs with $|V| = 500$ and $E(\theta) = 50$, with the buffer size fixed at 80 pages. The results are shown in Table 2. As can be seen, the amount of improvement over the COH heuristic is significant, but diminishes as the fixed buffer size decreases, since there are fewer opportunities for N-Release-($>N$) subsequences to be read in before the fixed buffer size is reached.

Table 2. Results of COH and LOCH on geometric graphs with $|V| = 500$, $E(\theta) = 50$ and $F = 80$, for OPAS2

Filename	COHopt (pages)	R(COH) (pages)	LOCHopt (pages)	R(LOCH) (pages)	Improvement (%)
Geo500_50_14	104	39	98	21	46.15
Geo500_50_17	95	18	92	12	33.33
Geo500_50_3	112	20	110	15	25.00
Geo500_50_19	106	41	103	31	24.39
Geo500_50_18	102	41	97	33	19.51
Geo500_50_4	102	28	93	25	10.71
Geo500_50_2	106	24	97	22	8.33
Geo500_50_16	130	38	89	36	5.26
Geo500_50_9	116	44	96	42	4.55
Geo500_50_1	119	48	105	46	4.17
Geo500_50_7	90	34	90	33	2.94
Geo500_50_12	109	77	109	76	1.30
Geo500_50_8	113	69	113	69	
Geo500_50_10	114	67	110	67	
Geo500_50_11	113	51	113	51	
Geo500_50_13	100	35	97	35	
Geo500_50_15	122	25	99	25	
Geo500_50_6	95	20	95	20	
Geo500_50_5	89	10	89	10	
Geo500_50_20	108	9	85	9	

The amount of improvement of the LOCH heuristic over the COH heuristic for general graphs is similarly minimal. In both the case of geometric graphs and general graphs, similar results were obtained for graphs with more vertices and/or edges.

5.3   Deficiencies of the LOCH Heuristic

There are some deficiencies of the LOCH heuristic which, have not been conclusively addressed here. They should be examined in future work.

One possible refinement is the detecting of N-Release-N subsequences as well. The arguments for the inclusion of N-Release-N subsequences before N-Release-($<N$) subsequences are similar to those for N-Release-($>N$) subsequences.

Another failing is that the LOCH heuristic only detects cases where the pages removed are all currently in the memory. In fact, there may be many cases of N-Release-($>N$) subsequences where not all the pages released are already in the memory, and these are not detected.

These deficiencies should eventually be addressed. Nonetheless, the existing LOCH heuristic gives us a platform to start new directions of research.

6   Conclusion

In this paper, we have attempted to find a heuristic for the OPAS1 and OPAS2 problems which performs better than the existing heuristics. En route to the creation of the algorithm, we examined the current best heuristics, the OH and COH heuristics, and examined their advantages and disadvantages.

We devised a new heuristic, LOCH, which performs better than existing heuristics, particularly in the case of geometric graphs. This is a useful result as it is our belief that geometric graphs is a good representation of possible real-life multi-relational joins. The LOCH heuristic is based on the concept of finding N-Release-($>N$) subsequences, such that the resultant buffer size after the entire sequence is fetched is less than before.

References

1. B. C. Desai, *Performance of a composite attribute and join index*, IEEE Trans. on Software Eng., 15 (1989), pp. 142–152.
2. P. Mishra and M. H. Eich, *Join processing in relational databases*, ACM Computing Surveys, 24 (1992), pp. 64–113.
3. E. R. Omiecinski, *Heuristics for join processing using nonclustered indexes*, IEEE Trans. Knowledge and Data Eng., 15 (1989), pp. 19–25.
4. B. C. Ooi and C. Y. Chan, *Efficient scheduling of page access in index-based join processing*, IEEE Trans. Knowledge and Data Eng., 9 (1997), pp. 1005–1011.
5. The Open University, *Networks 3 : Assignment and Transportation*, Walton Hall, Milton Keynes, MK7 6AA.
6. C. H. Papadimitriou and K. Steiglitz, *Combinatorial Optimization - Algorithms and Complexity*, Prentice Hall International, Inc, Englewood Cliffs, NJ 07632, USA, 1989.
7. P. Valduriez, *Join indices*, ACM Trans. on Database Systems, 12 (1987), pp. 218–246.

Data Organization Issues for Location-Dependent Queries in Mobile Computing[1]

Sanjay Kumar Madria[1], Bharat Bhargava[1], Evaggelia Pitoura[2], and Vijay Kumar[3]

[1]Department of Computer Science, Purdue University, West Lafayette, IN 47907.
{skm,bb}@cs.purdue.edu
[2]Computer Science Department, University of Ioannina, GR 45110, Greece,
pitoura@cs.uoi.gr
[3]Department of Computer Networking, University of Missouri-Kansas City, MO 64110,
kumar@cstp.umkc.edu

Abstract. We consider queries which originate from a mobile unit and whose result depends on the location of the user who initiates the query. Example of such a query is *How many people are living in the region I am currently in?"* We execute such queries based on location-dependent data involved in their processing. We build concept hierarchies based on the location data. These hierarchies define mapping among different granularities of locations. One such hierarchy is to generate domain knowledge about the cities that belong to a state. The hierarchies are used as distributed directories to assist in finding the database or relation that contains the values of the location-dependent attribute in a particular location. We extend concept hierarchies to include spatial indexes on the location-dependent attributes. Finally, we discuss how to partition and replicate relations based on the location to process the queries efficiently. We briefly discuss the implementation issues.

1 Introduction

Advances in wireless communication technology make it possible to realize a data processing paradigm that eliminates geographical constraints from data processing activities. In this environment, mobile users (mobile units) are not attached to a fixed location all the time. Instead their point of connection to the network changes as they move. A mobile unit is connected to a server, which manages the data processing activities in a well-defined region. When a unit moves out of one region, it gets connected to the server of a new region. The attachment to different servers is handled in a way that the mobile unit gets continuous service while moving. We envision a

---

[1] This research is partially supported by NSF under grant numbers 9805693-EIA, CCR-9901712 and IRI-9979453

J. Štuller et al. (Eds.): ADBIS-DASFAA 2000, LNCS 1884, pp. 142–156, 2000.

ubiquitous data processing system, which gives the impression that the desired data is available in the vicinity of a processing unit and can be accessed at anytime from anywhere.

The data processing mechanism in mobile environment is not fundamentally different from the conventional system [11]. However, the freedom of geographical mobility while processing information gives rise to a number of interesting and challenging problems, which can be categorized into application and system problems. In the application domain, one faces the problem of developing query structure and their processing, management of location-dependent data [1], accessing desired data, etc. System problems concern the consistency, serialization, system recovery and security.

We present research ideas for processing queries that deal with *location-dependent data* [1,2]. Such queries are refereed as location-dependent. The objective is to get the right data from different locations for processing a given query. The results returned in response to such queries should satisfy the location constraints with respect to the point of query origin, where the results are received, etc. We propose to build additional capabilities into the existing database systems to handle location-dependent data and queries.

We present several examples to recognize the problems of accessing correct data when the point of contact changes. Data may represent social security number (SSN) of a person, or maiden name, or sales tax of a city. In one representation the mapping of the data value and the object it represents is not subjected to any location constraints. For example, the value of SSN of a person remains the same no matter from which location it is accessed. This is not true in the case of sales tax data. The value of the sales tax depends on the place where sales query is executed. For example, sales tax value of Indiana is governed by a different set of criteria than the sales tax of Michigan. We can therefore, identify the type of data whose value depends on the set of criteria established by the location or not subject to the constraints of a location. There is a third type of data that is sensitive to the point of query. Consider a commuter who is travelling in a taxi and initiates a query on his laptop to find the nearby hotels in the area of its current location. The answer to this query depends on the location of the origin of the query. Since the commuter is moving she may receive the result at a different location. Thus, the query results should correspond either to the location where the result is received or to the point of the origin of the query. The difference in the two correct answers to the query depends on the location and not on the hotel. The answer to the query "find the cheapest hotel" is not affected by the movement. The former depends on the location where as later on the object characteristics.

Our focus in this paper is to model location-dependent data and execute queries processing them. To manipulate this kind of data we build *concept hierarchies* (based on the location) and extend them to include spatial indexes on the location-dependent attributes. For efficient query processing, we discuss the horizontal and vertical partitions and replication of relations based on location. We discuss how location-dependent data can be grouped or summarized. The partition tables and summarized relations can be cached at mobile unit so that location-dependent queries can be also processed locally.

The research on predicting, storing and querying the location of mobile objects has been discussed in [4,5,6,7,8]. Location-dependent data considered in this paper are stationary. They do not correspond to moving objects [4,5,6]. In moving object paradigm, objects are constantly moving and their location related data is constantly being updated in the database. We assume here that the location information about a mobile host is found with the help of a Global Positioning System (GPS) in conjunction with some of the methods used to predict future locations [5,9]. For example, Omnitracs developed by Qualcomm [10] is a commercial system used by transportation industry which provides location management by connecting vehicles such as trucks, via satellites, to company databases.

The research questions addressed in this paper are: (a) How to represent location-dependent data efficiently?, (b) Do we need to represent location differently or could it be represented in the schema?, (c) How to handle database partition and replication in the presence of location-dependent data?, (d) How to create index data using location and manage them for efficient query processing?

The remainder of this paper is structured as follows. In section 2, we discuss mobile database system architecture. Section 3 defines location-dependent data and query processing. We present a motivating example in Section 4. We discuss concept hierarchies in Section 5. Location-dependent indexing and summarization has been described in Section 6. Section 7 presents our discussion on replication and partitioning issues and implementation overview. We conclude in Section 8.

2 Mobile Database System Architecture

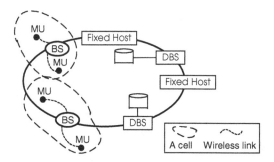

Fig. 1. Architecture of MDS

Figure 1 presents a general architecture of the Mobile Database System (MDS). A set of general purpose computers (PC, workstations, etc.) are interconnected through a high speed wired network. These computers are categorized into *Fixed hosts* (FH) and *Base Stations* (BS) or *mobile support stations* (MSS). A number of laptop computers, referred to as *Mobile Hosts* (MH) or *Mobile Units* (MU) are connected to the wired network components only through BSs via wireless channels. MUs are battery powered portable computers, which move around freely in a restricted area, which we refer to as the "geographical mobility domain" (G). In Figure 1, G is the total area covered by all BSs. This size restriction on their mobility is due to the limited bandwidth of wireless communication channels.

To support the mobility of MUs and to exploit frequency reuse, the entire G is divided into smaller areas called cells. Each cell is managed by a specific BS. The mobile paradigm requires that a MU must have unrestricted movement within G (inter-cell movement) and must be able to access desired data from any cell. The process of crossing a cell boundary by a MU and entering into another cell is referred to as a handoff. The entire process of handoff is transparent to a MU and is responsible for maintaining end-to-end data movement connectivity.

A database server (DBS) can either be installed at BSs or can be a part of FHs or can be a separate from BS or FH. In our MDS architecture, the *location-dependent* query arrives at MU and are processed with the help of MU, BS and DBS.

3 Location-Dependent Data

A location is a geographical area. Location may be expressed with various granularities. For instance it may be specified as a longitude-latitude pair, a city, a country or a region covered by a cell or a group of cells when referring to the cellular architecture in wireless communications. A data item is location- dependent if it takes on different values based on the location. For example, sale-tax rate is location-dependent while the authors of a book are not.

Definition 1. Location-dependent data - data whose value varies with location.

A location-dependent data item may have some value **a** in region **A** and some other value **b** in another region **B** at the same time. Both values are correct in their respective regions and represent the same data object. The value **b** may be related to value **a** by some functional mapping which may depend on factors such as the distance between the two regions or the two values may be independent. We assume that values in a location remain the same unless explicitly updated. We have not considered items whose value changes continuously with time.

Definition 2. Location attribute – an attribute whose domain consists of locations.

An example of a location attribute is the Location-address attribute in the relation shown in Figure 2. A location attribute may be *explicit* in the relation. The location attribute may be explicitly specified in the database scheme. However, there are cases in which there is no explicit location attribute, instead the location attribute is *implicitly* determined from the context. For example an implicit location attribute may be the location at which the database is stored. Such implicit attributes may be included as metadata or as part of an auxiliary schema.

Definition 3. Location-dependent attribute – an attribute whose value is associated with a location.

For example, both the Per day charges and the Tax attribute in the database instance in Figure 2 change based on the location attribute Location-address. A location-dependent attribute does not necessarily have different values at all different locations.

Definition 4 (a). Location-dependent query (type A) - A query Q is called location-dependent if its result depends on the location at which the query is originated.

Definition 4(b). Location-dependent query (type B) – A query Q that processes location-dependent data is also called location-dependent query. Location information may be in the form of longitude and latitude or in some other spatial parameter. The location information may be implicit or explicit in the query.

The query *"How many people are living in the region I am currently in?"* can be regarded as location-dependent because it must access the population of particular region. On the other hand *"List the SSN of people who are older than 50 years"*, is not a location-dependent query.

We propose approaches for processing queries which access location-dependent data under the following possible cases:

Location information is explicit in the query. For example, *"What is the humidity and temperature in Kansas City today?"* The location Kansas City may be presented in the *where* clause of SQL-syntax like *"where location = "Kansas City"*. The query must use Kansas City weather data and the result will be location specific. It is possible that the mobile unit could be in a different region when it receives the answer. Still the information is correct and can be used.

Location attribute is not explicit in the query, and query is evaluated for the location where it originated. The system can identify the implicit location by using longitude and latitude information, which can be available through GPS. There could be some other ways of identifying the location information such as the use of location directory or prediction with the help of the users past behavior. However, the problem with this answer is that the location information is not deterministic. Thus, the validity of this result cannot be accepted at a location with different longitude and latitude values.

Location is not explicit and the query is evaluated such that the results correspond to the current location where the user receives them. For example, suppose a salesman driving on a highway initiates a query *"Which is the nearest hotel?"* on his laptop. If the query is processed related to the current location of the salesman, then there may never be a precise answer, because by the time the distance is computed and relayed to the salesman, he might have changed his longitude and latitude. The value will be approximate and could be acceptable in certain cases. This processing mode, however, will require continuous monitoring of the mobile unit to identify its next location where the query result will be dispatched.

Location is not explicit and the query is evaluated at the time the query arrives at the database server. In this case, there are two issues. First, the query results reflect the current position of the user at the time query is evaluated. Second, the results reflect the current location associated with the location-dependent data. The first case is similar to the previous case; the query is evaluated with respect to the future location where the results will be received. However, the second case is different where the location information reflects the current state of the database. For example, the query "What is the destination of taxi with registration number CJ 213 will be evaluated with respect to its destination location at the *time* query is executed. However, when the results arrived, the target destination may change for that taxi in the database.

In such cases, the results returned to the user with respect to reference location (location used in the evaluation of the query) may be different but consistent and correct.

4 Location-Dependent Query Processing and Motivating Examples

Consider the following relational schema: Hotels (Hotel-name, Location-address, Per-day charges, Tax, Distance (from airport)). The relation is shown in Figure 2.

Hotel-Name	Location-address	Per day charges	Tax (%)	Rebate(%) (Oct.-March)	Distance (from-airport)
Holiday-Inn	San Jose, CA	110	5	10	5
Holiday-Inn	Palo Alto, CA	110	5	10	10
Holiday-Inn	Berkeley, CA	110	5	10	30
Holiday-Inn	Dallas, TX	100	7	0	40
Ramada-Inn	San Jose, CA	110	5	10	30
Ramada-Inn	Houston, TX	100	7	0	40

Fig. 2. Hotels

In Figure 2, there are two location-dependent attributes: Per day charges and Tax. They both depend on the location attribute Location-address. They depend indirectly on the Distance (from-airport) location attribute, since the distance from the airport can be computed from the Location-address attribute. Since the location attributes Location-address and Distance are part of the scheme, they are explicit location attributes.

We consider SQL-type location-dependent queries that include a location attribute in the where clause as well as queries that do not include such an attribute. Consider the following query:

Find the hotels in the area of California. This query can be translated into the following SQL-syntax

Q1 Select *Hotel-name, Location-address* from *Hotels* where *Location-address* like "CA";

This is an example of a query that includes a location-attribute namely the Location-address attribute. This query will return all tuples that contain "CA" in the Location-address in the relation Hotel in Figure 2. However, treating this as a location-dependent query, we expect to retrieve results depending on the location of the mobile user who posed the query. Assume that the user is willing to drive only k miles form its current position. Such user preferences may be a part of a user profile that maintains personalized information for each user. For example, lets assume that the user issues the query from the airport in CA, k = 12 and that the reference location is the location of the user when posing the query. Then, the first two tuples are returned to the user. If instead we consider as reference location the location of the user when it receives the result of its query, then different tuples may be returned since the user may have moved a few miles away form the airport.

In query Q1, one of the location attributes Location-address is part of the query whereas the other location attribute Distance does not appear in the query. In order to process such a query, the database needs another layer which can map the query with the help of the user movement information captured by a GPS system to another query like Q2.

Q2 Select *Hotel-name, Location-address* **from** *Hotels* **where** *Location-address* **like** *"CA"* **and distance from airport <= 12;**

A realistic query may not include a location attribute but queries for all hotels close to the user: *Find the hotel addresses in my area.* The equivalent query can be represented in SQL-syntax as follows:

Q3 Select *Hotel-name, Location-address* **from Hotels where** *location-attribute* **=** *current*;

The database system must complete this query with information about the location of the user by giving value to current before executing it.

Another issue arises if different notations are used for describing locations. Consider that the database does not contain the exact location of state such as CA, but suburbs such as Palo Alto or Berkeley. In that case, to execute the query Q1, the database system must first find which locations are in the CA state and then use the distance from the point of the origin of the query to find the exact location of the hotel.

Another example of the issues arising due to differences in describing location is the following query:

Find the hotels in Palo Alto area. The equivalent query in SQL-syntax can be as follows:

Q4 Select *Hotel-name, Location-address* **from Hotels where Location-address** **="Palo Alto";**

If query Q4 is executed using the relation **Hotels**, it will not return any hotels, as it does not match any of the tuples.

Yet another possibility is that the location attribute Address contains only CA. In this case, tuples in the relation Hotels can be grouped and replaced by one single tuple containing CA in the Location-address field (see Figure 4).

5 Concept Hierarchies

Concept hierarchies define a sequence of mappings from a set of lower-level concepts to their higher level correspondences [3,12,13] resulting in a hierarchy of concepts. In other words, concept hierarchies provide a set of predefined hierarchical relationships that generalize lower layer (i.e., primitive data) information to high layer. For example, a set {tennis, rugby, hockey, football} can be generalized as "sports" at a high level concept. A concept hierarchy can be defined on a single or on a set of attribute domains. For example, see the Location-address attribute in Figure 2.

5.1 Location-Based Concept Hierarchies

Concept hierarchies are data or application specific since they define mapping rules between different levels of concepts. The mapping of a concept hierarchy or some portion of it may be provided explicitly by a knowledge engineer or a domain expert. Many different concept hierarchies can be constructed based on different view points or users preferences. However, usually, many concept hierarchies can be associated with an attribute. In many implementations, it would be possible for a set of relatively stable and standard concept hierarchies to be made available as a common reference by all the databases. In [3], an automatic and dynamic generation of concept hierarchies is given.

Some of the issues in the construction of the location based concept hierarchies are as follows:

- Only set-valued domains of location attribute are considered. It is assumed that set-valued domains of attributes are simple structure-valued domains containing only discrete location values.
- The relational databases are summarized by using the location attribute's values at higher or the lower level concepts. Concept hierarchy can have any level of depth based on granularities of the location.
- There is no common region among two different locations. Thus, concept hierarchies are represented as trees.

Concept hierarchies can be generated among location attribute domains for the following:

- Within a domain itself, there may exist a concept hierarchy among the values in the location attribute. For example, a domain may be successively refined into more specialized location domain values.
- A concept hierarchy can be defined among location attributes using domains of attributes of a relation. For example, a concept hierarchy can relate attributes «City1» and «City2» with "State" at the root (since a state can have many cities).
- There may exist a concept hierarchy among domains of location attributes of different relations. For example, consider attributes "city" and "state" which may appear in two different relations. In that case, we can define a concept hierarchy across these two relations where "state" appears at higher level and "city" at lower level.

5.2 Constructing Concept Hierarchies

Concept hierarchies are constructed for each of the location attributes across all relations based on the domain values of those location attributes. The granularity of the concepts in the hierarchy may vary from that of the values of the domain of each individual attribute. For instance even if the domain of an attribute is a set of street addresses, the hierarchy may include only streets. Domain experts can be consulted to ensure that the hierarchies are complete and correct.

In general, concept hierarchies of domain values of location attributes are updated infrequently. Since they are constructed based on domain values, there is no need to incrementally update such hierarchies when:
- new values are inserted into a relation, or
- tuples are deleted from a relation.

Concept hierarchies need to be updated when attribute domains change or there is a need to include location attributes of new databases. For example, the introduction of a database that describes locations in USA necessitates that the concept hierarchy of Figure 3 is extended to include locations in USA. Note that one may construct concept hierarchies involving only instances of domain values that occur in a given relation instance. In this case, the insertion or deletion of tuples may cause the update of the concept hierarchy.

6 Location-Based Indexing and Summarization

Consider the concept hierarchy (CH) for each state in USA with the root as USA.

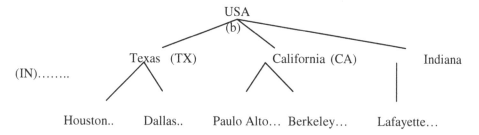

Fig. 3. Concept Hierarchy

Concept hierarchies are used to translate between different granularities used to represent locations. For instance, the concept hierarchy in Figure 3 can be used to determine that Palo Alto is a city in CA. Concept hierarchies can be used in conjunction with spatial indexes and for summarizing location information.

6. 1 Building Indexes

Concept hierarchies can be used as directories for direct processing using the appropriate database that includes values based on the reference location of a query. For instance, when a user issues a query similar to Q3 while the user is in California, the concept hierarchy can be used to direct to the Hotel relation that includes hotels in the California region.

In particular, we propose extending concept hierarchies to include information about the location of the database/relations that include location attributes. We build indexes for each location attribute in a relation. Such indexes may be spatial indexes, such as

R$^+$ trees. Nodes in the concept hierarchy point to the appropriate node of the spatial index. For instance, assume that we build a spatial index for the Address-Location attribute of the Hotel relation. In this case, the California node of the CH will include an entry (Hotel, Pointer) where Pointer points to the node of the spatial index on the Address-location attribute whose subnodes cover hotels in California.

In the case of a location-dependent query, the location of a moving user is commonly given as a pair of (latitude, longitude) values. This pair is mapped to the appropriate leaf of the concept hierarchy. In particular:

(a) If the reference location is the location of the user at the time the query is posed, then before sending the query for evaluation, the location of the user is estimated.

(b) If the reference location is the location of the user at the time the query arrives, then the estimation of the position of the user is initiated at the site at the static network that receives the query.

(c) If the reference location is the location of the user when the result arrives at its MH, the estimation of the location is again performed at the static site. However, estimating the location is now an involved procedure since this is a future location. This computation must also account for the time to transmit the result.

Once the location of the user is determined, this location is mapped to a leaf in the CH. For example, if the location is inside John Hopkins University, the location is mapped to the leaf "Baltimore". Then, we move up the CH tree until we find an entry for the requested relation. If the requested relation is the Hotel relation, then we end up at the node with label CA. This node points to the appropriate entries in the Hotel relation.

6.2 Location-Based Summarization

Another advantage of concept hierarchies is that the database relations can be condensed or summarized [13] using the location attributes. For example, suppose that the address field in the relation in Figure 2 contains no state such as CA and TX. This relation is summarized as follows using the CH in Figure 3. The Distance attribute now basically represents the aggregate operator maximum. It is applied here to the set of locations contained in the column and computes a new distance.

Hotel-name	Location -address	Per day charges	Tax (%)	Rebate(%) (Oct.- March)	Distance (from air- port)
Holiday-inn	CA	110	5	10	30
Holiday-Inn	TX	110	7	0	20
Ramada-Inn	CA	110	5	10	40
Ramada-Inn	TX	110	7	0	30

Fig. 4. Hotel 1: Summarized Relation Hotels

The relation in Figure 4 can be summarized as shown in Figure 5 using an aggregation operator like max for numeric values and conceptual summarization for location.

Another possibility is taking an aggregation operator like minimum. The error in the query can be generated if we know the maximum or minimum values for example of Per day Charges irrespective of locations then one can calculate the approximate answers [13]. For example, suppose that a mobile user has received a response to her earlier query about the Per day charges in CA area as 100 and tax as 5% for Holiday-Inn. Now she has received in response to the same query Per day charges as 110 max and tax as 7% max in another region A consisting of CA and TX using the relation shown in Figure 4. For simplicity, we assume that the query does not take into account rebates. With the help of earlier answer, she can approximately calculate that the error in per day charges between two locations CA and TX is (110 + 7%) - (100 +5%). This will be the error in the positive side. That is, user might have to pay minimum 0 dollars to maximum 12 dollars. If we use the aggregation operator min then error can be calculated on the negative side. User knows in this case he has to pay minimum amount as 100+5% and his earlier answer can be of no help. Thus, it is better to use aggregation operator max.

Hotel -name	Location -address	Max. Per day charges	Max. Tax (%)	Max. Rebate(%) (Oct.-March)	Max.Distance miles from airport)
Holiday - Inn	Region A	110	7	10	30
Ramada -Inn	Region A	110	7	10	40

Fig. 5. Hotel2 : Summarized relation Hotel1

Hotel-name	Location -address	Per day Charges Max.	Tax (%) Max.	Max. Rebate(%) (Oct.-March)	Max. Distance (from airport) in miles
Hotels	Region A	110	7	10	40

Fig. 6. Hotel3: Summarized relation Hotel2

By performing one more level of summarization and aggregation, we get the following relation as shown in Figure 6. Note that if the query is to find the Per day charges in Holiday-Inn, then the query in SQL-syntax will look like as follows:
Select Per day charges from Hotel2 where Location-address = "Region A".
The above query gives approximate answers that are valid in a much larger region A.

7 Replication and Partitioning

In mobile computing, replication of data can improve availability and allow a mobile host to operate even when disconnected from the fixed network. However, it incurs overheads since all replicas must be kept up-to-date. Our replication scheme is involves a hierarchical replication of database.

7.1 Data Partitioning Based on Location

To speed-up query processing, a relation may be partitioned based on the value of the location attribute. This partition may be physical or logical. In the case of a logical partition, the spatial index is used to define the tuples in the partition. A MH can store the part of the database that corresponds to its location. By doing so, queries can be answered locally on the MH. The relation Hotels shown in Figure 2 can be partitioned based on locations. We can get two partitions one for CA and another for TX. The partition (relation) for CA is in Figure 7.

The attributes such as Per day charges, Tax can be removed since they are redundant. Thus, we get the following relations as shown in Figures 8 and 9. The original relation can be obtained by taking the cross product of the relations shown in Figure 8 and 9. Note that Figure 7 corresponds to horizontal partition where as Figures 8 and 9 are with respect to vertical partitions of relation Hotels.

The Location-address can be removed and the location information can be augmented either with hotel name or using the concept hierarchies as shown in Figure 3 since we know that this relation is for locations in CA. Thus, we can again summarize the partition shown in Figure 8 as discussed in Section 6.2.

Hotel-name	Location-address	Per day charges	Tax	Distance
Holiday-Inn	San Jose , CA	110	5	5
Holiday –Inn	Palo Alto, CA	110	5	10
Ramada-Inn	San Jose, CA	110	5	30
Holiday-Inn	Berkeley, CA	110	5	30

Fig. 7. Hotel 4: Partition relation Hotels

Hotel-name	Location-address	Distance
Holiday-Inn	San Jose , CA	5
Holiday –Inn	Palo Alto, CA	10
Ramada-Inn	San Jose, CA	30
Holiday-Inn	Berkeley, CA	30

Fig. 8. Vertical partition 1: Hotels

Per Day Charges	Tax
110	5

Fig. 9. Vertical partition 2: Hotels

7.2 Hierarchical Replication Based on Location

Location dependency provides for an innovative replication scheme. We view a database as having multiple layers and we fully replicate *base data* (common at all the levels) at the lowest level. Base data is location-independent data. Replication of base data can be done at all the servers. At layer 0, we only replicate base data; data that do not depend upon location. At the next higher level, we have data that are the same for that set of locations and so on. Thus, we can replicate data in a hierarchical fashion.

Let us assume that Per day charges are same in all Holiday Inns in CA region as in Figure 2. We assume here that relation contains data about hotels in CA and TX only. We consider Hotel name and Per day charges as base relation and attach the CA and TX as location information with this relation. At next level, we create a relation with Tax, Address (location), Winter rebate and Distance (maximum) as attributes.

In Figure 2, Per day charges remain the same within the CA area, so there is no need to repeat this information for all the locations in CA, but it can be attached only to CA so that it will be valid for all the locations in CA. We can also replace the tuples that belong to different regions in CA by a single tuple with address CA as shown in Figure 11. This strategy avoids repeating information at all locations. However, note that some information may need to be repeated in case we need to join two relations linked to two different locations. We do not address this issue further in this paper.

Per day charges	Hotel names
110	Holiday-Inn
100	Ramada-Inn

Fig. 10. Level 0 – Base relation - location (CA, TX)

Tax(%)	Hotel address	Winter rebate(%)	Distance (maximum)
5	CA	10	30
7	TX	0	40

Fig. 11. Level 1 – relation at level 1- location CA

7. 3 Implementation Overview

One can store concept hierarchies and corresponding indexes at MUs. These concept hierarchies (CHs) and indicies correspond to the current location of MU. Once the MU moves to different location (note that many cells collectively may define a location), they need to be replaced by corresponding CHs and associated indexes. The CHs are stored at DBS (database servers) permanently. Since there are number of DBS, each one can have CHs and indexes corresponding to their location or they may also have replicated CHs and indexes. One advantage of replicating them is that MU can cache the CHs of next location before moving. However, in case there is a change in CHs and indexes at DBS, cache of MU needs to be made consistent. Normally CHs change infrequently since they are generated based on domain knowledge, not on instance level.

We assume here that MUs have some capabilities of processing a query. Once a query arrives at MU, it can reformulate the query with the help of CHs and then use indexes to find the corresponding database (relations). The query is then redirected to the corresponding DBS through BS which executes the query.

Another choice for storing CHs is DBS. Here it is we assumed that MUs have no capabilities of processing a query. Once the query arrives at MU, it is forwarded to DBS which then reformulate and executes the query.

Regarding the databases, each MU (if has database capabilities) can also store the partition tables (as shown in Figures 7, 8 and 9) with respect to its location. It then can execute the query locally. These partitioned tables however needs to be consistent with respect to original table at DBS. However, at the time disconnection, these tables can still be used to provide approximate answers [13].

8 Conclusions

We discuss location-dependent data and query evaluation. The modeling aspect and the data structures needed to implement location-dependent queries are given. The hierarchical replication scheme discussed is different than traditional replication of databases. Our location-dependent data and attribute concept is different than moving objects [4,5,6] where location-attribute is constantly changing (they call it dynamic attribute). We are currently working on building location-based indexing techniques. We plan to generate concept hierarchies based on location information given in the database. In the future, we plan to build location-dependent database query processing system, which can be placed on the top of any database management system.

References

[1]   Vijay Kumar and Margaret H. Dunham, "Defining Location Data Dependency, Transaction Mobility, and Commitment.   Technical Report 98-CSE-1, Southern Methodist University, February 1998.

[2]   Margaret H. Dunham and Vijay Kumar, "Location Dependent Data and its Management in Mobile Databases, Dexa '98, Austria 1998.

[3]   J. Han, and Y. Fu, Dynamic Generation and Refinement of Concept Hierarchies for Knowledge Discovery in Databases, in Proceedings AAAI'94 Workshop on Knowledge Discovery in Databases (KDD'94), Seattle, WA, 157-168. July, 1994.

[4]   Ouri Wolfson, Bo Xu, Sam Chamberlain, Liqin Jiang: Moving Objects Databases: Issues and Solutions. SSDBM 1998: 111-122

[5]   A.Prasad Sistla, Ouri Wolfson, Sam Chamberlain, Son Dao: Modeling and Querying Moving Objects. ICDE 1997: 422-432 .

[6]   George Kollios, Dimitrios Gunopulos and Vassilis J. Tsotras: On Indexing Mobile Objects. PODS 1999: 261-272.

[7]   Evaggelia Pitoura and Ioannis Fudos, An Efficient Hierarchical Scheme for Locating Highly Mobile Users. CIKM 1998: 218-225

[8]   Jamel Tayeb, Uzgur Ulusoy, Ouri Wolfson: A Quadtree-Based Dynamic Attribute Indexing Method. The Computer Journal 41(3): 185-200(1998)

[9]   Ouri Wolfson, Sam Chamberlain, Son Dao, Liqin Jiang, Gisela Mendez:
      Cost and Imprecision in Modeling the Position of Moving Objects. ICDE 1998: 588-596
[10] OmniTRACS. Communicating without Limits.
      http://www.qualcomm.com/ProdTech/Omni/ prodtech/omnisys.html.
[11] Margaret H. Dunham and A. Helan, "Mobile Computing and Databases: Anything
      New?", SIGMOD Record, Vol. 24, No. 4, December 1995.
[12] J. F. Roddick, N. G. Craske, and T. J. Richards, Hierarchical and set-valued Domains as
      an Approach to Summarization and Query Optimization in Databases, Department of
      Computer Science and Computer Engineering, La Trobe University, July, Technical
      Report, 12/93, 1993.
[13] S.K. Madria, Mukesh Mohania and J. Roddick, A Query Processing Model for Mobile
      Computing using Concept Hierarchies and Summary Databases, in proceedings of 5th
      Intl. Conference on Foundation for Data Organization (FODO'98), Japan, Nov. 1998.

Towards Intelligent Information Retrieval Engines: A Multi-agent Approach

Christos Makris[1], Athanassios Tsakalidis[1], and Bill Vassiliadis[1,2]

[1]Computer Technology Institute: Research Unit 5
P.O. Box 1122, 26110 Patras, Greece
{tsak,bb}@cti.gr
[2]ZEUS Consulting S.A.,
93 Riga Feraiou st., 26221, Patras, Greece.

Abstract: The amount of information available in on-line shops and catalogues is rapidly increasing. A single on-line catalogue may contain thousands of products thus posing the increasing need for fast and efficient methods for information filtering and retrieval. Intelligent agent communities may prove to be the needed item in transforming passive search and retrieval engines into active, evolving, personal assistants. In this paper we present a multi-agent architecture for an on-line shop and we propose new methods for performance balancing between filtering, retrieval, ranking, and server catalogue restructuring. This novel approach to multi-agent e-commerce systems provides intelligent, adaptive and personalised navigation within large hypertext environments useful for a wide range of Electronic Commerce applications.

1 Introduction

The amount of information available via e-shops and e-catalogues has rapidly increased in the last few years creating an information stress problem similar to that of the Internet: users cannot locate efficiently the information they need. This problem is crucial in on-line sales systems with thousands of products of different kinds and/ or categories. It is obvious that typical search methods are becoming less favourable as information increases resulting in money losses [1].

Autonomous, intelligent agents may prove to be the needed item in transforming passive e-commerce systems into active, personal shopping assistants. In hypertext situations such as searching and browsing, results must not only come quickly and require low cognitive load but must be tailored to user needs automatically [2].

In this paper we present a novel approach for the implementation of e-commerce systems that provide intelligent, adaptive and personalised services to their users. E-commerce functions are supported by a society of agents where a balance is achieved between filtering, retrieval, ranking through personalisation and web server restructuring. This collection of agents uses document content and context to structure the information space and to support the entire range of search activities. The interface

J. Štuller et al. (Eds.): ADBIS-DASFAA 2000, LNCS 1884, pp. 157–170, 2000.

allows potential customers to browse all available product information by using either an evolving subject based directory structure or an advanced information retrieval agent. The system architecture takes advantage of content representation and benefits from the interests of communities of users. Unlike traditional methods, an item is retrieved using not only its keyword description (content) but its context as well. The same principles are used for the reconstruction of the web server directory hierarchy. Our work also includes some preliminary results on an implementation which uses the described framework: a commercial on-line shop that sells greeting cards and posters, with over than 30.000 selections.

The structure of the paper is as follows: in section 2 an overview of related techniques and applications is provided. In section 3 the multi-agent architecture is examined and new algorithms for retrieval, filtering and ranking are described in detail. In section 4 some experimental results are presented and finally, in section 5 future directions are discussed.

2 Background

A significant issue that arises from the quantity of information available and the bandwidth limitations is the need for efficient methods that will keep retrieval latencies low and at the same time increase relevance quality of answers to user queries. There are several major techniques for retrieval and filtering of on-line catalogues in particular that contain pages that can be efficiently described by text. [4] presents a good description and analysis of information retrieval and filtering methods.

A very popular method is the Vector Representation model where web document filtering is based on the construction of indices that are representative of the content of the documents. Usually this involves filtering techniques such as TFIDF [5] where documents are transformed into weighted keyword vectors after stemming their keywords. Each keyword is weighted accordingly, depending on its frequency and its proximity to other keywords. Many popular techniques such as Inversion and Clustering are based on the vector representation model.

An approach widely advocated for special purpose search engines uses indexes based on the Signature File method. Signature file methods, in fact, have been proposed for various applications such as multikey and key retrieval for hypertext documents and multimedia systems. Although signatures files implementations have been proven to be less efficient than other methods in some applications, in situations where item entries tend to be short and of similar length or data have many attributes with a few distinct values [6], they are superior to both time response and storage needed. Especially when the vocabulary (in e-shops the number of products) is large this method is very competitive in size.

Information retrieval and filtering techniques have been extensively studied for a long time and numerous systems that use content based retrieval have appeared in the literature. Amalthea [7] is an evolving information filtering agent that monitors specific web sites for relevant information and uses user feedback/ recommendations for personalising search queries. Implementations such as WebACE [8] use clustering to construct clusters of training documents in order to form a user profile. Retriever [9] is an autonomous agents that tries to maximise its efficiency in one single search by learning the query domain. All the above mentioned filtering systems are based solely on content and not in context assuming that a web document has enough text density that can be used for running the classic frequency and proximity keyword algorithms. Also, user personalization is achieved by means of relevance feedback on how good or bad a retrieved item is. In on-line catalogues where web pages (describing a single product) contain only 2-3 sentences of text or even a few distinct keywords, these classic filtering techniques do not perform well. Furthermore, these agents perform their training and adaptation to specific users during the user query. Adding the train time to the retrieval and filtering delays results in systems that cannot be used efficiently in on-line sales systems.

From the above analysis we conclude that Information filtering and retrieval agents have received much attention in the last few years. Nevertheless, most implementations are best suited for filtering and retrieval of documents residing on the web or in digital libraries with high text density per document. They are not very well suited for on-line catalogues with special characteristics (low text density, many attributes per item etc.). Another disadvantage is that they usually do not take under consideration document context.

3   A Multi-agent Ecosystem

In order to understand the proposed framework and the need for a multi-agent approach, it is important to understand the type of information stored in an electronic catalogue (figure 1). The catalogue contains products that are described by a small set of keywords or a line of text (product description). In our use case this description was made available from a back-end application that is used for product management and logistic support. Each product is assigned in a catalogue web page where information such as price, size, category, product code, description and its image are stored. Products belong to thematic categories and subcategories.

A customer can access a product in two ways: using the search engine or using the directory structure. The search engine returns a ranked list of links directly to product web pages. The directory structure is used for narrowing selections through category browsing. When the user reaches the last sub-category level, the system presents a set of pages (called thumbnail pages) each one containing a small number of links (usually 6-8) in the form of image thumbnails to the corresponding product pages. The appearance of these thumbnails depends on the user e.g. users that belong to different user communities see different thumbnail pages.

A search sequence is performed as follows: the user submits a query, which is then handled autonomously by the system. An special purpose index is searched for filtering and retrieval of records that satisfy the query. Meanwhile an agent identifies the community in which the user belongs and retrieves a set of community weights

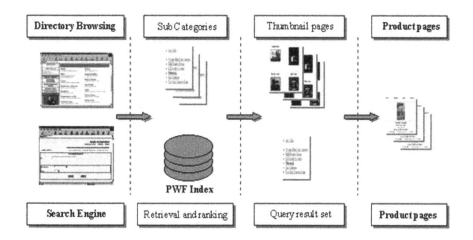

Fig. 1. Data representation and access methods

for the corresponding records. Another agent uses a ranking algorithm, which combines weights and records and presents the final result set to the user.

In this framework, information retrieval and filtering processes are viewed as a society of co-operative Intelligent Agents that interact with each other. Each agent is dedicated to a specific task. The model used defines a society of agents with complementary skills. The agents are built according to the architecture presented in figure 2. Each agent receives data from another agent operating under a point to point communication mode. There are six types of agents:

- *Search Agent.* Takes a user query as input and presents responses to these queries based on input from the Ranking agent.
- *Retrieval agent:* The retrieval agent accepts the query string from the search agent and retrieves the relevant documents from the catalogue index (called PWF Index) which is a high efficiency signature file structure. The retrieval agent co-operates with the User agent in order to feed the appropriate data to the Ranking agent.
- *User Agent:* this agent access information about the user (his profile), determines the community in which he belongs and returns a set of weights for all products retrieved by the Retrieval agent. This information is then passed to the Ranking agent.
- Ranking Agent: the ranking agent combines the returned list of products from the Retrieval agent with the corresponding weights provided by the User agent. The output is a ranked list of links to product pages.
- *Catalogue Agent:* the catalogue agent works offline (that is not during a query) for the reconstruction of thumbnail pages. Based on information provided by the user agent, thumbnail pages are reconstructed and reordered based on the preferences of all user communities. For this purpose a global community weight is extracted, and links to the most popular are placed in the top thumbnail pages.
- *Marketing Agent:* the marketing agent monitors the preferences of communities of users and performs a variety of promotion actions in order to increase sales. For

example the Marketing agent uses mail messages to inform identified groups of users about special offers in products similar to their recorded preferences or suggests new sales.

The agents interact with each other by exchanging messages according to a point to point communication mode. Messages are represented as cards that respect an interaction structure. This structure identifies the sender, the receiver, the nature and the data of the message. There are two different ways by which agents are linked to perform complicated tasks:

- *Succession*: the output of an agent is used as input to another agent. For example the User agent provides information (the member of the identified user communities) to the Marketing agent.
- *Validation*: several agents provide information about the same event (e.g. the query of a specific user) and their input is combined in a single output. For example the output of the User and Retrieval agents are combined by the Ranking agent to form the final result set.

3.1 The Search Agent

The Search agent provides the user interface by presenting a set of information retrieval options such as search, result set expansion, categorisation and ranking through personalisation. The user explicitly invokes all but the latter service via user interface operations. More specifically:

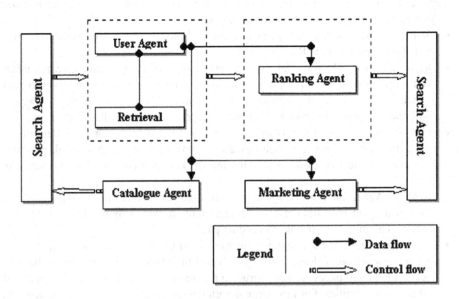

Fig. 2. The agent community.

- Search. Prunes the current result set to the retrieved file records and web page documents that match the given query. The Retrieval agent in invoked and relevant web pages are accessed through the PWF index.
- Expand. Broader and narrower terms are suggested by a thesaurus -based query refinement mechanism. Broader terms represent general concepts (product categories or commonly used keywords) related to the terms in the query and are expected to improve the quality of the result set. They provide a means of exploring the available dataspace. Narrower terms can improve precision by allowing specialisation of queries. The thesaurus mechanism is based on the automatic construction of thesaurus classes modified to consider categories of web pages (that is categories of products) rather than web pages themselves.
- Result set categorisation. To help potential customers to better understand the result set, the agent provides the option of categorisation of the result set. The agent organises and presents the result set web pages according to the categories that they belong to. Web pages with products that belong to the same categories (e.g. Christmas cards with Santa Claus) can be placed together in the user screen.

Each time a user visits the on-line shop for the first time, a personal record is created which stores all available user information. In the case of registered users personal information is requested and stored. In the case of unregistered users, information such as IP address, domain information etc is stored. All user transactions are logged and stored in a separate database for various purposes (personalisation, marketing analysis etc.).

3.2 Accelerating Document Filtering and Retrieval

Filtering and retrieval is based on an index structure that is based on a novel, high efficiency signature file method. This method extracts the signatures (hash code bit patterns) of product pages (represented by their set of keywords) and stores them in a two level signature file in order to accelerate retrievals. We use superimposed coding to create the signature of each product page. Each of the keywords yields a "word signature" which is a pattern of size F with m bits set to "1" while the rest are "0". F and m are design parameters. The keyword signatures are "ORed" together to form the page signature as it can be seen in table 1.

Table 1. The superimposed coding method for F =12 and m=5.

Keyword	Signature
"Christmas"	001 010 101 100
"Santa Claus"	101 011 001 000
Web page	**101 011 101 100**
superimposed signature	

The m bit positions to be set to "1" by each word are determined by a hash function. The PWF Index is a multilevel signature file where the web page signatures are grouped into partitions. More specifically the implementation uses the Parametric Weighted Filter technique (PWF) [10]. PWF incorporates the descriptive nature of multilevel organisations (and specifically the two-level organisation) and the partition capabilities of efficient implementation techniques such as Quick Filter [11]. The signature file is partitioned by applying linear hashing. The number of pages that a partition can have is variable and its maximum value is controlled by parameters of the scheme which are directly affected by the desired performance.

Each partition is characterised by a partition key. All signatures in the j-th partition share the same partition key. For each signature in a partition, the index stores its F-l_prefix where F is the fixed signature length, l denotes the current level of hashing and l_prefix the first l bits of the signature.

Every partition is organised using a two level method. The signatures in each partition (figure 4) are grouped randomly into groups of b signatures (b is called the grouping factor), which are called b_groups. Every b_group resides in only one disk page and it is characterised by a representative. A representative consists of two parts: the s_descriptor and the m_descriptor. The s_descriptor is formed by superimposing ('ORing') the signatures of the b_group, whereas the m_descriptor is a [logF] - tuple obtained by using the following procedure. Each signature of the b_group (figure 3) is conceptually divided into [logF] parts each F/[logF] bits long, except for the last one which is F- [F/[logF]([logF]-1) bits long (all logarithms are base-two). Then the i-th component of the m_descriptor is the maximum number of 1's (maximum weight), a signature in the b_group has in its i-th part. All representatives belonging to the same partition are stored into the same partition block. On the other hand, every partition block contains representatives of the same partition (consequently there is one to one correspondence between partitions and partition blocks). For each partition block (and therefore partition), there is auxiliary information stored in the main memory in the form of b_descriptor. A b_descriptor is formed by applying the same procedure followed in the case of m_descriptors but this time on the m_descriptors of the involved partition block, that is all signatures belonging to that partition are taken into account. From an abstract point of view the index implementation consists of a dynamically changing set of partitions organised as a forest of trees of height 1, with signatures being clustered into partitions by applying linear hashing.

This representation enables the Retrieval agent to efficiently handle information from two sources: the Product database and the PWF index. The Product database stores all available product information (a portion of that information is not available to the users) and the addresses (links) to product web pages. It must be noted database records do not contain images. The agent handles requests to the index from the Search, User and Ranking agents.

The Retrieval agent works as follows: the Search agent provides a set of keywords and logical operators (AND and OR) and the type of operation to be executed (search, expand or categorization). The Retrieval agent translates the query and initiates the appropriate index search sequence. This sequence locates the corresponding products by searching the PWF Index for the given set of keywords. The Index returns pointers

0000	0000	1100	0010
0000	0001	0000	0110
1000	1101	0001	0100
1	3	2	2

Fig. 3. The m_descriptor of a 3_group.

to the records that satisfy the query and the agent generates a initial result set of database records that satisfy the given query.

The basic retrieval algorithm is implemented as follows: given a query q, the Retrieval agent compares the query signature and obtains a set of qualified partitions. This set of partitions is restricted further by using the b_descriptors. Using the m_descriptor and s_descriptor the agent finds the qualified b_groups and fetches the corresponding record from the database. The algorithm is presented below:

```
1     S = {i / i ∧ (l_suffix(q)) = l_suffix(q)}
       p
               /* Obtain potential partitions */


2     S' ={ i ∈ S / b_descriptor(i) ≥ descriptor(q)}
       p          p
               /* Restrict partition set further */


3     S   = {x is a b_group i/ (m_descriptor(x) ≥
       p
       descriptor(q)) ∧ ((s_descriptor ∧ l_prefix(q))=
       l_prefix(q))}                       /*Retrieve all
       corresponding partition blocks*/


4     Return all pages contained in U   (S )
                                     i∈s i
```

During the insertion of a new product, its keywords are defined and the signature s is derived. The agent uses the PWF index in order to locate the partition to which s belongs. The signature s is inserted into the page of the partition with the least representatives. If all pages are full, s is inserted into an overflow area dedicated to the partition (each overflow area has only one representative stored in the partition block) and the number of partitions N is increased by 1. The next step is to reorganise the b_groups of the affected pages so that every page is full (except perhaps the last one). Finally, the descriptors are updated. The Delete algorithm follows similar steps. The Insert algorithm is presented below:

```
1     Find i where i = l_suffix(s)


2     IF pages(i) are full THEN


3     Place s in the overflow area


4     N = N +1
```

5   ELSE

6   Place s into the page with the least number of representatives

7   Reorganise the b_groups

8   Update the descriptors

3.2 A Context Based Method for Query Personalisation

There is an additional source of information that an agent filtering and retrieval system can use in Electronic Commerce transactions and that is the preferences of the users/customers, the opinion of the people that spend money on a e-shop. Users can be grouped into communities based on their preferences. Recommendations (purchases) of customers must be weighted accordingly and taken into account in any decision making process (searching, restructuring marketing etc.).

But how can the User agent distinct user communities, assign community weights and what is the most appropriate method to use this knowledge? We use an adaptation of Kleinberg's algorithm [3] for authoritative pages on the web. This algorithm uses a simple approach to take advantage of user opinions: if web document X has a link to document Y then the author of the X document thinks that Y contains useful information. Using the in-degree (authority score) one can measure the importance or

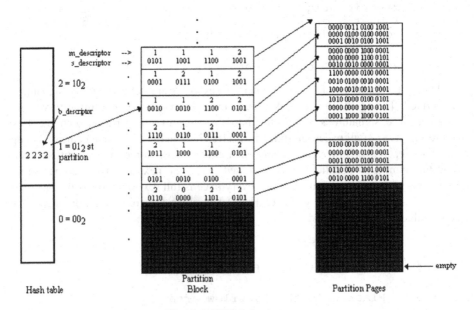

Fig. 4. A PWF index instance.

quality of a web document. Documents like X that point to many others are called hubs and documents that are pointed by many other are called authoritative. The main motivation is that a document that points to many good authorities is a good hub and a document that is pointed by many good hubs is a good authority. This way documents that have relevant information, with regard to a specific query, can be distinguished by their authority score. This algorithm can be used in search engines that retrieve information from the Internet.

In our case, we replace web documents with products and customers that buy them or access their web page. Similarly to Kleinberg's algorithm we associate a customer (hub) weight $cust(p)$ with each customer and a product (authority) weight $pr(p)$ for each product.

The next step is to construct a GxN matrix $A = [a_{ij}]$ which represents the directed graph of figure 5, that is the connection between the ith customer and the jth product. N can be the total number of products or the number of products of a specific category. G is the total number of customers. If customer i has purchased product j then $a_{ij} = 1$ else $a_{ij} = 0$. For every customer and product weight we apply the following update relations:

$$cust(p) = \sum_{p->q} pr(q) \quad , \quad pr(p) = \sum_{q->p} cust(q)$$

Kleinberg proves that after a number of iterations (usually 3-4) cust(p) and pr(p) converge and the algorithm terminates. Customer weights converge to the principal eigenvector of the matrix AA^T and product weights to the principal eigenvector of A^TA. The algorithm is as follows:

1   Let N be the set of products and G the set of customers in the graph.

2   For every node in G define cust(p) as the customer weight and for every node in N define pr(p) as the product weight.

3   Set cust(p) =1 and pr(p)=1.

4   Repeat

5   For every node in G do $cust(p) = \sum_{p->q} pr(q)$

6   For every node in N do $pr(p) = \sum_{q->p} cust(q)$

7   Normalise cust(p) and pr(p)

8   Until cust(p) and pr(p) converge.

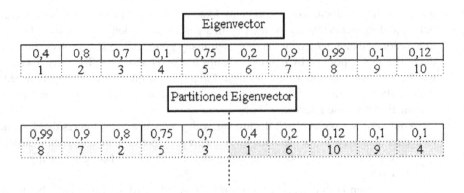

Eigenvector									
0,4	0,8	0,7	0,1	0,75	0,2	0,9	0,99	0,1	0,12
1	2	3	4	5	6	7	8	9	10

Partitioned Eigenvector									
0,99	0,9	0,8	0,75	0,7	0,4	0,2	0,12	0,1	0,1
8	7	2	5	3	1	6	10	9	4

Fig. 6. Partitioning non principal eigenvectors

By taking advantage of the information provided by the non-principal eigenvectors, it is possible to compute pairs of communities (X,Y). Y denotes a community of customers that have similar preferences and X their preferences and therefore the products that they have purchased. Eigenevectors are paired based on an association relationship. Each eigenvector of a pair is divided into two set of entries positive and negative (figure 6). These sets are the X and Y communities. The algorithm for computing these pairs is presented below:

1   Let X_i be the ith non principal eigenvector of $A^T A$

2   Compute Y_k = A * X_i

3   For each pair (X_i , Y_k) do

4   For the eigenvectors X_i ,Y_k

5   Compute pairs (X_i^+, X_i^-) and (Y_k^+, Y_k^-) by partitioning large positive and large negative values.

6   Construct pair (X_i^+, Y_k^+) and (X_i^-, Y_k^-)

7   Select the distinct pairs from all (X_i^+, Y_k^+) and (X_i^-, Y_k^-).

So, for each community of customers (Y) we have a set of values (X) that are actually the product weights *pr(p)* assigned by the community. Each such value is a community weight of a product.

The calculations of customer communities and community weights are performed by the User agent off-line and not during queries (usually during periods with reduced traffic). Each time a query is initiated, the User agent locates the community in which the customer belongs to and retrieves the community weights for the products that are returned by the Retrieval agent. The Ranking agent uses a simple process to order the returned set of products according to their community weights. A set of ranked links is generated and the result is passed to the Search agent for presentation.

3.3 Catalogue Restructuring

Catalogue browsing is also a service adapting to customer needs. When needed, restructuring is applied to the contents of thumbnail pages while the hierarchy of categories and sub-categories remains untouched.

Thumbnail pages appear in a sequential order to the user. The first page contains k links to the k most popular products of the category, the second the next k etc. Each thumbnail page has a fixed position (first, second etc.) in a row and that position never changes. The Catalogue agent continuously monitors customer weights by checking a weight threshold. When customer preferences (product weights) change significantly, then the product representation through the thumbnail pages is not ordered. The threshold is exceeded and the Catalogue agent initiates the reconstruction sequence.

The agent locates the categories or subcategories that must be restructured and reorders the links (figure 7). Thumbnail links, from all pages are retrieved and stored in a binary tree. Ordering is achieved using the total community weight of each product, that is the opinion of all customers for the product. For a total of N customer communities, the total community weight for a product is calculated by the following equation:

$$W = \sum w_i \Big/ N \quad , \quad \text{where } w_i \text{ is the community weight of community } I$$

The ordered set of links is assigned to the thumbnail pages (k per page).
The restructuring algorithm is a heap based process with the following steps (let U be the total number of products of the sub-category):

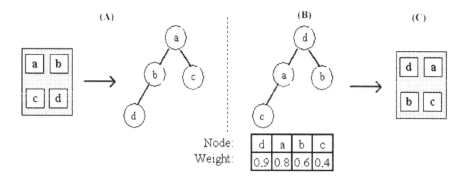

Fig. 7. Assigning links to a binary tree (A), reordering (B) and restoring links (C) for k=4.

1   For each thumbnail page store the link to a binary tree (Root, Left child, right child)

2   For i = 1 to U do

3   Find the link of the product with the largest Total Community Weight and place it at the root by exchanging places with other links in its path.

4   Traverse the tree (Root, Left child, right child) and store links to the thumbnail pages, k at a time.

4 Some Experimental Results

During the prototype implementation, only a portion of the product database was used (10.000 signatures). The page size was 2K with a load factor of about 0.75, pointer size 4 bytes and signature file size (F) 240 bits. The experiment included 1000 queries for various values of the grouping factor. Table 2 shows the experimental results for various values of the ratio of the average query weight L (number of bits of the query signature that are set to 1). From the results the following conclusion is derived: the higher the weights of the query signatures the better the performance of the Retrieval Agent. So this indexing technique is well suited for product catalogues where entries tend to be short and of similar length or multimedia data where items have many attributes with a few distinct values.

Also the vocabulary of products is large making this implementation very competitive in size. Furthermore storage requirements increase with higher values of the grouping factor. These above observations give designers the capability to choose a value suitable for different applications. For example, an implementation with small space and with high retrieval gains requires grouping factor values equal or greater than 4. Early experiments with a larger set of 100.000 signatures have shown that 3_groups are the more appropriate for balancing performance and space overhead.

Table 2. Storage requirements of the index (PWF) expressed in the form of partition pages.

Organisation	L				Storage
	1	*0.2*	*0.4*	*0.5*	
PWF (2_groups)	87.52	58.43	27.85	15.42	341
PWF (3_groups)	124.61	42.50	21.52	13.08	295
PWF (4_groups)	167.87	75.38	19.84	12.30	263

5 Conclusions and Future Work

The amount of information available through Internet based sales systems drives the need for intelligent and adaptive systems. In this paper we presented a multi-agent approach that uses cognitive and social filtering and retrieval methods in order to achieve a balance between time efficiency and quality of results. By incorporating new and adapting existing algorithms, we achieved to develop a framework that covers most needs of a modern information retrieval and filtering system.

Future work includes the development of flexible query mechanisms that can handle queries on both data and relationships. Further research includes new methods for customer clustering and personalisation.

References

[1]   Pyle, R.: Special Issue on Electronic Commerce on the Internet, Comm. of the ACM, vol 39, no6 (1996)
[2]   Adam, N., Yeshua, Y.: Electronic Commerce: Current Research Issues and Application, Springer Verlag, 155 pp. (1996)
[3]   Kleinberg, J.: Authoritative sources in a hyperlinked environment, Proc. ACM - SIAM Symposium on discrete Algorithms (1998)
[4]   Faloutsos, C.: A Survey of Information Retrieval and Filtering Methods, Technical Report CS-TR-3514, University of Maryland (1995)
[5]   Salton, G.: Automatic Text Processing, Reading, MA: Addison-Wesley (1989)
[6]   Zobel, J.R., Moffat, A., Ramamohanarao, K.: Inverted Files Versus Signature Files for Text Indexing, ACM Trans. On Database Systems, Vol. 23, No 4, pp. 863-896 (1998)
[7]   Moukas, A.: Amalthaea: Information Discovery and Filtering using a Multiagent Evolving Ecosystem, Applied Artificial Intelligence: An International Journal, Vol. 11, No. 5, pp. 437-457 (1997)
[8]   Han, S., Boley, D. et al.: WebACE: A Web Agent for Document Categorization and Exploration, Autonomous Agents 98 Conference (1998)
[9]   Fragoudis, D., Likothanassis, S.D.: Retriever: An Agent for Intelligent Information Discovery, Proceedings of the 20th Int. Conference on Information Systems (1999)
[10] Bozanis P., Makris C., Tsakalidis A.: Parametric Weighted Filter: An Efficient Dynamic Manipulation of Signature Files, The Computer Journal, vol. 38, No. 6, pp. 479-488 (1995)
[11] Zezula P., Rabitti F., Tiberio P.: Dynamic Partitioning of Signature Files, ACM Trans. on Inf. Systems, vol. 9, no. 4, pp. 336-367 (1991)

Design and Implementation of a Novel Approach to Keyword Searching in Relational Databases

Ute Masermann and Gottfried Vossen

Information Systems, University of Münster,
D-48149 Münster, Germany**

Abstract. The majority of the tools available for browsing and searching the Web is based on extracting information from *structured* documents. However, as information on the Web increasingly comes out of a database, it is crucial to be able to search *databases* when working with the Web. Due to the highly dynamic nature of the Web, it is unlikely ever to know the underlying schemata of those databases. We remedy this situation by introducing an extension of SQL called *Reflective SQL* (RSQL) which treats data and queries uniformly. Queries are stored in specific *program relations* and can be evaluated by a LISP-like operator called *eval*. Program relations cannot only be constructed for given queries, but their contents can also be generated dynamically based on the current contents of the underlying database. RSQL serves as a basis for a keyword-based search which renders it possible to formulate queries to databases in the absence of schema-knowledge. It is shown how this language can be exploited as a Web search engine that works on databases instead of documents.

1 Introduction

The problem of finding information disseminated over the Web is well-known. The current approach is mostly through keyword-based search engines that operate on suitable indexes. Their usage has shown that even inexperienced users are capable of formulating keyword-based queries to access Web data, and even though these queries may yield inexact results, users are willing to accept this vagueness due to the quick and convenient method of entering queries. However, as more and more Web sites are based on databases and generate their page contents dynamically, it becomes increasingly desirable to query data stored in databases. The language RSQL introduced in this paper serves this purpose, and forms the basis of a novel search tool for the Web.

Most existing search tools for the Web are based on extracting information from structured documents. A major problem is that, although database systems get increasingly employed for serving the Web, it is not possible to query them *directly* over the Web. The way of wrapping the database content in some kind of structured document and then querying those documents seems to be an

---

** Current address of 1st author: Deutsche Börse AG, D-60284 Frankfurt, Germany

J. Štuller et al. (Eds.): ADBIS-DASFAA 2000, LNCS 1884, pp. 171–184, 2000.

artificial technique; besides the fact that there is a vast amount of work in defining the document structure, the major disadvantage is in the loss of the semantics given by a database schema. In this paper, a solution to this problem is described, which renders it possible to formulate keyword-based queries *directly* to databases. We focus on *relational* databases and SQL, so our goal is to embed in this setting a way to query Web-interfaced databases in a declarative fashion.

As a motivating example, consider the situation where information on a particular person is desired; suppose the question of interest is "what is known about John?" (This query has repeatedly been studied in recent years, primarily in the context of database languages that are capable of generating dictionary queries dynamically [12,22].) If we enter the string "John" into the search field of a search engine, we will most likely be flooded with references to Web sites of people, animals, companies, etc. that come by the name "John." If we direct this query to a database where we assume that John is a person, we first have to inspect the dictionary for relations that may contain information about John, such as his address, his profession, or his hobbies. Next, if we direct this query to *two* databases simultaneously, we have to do the same for both database individually. Now suppose we do not have direct access to these databases, but approach them over the Web. In this situation, there is hardly a chance we get access to their respective dictionaries. So the best we can hope for is some form of local index that accepts the keyword "John" and then searches the respective site for relevant information. Several problems immediately arise: First of all, formulating an SQL query requires schema knowledge, which even varies from one database to the next. Also, experience with SQL shows that it is difficult for inexperienced ad-hoc users to deal with relations, attributes, and the syntax of SQL.

A way out of this situation (that bears resemblance with the idea of universal-relation interfaces that were studied in the mid-80s) is to find a way of querying relational databases *without* exact knowledge of the underlying schema. We propose such a way through our novel approach of keyword searching. A keyword expression which returns all facts about John simply looks as follows: `='John'`, i.e., like a common syntax used by search engines. When applied to a specific database, correct SQL statements are generated dynamically from such keyword expressions, using the respective data dictionary. Technically, this dynamic generation of queries is based on an SQL extension called *Reflective SQL*, which extends ordinary SQL by the possibility of handling procedural data. Reflective SQL is in turn a declarative counterpart of the *Reflective Relational Algebra* that was originally described in [22]. It uses a specific *program relation* for storing SQL expressions; program relations can be evaluated by a specific operator added to these languages; moreover, their contents can be created dynamically based on the underlying database or on the dictionary of the database. The keyword expressions are then processed by translating a given expression into Reflective SQL; the resulting expression(s) is/are then evaluated on the underlying databases.

The rest of the paper is organized as follows: We review related work that deals with searching information on the Web in Section 2. Section 3 lays the foundation for our keyword search, by dealing with reflection as a means to extend the query capabilities of SQL. Section 4 introduces a keyword-based query language, intended for accessing relational databases without schema-knowledge. In Section 5 we sketch an exploitation of the keyword search based on RSQL within a Web search engine that has been implemented in Java. The paper concludes with a short summary and directions for future work.

2   Related Work

Work related to ours is concerned with the development of *virtual systems* that integrate data for some specific purpose, and that are characterized by the fact that data always remains in the respective sources, queries get shipped to and operate on the sources, and the integration occurs during query *processing*. The original approach to gathering information on the Web has been through *search engines* like *Alta Vista* or *Yahoo!*, which build indexes of the contents of Web sites, and use techniques from information retrieval to extract keywords from structured HTML documents. A user can query those indexes by using Boolean formulas which contain one or more keywords; the result will be a list of relevant URLs. Due to the diversity of algorithms for extracting information from documents and of strategies for searching Web sites, distinct search engines commonly supply different results. Unlike our approach, no search engine is able to access information that is not stored in a document.

Multidatabase systems combine locally autonomous databases into a new one [4,8]. For querying a multidatabase, a global schema is required which is commonly built through several stages of integrating the local schemas of the underlying databases. Schema integration requires knowledge of all schemata and their semantics, which makes it difficult to exploit in the context of the Web, as Web servers are autonomous information sources without global administration. For being able to cope with schema heterogeneity, it is often left to the user to address individual databases in a federation appropriately when issuing a query. Indeed, multidatabase query languages are typically developed for specific systems [11,16]). *Schema-SQL* [13,21,14] on the other hand allows to query meta data and "ordinary" data in a uniform way, so one can build schema-independent queries. However, the user still has to work with individual tuple, relation, and database variables, so that some experience in database programming is required for being able to use this language.

As an aside, we mention that the problem of accessing database contents over the Web has technically been solved by all major database vendors by specific software. Most of them use HTML templates which are enriched by database queries. The queries are processed when accessing the templates so the user gets the actual data. The obvious disadvantage is the absence of declarative query capabilities.

A final approach to building virtual systems we mention is through *mediated integration systems* [23], which decompose queries according to the sources they wish to address, submit them individually, have them executed at local sites, gather results, and finally present them in a uniform way. Systems in this category include TSIMMIS [5] as well as Web-site management systems such as STRU-DEL [9,10], Araneus [3,20], or WebOQL [2]. These systems have brought along interesting conceptual issues, whose study helps in developing database techniques for the Web. Indeed, query languages like UnQL or LOREL [1] render it possible to query data sources whose structure is irregular, unknown, or hidden in the data itself. As the information available on the Web is also *semi-structured* in this sense, each source has to be described in a specific way before it can participate in an integration system; queries then work on such descriptions. Along similar lines is the approach to designing *webbases* reported in [7].

All known methods for querying heterogeneous data (on the Web, in multi-databases or in semi-structured data sources) are hence based on specific tools, such as schema-integration or a source description in a semi-structured data model. With every change in the underlying data this description has to be adapted appropriately; in the worst case, a new integration needs to be performed. This picture is easier for index servers, which process whatever they find when they perform an access, but they ignore semantic aspects. Finally, languages like Schema-SQL require detailed knowledge of the querying databases.

The language we are about to describe in the remainder of this paper bypasses all of the approaches described above in that (i) no additional or specifically prepared information is needed before a query to a hypothetical collection of databases can be stated, and (ii) semantics that is established in a given database schema is taken into account during query processing. As a result, whether the user works with a multidatabase system or the Web (or both), the language described here allows for a way of querying that retains the style of SQL, while at the same time providing high flexibility and even added expressive power.

3   Reflection and Reflective SQL

We now present the foundations upon which our schema-independent and key-word-based query language is based. We follow a bottom-up approach that first describes the underlying implementation vehicle. In particular, we present *Reflective SQL* (RSQL), a declarative way of making the paradigm of *reflection* available in a database query language. As will be seen, the main emphasis is on the use of meta-programming as a method for schema-independent database querying.

The central idea of *reflection* in the area of programming languages is the uniform treatment of programs and data. For languages which are *not* computationally complete, e.g., the relational algebra or SQL, reflection can enhance their expressiveness considerably. In case of the relational algebra this has been studied in [22], where the *Reflective Relational Algebra* ($\mathcal{RA}$) was introduced. $\mathcal{RA}$ uses particular relations to store queries; these *program relations* are evaluated by a new, LISP-style operator called *eval*. Program relations can be constructed for given queries, and they can be generated dynamically based on the current contents of the database. This makes it possible to show, for example, that bounded looping can be simulated in $\mathcal{RA}$; more generally, $\mathcal{RA}$ is capable of expressing the PTIME queries over ordered databases [22].

There are two drawbacks of $\mathcal{RA}$: First, it is an untyped language, meaning in particular that an evaluation of a program relation yields the empty relation in case the *eval* operator does not encounter a well-formed relational algebra expression; as long as the contents of a program relation is created automatically, however, this is not serious from a practical point of view. Second, programming in $\mathcal{RA}$ amounts to returning to some kind of "assembly-language programming." Indeed, writing even small programs can become a tedious task, so that a declarative counterpart is desirable. Note that this is entirely in line with the classical development that has led from relational algebra (as an implementation vehicle) to SQL (as a declarative query interface).

The result of a "transfer" of the concepts of $\mathcal{RA}$ to SQL is *Reflective SQL* (RSQL), a query language defined in the spirit of [6]: Queries are stored in program relations through an application of the new operator REIFY; the process of constructing data representations of programs and queries, respectively, is called *reification*. Finally, EVAL P evaluates such a program relation P. The following example informally explains the semantics of these new operators, details of which can be found in [18]:

REIFY	P	sno	pos	SQL-op	t1	c1	op	t2	c2	s	n	sno2

P	sno	pos	SQL-op	t1	c1	op	t2	c2	s	n	sno2
	1	1	SELECT	R	A				X		
	1	2	SELECT	S	A						
	1		FROM	R							
	1		FROM	S							
	1	1	WHERE	R	A	=	S	A			
	1	1	WHERE	R	B	>				100	
	1	2	WHERE	S	C	=			Y		

```
REIFY
    (SELECT R.A AS X, S.A
        FROM R, S
       WHERE R.A = S.A
         AND R.B > 100
          OR S.C = 'Y'
    )
    INTO P
```

The RSQL statement on the left reifies the given SQL statement into P. P is a program relation over the fixed scheme {*sno*, *pos*, *SQL-op*, *t1*, *c1*, *op*, *t2*, *c2*, *s*, *n*, *sno2*}. A query is reified straightforwardly: It is decomposed into its individual clauses (e.g., SELECT, FROM, WHERE), whose order is retained via appropriate statement numbers occurring in the first two columns of P; the clauses are identified by the SQL-op attribute. Every clause is then split into individual expressions to arrive at a representation which can be stored in a uniform way. Every expression has at most two tables to which it refers (t1, t2), and the same holds for column names (c1, c2). If the expression contains a condition, the operator is stored in the attribute op. If the second operand is another attribute, it is stored in c2 (possibly with t2 as qualifying table name). If it is a constant numeric value, it is stored in n; finally, a string is stored in s.

The use of attribute pos needs some explanation: In contrast to the expressions of the FROM clause, the sequence of the expressions in the SELECT clause is important because it constitutes the resulting schema. For example, if two relations are united they have to be relations over the same schema (i.e., the names, types *and* the order of the attributes have to be same); so we can assure an ordering using pos as an indicator of the position. In the case of a condition (in the WHERE clause) the position means that all conditions with the same position number are connected with AND, and different numbers indicate that subclauses are connected using OR. More complex conditions like subexpression put in brackets can be reduced to the ones mentioned above, so there is no restriction with respect to SQL expressions.

If more than one statement has to be reified into a single program relation, their ordering is established using the statement number sno that contains strings. The result of such a program is the union of the individual queries; if they do not have the same schema, the result will be the empty relation. Finally, we describe the use of sno2: In the case of nested queries, e.g., subqueries in the WHERE clause or when there are set operations like UNION, these subqueries need to be linked. This is done using sno2 which refers to the statement number sno of the corresponding statement.

The evaluation of a program relation P using the statement EVAL P evaluates the queries stored in P in the order of their statement numbers in column sno. Queries referenced by sno2 are evaluated in conjunction with the referring statement. Moreover, program relations can be queried and manipulated like ordinary relations: Searching all queries that access a specific relation is done by analyzing t1 and t2; selecting B instead of A means changing the corresponding value of c1 in a tuple where SQL-op equals 'SELECT'.

We now return to the motivating example we gave in the Introduction and show how to handle the query "what is known about John" for some database for which we do not provide schema information in the query. The strategy described next by way of this example will be the basis for evaluating keyword expressions as described in the next section. Suppose we are given a database with the following schema:

member	name address age		activity	name sport

We are interested in all facts about "John" that are stored in this database. Using standard SQL, a sequence of query expressions like the following would be needed for finding these facts, provided we know what relations contain which kind of information about persons:

```
SELECT * FROM member   WHERE name = 'John' OR address = 'John';
SELECT * FROM activity WHERE name = 'John' OR sport   = 'John';
```

The result of these SQL queries consists of relations with different schemas. We are more interested in a uniform representation of results and imagine results are returned as triples over attributes {rel, att, value}: rel contains the relation name of a resulting tuple, att marks the corresponding attribute, and value contains the value of this attribute.

We have to cope with the absence of schema-knowledge, and exploit the reflective capabilities of our language to this end: We use the data dictionary to *dynamically* generate queries from a query template. The results of those queries supply the generic schema as shown in the sample result relation above. The data dictionary DD of our sample database is shown below on the left. It contains the names of the relations, their attributes, and the data types of these attributes. The query template is shown on the right:

DD	rel	att	type
	member	name	string
	member	address	string
	member	age	number
	activity	name	string
	activity	sport	string

```
SELECT rel, att, [A] AS value
  FROM DD_View, [R]
 WHERE rel = '[R]'
   AND att  = '[A]'
   AND att1 = '[A1]'
   AND [A1] = 'John'
```

For every relation [R], every attribute [A] of [R], and every alphanumeric attribute [A1] of [R] a concrete query has to be derived from this template. The parameters are instantiated using a view created from the data dictionary; this view contains in each tuple one of the triples [R], [A], [A1] mentioned above. The SQL query deriving the view is as follows:

```
CREATE VIEW DD_View AS
   (SELECT DD.rel, DD.att, DD1.att AS att1 FROM DD, DD DD1
    WHERE DD.rel  = DD1.rel AND DD1.type = 'string')
```

The parameterized query is reified into an auxiliary program relation AP in the style of the one shown earlier. Finally, we are ready to instantiate the different parameters and build the concrete program relation using the view and the auxiliary program relation. An important aspect of dynamically creating program relations is the generation of new statement numbers. In our case this is done by using the unique tuples of the dictionary view: Each tuple serves as the identifier of a query, i.e., attribute sno consists of a concatenation of the attributes of the view in conjunction with the existing sno of the auxiliary program relation.

The concrete program relation is assembled with several subqueries: The first six of the subqueries shown below select the tuples that contain parameters. Each parameter is instantiated with the correct attribute value of the dictionary view while performing a join involving the auxiliary program relation and the dictionary view. With renaming the appropriate attribute of the view the parameter is replaced. Next, all tuples that do not contain a parameter are selected and "multiplied" for every tuple of the data dictionary. Finally, this program relation is evaluated.

```
EVAL (
  SELECT rel||att||att1||sno AS sno,pos,SQL-op,t1,att AS c1,op,t2,
       c2,s,n,sno2 FROM DD_View, AP WHERE c1 = '[A]'
  UNION
  SELECT rel||att||att1||sno AS sno,pos,SQL-op,t1,c1,op,t2,c2,
       att AS s,n,sno2 FROM DD_View, AP WHERE s = '[A]'
  UNION
  SELECT rel||att||att1||sno AS sno,pos,SQL-op,rel AS t1,c1,op,t2,
       c2,s,n,sno2 FROM DD_View, AP WHERE t1 = '[R]'
  UNION
  SELECT rel||att||att1||sno AS sno,pos,SQL-op,t1,c1,op,t2,c2,
       rel AS s,n,sno2 FROM DD_View, AP WHERE s = '[R]'
```

```
UNION
  SELECT rel||att||att1||sno AS sno,pos,SQL-op,t1,att1 AS c1,op,
       t2,c2,s,n,sno2 FROM DD_View, AP WHERE c1 = '[A1]'
UNION
  SELECT rel||att||att1||sno AS sno,pos,SQL-op,t1,c1,op,t2,c2,
       att1 AS s,n,sno2 FROM DD_View, AP WHERE s = '[A1]'
UNION
  SELECT rel||att||att1||sno AS sno,pos,SQL-op,t1,c1,op,t2,c2,
       s,n,sno2 FROM DD_View, AP
     WHERE c1 != '[A]' AND c1 != '[A1]' AND t1 != '[R]'
     AND s  != '[R]' AND s  != '[A]'  AND s  != '[A1]')
```

The part of the concrete program relation referring to the tuple *(member, address, name)* of the data dictionary view is shown next:

sno			pos	SQL-op	t1	c1	op	t2	c2	s	n	sno2
member	address	name	1	1	SELECT		rel					
member	address	name	1	2	SELECT		att					
member	address	name	1	3	SELECT		address		value			
member	address	name	1		FROM	DD_View						
member	address	name	1		FROM	member						
member	address	name	1	1	WHERE		rel	=		member		
member	address	name	1	1	WHERE		att	=		address		
member	address	name	1	1	WHERE		att1	=		name		
member	address	name	1	1	WHERE		name	=		John		

It represents the following SQL query:

```
SELECT rel, att, address AS value FROM DD_View, member
 WHERE rel = 'member' AND att = 'address'
   AND att1 = 'name'   AND name = 'John'
```

Notice that with this RSQL program, i.e., through (i) the statement to create the data dictionary view, (ii) the auxiliary program relation, and (iii) the construction/evaluation of the program relation, we achieve the goal of *schema-independent* querying. None of the three components uses schema-knowledge (besides the data dictionary), so this program can be applied to *any* database to return available facts about John.

If a user wants to query further information, e.g., if the values "John" *and* "Mary" shall both appear in one tuple, a different program has to be constructed. In addition, the user needs detailed knowledge about SQL, program relations, and meta-programming. Therefore RSQL itself is inconvenient for ad-hoc-users as a means for schema-independent querying. This motivates to extend the technique of parameterized queries and parameter instantiation to a more complex keyword search defined in the next section.

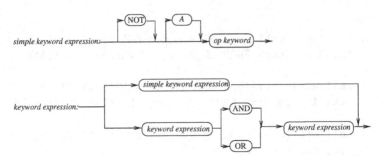

$op \in \{=, \texttt{LIKE}, <, >, <=, >=\}$, A is an attribute name and *keyword* has a data type known to the database.

Fig. 1. Syntax of keyword expressions.

4 Keyword Searching in Relational Databases

We now introduce an easy-to-use, yet powerful way of querying relational databases using keyword-based search. The syntax of keyword expressions follows the syntax of those Boolean expressions used as an interface for many of the search engines. During processing, expressions are transformed into RSQL programs, essentially along the lines exemplified in the previous section.

Our keyword search uses simple keywords combined with a preceding comparison operator. The sample query "what is known about john?" can be expressed by = 'John', i.e., all tuples are returned where at least one attribute equals 'John'. Other comparison operators may be LIKE, <, >, >= and >= with the obvious meaning. If attribute names of a schema are known, they can be used to indicate that *this* attribute has to comply with the given condition. Placing NOT in front of a simple keyword expression means that *none* of the attributes (of the same tuple) should meet the condition that follows. Two or more keyword expressions may be combined using Boolean AND and OR. The complete syntax is shown in Figure 1. We give some examples next:

1. = 'John' represents the query "what is known about John" that we have seen already.
2. NOT = 'John' AND > 35 returns all tuples where none of the attributes takes the values 'John' and another attribute of the same tuple has a value greater than 35. In our example database none of the tuples of the relation *activity* can meet the latter condition because there is no numerical attribute, so no query should be generated for this relation.
3. name like 'M%' means all tuples of those relations which have an attribute named 'name' whose value begins with 'M'.
4. = 'running' OR = 'rowing' AND NOT = 'Mary' results in all tuples with at least one attribute which takes one of the values 'running' or 'rowing' but where no attribute takes the value 'Mary'.

We now show how keyword expressions are transformed into RSQL programs, where we again follow the basic building blocks of their structure (see [18] for more details):

— *op keyword*: The transformation of this expression has been shown earlier with = as the comparison operator *op* and 'John' as keyword.
— *A op keyword*: In case the attribute name to be queried is known, the transformation becomes easy: the dictionary view contains all relation names and their corresponding attribute names which have an attribute *A*. It is no longer necessary to keep the attribute to be queried as an additional attribute in the view.
— NOT *A op keyword*: Placing NOT in front of a simple keyword expression with known attribute *A* only changes the operator to its negation. The dictionary view as well as the query template and the SQL statement for the generation of the concrete program relation remain the same as above.
— NOT *op keyword*: In contrast to *op keyword*, where a query is generated for each attribute which may satisfy the condition, we now have to generate *one* query whose WHERE clause contains *all* attributes in question.

As an example of the latter case, consider the expression NOT = 'John'; for which the query now looks as follows:

```
SELECT rel, att, name AS value FROM DD_View, member
 WHERE rel   = 'member' AND att      = 'name'
   AND name != 'John'    AND address != 'John'
```

That means that the last two rows of the query template shown earlier have to be handled in a different way than before: Row AND att1 = '[A1]' will be dropped whereas the last one has to be "multiplied" (and instantiated with the correct attribute name) with the number of attributes in question. We use a second data dictionary view *DD_View_NOT* to gather the relevant attributes for the last row. View *DD_View* is built like before (see *op keyword*), except that is does not contain an additional attribute *att1*. The two queries which establish both views are shown next.

```
CREATE VIEW DD_View_NOT AS          CREATE VIEW DD_View AS
 (SELECT DD.rel, DD.att              (SELECT DD.rel, DD.att
    FROM DD                             FROM DD);
  WHERE DD.type = type_of_keyword);
```

Notice that in this simple case *DD_View* contains the entire data dictionary — and we might use the original table — but as we will see during the transformation of complex expressions it will have to be restricted further.

We now look at the transformations relevant to complex keyword expressions. For every clause of a given *disjunction* the respective transformations to RSQL programs are performed, i.e., there are several data dictionary views and auxiliary program relations. One concrete program relation is generated for them so that the results of the subexpressions will be united.

Basically, transforming *conjunctions* may be done straightforwardly like for disjunctions: The individual expressions involved are transformed; after the evaluation of the program relations the intersection of their results is built. However, building the intersection of many sets with many tuples is costly and should therefore be avoided if possible. Furthermore it is unnecessary to generate queries which yield the empty set, e.g., for expressions like = 'John' AND NOT = 'John'. The same holds in case of tautologies where all tuples of all relations are building the result (e.g., =\,'John' OR NOT\,=\,'John'). These problems are solved with a parser which analyzes the Boolean expression in advance.

Another example is a conjunction where n different keywords (of the same type) are involved in the sense that n attributes are necessary to meet the complete expression: No queries have to be generated for relations with less than n attributes of this type. We have shown one example in the beginning of the section: Relation *activity* does not have a numerical attribute, so the expression >35 should not generate any query for this relation. On the other hand, one has to distinguish other cases, e.g., the expression LIKE '%a%' AND like '%r%' can be satisfied by only one alphanumerical attribute.

We next have to cope with the problem of reducing unnecessary queries by reducing the number of tuples contained in the data dictionary view: For every expression e_i of the form *op keyword* which appears in the conjunction a new attribute att_i is appended to the data dictionary view performing an appropriate join:

```
CREATE VIEW DD_View AS
    (SELECT DD.rel, DD.att, DD_1.att AS att_1,... DD_i.att AS att_i...
        DD_n.att AS att_n... FROM DD, DD DD_1,... DD DD_i..., DD DD_n
    WHERE DD.rel = DD_1.rel AND ... DD.rel = DD_i.rel AND...
        DD.rel = DD_n.rel AND DD_1.type = type_of_keyword_1 ...
    AND DD_i.type = type_of_keyword_i ...
    AND DD_n.type = type_of_keyword_n)
```

Though the execution of this view definition seems costly due the many joins, it is much cheaper to perform those joins (which involve only the tuple of the data dictionary, i.e., be far less than the "data tuples") than performing the previously discussed intersections. The query template is also expanded by AND [A_i] op keyword AND Att_i = '[A_i]' and for the instantiation of those additional parameters the correct subselects have to be formulated correspondingly.

5   Implementation of a Web Database Search Engine

We now sketch our implementation. Our prototypical system, whose overall architecture is shown in Figure 2, is written as a Java applet using JDBC to connect to relational databases. It uses a Web/JDBC connection to query heterogeneous databases without schema knowledge. A user can enter keyword expressions which are then processed by the underlying RSQL/Java system. The SQL statements generated are passed to the JDBC driver manager using JDBC methods

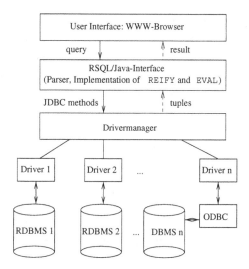

Fig. 2. Architecture of the RSQL/Java system.

so that all the connected databases are queried via their system-specific JDBC drivers. We mention that not only relational databases can be queried using JDBC, but any database having an ODBC interface; the only requirement for integrating a new database into this environment is the availability of this driver.

Keyword search assumes a data dictionary named DD with the attributes mentioned in the previous sections. Note that even though there is a data dictionary in every relational database, their naming and schemata do not follow uniform conventions. However, it is possible through specific JDBC methods of the package `java.sql` to obtain the relevant meta data from the different database systems in such a way that the required dictionary DD can uniformly be created. The problem of type safety in the generic schema (i.e., attribute `value` contains alphanumeric as well as numeric data) can also be solved with a JDBC method: The `ResultSet` which contains the resulting tuples of a query provides the method `getString` which converts every data value of the different attributes to a string value. This is sufficient for our goal of *querying* databases; if the values returned by a keyword query should be used for a subsequent calculation one has to find other ways of treating them appropriately.

The user interface of the search engine essentially has a query as well as a message field, where the former takes user input in the form of keyword expressions, and the latter indicates the database to which a user is currently connected. To which databases the client will connect is fixed by a user configuration file. Our system can be integerated with "ordinary" search engines, so that the result can be used as another search engine that accesses data stored in Internet databases. So far we have concentrated on querying the "original" data stored in databases and not the ones wrapped in structured documents. However, if the result should be presented as a structured document rather than a simple set of tuples, a reasonable extension to our prototype would be a wrapper that can cast results into that form. Note that this will be done *after* query execution so the database semantics will be preserved during the search. Another extension would be the exploitation of information retrieval techniques in the context of the keyword search in databases [15,17]: we would have to add ranking functions, do some linguistic work and define ontologies or thesauri to consider if documents (or more general: data) are related.

6   Conclusions

In this paper, we have presented a novel technique of querying databases by means of a keyword search. Importantly, our keyword search exploits reflection, which has recently been identified as a means to augment the expressive power of traditional relational query languages. In particular, languages such as the Reflective Algebra [22] or the more recent Reflective SQL [6,18] are able to generate database queries based on the contents of the underlying database itself. We here exploit this feature, among other things, for generating dictionary queries on the fly; this yields schema information which is then integrated into a dynamically generated ordinary database query implementing a given keyword expression.

Situations where keyword search is relevant typically arise in the context of the Web when searching for information that is kept in databases which in turn are connected to the Internet. Our approach is among the first to directly access database systems over the Web; moreover, our preliminary experience shows that even novice users can easily handle the language and the interface we have built for it. Since any number of databases can be addressed in one stroke, an application beyond Web searching is multidatabase access, a problem that has previously required complex query translation algorithms going through a hierarchy of schema layers.

An extension of the work described in this paper appears in [19]. There, we put another layer of abstraction atop RSQL, which contains a "stripped-down" version of SQL that is *schema-independent*, i.e., essentially can do without a `from` clause and can do without attribute knowledge. Schema-Independent SQL (SISQL) is a way to circumvent a search engine, and to query databases connected to the Web directly through a browser interface. SISQL queries are mapped to RSQL queries and then processed in the way described in this paper. A net effect of introducing this additional layer is that query results obtained from SISQL are often more precise than those obtained from RSQL.

Another extension of the work reported in this paper would be to base the approach on XML-DTDs [1] instead of data dictionaries; this would render it possible to generate relational schemas out of DTDs and subsequently generate correct database queries from RSQL queries in a dynamic fashion.

References

1. S. Abiteboul, P. Buneman, D. Suciu. *Data on the Web*. Morgan Kaufmann, 2000.

2. G. O. Arocena and A. O. Mendelzon. WebOQL: Restructuring Documents, Databases, and Webs. In *Proc. 14th ICDE*, 24–33, 1998.
3. P. Atzeni, G. Mecca, and P. Merialdo. Design and Maintenance of Data-Intensive Web Sites. In *Proc. 6th International Conference on Extending Database Technology (EDBT)*, 436–450, 1998.
4. O. A. Bukhres and A. K. Elmagarid. *Object-Oriented Multidatabase Systems*. Prentice-Hall, 1996.
5. S. S. Chawathe, H. Garcia-Molina, J. Hammer, K. Ireland, J. Papakonstantinou, Y. Ullman, and J. Widom. The TSIMMIS Project: Integration of Heterogeneous Information Sources. In *Proc. 10th Meeting of the Information Processing Society of Japan (IPSJ)*, 7–18, 1994.
6. M. Dalkilic, M. Jain, D. Van Gucht, and A. Mendhekar. Design and Implementation of Reflective SQL. TR451, Indiana University, Computer Science, 1996.
7. H. Davulcu, J. Freire, M. Kifer, and I. V. Ramakrishnan. A Layered Architecture for Querying Dynamic Web Content. In *Proc. ACM SIGMOD*, 491–502, 1999.
8. A. K. Elmagarid, M. Rusinkiewicz, and A. Sheth (eds.). *Management of Heterogeneous and Autonomous Database Systems*. Morgan Kaufmann, 1998.
9. M. Fernandez, D. Florescu, J. Kang, A. Levy, and D. Suciu. STRUDEL: A Web-Site Management System. In *Proc. ACM SIGMOD*, 549–552, 1997.
10. M. Fernandez, D. Florescu, A. Levy, and D. Suciu. Web-Site Management: The Strudel Approach. *IEEE Data Engineering Bulletin*, 21(2):14–20, 1998.
11. J. Grant, W. Litwin, N. Roussopoulos, and T. Sellis. Query Languages for Relational Multidatabases. *The VLDB J.*, 2(2):153–171, 1993.
12. L. V. S. Lakshmanan, F. Sadri, and I. N. Subramanian. On the Logical Foundations of Schema Integration and Evolution in Heterogeneous Database Systems. In *Proc. 3rd DOOD*, 81–100, 1993.
13. L. V. S. Lakshmanan, F. Sadri, and I. N. Subramanian. SchemaSQL – A Language for Interoperability in Relational Multi-Database Systems. In *Proc. 22nd VLDB*, 239–250, 1996.
14. L. V. S. Lakshmanan, F. Sadri, and I. N. Subramanian. On Efficiently Implementing SchemaSQL on an SQL Database System. In *Proc. 25th VLDB*, 271–282, 1999.
15. S. Lee. An Extended Relational Database Model For Uncertain And Imprecise Inormation. In *Proc. 18th VLDB*, 211–220, 1992.
16. W. Litwin, L. Mark, and N. Roussopoulos. Interoperability of Multiple Autonomous Databases. *ACM Computing Surveys*, 22(3):267–293, 1990.
17. C. Lynch. Nonmaterialized Relations and the Support of Information Retrieval Application by Relational Database Systems. *J. American Society for Information Science*, 42(6):389–398, 1991.
18. U. Masermann. *Schema-independent Query Languages for Relational Databases*. Ph.D. thesis (in German). infix, DISDBIS No. 60, 1999.
19. U. Masermann, G. Vossen. SISQL: Schema-Independent Database Querying (on and off the Web). To appear in *Proc. 4th IDEAS*, Yokohama 2000.
20. G. Mecca, P. Atzeni, A. Masci, P. Merialdo, and G. Sindoni. The Araneus Web-Base Management System. In *Proc. ACM SIGMOD*, 544–546, 1998.
21. R. J. Miller. Using Schematically Heterogeneous Structures. In *Proc. ACM SIGMOD*, 189–200, 1998.
22. J. Van den Bussche, D. Van Gucht, and G. Vossen. Reflective Programming in the Relational Algebra. *JCSS*, 52(3):537–549, 1996.
23. G. Wiederhold. Mediators in the Architecture of Future Information Systems. *IEEE Computer*, March:38–49, 1992.

A Rule-Oriented Architecture to Incorporate Dissemination-Based Information Delivery into Information Integration Environments

Hironori Mizuguchi[1]*, Hiroyuki Kitagawa[2],
Yoshiharu Ishikawa[2], and Atsuyuki Morishima[2]

[1] Doctoral Degree Program in Engineering, University of Tsukuba
[2] Institute of Information Sciences and Electronics, University of Tsukuba
1-1-1 Tennoudai, Tsukuba, Ibaraki, 305-8573, Japan
{hironori,kitagawa,ishikawa,mori}@dblab.is.tsukuba.ac.jp,
WWW page: http://www.dblab.is.tsukuba.ac.jp/projects/kde/

Abstract. Integration of heterogeneous information sources has been one of important research issues in recent advanced application environments. Today, various types of information sources are available. Dissemination-based information delivery services that autonomously deliver information from the server sites to users are among the useful and promising information sources. In this paper, we present incorporation of dissemination-based information delivery into information integration environments. The integration here has two goals: (1) Users can utilize dissemination-based information services as other information sources such as databases and the Web. Namely, they can be sources of information integration. (2) Users can obtain integrated information through dissemination-based delivery. We explain this requirement can be met by a combination of an information integration engine and event-driven rule processing scheme. We also explain prototype system development.

1 Introduction

The recent development of network technology has enabled us to access various information sources easily. Due to the need for the integration facility of heterogeneous information sources, *information integration* (*mediation*) has been one of important research issues in advanced application environments [3,4,6,7,8,9,12,13,14,18]. An information integration system provides an environment by which information in heterogeneous sources, such as relations in RDBs, structured documents in document repositories, and Web servers, can be uniformly treated. Most of the existing information integration systems are based on the *mediator/wrapper* paradigm [18,23], where information sources are "wrapped" so that uniform interfaces are provided to the mediator. A mediator integrates such information sources and provides mediation services.

Although the recent development of technology has made it possible to integrate existing heterogeneous information sources, we still have to cope with a new kind of information source—*dissemination-based information services* [5,11,17,20]. Dissemination-based information services that deliver information directly to the users are considered

---

* Current affiliation: NEC Corporation

J. Štuller et al. (Eds.): ADBIS-DASFAA 2000, LNCS 1884, pp. 185–199, 2000.

to be useful and promising information sources. In dissemination-based information services, servers actively deliver information to the clients. Therefore, the users can receive up-to-date information automatically, and do not have to worry about where the information services are located or when they are updated. Since the current dissemination-based information services use various information delivery methods such as the Internet and wireless data broadcasting, information integration systems that incorporate dissemination-based information services have to take their characteristics into account and deal with various information delivery methods.

We identify the following two types of features that information integration systems incorporating dissemination technology should provide, and integrate them into our unified framework.

1. *Integration of dissemination-based services*: Users can use dissemination-based services via an information integration system without considering their dissemination-based nature. Namely, they can regard the dissemination-based services as conventional information sources such as databases and Web servers.
2. *Dissemination-based delivery of the integrated information*: Users can access an information integration system as if the system is a dissemination-based information service. Namely, they can obtain the integrated information through the dissemination service.

The former enables user-specified selection of the delivered information incoming from diverse dissemination-based information services and integration of dissemination-based services with other information sources such as relations in RDBs and documents on the Web. The latter enables effective information delivery of the integrated results from the integration system based on the timing requirement specified by the users. Using these facilities, we can access integrated information efficiently and can construct value-added applications more easily. For example, it is possible to extract interesting portions from the disseminated information, integrate them with existing information sources such as relational databases, and then periodically deliver the integrated results to the users using the dissemination facility.

Needless to say, the above two features are independent inherently. However, both require "active" features such as event handling, support for timing constraints, and dynamic rule invocation to integrate and deliver information. In this research, we realize these features by adding ECA rule [15,24] handling function to an information integration system *InfoWeaver* [7,13]. *InfoWeaver* has been developed in our research group, and is based on the mediator/wrapper paradigm. In this paper, we introduce *wrapping facility* for dissemination-based information services, a *dissemination subsystem*, and an *ECA rule subsystem* into the current *InfoWeaver* system. Features provided by the wrapping facility and the ECA rule subsystem make it possible to integrate dissemination-based information services. Also, we can deliver integrated results using the ECA rule subsystem and the dissemination subsystem.

The remaining part of this paper is organized as follows. In Sect. 2, we explain the notion of dissemination-based information services, and show a motivating example to integrate dissemination-based information services. The overview of our approach is shown in Sect. 3. Section 4 describes the *InfoWeaver* system. Section 5 introduces three new features, the wrapping facility for dissemination-based information services, the dissemination subsystem, and the ECA rule subsystem. Section 6 illustrates specification of information integration in our prototype system using the motivating example in Sect. 2. Section 7 discusses the related works. Finally, Section 8 presents the conclusion.

2   Integration of Dissemination-Based Information Sources

2.1   Dissemination-Based Information Sources

In this section, we first introduce the notion of *dissemination-based information services*, on which this research is based. A dissemination-based information service actively delivers information such as news articles to the clients so that the users can obtain the latest information without any efforts. An information dissemination system generally provides multiple information dissemination services (e.g., a stock price news and a product information delivery service). In the following, we sometimes call each information dissemination service a *channel*. We also use the term *dissemination-based information source*, when we regard a dissemination-based information service as an information source.

We can characterize each dissemination-based information service (channel) from the following three viewpoints. First, we can classify information dissemination services according to the types of data they deliver. For example, PointCast [17] mainly uses HTML documents for its service. Castanet [11] can deliver binary data such as Java programs in addition to documents. Second, we can characterize a dissemination-based information service by the granularity of the delivered data items (e.g., a document, a set of documents, and so on). We call the granularity of the data sent at an information delivery event a *delivered item*. Third, we can use delivery methods to classify dissemination services; current dissemination services use a variety of delivery methods such as e-mails, delivery based on the Internet technology, and data broadcasting using electric waves.

2.2   Motivating Example

As described in Sect. 1, our goal in this paper is to incorporate information dissemination features into an existing information integration system *InfoWeaver*. The enhanced *InfoWeaver* system will have two types of additional facilities: (1) integration of channels (dissemination-based services) as information sources, and (2) dissemination-based delivery of the integrated information. The next motivating example is based on the above two additional features and used throughout this paper.

Figure 1 illustrates our motivating example. We assume that there exist two channels:

1. *Product information news channel*: This channel periodically sends new product information to the clients using e-mails. It uses XML [22] as its news document format.
2. *Stock price information feed channel*: This channel provides the latest stock price information over the Internet. The delivery of stock price information is not periodic (i.e., irregular), and the delivery is performed on a per-company base. Namely, it sends a record that consists of a company name, its category of business, and its current stock price on each delivery.

In addition to these channels, we assume the existence of the following information source:

3. *Stockholder database*: For each stockholder, the information of the stock items that he or she owns is managed in a relational table. A tuple in the relational table contains information such as the company name, the purchase price, the number of stocks, and a threshold value specified by the owner (described below).

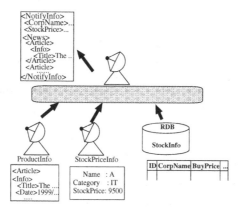

Fig. 1. Motivating Example

To show an information integration example, suppose a user owns stocks of companies in the IT (information technology) category, and their information is managed in the stockholder database. Assume that the user has the following demands:

– When a new stock price for an IT category company has arrived, check it and send a notification to the user if it exceeds its *threshold value*. The threshold value is specified by the user for each IT stock item and stored as an attribute value in the stockholder database table.
– The notification should include the product information of the company, extracted from the product information news articles within the last one week, and the stock item information for the company, which is stored in the stockholder database table.

To satisfy the above demands, we need to provide a unified framework that has the following functions to:

1. Detect an event such that a new stock price has arrived.
2. Access the underlying information sources (e.g., databases), check whether the specified condition is satisfied or not, and trigger a dissemination process if the condition is satisfied.
3. Archive the delivered items (e.g., product information news articles) while they have the possibilities of use, and extract the specified portions from them on demand.
4. Integrate information obtained from multiple information sources (including channels), and deliver the integrated result to the user based on the specified method.

In the next section, we describe our approach to realize these functions.

3   Overview of Our Approach

3.1   Requirements and Our Approach

As described in the previous section, the aim of this research is to extend an existing information integration system by incorporating the information dissemination function and to provide two new features: integration of dissemination-based information sources and dissemination-based delivery of the integrated information. The required additional facilities to realize the goals and the approaches adopted in this research are as follows:

1. *Wrapping facility for dissemination-based information sources*: The information integration system used in this research (*InfoWeaver*) is based on the mediator/wrapper paradigm, which is commonly used in various information integration systems. We also employ this paradigm to incorporate dissemination-based information sources and provide the wrapping facility. A wrapper for a dissemination-based information source "wraps" the non-essential details of the source and provides a uniform interface for the mediator. Besides, the wrapping facility has an additional function to provide a common abstract interface for dissemination-based information sources, such as an event generation function to support the notification service.
2. *Dissemination-based delivery of the integrated information*: To support this facility, we introduce a dissemination subsystem that delivers the integrated information to the user based on the specified delivery method.
3. *Event and time management*: An event generation and processing function is required to support the notification service. In our approach, a wrapper for a dissemination-based information source generates arrival events[1], and they are handled in the rule processing facility described below. In addition, the event facility is also used in the *timer module*. It generates timer events according to the given timer specification to trigger information delivery such as sending information at a specified time and periodic delivery.
4. *ECA rule processing*: To specify the processing instructions for targeted events, the enhanced *InfoWeaver* system allows *ECA rule-based declarative descriptions* of event handling. ECA rules are commonly used in active databases [15,24] and consist of event, condition, and action parts. Specified ECA rules are handled in the *rule subsystem*.

3.2   System Architecture

The system architecture enhanced to incorporate information dissemination features is shown in Fig. 2. The core of the architecture is the *InfoWeaver* information integration system based on the mediator/wrapper paradigm. We have introduced additional modules such as the wrapping facility for dissemination-based information sources, the dissemination subsystem, and the rule subsystem to extend *InfoWeaver*'s basic functions.

Using the motivating example shown in Subsect. 2.2, we briefly illustrate the function of each subsystem.

---

[1] Our model can easily be extended to allow wrappers of any type to generate events depending on states of the underlying information sources.

1. When a new stock price has arrived, the wrapper for the stock price information feed channel detects the arrival as a new event, and notifies the event to the rule subsystem.
2. The rule subsystem invokes the ECA rule corresponding to the notified event, and sends a query to the mediator to evaluate the condition part of the rule to check whether the company belongs to the IT category and whether the price exceeds the threshold value.
3. If the condition part is satisfied, the rule subsystem issues another query to the mediator to integrate the user's stock information about the company and the the product news articles on the company delivered within the last one week.
4. The mediator processes the query to integrate information. When its query processing is finished, the mediator notifies the completion to the rule subsystem.
5. Then, the rule subsystem orders the dissemination subsystem to deliver the integrated result to the user.
6. The dissemination subsystem receives the integrated result from the mediator, transforms it into an appropriate format, and then delivers it to the user.

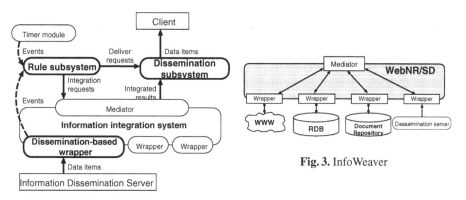

Fig. 2. System Architecture

Fig. 3. InfoWeaver

4   InfoWeaver

In this section, we describe the core part of the system, the *InfoWeaver* information integration system. *InfoWeaver* can integrate heterogeneous information sources such as relational databases, structured documents (XML and SGML), and Web pages (Fig. 3). Information integration in *InfoWeaver* is performed based on its common data model *WebNR/SD*. In the following, we introduce some notions and terminology related to this paper. See [7,12] for more details.

4.1   WebNR/SD Data Model

Figure 4 illustrates data representation in the common data model WebNR/SD. *WebNR/SD* is based on the *nested relational data model* [19] and provides nested relational algebra operators shown in Fig. 5. A feature of WebNR/SD is that it provides an abstract data type, called *SD type* (*Structured Document type*), to store and manipulate structured documents such as XML, SGML, and HTML. An instance of SD type is called an *SD value* and treated as an attribute value in a nested relation. An SD value consists of a DTD (Document Type Definition) representing the document structure and a structured document (e.g., XML) that conforms to the DTD (Fig. 4). WebNR/SD provides a selection operator to manipulate SD values and converter operators (described below) to transform SD value structures. In addition, WebNR/SD has special SD values to represent Web link structures. It enables navigation and manipulation of Web data.

Data integration in the mediator is based on WebNR/SD, and wrappers translate data in the underlying sources into nested relations which may contain SD values. The mediator can maintain temporary relations to store intermediate integration results if necessary.

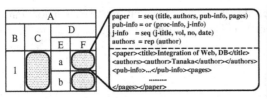

Selection	$\sigma_p(r)$
Projection	$\pi_{A_1, \ldots, A_n}(r)$
Cartesian product	$r_1 \times r_2$
Nest	$\nu_{A=(B_1, \ldots, B_m)}(r)$
Unnest	$\mu_A(r)$
Union	$r_1 \cup r_2$
Difference	$r_1 - r_2$

Fig. 4. Data Representation in WebNR/SD (right: an SD value)

Fig. 5. Nested Relational Algebra Operators

4.2 Converter Operators

WebNR/SD provides two *converter operators*, *Unpack* (**U**) and *Pack* (**P**), to attain bi-directional conversion between SD values and nested table structures. Unpack decomposes SD values and constructs nested subrelations. On the other hand, Pack composes SD values by embedding given subrelations into "template" SD values.

The following examples illustrate the usage of Unpack and Pack, where the relations r_1 and r_2 are shown in Fig. 6. We omit DTDs and only present document instances in this figure to simplify the presentation.

$$r_2 := \mathbf{U}_{Articles \to As(O, Article)}(r_1) \tag{1}$$

$$r_1 := \mathbf{P}_{As(O, Article\ as\ x) \to Articles}(r_2) \tag{2}$$

In Eq. (1), Unpack decomposes the SD value in the *Articles* attribute. The resulting relation r_2 contains extracted articles in the *As.Article* attribute. To preserve the original document structures, r_2 contains reference values (e.g., &x.1;) that point the corresponding nested tuples in the *As* attribute. These reference values are called *SD references*. Eq. (2) plays the inverse role and recovers r_1 using the Pack operator. It uses the *Articles* attribute values of r_2 as templates, and embeds each referenced subtuple into the corresponding position.

Composite operators are defined as combinations of the primitive operators. Some composite converters are as follows. They are used for specifying data integration in the motivating example.

Fig. 6. Sample Relations r_1 and r_2

- $\mathbf{U}_{A_i \to (B_1[e_1]\ as\ x_1, ..., B_n[e_n]\ as\ x_n)}$: It is an extended version of Unpack, and represents a sequence of primitive Unpacks. Figure 7 shows an example, where
  $r_4 := \mathbf{U}_{B \to (C[author]\ as\ x,\ D[title]\ as\ y)}(r_3)$.
- $\mathbf{P}_{(A_i, ..., A_j) \to B, G}$: It is an extended version of Pack, and creates new SD values in attribute B using SD values in attributes $A_i, ..., A_j$. $\mathbf{P}_{(C, D) \to B, G}(r_5)$ yields the relation r_3 in Fig. 7.
- $\mathbf{P}_{A_i(D) \to B, G}$: It is another extended version of Pack, and creates new SD values in attribute B using SD values in attribute D. For example, $r_7 := \mathbf{P}_{B(C) \to D, G}(r_6)$ in Fig. 7.

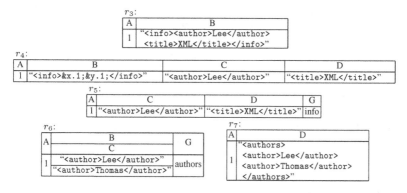

Fig. 7. Composite Operators

5   System Enhancements

In this section, we describe the enhanced portions to incorporate information dissemination features into the *InfoWeaver* system.

5.1   Wrapping Facility for Dissemination-Based Information Sources

A wrapper for a dissemination-based information source translates delivered items into the WebNR/SD model and provides them to the mediator. Also, it generates an arrival event when a new delivered item has arrived. The wrapper provides an abstract uniform interface to the wrapped channel so that every channel in our framework is modeled as a *stream relation*.

Figure 8 illustrates the idea of a stream relation. A *stream relation* is a special kind of relation and holds the latest delivered item. When a new item arrives, the content of a stream relation is totally replaced by the incoming item. A stream relation has an additional attribute *TS* to store the timestamp value of information delivery.

As shown below, some rules are usually specified to process arrival events. They may trigger actions of the mediator to check the contents of the new delivered items and/or to copy them into temporary relations in the mediator for storage and archival.

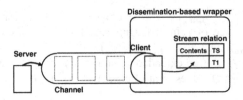

Fig. 8. Stream Relation

5.2 Dissemination Subsystem

The dissemination subsystem receives a delivery request from the rule subsystem, and retrieves the information to be delivered (represented as nested relations which may contain SD values) from the mediator. It converts the obtained information into an appropriate delivery format and then delivers it to the user. To describe delivery specifications, we introduce a new operator, the *delivery specifier* **Deliver**. The following example shows a delivery specification for a relation R.

$$\mathbf{Deliver}_{'MAIL'}(\text{'hiro@x.ac.jp', 'Notify From Rule', } C)[R]$$

It is intended that an e-mail notification is used for delivery, and the content value of attribute C in relation R is delivered. Other parameter values, "hiro@x.ac.jp" and "Notify From Rule", are the destination address and the e-mail subject, respectively.

5.3 Rule Subsystem

In this subsection, we first describe ECA rules used in the system, and then show some examples of rules.

ECA Rule An ECA rule consists of three parts: the event, condition, and action parts. Each part is described below.

Event There are two kinds of events: *primitive event* and *composite event*. The current system allows the following three primitive events:

1. arrival(S): this event notifies an arrival of a new delivered item through the channel S.
2. interval(int): this event represents that the time interval int has passed since the alarm was set; it is used to represent a timer event.
3. alarm(T): this event alarms when it is time T.

A composite event is constructed from primitive events and/or other composite events. Details are omitted here.

Condition The condition part of an ECA rule is evaluated by the mediator when the rule is invoked. We can use any conditions specifiable as a selection condition in the selection operator and a join condition in the join operator in WebNR/SD. For example, the condition $R.Name = 'A'$ becomes true if the *Name* attribute in relation R contains the value A.

Action In the action part, we can use WebNR/SD algebra expressions to specify integration instructions. These expressions are evaluated by the mediator. We can also specify manipulation of temporary relations using notations shown in Fig. 9. They denote assignment of relations and append/deletion of tuples. The action part may include specification of dissemination-based delivery. The delivery specifier Deliver is used for this purpose.

$R_1 := R_2$ Assign relation R_1 to relation R_2.
$R_1 += R_2$ Tuples of R_2 are appended to relation R_1.
$R_1 -= R_2$ Tuples of R_2 are subtracted from relation R_1.

Fig. 9. Additional Notations Allowed in an Action Part

Example of Rules Now we explain how ECA rules are specified. To denote an ECA rule, we use the following syntax: a rule name is specified after the keyword **Rule**, and the event, condition, and action parts are specified in **on**, **if**, and **do** clauses, respectively. We can include multiple actions in a **do** clause, and they are sequentially executed. When an **if** clause is omitted, we assume that the condition true is specified.

First, we show the rule Receiving_ACorpStock:

Rule Receiving_ACorpStock
on: arrival(StockPriceInfo)
if: StockPriceInfo.Name = 'A'
do: SelectA += $\sigma_{Name = 'A'}$(StockPriceInfo);
     SelectA := $\sigma_{TS > now - 1day}$(SelectA);

In this rule, StockPriceInfo plays two roles: the one in the **on** clause represents the stock information feed channel, and these in the **if** and **do** clauses denote the stream relation corresponding to the channel. This rule is invoked when a new item has arrived through the StockPriceInfo channel. Then, we can access the delivered item as a new tuple in the stream relation StockPriceInfo. Actions in the **do** clause are executed when the current StockPriceInfo relation contains a tuple with the value A in attribute *Name* (meaning that the stock price is for the company 'A'). If the condition is met, first, the tuple is appended to the temporary relation SelectA. Then, only tuples delivered within the last 24 hours are selected and maintained in SelectA.

The following rule gives an example of periodic delivery.

Rule Disseminating_ACorpStock
on: alarm(8 am)
do: **Deliver**$_{'DailyStock'('ACorp.', TS, Price)}$[SelectA];

Based on the **on** clause, the action part of this rule is executed at 8 o'clock every morning. The rule sends the latest stock price information accumulated in the temporary relation SelectA, described above, through the DailyStock channel. Namely, the two ECA rules shown here implement the task to send a daily report that contains the stock price information of the company A delivered within the last 24 hours at 8 o'clock every morning.

6   Running Example and Its Implementation

In this section, we show rule specifications for the motivating example in Sect. 2 using the enhanced *InfoWeaver* functions. Then, we describe some implementation details.

6.1   Rule Specifications

Before showing rule specifications, the underlying assumptions are described. First, we assume that the data in the stockholder database is stored in the relation StockInfo, whose schema is shown in Fig. 10. Second, we assume that the documents delivered through the product information news channel are XML documents conforming to the DTD shown in Fig. 11. The wrapper for this channel creates a stream relation whose tuples have SD values corresponding to the XML documents. Third, we assume that the wrapper for the stock price information feed channel encapsulates the channel as a stream relation with the schema shown in Fig. 12. Finally, we assume that the stockholder has the demands of information integration and notification described in Subsect. 2.2.

To specify the integration and delivery requirements, the stockholder writes the first rule in Fig. 13. It archives the news articles delivered within the last one week through the product news information channel. Next, the stockholder specifies the second rule to integrate three information sources and to deliver the integration results using e-mails. In the second rule, delivery is performed only for the companies such that their delivered stock prices are higher than the corresponding threshold values stored in the StockInfo relation.

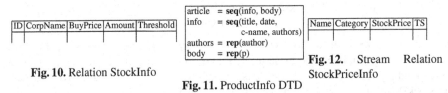

Fig. 10. Relation StockInfo

Fig. 11. ProductInfo DTD

Fig. 12. Stream Relation StockPriceInfo

6.2   Prototype Implementation

We have implemented the additional modules of the enhanced *InfoWeaver* system in Java programming language (the original *InfoWeaver* system is also implemented in Java), and developed an integrated prototype including information sources. Figure 14 shows the screen shot of the prototype system. Along the motivating example, the information sources in the current implementation consist of two dissemination-based information sources and a relational database.

Oracle is used as the underlying relational database system. The mediator uses *JDBCWrapper* to access Oracle relational databases through the JDBC protocol. For the

Rule OneWeekProductNews
  on: arrival(ProductInfo)
  do: `#Archives product information news articles`
      `#within last one week`
    LastOneWeekNews += ProductInfo;
    LastOneWeekNews := $\sigma_{TS > now - 1week}$(LastOneWeekNews);

Rule NotifyStock
  on: arrival(StockPriceInfo)
  if: StockPriceInfo.Category = 'IT'
               $\wedge$ StockPriceInfo.StockPrice > StockInfo.Threshold
  do:`#Integration of three information sources`
    CorpNews :=
        $\mathbf{P}_{ns(News)} \rightarrow$ CorpNews$(\nu_{ns = (News)}(\pi_{C\text{-}name, News}($
        $\mathbf{P}_{(Title, Date, Body)} \rightarrow$ News$(\mu_{cs}($
        $\mathbf{U}_{Info} \rightarrow {}_{(Title, Date, C\text{-}name)}($
        $\mathbf{U}_{Article} \rightarrow {}_{(Info, Body)}$(LastOneWeekNews)))))));
    NotableStockInfo :=
        $\pi_{CorpName, StockPrice, BuyPrice}$(StockInfo
        $\bowtie_{Threshold < StockPrice \wedge CorpName = Name}$ (
        $\sigma_{Category = 'IT'}$(StockPriceInfo)));
    NewsAndStockInfo := $\pi_{NotifyInfo}($
        $\mathbf{P}_{(CorpName, StockPrice, BuyPrice, CorpNews)} \rightarrow$ NotifyInfo$($
        NotableStockInfo$\bowtie_{CorpName = C\text{-}name}$CorpANews);
    `#Delivery of integrated results by e-mails`
    $\mathbf{Deliver}_{Mail('hiro@x.ac.jp', 'StockPrice has changed', NotifyInfo)}$[NewsAndStockInfo];

Fig. 13. Rule Specifications for the Motivating Example

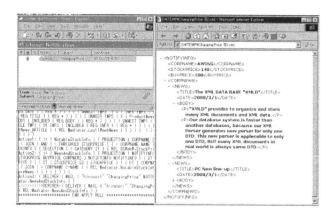

Fig. 14. Screen Shot

product information news channel, we simulated its role by e-mail services. *MailPop-Wrapper* for e-mail-based channels obtains delivered information (e-mails) by the POP protocol. To simulate the stock price information feed channel, we constructed *DS-*

Wrapper. It can handle information feed services that deliver uniform data items over the network, and provides a stream relation view to the mediator. We also implemented the information dissemination facility to deliver integrated information. The current implementation only supports e-mail-based delivery; when the dissemination subsystem obtains integrated information (represented as a relation), it converts the information into text strings and sends it using the SMTP protocol.

The rule subsystem is also implemented in Java[2]. The event handling service in this subsystem works as follows. Given an ECA rule, it analyzes the event part of the rule and generates an *event listener*. If the event is an arrival event, the event listener is registered in the corresponding wrapper that will generate arrival events. If the event is a timer event, the generated event listener is registered in the timer module. When an event occurs, the corresponding event listener notifies the event to the rule subsystem by pushing it into the event queue.

7   Related Works

In this research, we have realized a unified framework that provides the following two features: (1) integration of dissemination-based information sources and (2) dissemination-based delivery of the integrated results. To the best of our knowledge, there is no work that can support both of them.

PointCast [17] and *Castanet* [11], described in Sect. 2, are commercial dissemination-based information services. Although these services can deliver information autonomously to users, they cannot issue queries to extract interesting information from various dissemination-based services.

DBIS [1,2] and *Muffin* [16] aim to extract information from multiple dissemination-based information services. DBIS use a software module called *Information Broker* to access multiple dissemination-based sources transparently and to select information based on user profiles. Muffin can create a new *virtual channel* based on the user profile. An interesting feature of Muffin is its support of multiple rating criteria. To select information from multiple information services, it uses frequency of delivery, freshness, and popularity as well as similarity. In contrast to our approach, these two researches only consider information selection from multiple dissemination-based information sources, and do not support integration of dissemination-based services with other existing information sources.

OpenCQ [10] is an information integration system for distributed heterogeneous information sources. This system is based on the event-driven approach and supports continual queries. A *continual query* consists of three components, a query, a trigger condition, and a termination condition. Whenever a trigger condition such as update in an information source becomes true, this system repeatedly executes the query until the stop condition holds. As a result of the query, the difference between the current query execution and the previous one is reported. This work is related to our approach because it follows an event-based approach and discusses the issue of information integration. However, OpenCQ considers only a particular case of the dissemination-based delivery of the integration results. Moreover, its mediator cannot store integration results. Therefore, OpenCQ cannot support integration of dissemination-based information sources

---

[2] Java-based rule engine shells could have been used as a core engine.

or complex delivery requirements shown in this paper, and its functionality is limited compared to our approach.

Tapestry [21] also supports continual execution of queries for append-only relational databases. A *continual query* in Tapestry is an SQL query including time conditions in the WHERE clause. Like OpenCQ, this system reports the difference from the previous result to the user. Although an append-only database can be seen as a dissemination-based service, the queries allowed in Tapestry is limited to special cases. Moreover, Tapestry does not provide event-driven data processing and information integration facilities.

8   Conclusions

In this research, we have incorporated information dissemination features into an existing information integration system *InfoWeaver*. We set two goals: (1) integration of dissemination-based information services as other conventional information sources, and (2) dissemination-based delivery of the integrated information. To achieve these goals, we used ECA rules to describe processing instructions. Also, we enhanced the *InfoWeaver* system to support event handling and rule processing functions. Using ECA rules, the user can specify event-driven integration of information sources and delivery of the integration results.

In this paper, we have described our approach to realize the goals, the enhanced system architecture, and the rule system to specify integration and delivery requirements. We have also shown the overview of the prototype implementation. We introduced additional modules, wrappers for dissemination-based information sources, the rule subsystem, and the dissemination subsystem, into the existing *InfoWeaver* system. In short, this work provides a novel framework of information integration by incorporating dissemination features, and has realized it by constructing a prototype system.

The *InfoWeaver* project is ongoing in our group. The future work includes more sophisticated management of information delivery scheduling and maintenance of archived data items. Development of a user-friendly specification scheme of integration requirements is another important research issue.

Acknowledgment. This research was supported in part by the Grant-in-Aid for Scientific Research from the Ministry of Education, Science, Sports and Culture, Japan.

References

1. D. Aksoy, M. Altinel, R. Bose, U. Cetintemel, M. Franklin, J. Wang, and S. Zdonik, "Research in Data Broadcast and Dissemination", *Proc. the First Intl. Conf. on Advanced Multimedia Content Processing (AMCP'98)*, Osaka, Japan, Nov. 1998. *LNCS* 1554, Springer-Verlag, 1999.
2. M. Altinel, D. Aksoy, T. Baby, M. Franklin, W. Shapiro, and S. Zdonik, "DBIS-Toolkit: Adaptible Middleware for Large-Scale Data Delivery", *Proc. ACM SIGMOD*, pp. 544–546, Jun. 1999.
3. C. K. Baru, A. Gupta, B. Ludäscher, R. Marciano, Y. Papakonstantinou, P. Velikhov, and V. Chu, "XML-Based Information Mediation with MIX," *Proc. ACM SIGMOD*, pp. 597–599, Jun. 1999.

4. R. Domening and K. R. Dittrich, "An Overview and Classification of Mediated Query Systems", *ACM SIGMOD Record*, Vol. 28, No. 3, pp. 63–72, 1999.

5. M. Franklin and S. Zdonik, "Data in Your Face: Push Technology in Perspective", *Proc. ACM SIGMOD*, pp. 516–519, Jun. 1998.

6. M. R. Genesereth, A. M. Keller, and O. M. Duschka. "Infomaster: An Information Integration System," *Proc. ACM SIGMOD*, pp. 539–542, May 1997.

7. H. Kitagawa, A. Morishima, and H. Mizuguchi, "Integration of Heterogeneous Information Sources in InfoWeaver", *Advances in Database and Multimedia for the New Century — A Swiss/Japanese Perspective*, World Scientific Publishing, 2000. (to appear)

8. Y. Lee, L. Liu, and C. Pu, "Towards Interoperable Heterogeneous Information Systems: An Experiment Using the DIOM Approach," *Proc. ACM Symp. on Applied Computing (SAC'97)*, pp. 112–114, Feb./Mar. 1997.

9. A. Y. Levy, A. Rajaraman, and J. J. Ordille, "Querying Heterogeneous Information Sources Using Source Descriptions," *Proc. VLDB*, pp. 251-262, Sept. 1996.

10. L. Liu, C. Pu, and W. Tang, "Continual Queries for Internet Scale Event-Driven Information Delivery" *IEEE Trans. on Knowledge and Data Engineering*, Vol. 11, No. 4, pp. 610–628, 1999.

11. Marinba Inc., "Castanet", http://www.marimba.com/products/castanet-intro.htm.

12. A. Morishima and H. Kitagawa, "Integrated Querying and Restructuring of the World Wide Web and Databases", *Proc. Intl. Symp. on Digital Media Information Base (DMIB'97)*, pp. 262–271, Nara, Japan, Nov. 1997, World Scientific.

13. A. Morishima and H. Kitagawa, "InfoWeaver: Dynamic and Tailor-Made Integration of Structured Documents, Web, and Databases", *Proc. ACM Digital Libraries '99*, pp. 235–236, Aug. 1999.

14. Y. Papakonstantinou, H. Garcia-Molina, and J. Widom, "Object Exchange Across Heterogeneous Information Sources," *Proc. 11th Intl. Conf. on Data Engineering (ICDE'95)*, pp. 251–260, Mar. 1995.

15. N. W. Paton and Oscar Díaz, "Active Database Systems", *ACM Computing Surveys*, Vol. 31, No. 1, pp.63–103, 1999.

16. M. Qiang, H. Kondo, K. Sumiya, and K. Tanaka, "Virtual TV Channel: Filtering Merging and Presenting Internet Broadcasting Channels", *ACM Digital Library Workshop on WOWS (Workshop on Organizing Web Space)*, Berkeley, CA, Aug. 1999.

17. S. Ramakrishnan and V. Dayal, "The PointCast Network", *Proc. ACM SIGMOD*, pp. 520, Jun. 1998.

18. M. T. Roth and P. M. Shwarz, "Don't Scrap It, Wrap It! A Wrapper Architecture for Legacy Data Sources," *Proc. VLDB*, pp. 266–275, Sept. 1997.

19. H.-J. Schek and M. H. Scholl, "The Relational Model with Relation-valued Attributes," *Information Systems*, Vol. 11, No. 2, pp. 137–147, 1986.

20. K. Sumiya and Y. Miyabe, "Models and Systems for Information Breadcast", *Information Processign Society of Japan Transactions on Databases*, Vol. 40, No. SIG8(TOD4), pp.141–157, Nov. 1999. (in Japanese)

21. D. B. Terry, D. Goldberg, D. Nichols, and B. M. Oki, "Continuous Queries over Append-Only Databases", *Proc. SIGMOD*, pp.321–330, Jun. 1992.

22. W3C, *Extensible Markup Language (XML) 1.0*, W3C Recommendation, 1998.

23. G. Wiederhold, "Mediators in the Architecture of Future Information Systems," *IEEE Computer*, Vol. 25, No. 3, pp. 38–49, 1992.

24. J. Windom and S. Ceri (eds.), *Active Database Systems,* Morgan Kaufmann, 1996.

Hierarchical Materialisation of Method Results in Object–Oriented Views*

Tadeusz Morzy, Robert Wrembel, and Tomasz Koszlajda

Poznań University of Technology, Institute of Computing Science
Piotrowo 3A, 60-965 Poznań, Poland
morzy@put.poznan.pl
{Robert.Wrembel, Tomasz.Koszlajda}@cs.put.poznan.pl

Abstract. In this paper we propose a framework for the materialisation of method results in object–oriented views. When the result of a given method is materialised, then it has to be kept up to date after objects used to compute the value of this method were updated. To this end we use additional data structures representing links between materialised methods and objects used to compute these methods. When such an object is updated, the system examines an appropriate data structure in order to find out which materialised methods have to be recomputed. When a given method m is materialised, it may be reasonable to materialise also the intermediate results of methods called from m. We call this technique *hierarchical materialisation*. When an object used to materialise the result of m is updated, then m has to be recomputed. This recomputation can use unaffected intermediate materialised results, thus reducing the recomputation time.

1 Introduction

Views in relational, object–relational, or object–oriented database systems are important mechanisms which provide among others: logical data independence, simplification of a database schema, shorthand for queries, and which are used for hiding data and implementing security policies.

Another important task performed by views is the integration of information coming from different homo– and heterogeneous distributed sources. Contemporary enterprises collect large amounts of data of different format and complexity (e.g. relational, object–relational, and object–oriented databases, on-line multimedia data stores, HTML and XML data, spreadsheets, flat files etc.). Therefore, one of the important issues is to provide an integrated access to all these heterogeneous data sources.

---

* This work is partially supported by the grant No. 8T11C04315 from the State Committee for Scientific Research (KBN), Poland

J. Štuller et al. (Eds.): ADBIS-DASFAA 2000, LNCS 1884, pp. 200–214, 2000.

There are two basic approaches to data integration: the *mediated* approach and the *data warehousing* approach [7]. In both of these approaches views are applied to data integration. As the information being processed is of a complex structure and behaviour, traditional relational database and data warehousing systems are not sufficient. Therefore, more and more often object–oriented or object–relational databases are used. The next step towards storing, processing, and analysing data of a complex structure is the development of object–relational data warehousing systems. In such systems object–oriented views are important mechanisms providing an integrated access to data of an arbitrary complex structure and behaviour. Due to a powerful object–oriented data model, object–oriented views are well suited for transforming other models to a common model used by an integrating database.

Views serve also as the means of data materialisation, which is an important technique used in: (1) distributed databases in order to reduce access time to remote data and to tackle the problem of temporary unavailability of data sources; (2) in data warehousing systems in order to speed up the execution of complex analytical queries [6]. Data materialisation requires mechanisms that will propagate modifications of a database to materialised views. A lot of work has been done to maintain relational materialised views, where efficiency is achieved by using *incremental propagation* [6]. Much less work has been done to support object–oriented views materialisation [4] and maintenance [9, 10]. Moreover, the existing approaches to materialised object–oriented views so far considered only the structural parts of view objects.

In this paper we propose a framework for the materialisation of method results in object–oriented views. This framework extends our previous work on the materialisation and maintenance of structural parts of views [13].

The materialisation of a method consists in computing the result of this method once, storing it persistently in a database, and then using the persistent value when the method is invoked, rather than computing the result each time the method is called. On the one hand, this technique allows to reduce access time to the result of a method. But on the other hand, when a method result is made persistent it has to be kept up to date when data used to compute this result change. To this end, we use additional data structures representing links between materialised methods and objects used to compute these methods. When such an object is updated, the system examines an appropriate data structure in order to find these materialised methods that have to be recomputed. Methods invocations form a graph of dependencies. When method m is materialised, it may be reasonable to materialise also the intermediate results of methods called from m. We call this technique *hierarchical materialisation*. In order to maintain the chain of methods invocations we introduced a data structure, called the *Graph of Method Calls*. When an object used to materialise the result of method m is updated, then m has to be recomputed. This recomputation can use unaffected intermediate results that has already been materialised, thus reducing the time spent on recomputation.

This paper is organised as follows: Section 2 discusses related approaches to object–oriented views materialisation and methods materialisation. Section 3 outlines our concept of views. Sections 4 and 5 describe our framework of materialisation and maintenance of structural and behavioural parts of views, respectively. Section 6 summarises the paper and points out the area for future work.

2 Related Work

Several approaches to object–oriented views have been proposed in scientific publications (see [11] for an overview). As it concerns materialised object–oriented views few approaches have been proposed so far that support their materialisation [4] and maintenance [9, 10]. In [4] an arbitrary portion of a source database schema can be replicated (together with associated class instances) into a materialised view, called replica. However, the system does not keep consistency between a database and replicas. The *MultiView* system [9, 10] supports incremental view maintenance. But the system materialises only pointers to base objects, and, therefore, it may not be suitable either for distributed databases or for data warehousing systems where integrated data should be stored/materialised locally in a warehouse for the sake of efficiency, rather than accessed remotely.

The materialisation of methods and their maintenance was investigated in the context of indexing techniques and query optimisation, c.f. [1, 3, 8]. The main problem with materialised methods concerns the consistency maintenance between a materialised result of a method m and objects used to compute the value of m. To this end, these approaches use additional data structures that store references from objects used to compute a given method to this method. The concept of [8] uses the so called *Reverse Reference Relation*, which contains the tuples in the form of: [*object used to materialise method m, the name of a materialised method, the set of objects passed as arguments of m*]. Furthermore, this approach maintains also the information about the attributes, called *relevant attributes*, whose values were used to materialise method m. Method m has to be recomputed only when the value of a relevant attribute of an object used in m was updated.

Another approach to methods precomputation was discussed in [5]. The authors developed the concept of the so called *inverse methods* in order to alleviate the need to compute a given method for each instance of a given class. The result of an inverse method is stored in the memory and is accessible only for the current query.

3 The Concept of an Object–Oriented View Schema

In our approach, an *object–oriented view* is defined as a *view schema* of an arbitrary complex structure and behaviour. A view schema is composed of view classes. Each *view class* is derived from one or more *base classes*, i.e. classes in a database schema, called *base schema*. View classes in a view schema are connected by inheritance and aggregation relationships. Several view schemas can be created from the same base schema. A view schema creation process was described in [12].

Example 1. Let us consider a base schema composed of eight classes. The class diagram, in UML notation, is presented in Figure 1. The *Computer* class is composed of three classes, namely *CDDrive*, *Disk*, and *MainBoard*. *MainBoard*, in turn, is further composed of *CPURadiator*, *CPU*, and *RAMSlot*. *RAMSlot* references another class, i.e. *RAMModule*.

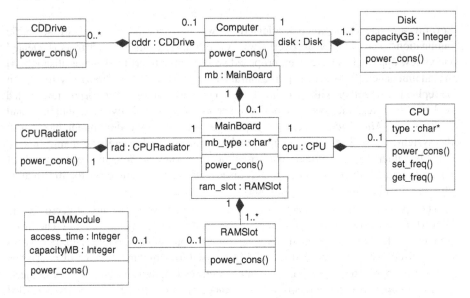

Fig. 1. An example of a database schema

A view schema composed of six view classes was derived from this base schema (cf. Figure 2). *V_Computer*, *V_CDDrive*, *V_Disk*, and *V_CPU* view classes were derived from *Computer*, *CDDrive*, *Disk*, and *CPU* base classes, respectively.

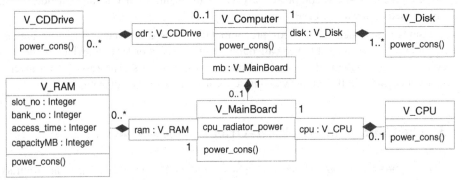

Fig. 2. An example of a view schema derived from a base schema in Figure 2

V_RAM merges information from two base classes, i.e. it takes some attributes from *RAMSlot* as well as from *RAMModule*. *V_MainBoard* merges information from two base classes, namely *MainBoard* and *CPURadiator*. The *V_MainBoard* view class was derived from base class *MainBoard* with the predicates allowing to access only these main boards that are of ATX type and use Intel processors, i.e. *mb_type='ATX' and cpu.type='Intel'*. Additionally, *V_Computer* was derived with the predicate allowing to access only these computers that use hard disks with the capacity grater that 10GB, i.e. *disk.capacityGB>10*. □

A view class is derived and placed in a selected view schema by the OQL–like command:

```
create view class vc_name ...;
```

that allows to define the structure of a view class, its behaviour, and the set of instances. The full syntax of this command is presented in [13]. Due to space limitations we shall not describe it here.

4   The Structural Part of a View Schema Materialisation

The persistence of base as well as view objects is realised by the so called *roots of persistence*. The root of persistence is a schema element that attributes persistence to objects. An object becomes persistent only when: (1) it is explicitly attached to the root of persistence or (2) it is referenced by another persistent object, otherwise an object is temporary.

Instances of a view class are called *view objects*. View objects are not persistent by default and they are recomputed each time the application (query) addresses a view class. A given view schema can be explicitly materialised, meaning that the instances of view classes become persistent. In order to materialise a view schema the following command is used:

```
materialise view schema vs_name;
```

In our approach we use the object generating semantics of all view classes, i.e., the instances of each view class are new objects and each view object is assigned new *view object identifier – vOid*. This policy is required when performing complex restructuring of base objects in a view class. Furthermore, object generation is suitable for materialising instances of view classes.

In order to propagate changes from base objects to their materialised counterparts in view schemas, two additional data structures have to be maintained by the system. These structures, which are briefly described below, are called *Class Mapping Structure* and *Object Mapping Structure* cf. [13].

4.1   Class Mapping Structure

When view classes are derived from a given base class C_i, the system maintains mappings between C_i and all view classes that were derived from it. The structure used to store derivation links is called *Class Mapping Structure*. It is used among others while propagating changes from base to materialised view objects.

Class Mapping Structure (shortly **CMS**) is defined as the set of tuples having four fields. The first field stores the name of a base class C_i, the second field stores the array of attribute names of C_i that are used in the definition of view class V_i. The third field stores the name of view class V_i derived from C_i and the fourth field stores the array of attribute names used in V_i (details can be found in [13]).

4.2 Object Mapping Structure

The update of base object o_i should be propagated only to those view objects that were created from o_i. Therefore, one important issue that must be solved is the identification of these materialised view objects that are affected by the update of o_i. To this end the *Object Mapping Structure* is used.

Object Mapping Structure (**OMS** for short) provides the mapping between a base object and all view objects created from it. The **OMS** is created and maintained by the system for each base class C_i. All view classes derived from C_i also have access to **OMS**. This structure is organised as the set of tuples where the first field stores base object identifier (*oid*) and the second field stores the set of all view object identifiers (*vOid*) created from this base object. The system examines the content of a given *Object Mapping Structure* among others while propagating changes from base to view objects (details can be found in [13]).

5   The Behavioural Part of View Schema Materialisation

By default, methods defined in a view class are computed each time they are invoked. In order to make the result of a method persistent (materialise the method), a database designer has to explicitly invoke the following command:

```
materialise method view_class_name::method_name
in view schema vs_name;
```

After that, the result of the first invocation of a method m_i for a view object vo_i is stored persistently. Each subsequent invocation of m_i for the same object vo_i uses the already materialised value. The materialisation of methods in a given view schema is allowed only when this schema was previously materialised (cf. Section 4).

We assume the full encapsulation of view objects, i.e. the value of each attribute a_i of a view class V_i is accessed by a *readA_i* method, called *read method*. The information about a read method and an attribute whose value is provided by this method is stored in each view class. Read methods are not materialised, as they simply provide the value of an attribute. The *readMethod(attribute_name)* function returns the name of a read method for an attribute passed as the argument.

5.1 Method Persistence Structure

The information about methods whose results have to be persistent is stored in additional data structure, called *Method Persistence Structure* (***MPS*** for short). Each instance of ***MPS*** is a tuple with the following fields:

```
[method_name, view_class_name, view_schema_name]
```

For example, the following command is used to make persistent the result of the *power_cons* method in the *V_CPU* view class (defined in view schema *VS1*).

materialise method V_CPU::power_cons
in view schema VS1;

However, no method result is materialised yet. The command informs the system that the next invocation of this method for a given object vo_i should be materialised. To this end, appropriate information is inserted to ***MPS***, i.e.:

```
[power_cons,V_CPU,VS1]
```

When the *power_cons* method is invoked for the instance vo_i of the *V_CPU* view class, the system checks whether the result of this method should be made persistent by examining *Method Persistence Structure*. To this end the following function is used:

```
CheckMPS(method_name,view_class_name,view_schema_name)
```

CheckMPS returns *true* if the result of a given method (passed as the first argument) in a given view class (passed as the second argument) in a given view schema (passed as the third argument) should be made persistent. Otherwise the function returns *false*.

5.2 Materialised Method Results Structure

As the same method can be invoked for different instances of a given view class and the same method can be invoked with different values of input arguments, the system has to maintain the mappings between: (1) the materialised value of a method, (2) object for which it was invoked, and (3) values of input arguments. We use here the mechanism similar to those proposed in [3, 8]. The mappings are represented in the structure, called the *Materialised Method Results Structure* (***MMRS***). Each instance of ***MMRS*** is a tuple with the following fields:

```
[method_name,
          {input_argument_value}, {[vOid, result]}
          view_class_name, view_schema_name]
```

The second field of this structure represents the set of input argument values that can be simple values or view objects. A given method can be invoked with the same set of input argument values, but for different objects, therefore, the third field is defined as the set of tuples [*vOid, result*]. *vOid* is the view object identifier for which a given method was invoked, and *result* is the result of the method.

For example, let us assume that the *power_cons* method in the *V_CPU* view class may be invoked with the argument representing the frequency of a processor clock. The invocation of *power_cons(233)* for the instance identified by $vCpu_1$ (results in 21W) and $vCpu_{23}$ (results in 25W) causes that the following tuple is inserted in *MMRS*:

```
[power_cons,{233},{(vCpu₁, 21),(vCpu₂₃, 25)},V_CPU,VS1]
```

5.3 The Graph of Method Calls

A method defined in one view class can invoke other methods defined in other view classes. For example, in order to compute the consumption of power by the instances of *V_Computer*, the *power_cons* method (in *V_Computer*) calls *power_cons* methods defined in *V_Disk*, in *V_CDDrive*, and in *V_Main_Board*.

The chain of method dependencies, where one method calls another, is called the *Graph of Method Calls* (*GMC* for short), i.e. *GMC* = *(M, E)*, where *M* is the set of nodes, each of them representing a method defined in a view class, in a given view schema VS_i, and *E* is the set of edges. An edge is a pair of nodes *(m_i, m_j)* where m_i calls m_j.

The *GMC* is implemented as a structure whose entries are tuples of the following format:

```
[calling_method_name, calling_class_name,
        called_method_name, called_class_name,
        view_schema_name]
```

Such a representation allows to traverse the graph in both directions. The direction from a called method to its calling method is used while finding these calling methods whose materialised values became no longer valid (cf. Section 5.5).

For a given method m_i, being called from other methods, the *findCallingMethods* function is used in order to find all the names (preceeded with view class name) of methods calling m_i. The name of the called method name is passed as the first argument of this function.

```
findCallingMethods
    (called_method_name,view_class_name,view_schema_name)
```

Example 2. As an example let us consider the view schema presented in Figure 2. Each view class in this view schema has a method called *power_cons* that returns the consumption of electricity power by a computer component. The consumption of power by each composite instance of *V_Main_Board* is computed as the sum of power consumed by each component object, i.e. instances of *V_RAM* and *V_CPU*. Similarily, the consumption of power by each instance of *V_Computer* is the sum of power consumptions by the component instance of *V_CDDrive*, *V_MainBoard*, and *V_Disk*.

The example of the *Graph of Method Calls* for the view schema presented in Figure 2 is shown in Figure 3. The name of each method is preceded with the name of a class in which it was defined.

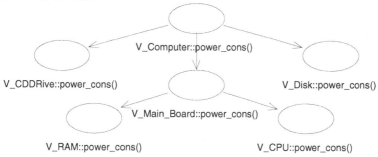

Fig. 3. An example of the *Graph of Method Calls*

□

The extraction of **GMC** nodes and edges should be performed automatically by the system during the creation of view methods. However, we do not provide the method for doing it automatically. So far we considered a database designer as a person responsible for managing the **GMC**. The automatic maintenance of **GMC** is the subject of further investigation.

5.4 Hierarchical Materialisation

When method m is materialised, it may be reasonable to materialise also the intermediate results of methods called from m. When a view object vo_i, used to materialise the result of method m, is updated, then m has to be recomputed. This recomputation can use unaffected intermediate materialised results, thus reducing the recomputation overhead.

We call this technique *hierarchical materialisation*. In order to maintain the chain of method invocations the system uses the *Graph of Method Calls*. In our framework all the intermediate results up to leaf nodes are materialised.

Example 3. Figure 4 presents, in the UML notation, the materialised instances of the view schema from Figure 2. One instance of *V_Computer* was materialised, namely the object identified by OID $vCom_1$. It is further composed of objects vCD_1 (the instance of view class *V_CDDrive*), vD_{20} (the instance of view class *V_Disk*), and vMB_{100} (the instance of *V_MainBoard*), which in turn is composed of: vR_{200}, vR_{201}, vR_{202}, and vP_{10}.

As an example illustrating the concept of *hierarchical materialisation* and its advantage let us consider the materialisation of methods initiated by the command:

```
materialise method V_Computer::power_cons
in view schema VS1;
```

As it was pointed in Section 5.1, the result of *V_Computer::power_cons* is materialised for the instance of *V_Computer* only when this method is invoked for this instance. Furthermore, all the methods called from *V_Computer::power_cons* are also materialised.

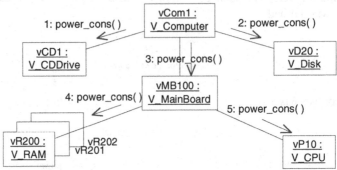

Fig. 4. An example of materialised view schema instances

Let us assume that the *power_cons* method was invoked for $vCom_1$. In our example the hierarchical materialisation mechanism results in materialising values of the following methods: *V_RAM::power_cons* for objects identified by vR_{200}, vR_{201}, vR_{202}, *V_CPU::power_cons* for object vP_{10}, *V_MainBoard::power_cons* for object vMB_{100}, *V_Disk::power_cons* for object vD_{20}, *V_CDDrive::power_cons* for object vCD_1, and finally *V_Computer::power_cons* for object $vCom_1$.

The contents of *Method Persistence Structure*, *Materialised Method Results Structure*, and *Graph of Method Calls* are presented below.

Table 1. Method Persistence Structure

method name	view class name	view schema name
power_cons	V_Computer	VS_1
power_cons	V_CDDrive	VS_1
power_cons	V_Disk	VS_1
power_cons	V_MainBoard	VS_1
power_cons	V_RAM	VS_1
power_cons	V_CPU	VS_1

Having materialised the methods mentioned in Example 3, let us assume that the component object vD_{20} was replaced with another disk instance, say vD_{301}, with greater consumption of power. Thus, the materialised result of *V_Computer::power_cons* is no longer valid and it has to be recomputed. However, during the recomputation of $vCom_1.power\_cons$ the unaffected materialised results of methods can be reused, i.e. $vCD_1.power\_cons$, $vMB_{100}.power\_cons$ did not change and they can be used to compute a new value of $vCom_1.power\_cons$.

Table 2. Graph of Method Calls

calling method	calling class	called method	called class
power_cons	V_Computer	power_cons	V_CDDrive
power_cons	V_Computer	power_cons	V_Disk
power_cons	V_Computer	power_cons	V_MainBoard
power_cons	V_MainBoard	power_cons	V_RAM
power_cons	V_MainBoard	power_cons	V_CPU
power_cons	V_RAM	readU	V_RAM
power_cons	V_RAM	readI	V_RAM
power_cons	V_CPU	readU(int frequency)	V_CPU
power_cons	V_CPU	readI(int frequency)	V_CPU
power_cons	V_CDDrive	readU	V_CDDrive
power_cons	V_CDDrive	readI	V_CDDrive
power_cons	V_Disk	readU	V_Disk
power_cons	V_Disk	readI	V_Disk

readU and *readI* functions are read methods for *voltage* and *current_intensity* attributes, respectively.

Table 3. Materialised Method Results Structure

method name	{input argument values}	{vOid, value}	view class name	view schema name
power_cons	null	vR_{200}, 2 vR_{201}, 2 vR_{202}, 2	V_RAM	VS_1
power_cons	233	vP_{10}, 25	V_CPU	VS_1
power_cons	null	vMB_{100}, 71	V_MainBoard	VS_1
power_cons	null	vCD_1, 15	V_CDDrive	VS_1
power_cons	null	vD_{20}, 22	V_Disk	VS_1
power_cons	null	$vCom_1$, 108	V_Computer	VS_1

□

Without having materialised the power consumption of each component object, all the methods called from *V_Computer::power_cons* would have to be computed.

In our approach we assume that the decision whether a method should be materialised or not is explicitly made by a database designer/administrator during the system tuning activity.

5.5 The Maintenance of Materialised Methods

View objects in a materialised view schema have to be kept up to date with their corresponding base objects. The framework that we developed in [13] allows to propagate updates to each view object immediately after the corresponding base object was updated.

When the result of a given method is materialised, then it also has to be kept up to date after objects used to compute the value of this method were updated. The result of materialised method m_i becomes obsolete when:

- m_i, defined in view class vc_i, uses the attribute (by means of invoking its read method) of an instance of vc_i whose value was changed;
- a view object vo_i, used as the input argument of m_i, was updated;
- the materialised value of any method called from m_i was changed.

The update of a base object o_i triggers the following actions: (1) the propagation of an update to a view object vo_i that represents o_i in a view, (2) the invalidation of these materialised method results, whose values depend on vo_i.

The invalidation of a materialised method result has to be propagated up to the top of the *Graph of Method Calls*. Assuming that an update to an attribute a_i of the instance vo_i of view class vc_i in view schema VS_j was updated, the following actions are taken.

1. The read method for attribute a_i is found by invoking:

```
rMname: string;
rMname = readMethod(a_);
```

2. All the materialised methods that directly call the above read method are found by invoking:

```
callingMeth: array of string;
callingMeth = findCallingMethods(rMname, vc_, VS_);
```

3. For an updated view object vo_i the list of composite objects referencing vo_i is checked.

   In order to find a composite object vo_r for a component vo_i the system must maintain additional links from component objects to their composite objects. In our framework each view object has the so called *inverse relationship* associated with it (cf. [2]). The list of composite objects referencing vo_i is returned by invoking the *findReferencingObj* function:

```
composite_ref_object: list of OID;
composite_ref_object = vo_.findReferencingObj();
```

4. The following entries are removed from ***MMRS***:

   a) for a view object vo_i, if a read method and a method calling it are defined in the same view class:

```
for each m in callingMeth
   removeMMRSentry(m, vo_, vc_, VS_);
```

The *removeMMRSentry* procedure requires four input arguments: the name of a method, whose materialised result is to be removed, the identifier of a view object for which *m* was materialised, the name of a view class in which *m* is defined, and the name of a view schema in which this view class is defined.

b) for a component view objects referencing vo_i if a read method is called from a composite view class:

```
for each m in callingMeth
{ for each vo_r in composite_ref_object
    removeMMRSentry(m, vo_r, getViewClass(vo_r), VS_j);}
```

In this case, *removeMMRSentry* removes from **MMRS** the materialised result of method *m*, for a composite object vo_r that is composed of vo_i. The name of a view class is fetched by function *getViewClass* that requires the identifier of a view object as an input argument.

5. Steps 2-4 are repeated recursively for each method in *callingMeth* until the root of **GMC** is reached.

Having removed all the invalid entries to **MMRS**, the next invocation of a previously materialised method m_i results in a new materialisation of its result.

6   Conclusions and Future Work

The support for view materialisation and maintenance is required when applying object–oriented views in data warehousing systems or in distributed environments. In this paper we presented a framework for object–oriented view materialisation and maintenance with respect to behavioural parts of view classes. To the best of our knowledge, the materialisation of methods in object–oriented views has not been considered so far in scientific research.

In our framework, we proposed the mechanism of hierarchical materialisation of methods. This technique allows to reduce the maintenance cost of materialised methods, as unaffected intermediate results do not have to be recomputed and can thus be reused during the recomputation of another affected method. However, the maintenance of materialised methods requires look–ups to **MPS**, **GMC**, and **MMRS** structures. Accessing them and searching for the information consume additional time, slowing down the process of method maintenance and computation. Indexing techniques can be used in order to reduce the time of accessing information in these structures.

The decision which method to materialise is made by a database designer/administrator during the system tuning process. He or she has to carefully select the methods for materialisation. Good candidates are those methods that do not have input arguments or have input arguments with a small, discrete domain. Otherwise, the *Materialised Method Results Structure* may grow rapidly and diminish the system performance.

Another factor that deteriorates the system performance is the frequency of updates to these objects that were used to materialise methods. When the immediate maintenance strategy is used, the more frequently object are being updated, the more time is spent by the system on maintaining materialised methods.

The issues that need further investigation are as follows:

- the development of a mechanism that would allow to construct automatically the *Graph of Method Calls* by analysing the codes of view methods;
- the optimisation of data structures (*MPS*, *MMRS*, and *GMC*) and techniques of accessing these structures;
- the implementation of our framework in the ObjectStore system;
- the experimental evaluation of our mechanism of methods materialisation and maintenance in order to: (1) measure how far the method materialisation can speed up the access to data, with comparison to non materialised methods approach, (2) measure additional time used for maintaining the materialised results of methods.

References

1. Bertino E.: Method precomputation in object–oriented databases. *Proceedings of ACM–SIGOIS and IEEE–TC–OA International Conference on Organizational Computing Systems*, 1991

2. Cattell R., G., G., Barry D., Berler M., Eastman J., Jordan D., Russel C., Shadow O., Stanienda T., Velez F.: Object Database Standard: ODMG 3.0, *Morgan Kaufmann Publishers*, 2000

3. Clement T. Yu, Weiyi M.: Principles of Database Query Processing for Advanced Applications, *Morgan Kaufmann Publishers, Inc.*, 1998

4. Dobrovnik M., Eder J.: Partial Replication of Object–Oriented Databases. *Proceedings of Second East-European Conference on Advances in Databases and Information Systems – ADBIS'98*. Poland, 1998, LNCS No. 1475, pp. 260-271

5. Eder J., Frank H., Liebhart W.: Optimization of Object–Oriented Queries by Inverse Methods. *Proceedings of East/West Database Workshop*, Austria, 1994

6. Gupta A., Mumick I.S. (eds.): Materialized Views: Techniques, Implementations, and Applications. The MIT Press, 1999

7. Hammer J., Garcia–Molina H., Widom J., Labio W., Zhuge Y.: The Stanford Data Warehousing Project. *Data Engineering Bulletin*, Vol. 18, No. 2, June 1995, pp. 40-47

8. Kemper A., Kilger C., Moerkotte G.: Function Materialization in Object Bases: Design, Realization, and Evaluation. *IEEE Transactions on Knowledge and Data Engineering*, Vol. 6, No. 4, 1994

9. Kuno H. A., Rundensteiner E.: Materialised Object-Oriented Views in MultiView. *Proceedings of the ACM Research Issues in Data Engineering Workshop*, 1995

10. Kuno H. A., Rundensteiner E.: Using Object-Oriented Principles to Optimize Update Propagation to Materialised Views. *Proceedings of Int. Conf. on Data Engineering*, 1996, pp. 310-317

11. Wrembel R.: Object–Oriented Views: Virtues and Limitations. *Proceedings of the 13th International Symposium on Computer and Information Sciences – ISCIS'98*, Turkey, 1998, pp. 228-235

12. Wrembel R.: Deriving consistent view schemas in an object-oriented database. *Proceedings of the 14th International Symposium on Computer and Information Sciences – ISCIS'99*, Turkey, 1999, pp. 803-810

13. Wrembel R.: On Materialising Object–Oriented Views. *Proceedings of the Fourth IEEE Baltic Workshop on Databases and Information Systems*, Lithuania, 2000, pp. 38-51

Finding Generalized Path Patterns
for Web Log Data Mining *

Alex Nanopoulos and Yannis Manolopoulos

Data Engineering Lab,
Department of Informatics, Aristotle University
54006 Thessaloniki, Greece
{alex,manolopo}@delab.csd.auth.gr

Abstract. Conducting data mining on logs of web servers involves the determination of frequently occurring access sequences. We examine the problem of finding traversal patterns from web logs by considering the fact that irrelevant accesses to web documents may be interleaved within access patterns due to navigational purposes. We define a general type of pattern that takes into account this fact and also, we present a level-wise algorithm for the determination of these patterns, which is based on the underlying structure of the web site. The performance of the algorithm and its sensitivity to several parameters is examined experimentally with synthetic data.

1   Introduction

Log data which are collected by web servers contain information about user accesses to the web documents of the site. The size of logs increases rapidly due to two reasons: the rate that data are collected and the growth of the web sites themselves. The analysis of these large volumes of log data demands the employment of data mining methods.

Recently, several methods have been proposed for mining web log data [10, 14,16]. Following the paradigm of mining association rules [1], mined patterns are considered to be frequently occurring access sequences. An example of this kind of pattern is a sequence $\langle D_1, \ldots, D_n \rangle$ of visited documents in a web site. If such a sequence appears frequently enough, then it indicates a pattern which can be useful for designing purposes of the web site (advertising), users motivation with dynamic web documents, system performance analysis, etc.

The transformation of web log files to a data format similar to basket data is discussed in [9]. Each user session is split into several transactions, requiring that all accesses inside each transaction are close in time. Then, existing algorithms for mining association rules (e.g. Apriori) are used over the derived transactions. In [7], a more sophisticated transformation (algorithm *MF*) is proposed which identifies inside a transaction all *maximal forward sequences*, i.e. all sequences comprising accesses which have not been made by a backward movement. In

---

* Work supported by a national PABE project.

J. Štuller et al. (Eds.): ADBIS-DASFAA 2000, LNCS 1884, pp. 215–228, 2000.

the same paper, a variation of mining association rules with hash filtering and transaction trimming is proposed (algorithm *Full Scan–FS*). Also, by exploiting main memory, another algorithm is proposed (*Selective Scan – SS*), which is able to skip several database scans and count candidates belonging to many phases, within the same database scan. Finally, a different approach is followed in [5]. More specifically, one database scan is performed and the number of occurrences of each pair of accesses is determined, i.e. for each pair of web documents A and B the number of times pair AB occurred is counted. Then, the notion of *composite association rule* is defined which is based on the frequencies counted at the previous step. Two algorithms are proposed (*Modified DFS* and *Incremental Step*) for finding composite association rules.

Although all previous approaches mine patterns from access information contained in a log file, these patterns differ significantly. For the first approach, the patterns are standard association rules which are mined with existing algorithms. These rules do not take into account the web site structure. Thus, this approach may overevaluate associations, which do not correspond to the actual way of accessing the site. The method of maximal references finds frequently occurring sequences of consecutive accesses. As will be presented in more detail in Section 2.2, this approach is sensitive to noise, since patterns which are corrupted by noisy accesses, loose the property of consecutiveness. The composite-association rules method counts the frequencies of sequences of length two and, based on these frequencies, estimates the remaining ones of larger sequences, without verifying the estimates with the database contents. This approach is based on the assumption that the probability of an access depends only on the previous access (first-order markov property), which does not hold in all cases.

In this paper, we give a definition of traversal pattern, adopting the meaning given in [7], but we do not pose the constraint that accesses should be consecutive inside the patterns during the frequency counting procedure. These differences from the existing approach require the development of a new algorithm for finding such traversal patterns. We present an algorithm for generating and counting the support of candidate patterns that is level-wise, as the Apriori-like methods, which takes into account the underlying web site structure. Although the general structure of the proposed algorithm is Apriori-like, the data structures and the procedures for support counting and candidate generation differ significantly and these operations are performed efficiently by considering the site structure. The performance of the algorithm is examined experimentally, using synthetic data.

The rest of this paper is organized as follows. Section 2 gives background information and a brief overview of algorithms *Full Scan* and *Selective Scan* [7]. The problem statement is given in Section 3. Section 4 presents the level-wise algorithm, whereas Section 5 contains the performance results of the algorithm. Finally, Section 6 gives the conclusions and directions of future work.

2   Background

2.1   Definitions

A web site can be abstractly viewed as a set of web documents connected with hypertext links. The site can be represented by a simple unweighted directed graph, which is a finite set of vertices and arcs. A vertex corresponds to a document and an arc to a link. Each arc joins an ordered pair of vertices. The graph contains no loops (i.e. arcs joining a vertex with itself), no parallel arcs (i.e. arcs joining the same ordered pair of vertices), whereas no weight (e.g. distance, cost, etc.) is associated with any arc. Since traversal patterns contain information about user access, no quantitative (e.g. weights) or duplicate (e.g. loops, parallel arcs) information has to be considered [1]. An example of a simple, directed graph is illustrated in Figure 1.

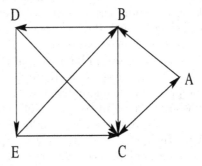

Fig. 1. A directed graph.

A traversal in the site is a sequence of consecutive arcs, i.e. links, that can be represented with the sequence of the terminating vertices of each arc. The length of the traversal is defined by the number of contained vertices. The traversals are contained in the log file. Each entry in the log is of the form (*userID*, *s*, *d*), which denotes the user identification number, the starting position *s* and the destination position *d*. Although the actual representation of a log may be different, since it contains additional information, for the purpose of mining traversal patterns, the log can be abstractly viewed as described previously. The beginning of a new traversal is marked with a triplet (*userID*, *null*, *d*). All pairs corresponding to the same user identification number are grouped together to form a traversal.

In many cases, duplicate arcs or vertices inside the traversal do not contain useful information, like backward movements [7]. This type of traversal where each arc and vertex is distinct, is called a *path*. In the example of Figure 1, $\langle A, B, D, C \rangle$ is a path, whereas $\langle B, D, E, B, C \rangle$ is not.

---

[1] In case the graph structure is not simple, a simple graph can be derived by omitting loops, multiple edges and weights

Definition 1 *Any subsequence of consecutive vertices in a path is also a path and is called a section. A section is contained in the corresponding path. If P represents a path $\langle p_1, \ldots, p_n \rangle$, then $S = \langle s_1, \ldots, s_m \rangle$ is a section of P, if there exist a $k \geq 0$ such that $p_{j+k} = s_j$ for all $1 \leq j \leq m$.*   □

In the example of Figure 1, $\langle A, B, D \rangle$ is a section of path $\langle A, B, D, C \rangle$. The criterion of section containment requires that the vertices (and the corresponding arcs) are consecutive in the path. If this is not required then we define a *subpath*.

Definition 2 *Given a path $P = \langle p_1, \ldots, p_n \rangle$ in a graph G, we call subpath of P, the sequence $SP = \langle sp_1, \ldots, sp_m \rangle$ for which:*

- $\forall \, sp_i \in SP \Rightarrow sp_i \in P$
- $sp_i = p_k$ and $sp_j = p_l$ and $i < j \Rightarrow k < l, \forall i < j$ □

In other words, the vertices (and arcs) of the subpath belong also to the corresponding path and the order of their appearance in the path is preserved in the subpath. Additionally, the subpath itself is a path in the corresponding graph. In the example of Figure 1, $\langle A, B, C \rangle$ is a subpath of $\langle A, B, D, C \rangle$. The following lemma shows that the notion of subpath is a generalization of that of section.

Lemma 1 *If $P = \langle p_1, \ldots, p_n \rangle$ is a path and $S = \langle s_1, \ldots, s_m \rangle$ a section of P, then S is also a subpath of P.*

Proof. Since P is a path, S is also a path. Also, since S is a section of P, then it holds that: $\forall \, s_i \in S \Rightarrow s_i \in P$. Finally, there exist a $k \geq 0$ such that: $p_{j+k} = s_j$ for all $1 \leq j \leq m$. If $s_j = p_{j+k}$ and $s_{j+1} = p_{j+k+1}$, then for $j < j+1 \Rightarrow j + k < j + k + 1$, which is true for all $1 \leq j \leq m$.   □

Next, we present some quantitative conclusions regarding the number of subpaths. The proofs can be found in [12].

Lemma 2 *A path $P = \langle p_1, \ldots, p_n \rangle$ of length n has at least $n - k + 1$ and at most $\binom{n}{k}$ subpaths of length k.*   □

Corollary 1 *A path $P = \langle p_1, \ldots, p_n \rangle$ of length n has at least two and at most n subpaths of length $n - 1$.*   □

Corollary 2 *A path $P = \langle p_1, \ldots, p_n \rangle$ of length n has exactly two sections of length $n - 1$.*   □

2.2   Overview of Maximal Reference Sequences

In *algorithm MF* [7], a preprocessing of the log file is performed to extract *maximal forward references*. First, each user session is identified. A session is further decomposed into a number of transactions, [2] which are the paths resulting after

---

[2] In the sequel, terms transaction and path are used interchangeably.

discarding all backward movements. After this step, a modified algorithm for mining large itemsets is used. This algorithm is called *Full Scan* and resembles *DHP* [13], an Apriori-like algorithm which uses hash-pruning and transaction trimming. Also, algorithm *Selective Scan* is proposed, which exploits the available main memory and merges several phases of the Apriori-like algorithm.

Algorithms *Full Scan* and *Selective Scan* do not find the supports of arbitrary sets of vertices, as the standard algorithms for association rules do, but they take into account the ordering of vertices inside the transactions. These algorithms determine all large *reference sequences*, i.e. all *sections* (see Definition 2) of the graph *contained* in a sufficient number of transactions. Recall that a candidate S is contained as section in a path (transaction) P, if S is a section of P, i.e. $p_{j+k} = s_j$ for some $k \geq 0$. For the candidate generation, a candidate $S = \langle s_1, \ldots, s_{k+1} \rangle$ of length $k+1$ is generated by joining $S' = \langle s_1, \ldots, s_k \rangle$ and $S'' = \langle s_2, \ldots, s_{k+1} \rangle$, if both these sections of S with length k were found large. With respect to Corollary 2, S has only two sections of length k, i.e. S' and S''. In [7] it is not explained if any candidate pruning takes place, like in Apriori and DHP where every subset is tested if it is large. Since S' and S'' are the only sections of S, any other combination of k vertices of S, even if it is a path in the graph, will not be supported by the same transactions which support S. If a transaction P contained S and a combination of k vertices S''' from S, then S''' would be contained as a section by S, which contradicts with Corollary 2. Therefore, no further candidate pruning can take place.

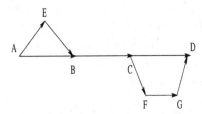

Fig. 2. A transaction corrupted by irrelevant accesses during navigation.

The resulting patterns are all large *maximal reference sequences*, i.e. all paths with the maximum possible length, contained as sections in a number of transactions which is larger than *minSupport*. Compared to standard association rules, maximal reference sequences are traversal patterns. However, patterns may be corrupted by noisy accesses which are random accesses, not parts of a pattern, which are done during user navigation. Thus, inside a user traversal, patterns are interleaved with noise. Figure 2, illustrates a transaction $T = \langle A, E, B, C, F, G, D \rangle$. If $P = \langle A, B, C, D \rangle$ is the pattern (maximal reference sequence), then P is not a section of T and thus, it is not supported by transaction T. If many transactions are corrupted, then pattern P will not have adequate support and will be missed. Therefore, irrelevant accesses for navigational purposes have an impact on the support of the patterns and their determination.

3   Mining Access Patterns Based on Subpath Definition

3.1   Problem Statement

Given a collection of transactions which are paths in a web site represented by a graph, all paths contained as subpaths by a fraction of transactions which is larger than *minSupport* are found. Following the notation of standard association rules, this fraction is called *support* and all such paths are called *large*. As described in Section 2.1, in the sequel we use the terms of vertex and arc instead of web document and hypertext link. Finally, as a post-processing step, the large paths of maximal length can be determined. Since this is a straightforward operation, it will not be considered any further.

The database consists of paths in the given graph which can be derived from the log file using algorithm *MF* [7]. A candidate path P is supported by a transaction T, if P is a subpath of T. Thus, vertices corresponding to noisy accesses in T do not affect the support of P. In the example of Figure 2, pattern $P = \langle A, B, C, D \rangle$ is a subpath of transaction $T = \langle A, E, B, C, F, G, D \rangle$ although it is not its section. Recall that P is a path in the graph and the ordering of vertices in T is preserved. Following Lemma 1, the set of all large paths with the subpath-containment criterion is a superset of all large references sequences with the section-containment criterion. Figure 3 illustrates an example with a database of five path transactions from the graph of Figure 1 with *minSupport* equal to two.

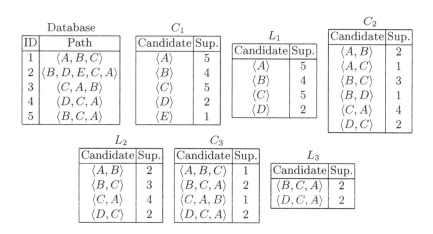

Fig. 3. Example of large path generation.

The differences in mining large paths compared to mining standard association rules and reference sequences, require the development of a new algorithm which has to be based on the graph structure and take into account the notion of subpath containment.

3.2   Pruning with the Support Criterion

Apriori pruning criterion [1] requires that a set of items $I = \{i_1, \ldots, i_n\}$ is large only if every subset of I of length $n - 1$ is also large. In case of a path $S = \langle s_1, \ldots, s_n \rangle$, pruning can be performed based on the following lemma:

Lemma 3 *A path $S = \langle s_1, \ldots, s_n \rangle$ is large only if every subpath S' of S, with length $n - 1$ is also large.*

Proof. See [12].   □

With respect to Corollary 1, a path of length n has at least two and at most n subpaths of length $n - 1$. Notice that in case of mining large reference sequences [7], only the two sections of the path are considered (see Corollary 2). For the determination of large paths, only the subpaths have to be tested, whose number may be less than $\binom{n}{n-1} = n$, as it is the case for itemsets. Therefore, not any other combination of vertices, besides the subpaths, should be tested.

4   Determination of Large Paths

The determination of large paths can be performed in a level-wise manner, as in the Apriori algorithm [1]. The general structure of the algorithm is given bellow. The minimum required support is denoted as *minSupport*. C_k denotes all candidates of length k, L_k the set of all large paths of length k, D the database and G the graph.

Algorithm 1: Level-wise determination of large paths over a graph G
1) $C_1 \leftarrow$ the set of all paths of length 1
2) $k = 1$
3) **while** $(C_k \neq \emptyset)$ {
4)   **for each** path $p \in D$ {
5) $S = \{s | s \in C_k, s \text{ is subpath of } p\}$
6)   **for each** $s \in S$, s.count++
7)   }
8) $L_k = \{s | s \in C_k, s.\text{count} \geq minSupport \}$
9) $C_{k+1} \leftarrow$ genCandidates(L_k, G)
10)   k++
11) }

Although the general structure of the level-wise algorithm is similar to Apriori, its components for

  a. candidate support counting (steps 5 and 6), and
  b. the generation of the candidates of the next phase (step 9)

differ significantly since the problem of determining large paths, as stated in Section 3.1, presents several differences compared to the one of finding large itemsets. First, candidates have to be paths in the graph and not arbitrary combination of vertices. Thus, the procedure of candidate generation (step 9) has to form only valid candidates. It also has to perform apriori pruning with respect to Lemma 3. For support counting (steps 6 and 7), the subpath containment has to be performed with respect to Definition 2. These differences require an algorithm which takes into account the graph structure. Additionally, although existing data structures like the *hash-tree* and *hash-table* can be used for determining large paths, as in [1,7], we use a trie data structure for counting the supports and for storing the large paths. The procedure of generating candidate paths for the next phase of the algorithm is performed with an efficient recursion manner over the trie. It is necessary to notice that all improvements to the Apriori algorithm, as in [13], are also applicable to *Algorithm 1*. Therefore, they are not used in order to make the differences more clear.

4.1 Data Structures

First, we need to store the graph in a main memory data structure. Although several approaches for the representation of graphs in secondary storage have been reported [8,11], however, we assume that the graph size is such that the graph can fit in main memory. The reason is that for the typical example of a web site, the total number of graph vertices is less than a few thousands. The graph is represented with its *adjacency lists*, which hold a list with all vertices connected with an arc starting from graph vertex v, for each v. This list is denoted as $N^+(v)$ and is called the *positive neighborhood* of v [3]. The adjacency list representation is more appropriate for less dense graphs, i.e. graphs with not many arcs.

The candidate paths are held in a trie, an approach which is also followed in [6,15] for itemsets. An important difference is that the fanout (i.e. the number of branches from a trie node) in the case of paths is much smaller, compared to the case of itemsets where any combination of items forms an itemset. This way, the trie occupies less space. Large paths remain in the trie to advocate the procedure of candidate generation.

4.2 Support Counting

The support counting for candidate paths (steps 5 and 6 in algorithm) is the most computationally intensive part of *Algorithm 1*. At the k-th database scan, the support of candidates of length k is counted. For each transaction P with length n that is read from the database, all possible subpaths of length k have to be determined (if P's length is less than k, it is ignored). P is decomposed into all its $\binom{n}{k}$ possible combinations of vertices (see Lemma 2) and each one is searched. For those which exist in the trie, i.e. they are subpaths of P, their

---

[3] The negative neighborhood $N^-(v)$ consist of all vertices w for which there is a vertex from w to v.

support is increased by one. For example, if path $P = \langle A, B, C, D \rangle$ and $k = 3$, then $\langle A, B, C \rangle$, $\langle B, C, D \rangle$, $\langle A, B, D \rangle$ and $\langle A, C, D \rangle$ are searched.

Since, in general, P has less than $\binom{n}{k}$ subpaths, an unsuccessful search is performed for each combination which is not a subpath. In the previous example, $\langle A, B, C \rangle$ and $\langle B, C, D \rangle$ are definitely subpaths (see Corollary 1), while the remaining two may not be subpaths. In the worst case, the complexity of each unsuccessful search is $O(k)$. Thus, the total cost in the worst case is $O(k \cdot [\binom{n}{k} - 2])$. The search for those combination of vertices, which are not subpaths, could be avoided only if for any combination of k vertices, it can be known that there exist a path in the graph connecting these vertices. Algorithms which find the closure of the graph can recognize if there exist a path connecting only two vertices. Since the determination of the path existence would perform a search in the graph with cost $O(k)$ at the worst case, the total cost would again been equal to $O(k \cdot [\binom{n}{k} - 2])$.

As mentioned earlier, the advantage of the trie over the hash-tree, is that, since candidates in hash-tree are only at leafs, at best k and at worst $k + k \cdot m$ comparisons are required for looking up a candidate, where m is the number of candidates stored in a leaf of the hash-tree [1]. On the other hand, in case of a trie, this operation requires k comparisons at the worst case. Apparently, hash-tree requires less memory but, as explained, by storing only paths instead of all arbitrary vertex combinations, memory requirements for the trie are reduced significantly.

4.3   Candidate Generation

After having scanned the database, all large candidates of this phase have to be determined (step 8) and all candidates for the next phase have to be generated (step 9). In Apriori [1], these two steps are performed separately. First, all large candidates L_k at phase k are determined and stored in a hash table. Then, a join $L_k \bowtie L_k$ is performed, using the hash table, for the generation of candidates of phase $k + 1$. For each candidate of length $k + 1$, which belongs to the result of $L_k \bowtie L_k$, all its k subsets of length k are searched whether they belong to L_k (using again the hash table).

Joining $L_k \bowtie L_k$ is done with respect to the first $k - 1$ items of the itemset. For example, if $k = 3$ and two itemsets $I_1 = \{1, 2, 3\}$ and $I_2 = \{1, 2, 4\}$ are large, then they are joined to form a possible candidate $C = \{1, 2, 3, 4\}$. If I_1 or I_2 does not exist, then C will not be a candidate since not all its subsets are large (I_1 or I_2 are not large). Therefore, joining is performed for avoiding generating candidates which will be pruned by the apriori-pruning criterion. As it is easy to show, it is equivalent as if joining on any fixed $k - 1$ items was done, instead of the first $k - 1$ ones.

In case of path candidates, their generation cannot be based on joining $L_k \bowtie L_k$, on a fixed combination of $k - 1$ vertices, because each candidate path C has a different number of large subpaths. For example, the first $k - 1$ vertices (as in Apriori) may not be present in any other subpath besides the one of the two sections of C (see Corollaries 1 and 2). Moreover, this joining in Apriori is performed to reduce the number of examined possible candidates, since any item can be appended to a candidate of length k to produce a possible candidate of length $k + 1$. On the other hand, for candidate paths, only the extensions from the vertices in the positive neighborhood of the last vertex are considered, whose number is much less compared to the case of itemsets.

Therefore, for the generation of candidates of the next phase for *Algorithm 1*, a different approach is followed and steps 8 and 9 are performed together. By visiting all trie leaves, if a candidate $L = \langle \ell_1, \ldots \ell_k \rangle$ is large, then the adjacency list of $N^+(\ell_k)$ (last vertex) is retrieved. For each vertex v in the adjacency list, which does not belong to path L and subpath $L' = \langle \ell_2, \ldots, \ell_k, v \rangle$ is large, a possible candidate $C = \langle \ell_1, \ldots, \ell_k, v \rangle$ of length $k + 1$ is formed by appending v at the end of L. Then, all subpaths of C of length k, besides L', are searched in the trie and if all are large, then C is considered to be a candidate of length $k + 1$ by adding a branch in the trie from vertex ℓ_k to vertex v. The following algorithm describes the candidate generation procedure.

Procedure: genCandidates(L_k, G)
//L_k is the set of large paths of length k and G is the graph
for each large leaf $L = \langle \ell_1, \ldots, \ell_k \rangle$ of trie {
    $N^+(\ell_k) = \{v \mid$ there is an arc $\ell_k \to v$ in $G\}$
    for each $v \in N^+(\ell_k)$ {
        if (v not already in L) and $L' = \langle \ell_2, \ldots, \ell_k, v \rangle$ is large {
            $C = \langle \ell_1, \ldots, \ell_k, v \rangle$
            if ($\forall$ subpath $S \neq L'$ of $C \Rightarrow S \in L_k$)
                insert C in the trie by extending ℓ_k with a branch to v
        }
    }
}

Correctness. See [12].   □

All $k - 2$ possible subpaths $S \neq L'$ of length k of a candidate C have to be searched in the trie structure to verify if they are large. During an unsuccessful search of a possible subpath S, it has to be determined if it is not in the trie because it is not large or because it is not a valid subpath. Thus, if $S = \langle s_1, \ldots, s_k \rangle$ and vertex s_i is not present, then it has to be tested if there is an arc $s_{i-1} \to s_i$ in the graph. If not, then S is not a valid subpath and is ignored. Otherwise, S does not exist, because vertex s_{i-1} was not expanded in a previous phase since subpath $\langle s_1, \ldots, s_{i-1} \rangle$ was not large therefore, S is also not large and thus, C is pruned.

With regards to the efficiency of the procedure *genCandidates* we notice the following. For testing if the subpaths of a candidate are large, there is no need to create a separate hash table (as in case of Apriori) because large candidates are already present in the trie. Testing if a vertex from the adjacency list is already present in the candidate path is done by using a temporary bitmap, which is maintained during the visit of the trie leaves. This way, testing containment is done in O(1). The way trie leaves are expanded by using the adjacency list of their terminating vertex justifies the selection of the graph representation with its adjacency lists. Finally, the trie grows dynamically with simple leaf extensions and there is no need to create a hash-tree from the beginning, as in Apriori.

5   Performance Results

This section contains the results of the experimental evaluation of *Algorithm 1* using synthetic data. The experiments were run in a workstation with one Pentium III processor 450 MHz, 256 MB RAM, under Windows NT 4.0.

5.1   Synthetic Data Generator

First, the site structure has to be generated. Two significant parameters are the total number N of web documents and the maximum number F of hypertext links inside a document. Following the results of [3,4], each web document has a size (in KB) which follows a mixed distribution: Lognormal, for sizes less than 133 KB and Pareto for larger ones. This way, as presented in [4], 93% of the documents are html documents and the remaining ones are large binary objects (images, sounds, etc). For each document, its fanout, i.e. the number of its hypertext links, is determined following a uniform distribution between 1 and F. Documents with sizes larger than 133 KB do not have links because we assume they correspond to large binary objects.

Table 1. Symbols representing parameters of synthetic data.

Symbol	Definition
N	number of vertices
F	maximum fanout
L	average pattern length
P	total number of patterns
C	corruption level

Large paths are chosen from a collection of P paths which represent the patterns. The length of each path pattern is determined by a Poisson distribution with average length L. For the formation of each transaction, representing a user traversal, one of the P path patterns is chosen with uniform distribution. The corruption of patterns is represented with the corruption level C, which is the number of vertices from the path pattern which will be substituted. This number follows a Poisson distribution with average value C. Table 1 presents all the symbols used in the following. Datasets are characterized by the values for parameters L, F and D. For example, $L5F3D100K$ denotes a dataset with average path pattern length 5, maximum fanout 3 and 100,000 transactions. More details for the synthetic data generator can be found in [12].

5.2   Results

First, we examined the scale-up properties of *Algorithm 1* with respect to the number of database path transactions. Figure 4a illustrates the execution times for databases with 1×10^6, 2.5×10^6 and 5×10^6 transactions. For this experiment, the average pattern length $L = 7$, the number of patterns $P = 1,000$, the maximum fanout $F = 15$, and the corruption level $C = 25\%$. Thus, these sets can be denoted as $L7F15D1M$, $L7F15D2.5M$ and $L7F15D5M$. Results are represented for three characteristic values of *minSupport*. As it can be noticed from Figure 4a, *Algorithm 1* presents a linear scale-up with respect to database size.

Also, we examined the scale-up properties of *Algorithm 1* with respect to the site size, i.e. the number of the graph vertices. We used $P = 1,000$, $L = 7$ and $D = 100,000$ transactions. The maximum fanout $F = 15$, since for large graphs we would like that they are not very sparse, whereas $C = 25\%$. The dataset is denoted as $L7F15D100K$ and Figure 4b illustrates the results for three number of vertices: 1000, 2500 and 5000, again for the same three *minSupport* values. As it can be seen, the execution times increases with respect to the number of vertices since there are more candidates to be examined.

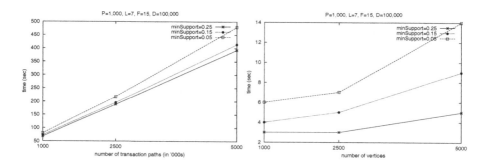

Fig. 4. Scale-up results w.r.t.: **a.** number of transactions, **b.** number of web documents (graph vertices).

Then, we examined the properties of *Algorithm 1* with respect to the pattern length. For this experiment, $P = 1000$ patterns, $N = 1000$ vertices, $D = 100,000$ transactions, the maximum fanout $F = 15$ and the corruption level $C = 25\%$. Figure 5a illustrates the results for three average pattern lengths: 5, 10 and 15. As shown, the execution time increases for larger lengths, especially for lower *minSupport* values, since more phases and thus, database scans are required.

Finally, we tested the impact of the corruption level. Recall that this parameter represents the expected number of vertices within a pattern which are corrupted with other vertices (i.e. not part of the pattern). Figure 5b illustrates the number of large paths founded in the result with respect to three values of corruption level: 0.1%, 0.25% and 0.4%. The dataset was $L7F15D100K$ with

$P = 1000$ patterns. As it is expected, the number of large paths reduces with respect to the corruption level because patterns are changed. However, the reduction is not remarkable since pattern identification is not affected significantly by the corruption.

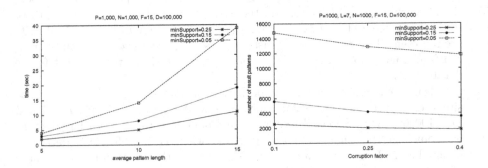

Fig. 5. a. Execution time w.r.t. average pattern length. **b.** Number of large paths w.r.t. the corruption level.

6   Conclusions

We examined the problem of determining traversal patterns from web logs. These patterns take into account the fact that irrelevant accesses, made for navigational purposes, may be interleaved with accesses which are not part of the pattern. We presented a level-wise algorithm for counting the support of these patterns. This algorithm differs from the existing Apriori-like algorithms because it has to take into account the graph structure which represents the web site. The performance of the algorithms is tested experimentally with synthetic data which are produced following several results on recent web statistics.

The quality of the patterns can only be tested within the framework of a specific application. In the future, we plan to test the proposed patterns for the purpose of web prefetching, i.e. the prediction of forthcoming web document requests of a user. For such an application, the impact of noise, as defined in this paper, will be tested more precisely.

Acknowledgments. We would like to acknowledge the effort of Mr. Dimitrios Katsaros on the development of the synthetic data generator.

References

1. R. Agrawal and R. Srikant: "Fast Algorithms for Mining Association Rules", *Proceedings Very Large Data Bases Conference (VLDB'94)*, pp.487-499, 1994.
2. R. Agrawal and R. Srikant: "Mining Sequential Patterns", *Proceedings International Conference on Data Engineering (ICDE'95)*, pp.3-14, 1995.

3. M. Arlitt and C. Williamson. "Internet Web Servers: Workload Characterization and Performance", *IEEE/ACM Transactions on Networking*, Vol.5, No.5, 1997.

4. P. Barford and M. Crovell: "Generating Representative Web Workloads for Network and Server Performance Evaluation", *Proceedings ACM Conference on Measurement and Modeling of Computer Systems (SIGMETRICS'98)*, pp.151-160, 1998.

5. J. Borges and M. Levene: "Mining Association Rules in Hypertext Databases", *Proceedings Conference on Knowledge Discovery and Data Mining (KDD'98)*, pp.149-153, 1998.

6. S. Brin, R. Motwani, J. Ullman and S. Tsur: "Dynamic Itemset Counting and Implication Rules for Market Basket Data", *Proceedings ACM SIGMOD Conference (SIGMOD'97)*, pp.255-264, 1997.

7. M.S. Chen, J.S. Park and P.S. Yu: "Efficient Data Mining for Path Traversal Patterns", *IEEE Transactions on Knowledge and Data Engineering*, Vol.10, No.2, pp.209-221, 1998.

8. Y. Chiang, M. Goodrich, E. Grove, R. Tamassia, D. Vengroff and J.S. Vitter: "External-Memory Graph Algorithms", *Proceedings Symposium on Discrete Algorithms (SODA'95)*, pp.139-149, 1995.

9. R. Cooley, B. Mobasher and J. Srivastava: "Data Preparation for Mining World Wide Web Browsing Patterns", *Knowledge and Information Systems*, Vol.1, No.1, pp.5-32, 1999.

10. K. Joshi, A. Joshi, Y. Yesha and R. Krishnapuram: "Warehousing and Mining Web Logs", *Proceedings Workshop on Web Information and Data Management*, pp.63-68, 1999.

11. M. Nodine, M. Goodrich and J.S. Vitter: "Blocking for External Graph Searching", *Proceedings ACM PODS Conference (PODS'93)*, pp.222-232, 1993.

12. A. Nanopoulos and Y. Manolopoulos: "Finding Generalized Path Patterns for Web Log Data Mining", Technical report, Aristotle University, http://delab.csd.auth.gr/publications.html, 2000.

13. J.S. Park, M.S. Chen and P.S. Yu: "Using a Hash-based Method with Transaction Trimming for Mining Association Rules", *IEEE Transactions on Knowledge and Data Engineering*, Vol.9, No.5, pp.813-825, 1997.

14. J. Pei, J. Han, B. Mortazavi-Asl and H. Zhu: "Mining Access Patterns Efficiently from Web Logs", *Proceedings Pacific-Asia Conference on Knowledge Discovery and Data Mining (PAKDD'00)*, 2000.

15. Y. Xiao and M. Dunham: "Considering Main Memory in Mining Association Rules", *Proceedings Conference on Data Warehousing and Knowledge Discovery (DaWaK'99)*, pp.209-218, 1999.

16. O. Zaiane, M. Xin and J. Han: "Discovering Web Access Patterns and Trends by Applying OLAP and Data Mining Technology on Web Logs", *Proceedings on Advances in Digital Libraries (ADL'98)*, pp.19-29, 1998.

Size Estimation of the Intersection Join between Two Line Segment Datasets*

Enrico Nardelli[1,2] and Guido Proietti[1,2]

[1] Dipartimento di Matematica Pura ed Applicata, Università di L'Aquila,
Via Vetoio, 67010 L'Aquila, Italy.
{nardelli,proietti}@univaq.it.
[2] Istituto di Analisi dei Sistemi e Informatica, Consiglio Nazionale delle Ricerche,
Viale Manzoni 30, 00185 Roma, Italy.

Abstract. In this paper we provide a theoretical framework for estimating the size of the intersection join between two line segment datasets (e.g., roads, railways, utilities). For real datasets, it has been pointed out that the line segment lengths and slopes are distributed according to specific mathematical laws [14]. Starting from this result, we show how to predict the size of the intersection join between two line segment datasets. We evaluate our formula through several experimentations, showing that the estimation is accurate, as compared to that obtained by using a naive uniform model.

1 Introduction

The *spatial join* between two spatial datasets is one of the most popular spatial operation. It can be defined as follows: Given two datasets S and S' of spatial objects and a binary spatial predicate $\theta : S \times S' \rightarrow \{$false, true$\}$, find all pairs of objects $(s, s') \in S \times S'$ such that $\theta(s, s') =$ true. Among the most common spatial predicates, we recall *intersects, crosses, contains, near, adjacent, northwest, meets* and many others [7]. Among them, the most popular is certainly the *intersects* predicate, since it plays a crucial role for the computation of all kinds of joins [8].

In the past, several processing techniques of the intersection join have been developed. In particular, these techniques deal both when S and S' are indexed through an R-tree [2], and when S and S' are not indexed [11,12]. Recently, attention has been posed towards the more general problem of optimizing the processing of *multiway spatial join* [13], where the number of datasets involved in the join operation is larger than 2.

In recent years, *line segment* datasets (e.g., roadmaps, drainage systems, railways, utility networks and many others) are appearing more and more frequently in numerous applications involving spatial data, such as GIS [8,10], multimedia [4], and even traditional databases. This is especially true with the advent

---

* This work has been partially supported by the EU TMR Grant CHOROCHRONOS.

J. Štuller et al. (Eds.): ADBIS-DASFAA 2000, LNCS 1884, pp. 229–238, 2000.

and the rapid growing of spatio-temporal databases, where, for instance, moving points can be represented by means of polylines [5,6]. Therefore, database management systems are usually concerned with intersection join operations involving two datasets of this category, like for instance *"Find all the roads that are crossed by a drain in a given area"*.

Since usually data are stored through their minimum bounding rectangles (MBRs), together with a pointer to the corresponding database entry containing a detailed description of the object, the first step in order to optimize the operation is to retrieve all possible candidates to the output of the join, through a join performed over the MBRs of the objects: this is the so-called *filter step*. Afterward, a *refinement step* takes place, where candidate objects retrieved from the filter step are selected on the basis of effective intersection.

Therefore, to the aim of characterizing the computational effort required by an intersection join and to optimize it as a whole, it is of primary importance to estimate the *size* of the output of the refinement step, that is the number of mutual intersections between the objects in $\mathcal{S}$ and $\mathcal{S}'$. Known techniques for solving this problem generally assume that objects in $\mathcal{S}$ and $\mathcal{S}'$ are *uniformly* and *independently* distributed, although it is well known that this assumption is too restrictive when dealing with real spatial datasets [3]. In this paper we abandon this assumption, and we instead make use of an *exponential law* discovered in the past [14], and concerned with the *complementary cumulative distribution function*[1] (CCDF) of the line segment lengths (expressing the number of line segments $F(\ell)$ having length at least ℓ). We will show that using such a law, we can obtain good estimations, by knowing only few and easy-to-retrieve parameters. More precisely, we will present a large collection of experiments on several line segment datasets, showing that our prediction is usually 40% far from the reality, while the uniform model provides unreliable estimations, with a relative error of up to 5000%. Since the intersection join is the most popular join operation, and given that line segment datasets are among the largest commonly appearing spatial datasets, we conclude that we move an important step forward in the hard task of estimating the size of spatial join operations.

The paper is organized as follows: Section 2 recalls some results achieved in the past on the topic of query optimization and data modelling for multi-dimensional data, and gives a short insight into the mathematical laws that are used throughout the paper. In Section 3 we develop two formulae that can be used to estimate the size of an intersection join between two line segment datasets: the first one is based on a uniform model, while the second one is based on the above mentioned laws. Section 4 provides a collection of experimental results on real datasets, performed to measure the quality of the estimation provided by our model as compared to the uniform model, and suggests some ideas for a possible future improvement of our model. Finally, Section 5 contains some open problems and concluding remarks.

---

[1] Remember that the cumulative distribution function of $f(x) : \Re \to \Re$ is defined as $F(x) = \int_{-\infty}^{x} f(t)dt$, while the complementary cumulative distribution function is defined as $\overline{F}(x) = \int_{x}^{+\infty} f(t)dt$.

2   Previous Work

The main topic within the spatial database field which is related to our present work is *query optimization*, and, more specifically, *size estimation* of the intersection join between two line segment datasets. As we will show in the following, we will develop an analytical formula based on a non-uniform distribution of the underlying data. In fact, the uniformity assumption generally lead to pessimistic results [3].

Whereas for one-dimensional data some developed non-uniform distributions (like for example the Zipf distribution [16]) have met with success, for multi-dimensional data difficulties have not been overcome yet. Most of the previous analysis efforts have focused on point data [1]. In fact, for point data, the count and the fractal dimension of the dataset are sufficient to accurately estimate selectivities for window queries, spatial joins and nearest neighbor queries. For region data, novel results have been proposed in [15], where the authors developed a realistic statistical model, and showed how to use it to compute the selectivity of window queries.

Concerning *line segment data*, the selectivity of window queries has been estimated making use of an exponential law for the CCDF of the segment lengths [14]. More formally, given two points $p_1 = (x_1, y_1)$ and $p_2 = (x_2, y_2)$ in the Euclidean plane $\mathbb{E}^2$, a *convex combination* of p_1 and p_2 is a point $p = (x, y)$ such that

$$x = (1 - \alpha) \cdot x_1 + \alpha \cdot x_2 \quad \text{and} \quad y = (1 - \alpha) \cdot y_1 + \alpha \cdot y_2,$$

with $\alpha \in \mathbb{R}, 0 \leq \alpha \leq 1$. A *line segment* (or simply segment) $s = \overline{p_1 p_2}$ is the set of convex combinations of its *endpoints* p_1 and p_2. Without loss of generality, we will assume in the rest of the paper that $x_1 \leq x_2$ (if $x_1 = x_2$, then we assume that $y_1 \leq y_2$). The *length* of s is

$$\ell(s) = \sqrt{(x_1 - x_2)^2 + (y_1 - y_2)^2},$$

while its *slope* $\theta(s)$ is the angle that s forms with the *horizontal ray*

$$\rho(s) = \{(x, y) \in \mathbb{E}^2 | x \geq x_1, y = y_1\}.$$

Therefore, we have $-\frac{\pi}{2} < \theta(s) \leq \frac{\pi}{2}$. Let $\mathcal{S} = \{s_1, s_2, \ldots, s_n\}$ be a real dataset of line segments. In [14], it has been observed that the CCDF of the segment lengths, say $F(\ell)$, obeys to the following exponential law

$$F(\ell) = n \cdot \left(n^{\frac{1}{\ell_{\max}}}\right)^{-\ell} \quad \ell \geq 0, \tag{1}$$

where $\ell_{\max}$ is the length of the longest line segment in $\mathcal{S}$. Hence, the CCDF of the lengths of $\mathcal{S}$ can be synthetically described by means of a mathematical law (named *SLED law*) containing only two constants that can be easily determined: the count of objects n and the length $\ell_{\max}$ of the longest line.

Moreover, in the same paper it has been observed that in many real line segment datasets the orientation of the segments is uniformly distributed. This has been named the *SUD law*. In the next section, we will use both the SLED and the SUD law to predict the size of the *intersection join* between two line segment datasets.

3   Proposed Method

In this section, we first give the problem definition, and we then propose two estimations of the intersection join between two line segment datasets: the first one is based on a naive uniform model, while the second one makes use of the above mentioned laws.

3.1   Problem Definition

Let us rigorously state the problem we are concerned with. For the sake of clarity, we focus on the 2-dimensional space, but all the results can be extended to the d-dimensional space.

PROBLEM: size of the intersection join between two line segment datasets

Given: In the address space $U = [0,1] \times [0,1]$, two line segment datasets $\mathcal{S} = \{s_1, s_2, \ldots, s_n\}$ and $\mathcal{S}' = \{s_1', s_2', \ldots, s_m'\}$, whose longest segments have length $\ell_{\max}$ and $\ell_{\max}'$, respectively;

Find: the size of the *intersection join* between $\mathcal{S}$ and $\mathcal{S}'$, that is the number of mutual intersections between segments of $\mathcal{S}$ and $\mathcal{S}'$, say $Size(\mathcal{S} \cap \mathcal{S}')$.

3.2   A Naive Estimation Based on the Uniform Model

Assuming that $\mathcal{S}$ and $\mathcal{S}'$ obey to a uniform model, we have that each segment in $\mathcal{S}$ has length $\ell_{\max}$, while each segment in $\mathcal{S}'$ has length $\ell_{\max}'$. The following can be proved:

Theorem 1. *Let be given in $U = [0,1] \times [0,1]$ two line segment datasets $\mathcal{S} = \{s_1, s_2, \ldots, s_n\}$ and $\mathcal{S}' = \{s_1', s_2', \ldots, s_m'\}$, whose longest segments have length $\ell_{\max}$ and $\ell_{\max}'$, respectively. If we assume that segments in $\mathcal{S}$ and $\mathcal{S}'$ are distributed according to a uniform model, then we have*

$$Size(\mathcal{S} \cap \mathcal{S}') = \frac{2}{\pi} \cdot n \cdot m \cdot \ell_{\max} \cdot \ell_{\max}'. \tag{2}$$

Proof. To estimate $Size(\mathcal{S} \cap \mathcal{S}')$, we handle the spatial join operation as a sequence of intersection queries posed on $\mathcal{S}'$ of each segment belonging to $\mathcal{S}$. Firstly, observe that given two segments s and s' in U, the probability they intersect is

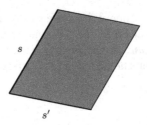

Fig. 1. Two segments s and s' intersect iff the right endpoint of s falls into the grey area.

$$p(s \cap s') = \ell(s) \cdot \ell(s') \cdot |\sin(\theta(s) - \theta(s'))|.$$

In fact, this is the probability that the right endpoint of s falls into the grey polygon depicted in Figure 1.

It follows that the expected number of segments in $\mathcal{S}'$ intersected in U by s_1, say $T(s_1, \mathcal{S}')$, is

$$T(s_1, \mathcal{S}') = \sum_{j=1}^{m} p(s_1, s'_j) = \ell(s_1) \cdot \sum_{j=1}^{m} \ell(s'_j) \cdot |\sin(\theta(s_1) - \theta(s'_j))|.$$

Analogously, when considering the i-th segment in $\mathcal{S}$, we have that

$$T(s_i, \mathcal{S}') = \sum_{j=1}^{m} p(s_i, s'_j) = \ell(s_i) \cdot \sum_{j=1}^{m} \ell(s'_j) \cdot |\sin(\theta(s_i) - \theta(s'_j))|.$$

Therefore, we have that

$$Size(\mathcal{S} \cap \mathcal{S}') = \sum_{i=1}^{n} T(s_i, \mathcal{S}') = \sum_{i=1}^{n} \ell(s_i) \cdot \left(\sum_{j=1}^{m} \ell(s'_j) \cdot |\sin(\theta(s_i) - \theta(s'_j))| \right). \quad (3)$$

Since segments in $\mathcal{S}$ and $\mathcal{S}'$ are oriented according to a uniform model, we have that the average value of $|\sin(\theta(s_i) - \theta(s'_j))|$ equals the average value of $\sin \theta$ in $[0, \pi/2]$, that is $2/\pi$ [14]. Moreover, since segment lengths in $\mathcal{S}$ and $\mathcal{S}'$ are uniformly distributed as well, we have that $\ell(s_i) = \ell_{max}$ and $\ell(s'_j) = \ell'_{max}$, for all i and j. Hence, we eventually have that

$$Size(\mathcal{S} \cap \mathcal{S}') = \frac{2}{\pi} \cdot n \cdot m \cdot \ell_{\max} \cdot \ell'_{\max}. \quad (4)$$

$\square$

3.3 A More Accurate Estimation

A more accurate estimation for real line datasets can be obtained by assuming that segments in $\mathcal{S}$ and $\mathcal{S}'$ obey to the SLED and to the SUD law. Let $F(\ell)$ and $F'(\ell)$ be the CCDFs associated with $\mathcal{S}$ and $\mathcal{S}'$, respectively. ¿From our assumptions, we have that

$$F(\ell) = n \cdot \left(n^{\frac{1}{\ell_{\max}}} \right)^{-\ell} \quad F'(\ell) = m \cdot \left(m^{\frac{1}{\ell'_{\max}}} \right)^{-\ell} \quad \ell \geq 0. \tag{5}$$

The following can be proved:

Theorem 2. *Let be given in $U = [0,1] \times [0,1]$ two line segment datasets $\mathcal{S} = \{s_1, s_2, \ldots, s_n\}$ and $\mathcal{S}' = \{s'_1, s'_2, \ldots, s'_m\}$, whose longest segments have length $\ell_{\max}$ and $\ell'_{\max}$, respectively. If we assume that segments in $\mathcal{S}$ and $\mathcal{S}'$ are distributed according to the SLED and to the SUD law, then we have that* [2]

$$\boxed{Size(\mathcal{S} \cap \mathcal{S}') \approx \frac{2}{\pi} \cdot \frac{\ell_{\max}}{\ln n} \cdot \frac{\ell'_{\max}}{\ln m} \cdot (m - \ln m - 1) \cdot (n - \ln n - 1).} \tag{6}$$

Proof. The proof is based on the approach used for Theorem 1. Without loss of generality, let us assume that the segments in $\mathcal{S}$ and $\mathcal{S}'$ are sorted in decreasing order according to their length, that is $\ell(s_1) = \ell_{\max}$ and $\ell(s'_1) = \ell'_{\max}$. ¿From the inverse relation[3] of (5), we have that

$$\ell(F) = \frac{1}{\ln \left(n^{\frac{1}{\ell_{\max}}} \right)} \cdot \ln \frac{n}{F} = \frac{\ell_{\max}}{\ln n} \cdot \ln \frac{n}{F}$$

and analogously for $\ell(F')$

$$\ell(F') = \frac{\ell'_{\max}}{\ln m} \cdot \ln \frac{m}{F'}.$$

Following (3), and given that $\mathcal{S}$ and $\mathcal{S}'$ obey to the SUD law, we have that

$$Size(\mathcal{S} \cap \mathcal{S}') = \frac{2}{\pi} \cdot \sum_{i=1}^{n} \sum_{j=1}^{m} \ell(s_i) \cdot \ell(s'_j). \tag{7}$$

To estimate $Size(\mathcal{S} \cap \mathcal{S}')$, we replace the above summation by an integral. This approximation is based on the Euler's summation formula, which for sufficiently smooth functions (like $F(\ell)$ and $F'(\ell)$ are) turns out to be very accurate [9]. Therefore, we have that (7) can be rewritten as follows

---

[2] In the rest of the paper, all logarithms are natural.

[3] Remember that given a one-to-one function $f(x) : \Re \to \Re$, its inverse $f^{-1}(x)$ is defined by $f(f^{-1}(x)) = f^{-1}(f(x)) \equiv x$.

$$Size(\mathcal{S} \cap \mathcal{S}') \approx \frac{2}{\pi} \cdot \int_1^n \int_1^m \ell(F) \cdot \ell(F') dF\ dF' =$$

$$\frac{2}{\pi} \cdot \frac{\ell_{\max}}{\ln n} \cdot \frac{\ell'_{\max}}{\ln m} \cdot \int_1^n \int_1^m \ln \frac{n}{F} \cdot \ln \frac{m}{F'} dF\ dF' =$$

$$\frac{2}{\pi} \cdot \frac{\ell_{\max}}{\ln n} \cdot \frac{\ell'_{\max}}{\ln m} \cdot (m - \ln m - 1) \cdot (n - \ln n - 1).$$

$\square$

4   Experiments on Real Datasets

To assess experimentally the accuracy of our formula (6), we have tested it on different line segment datasets scattered all around the world (Italy, Germany, Japan, California, Russia, etc.), available at `http://www.gisdatadepot.com`. More precisely, we have downloaded all the line segment datasets available for several different countries. Afterwards, we have computed the intersection join between all pairs of datasets of each country, since it does not make much sense to intersect two datasets from two different countries. Due to space limitations, we here provide a small subset of the experiments, concerned with the following data of North Italy:

- Drainage system (DRAIN), consisting of 18,923 segments;
- Railways network (RAIL), consisting of 4,469 segments;
- Roadmap (ROAD), consisting of 9,732 segments;
- Utility network (UTIL), consisting of 2,070 segments.

All the datasets were stored in vectorial format on a Digital DEC 3000 running UNIX V4.0B. Preliminarily, we have computed all the relevant features needed for checking our results. Such a computation is very fast, since it can be performed by means of a single scan of the datasets. These data are summarized in Table 1. Figure 2 depicts the datasets, along with the CCDF of their segment lengths. Notice that CCDFs are plotted in a log-linear diagram: The pictures confirm that the CCDFs follow very well an exponential law, since they appear as straight lines in the log-linear diagram.

To ascertain the accuracy of our formula (6) as compared with the estimation provided by the uniform model (2), we have opposed them to the real size of the

Table 1. Datasets features.

Dataset	Count	ℓ_{max}	Image Space Area
DRAIN	18,923	0.09961	23.842
RAIL	4,469	0.15468	23.242
ROAD	9,732	0.14578	23.529
UTIL	2,070	0.41221	22.342

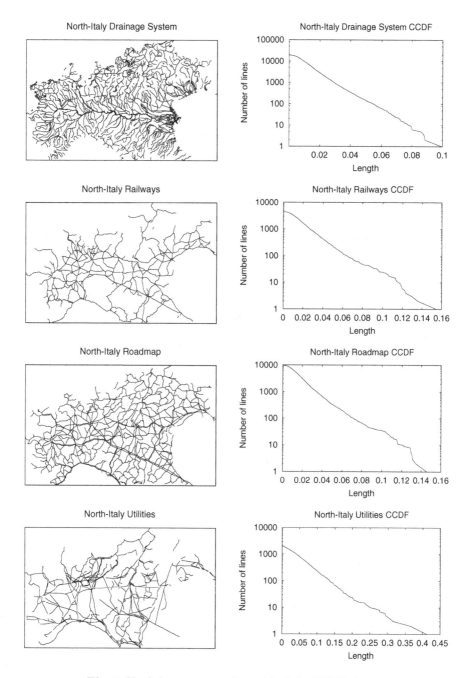

Fig. 2. Used datasets, together with their CCDF plots.

Table 2. Experimental results: real size of the joins versus estimated ones using the proposed technique (NEW) and the uniform model (OLD), together with their respective relative errors.

Dataset	Actual	NEW	OLD	% Err NEW	% Err OLD
DRAIN ∩ RAIL	625	367.1	30482.9	-70.1	4777.2
DRAIN ∩ ROAD	1202	683.9	61956.2	-75.7	5054.4
DRAIN ∩ UTIL	875	510.8	38593.0	-71.2	4310.6
RAIL ∩ ROAD	601	347.0	26861.3	-42.2	4369.3
RAIL ∩ UTIL	385	250.2	16155.2	-38.5	4515.7
ROAD ∩ UTIL	675	489.6	34493.6	-27.5	5010.0

intersection joins between all possible pairs of datasets. The intersection join has been performed by using segment trees implemented in C language. Given the size of some datasets (of the order of several thousands of line segments), the results have been obtained by paying a severe cost in terms of CPU time (up to a hour). This confirms that the size estimation of spatial join operations is a very crucial step in query optimization. Table 2 contains the obtained results and their relative errors, both for our model (NEW) and the uniform one (OLD).

A first comment on the results is that our estimation maintains the error within 75%, achieving an accuracy of 27%, while the uniform model is totally unreliable, with an error in the (over)estimation up to 5,000%. Notice that our model tends to underestimate the actual size of the intersection. Our explanation for this fact is that the datasets from a given country tend to overlap (given that they are defined over the same geographic space and therefore there is a strong correlation among them). In some sense, we could interpret the deviation from the predicted value as a measure of the correlation between the datasets!

We leave as a future study the problem of correcting our formulas so that they take into account from the beginning of the correlation between the two datasets that are going to be joined.

5   Conclusions

The main contribution of this paper is the estimation of the size of the intersection join between two spatial datasets containing line segments.

We showed that very few measures are needed (essentially the count of segments and the length of the longest segment), to achieve quite accurate results. Our experiments on diverse, real datasets, scattered around the world showed that our approach achieves estimates pretty close to the reality, while a straightforward estimation based on a uniform model provides result totally unreliable.

Promising future directions include the study of the intersection join on spatial datasets other than line datasets, the extension to the case of multiway intersection join, and the analysis of other spatial join operations. We also look forward to improve our formulas by taking into account of a *correlation factor* between the datasets.

References

1. A. Belussi and C. Faloutsos. Estimating the selectivity of spatial queries using the 'correlation' fractal dimension. In *21th Conference on Very Large Data Bases (VLDB'95)*, pages 299–310, Zurich, Switzerland, 1995.
2. T. Brinkhoff, H.P. Kriegel, and B. Seeger. Efficient processing of spatial joins using R-trees. In *19th ACM Int. Conf. on Management of Data (SIGMOD'93)*, pages 237–246, 1993.
3. S. Christodoulakis. Implication of certain assumptions in database performance evaluation. *ACM TODS*, 9(2):163–186, June 1984.
4. C. Faloutsos, M. Ranganathan, and Y. Manolopoulos. Fast subsequence matching in time-series databases. In *20th ACM Int. Conference on Management of Data (SIGMOD'94)*, pages 419–429, Minneapolis, MN, May 1994.
5. L. Forlizzi, R.H. Güting, E. Nardelli, and M. Schneider. A data model and data structures for moving objects databases. In *26th ACM Int. Conf. on Management of Data (SIGMOD 2000)*, pages 319–330, 2000.
6. A.U. Frank, S. Grumbach, R.H. Güting, C.S. Jensen, M. Koubarakis, N.A. Lorentzos, Y. Manolopoulos, E. Nardelli, B. Pernici, H.J. Schek, M. Scholl, T.K. Sellis, B. Theodoulidis, and P. Widmayer. Chorochronos: A research network for spatiotemporal database systems. *SIGMOD Record*, 28(3):12–21, 1999.
7. V. Gaede and O. Günther. Multidimensional access methods. *Computing Surveys*, 30(2):170–231, 1998.
8. V. Gaede and W.F. Riekert. Spatial access methods and query processing in the object-oriented GIS GODOT. In *AGDM'94 Workshop*, pages 40–52, Delft, The Netherlands, 1994.
9. R.L. Graham, D.E. Knuth, and O. Patashnik. *Concrete Mathematics*. Addison-Wesley Publishing Company, New York, 1989.
10. R.H. Güting. An introduction to spatial database systems. *VLDB Journal*, 3(4):357–399, 1994.
11. N. Koudas and K.C. Sevcik. Size separation spatial join. In *23th ACM Int. Conf. on Management of Data (SIGMOD'97)*, pages 324–335, 1997.
12. M.L. Lo and C.V. Ravishankar. Spatial joins using seeded trees. In *20th ACM Int. Conf. on Management of Data (SIGMOD'94)*, pages 209–220, 1994.
13. D. Papadias, N. Mamoulis, and Y. Theodoridis. Processing and optimization of multiway spatial joins using R-trees. In *18th ACM Symp. on Principles of Database Systems (PODS'99)*, pages 44–55, 1999.
14. G. Proietti and C. Faloutsos. Selectivity estimation of window queries for line segment datasets. In *7th ACM Conference on Information and Knowledge Management (CIKM'98)*, pages 340–347, Washington, DC, 1998.
15. G. Proietti and C. Faloutsos. Accurate modeling of region data. *IEEE Trans. on Knowledge and Data Engineering,* in press, 2000. Also available as CMU-TR-98-126, Dept. of Computer Science, Carnegie Mellon University, Pittsburgh, PA.
16. G.K. Zipf. *Human behavior and principle of least effort: an introduction to human ecology*. Addison Wesley, Cambridge, MA, 1949.

Distributed Searching of k-Dimensional Data with Almost Constant Costs

Adriano Di Pasquale[1] and Enrico Nardelli[1,2]

[1] Dipartimento di Matematica Pura ed Applicata, Univ. of L'Aquila,
Via Vetoio, Coppito, I-67010 L'Aquila, Italia.
{dipasqua,nardelli}@univaq.it

[2] Istituto di Analisi dei Sistemi ed Informatica, Consiglio Nazionale delle Ricerche,
Viale Manzoni 30, I-00185 Roma, Italia.

Abstract. In this paper we consider the dictionary problem in the scalable distributed data structure paradigm introduced by Litwin, Neimat and Schneider and analyze costs for insert and exact searches in an amortized framework. We show that both for the 1-dimensional and the k-dimensional case insert and exact searches have an amortized almost constant costs, namely $O\left(\log_{(1+A)} n\right)$ messages, where n is the total number of servers of the structure, b is the capacity of each server, and $A = \frac{b}{2}$. Considering that A is a large value in real applications, in the order of thousands, we can assume to have a constant cost in real distributed structures.

Only worst case analysis has been previously considered and the almost constant cost for the amortized analysis of the general k-dimensional case appears to be very promising in the light of the well known difficulties in proving optimal worst case bounds for k-dimensions.

Keywords: distributed data structure, message passing environment, multi-dimensional search.

1 Introduction

The constant increase of PCs and workstations connected by a network and the need to manage greater and greater amount of data motivates the research focusing on the design and analysis of distributed databases. The technological framework we make reference to is the so called *network computing*: fast communication networks and many powerful and cheap workstations. There are several aspects making this environment attractive. The most important one is that a set of sites has more power and resources with respect to a single site, independently from the equipment of a site. Moreover the network offers a transfer speed that is not comparable with the magnetic or optical disks one. Therefore this framework is a suitable environment for the newer applications with high performance requirements, like, for example, spatio-temporal databases [14,3].

In this work we consider the dictionary problem in a message passing distributed environment and we follow the paradigm of the SDDS (*Scalable Distributed Data Structure*) defined by Litwin, Neimat e Schneider [8]. The main properties of SDDS paradigm are:

J. Štuller et al. (Eds.): ADBIS-DASFAA 2000, LNCS 1884, pp. 239–250, 2000.

1. Keep a good performance level while the number of managed objects changes.
2. Perform operations locally.

We assume that data are distributed among a variable number of servers and accessed by a set of clients. Both servers and clients are distributed among the nodes of the network. Clients and servers communicate by sending and receiving *point-to-point* messages. We assume network communication is free of errors. Servers store objects uniquely identified by a key. Every server stores a single block (called *bucket*) of at most b data items, for a fixed number b. New servers are brought in as the volume of data increases to maintain the performance level.

The fundamental measure of the efficiency of an operation in this distributed context is the number of messages exchanged between the sites of the network. The internal work of a site is neglected. In order to minimize the number of messages, in a search operation it is possible to use some index locally to a site to better address the search towards another site. The search process in the local index performed by a site is not accounted in the complexity analysis.

The clients are not, in general, up-to-date with the evolution of the structure, in the sense they have some local indexing structure, but do not know, in general, the overall status of the data structure. Different clients may therefore have different and incomplete views of the data structure.

In an extreme case we can design the following distributed structure: there is a server *root* knowing all the other servers. When a split occurs, the new server which is brought in sends a messages to *root* to communicate its presence. When a server is not pertinent for a request, it sends the request to *root*, that looks for the correct server in its local index and sends it the request. Each access has thus a cost of at most 2 messages. But with this solution *root* is a bottleneck, because it has to manage each address error, and this violates the basic scalability requirement of the SDDS paradigm.

However, the above example shows that we can have, within this distributed computing framework, a worst case constant cost for the search process, while in the centralized case the lower bound is well known to be logarithmic.

There are various proposal in the literature addressing the dictionary problem within the paradigm of the SDDS: LH* [8], RP* [9], DRT [7], lazy k-d-tree [10], RBST [1], BDST [4] distributed B+-trees [2].

In this work we propose a variant of the management technique for distributed data used in the DRT [7]. We conduct an amortized analysis of the proposed strategy showing it has an almost constant cost for insert and search and we show how to adapt the strategy to the multi-dimensional case.

2   Description of the Structure

2.1   Split Management

Servers manage their bucket in the usual way. We say a server goes in overflow when it is managing b keys and a new one is sent to it, where b is the capacity of a server. For the sake of simplicity, we assume b is even. When a server goes in overflow it has to split: it finds a new server to bring in (for example asking to a special site, called Split Coordinator), and sends it half of its keys.

The interval of the keys managed by s is divided by the *split* in two sub-intervals. From now on, the server s manages one of this sub-intervals (the one that contains the keys remaining in s), while s' manages the other one. We assume that after a *split* the splitting server s always manages the lower half of the two intervals resulting from the *split* and the new server s' manages the upper half. Also, after this *split*, s knows that s' is the server brought in by itself.

After a *split*, one of the two resulting servers manages $\frac{b}{2}$ keys and the other one $\frac{b}{2}+1$ keys. Let $A = \frac{b}{2}$. Whit m requests, it follows directly that we can have at most $\lfloor \frac{m}{A} \rfloor$ *splits*.

2.2   Local Tree

The clients and the servers have a local indexing structure, called *local tree*. From a logical point of view this is a tree composed by an incomplete collection of servers. For each server s the managed interval of keys $I(s)$ is also stored. The local tree of a client can be wrong, in the sense that in the reality a server s is managing an interval smaller than what the client currently knows, due to a *split* performed by s and unknown to the client. In particular, given the split management policy above described, if $I_r = [a, b)$ is the real interval of s, and $I_{lt} = [c, d)$ is the interval of s in some local tree, then $a = c$ and $b \leq d$. For example in reality $I_r(s) = [100, 200)$, while in a local tree we could have $I_{lt}(s) = [100, 250)$. The local tree can be managed internally with any data structure: list, tree,etc.

Note that for each request of a key k received by a server s, k is within the interval I that s managed before its first division. This is due to the fact that if a client has information on s, then certainly s manages an interval $I' \subseteq I$, due to the way overflow is managed through *splits*. Therefore if s is chosen as server to which to send the request of a key k, it means that $k \in I' \Rightarrow k \in I$.

The local tree of a client c is set up and updated using the answers of servers to request of c. The local tree of a server s is composed at least by the servers generated by s through a *split*. In particular, since a server always knows the next ones brought in by itself through its *splits*, this always guarantees the existence of a path between the initial server and any other server. A server always adds its *local tree* in every message to update clients with information about its view of the overall structure.

2.3   Requests Management

A client c that wants to perform a request chooses in its local tree the server s that should manage the request and sends it a *request message*.

If s is pertinent for the request then performs it (see figure 1-a). In general, if the request is a search operation then an answer is always sent back to the client; if it is an insert no answer is sent.

If s is not pertinent we have an *address error*. In this case s looks for the pertinent server s' in its *local tree* and forwards it the request.

Since also s' can be not pertinent, thus forwarding the request to still another server, in general we can have a series of *address error* that causes a chain of messages between the servers $s_1,s_2,..,s_k$. Finally, server s_k is pertinent and can satisfy the request. Moreover, s_k receives the local trees of the server $s_1,s_2,..,s_{k-1}$ which have been traversed by the request. It first builds a correction tree C aggregating the local trees received and its own one, and then sends Local Tree Correction (LTC) messages with C to the client (even if it was an insert operation) and to all servers $s_1,s_2,..,s_{k-1}$, so to allow them to correct their local trees (see figure 1-b).

In figure 1 the possible cases of search process are shown. We have that each request has a cost, without counting the initial request and the final answer messages, either 0 (case a) or $2(k-1)$(case b).

This strategy to manage the distributed structure, is very similar to the one defined by Kröll and Widmayer for DRT [7] and therefore we call it DRT*.

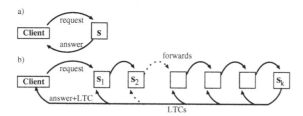

Fig. 1. Possible cases of the search process.

2.4   Split Tree

From the description above of the local trees and how they change due to the distribution of information about the overall structure through LTC messages, it is clear that the number of messages needed to answer a request changes with the increase of the number of requests. To analyze how changes in the content and structure of local trees affect the cost of answering to requests we associate to each server s of DRT* a rooted tree $ST(s)$, called the *split tree* of s. The nodes of $ST(s)$ are the servers pertinent for a request arriving to s. The tree has an arbitrary structure except that the root is s. An arc (s_1, s_2) in $ST(s)$ means that s_1 is in the local tree of s_2. When a server updates its local tree using LTC messages the structure of $ST(s)$ changes.

We call $ST_0(s)$ the split tree of server s obtained from a sequence of requests over a DRT* without applying the correction of the local trees of the servers using LTC messages, i.e. $ST_0(s)$ is shaped only by *splits* of the servers. Initially $ST_0(s)$ is made up only by s. Whenever s splits, with s' as new server, the node s' and a new arc (s', s) are added to $ST_0(s)$. The same holds for the splits of servers which are nodes in $ST_0(s)$ (for example, in figure 2-center, the split of server e adds the node s' and the arc (s', e) in $ST_0(a)$).

Since each server s' in $ST_0(s)$ was created by a chain of splits emanating from s, then s' manages a sub-interval of the initial interval managed by s.

If we consider the correction of local trees, the structure of the split tree of s changes. Infact, due to the correction, after a request to a server d, s adds all the servers in the path between s and d in its local tree. The consequence is that now s can address directly these servers in the future. In order to describe this new situation in the split tree of s, we delete the arcs of the traversed path and add to s the arcs between s and the traversed servers. The result is a compression of the path between s and d (see figure 2-right).

We denote with $ST(s)$ the split tree of s whose structure has been determined by the use of LTC messages. We denote with $T_s(s')$ the sub-tree of $ST(s)$ rooted at server s'. We give some immediate properties of split trees:

Lemma 1. *Each request arriving to s is pertinent for a server in $ST(s)$.*

Lemma 2. *Let s' be a server in $ST(s)$. Let $Q_s(s')$ be the set of servers in the sub-tree of $ST_0(s)$ rooted at s', but for s' itself. Let $p(s', s)$ be the set of servers belonging to the path in $ST_0(s)$ from s' (excluded) to s (included).*

As long as no request pertinent for a server $x \in Q_s(s')$ arrives to a server $y \in p(s', s)$, it is $ST(s') = T_s(s')$.

For example, by comparing figure 2-left and figure 2-right, you can check that $ST(c)$ does not correspond anymore with the sub-tree $T_a(c)$ of $ST(a)$ after the request pertinent for d arrives to a and is forwarded to d.

We use the split trees to takes into account in the amortized analysis the use of LTC messages to reduce the cost of satisfying the request.

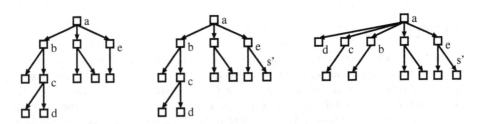

Fig. 2. The splits build up $ST_0(a)$ (e splits, with s' as new server)(left and center). The effect of a compression after a request pertinent for d and arrived to a (right). $ST(c)$ does not correspond anymore to the sub-tree $T_a(c)$ of $ST(a)$. The same for b.

3   Amortized Analysis

Since the way local trees change during the evolution of the overall structure is similar to the structural changes happening in the *set union problem* we now first briefly recall it and then analyze amortized complexity of operations in DRT*.

3.1   The Set Union Problem

The set union is a classical problem that has been deeply analyzed [13,15]. It is the problem of maintaining a collection of disjoint sets of elements under the operation of union. All algorithms for the set union problem appearing in the literature use an approach based on the *canonical element*. Within each set, we distinguish an arbitrary but unique element called the *canonical element*, used to represent the set. Operations defined in the set union problem are:

- *make-set(e)*: create a new set containing the single element e, which at the time of the operation does not belong to any set. The canonical element of the new set is e.
- *find(e)*: return the canonical element of the set containing element e.
- *union(e,f)*: combine the sets whose canonical elements are e and f into a single set, and make either e or f the canonical element of the new set. This operation requires that $e \neq f$.

We represent each set by a rooted tree whose nodes are the elements of the set and the root is the canonical element. Each node x contains a pointer $p(x)$ to its parent in the tree; the root points to itself. This is a *compressed tree* representation [6].

To carry out *find(e)*, we follow parent pointers from e until the root, which is then returned. While traversing parent pointer, one can apply some techniques for compressing the path from the elements to the root: *compression*, *splitting*, and *halving* (see figure 3).

To carry out *union* various techniques can be applied: *naive linking*, *linking by rank* and *linking by size*.

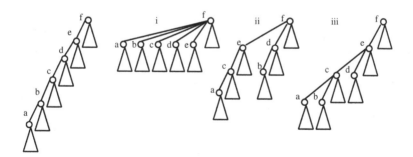

Fig. 3. The compression (i), the splitting (ii), and the halving (iii) of a path a,b,c,d,e,f
.

In [15], Tarjan and Van Leeuwen have conducted a worst-case analysis on the set union problem. In particular, they have shown that *naive linking* coupled with any of the three above described path compression techniques gives a worst-case running time of the set union problem of $\Theta\left(m \log_{(1+m/n)} n\right)$, where m is the number of finds and n is the number of elements, and it is assumed that $m \geq n$.

3.2 Upper Bound

For shortness of space, in this paper we suppose to operate in an environment where the clients work slowly. More precisely, we suppose that between two requests the involved servers have the time to complete all updates of their local tree. This restriction can be easily overcome through the introduction of a suitable lock mechanism [5] providing similar complexity result.

The cost of a sequence of operations is the sum of the cost of each operation. For the complexity analysis we can view insert and search operations as composed by two parts: the request part, possibly with forwarding and LTC messages, and the split part. Then the cost of an operation is the sum of the cost for the request part and of the cost for the split part. The cost of the request part is the number of messages needed to answer it. We do not count the two messages of request from the client and of answer to it, since these are always present in any operation and add only a constant term to the analysis. For the cost of the split part we assume that a *split* takes 4 messages (like in the DRT [7]).

In order to give an upper bound on the complexity of queries on DRT*, we show an equivalence between split trees and the compressed trees used for the set union problem solved by means of *naive linking* coupled with the *compression* technique. In particular we show that there is an equivalence between:

- A server and an element.
- A compressed tree $CT(s)$ with canonical element s and the split tree $ST(s)$ of the server s.
- A $find(s')$, where s' is in the compressed tree $CT(s)$ with canonical element s, and a request (insert or search) pertinent for a server s', where s' is in the split tree $ST(s)$, and arriving to a server s.
- A $make\text{-}set(s')$ and a $split$ of a server s, where s' is the new server.

Please note that in $union(e, f)$ with the *naive linking* technique we always make e point to f. We now show that for each sequence of requests in a DRT* there is a specific sequence of *finds*, *make-sets* and *unions* in the set union problem whose complexity bounds the DRT* one.

Let us consider a request arrived at server s and pertinent for s'. This can be a search or an insert of a key in a server s'. We can view this request as the search of the server s' in $ST(s)$ and we call this view *server search*(s', s). Please note that a request and its view as a *server search* in the split tree have the same cost. Therefore, in order to calculate the cost of a sequence of requests in a DRT* we can consider a corresponding sequence of operations in split trees, made up by *server searches* and *splits*, and calculate the cost of this sequence.

Lemma 3. *Let σ be a sequence of requests in a DRT* and σ' the corresponding sequence of splits and server searches in split trees. Let σ'' be a permutation of σ', keeping the relative order between the splits and between the server searches, and such that all the splits are at the beginning of the sequence. Then σ' and σ'' have the same cost.*

Proof. Note that since split is a local operation its cost does not depend on its position in the sequence of operations on the split tree. Moreover its advance in the sequence of operations on the split tree does not affect the cost of any *server searches*.

Lemma 4. *Let σ'' be a sequence of operations in split trees, where all splits are at beginning. The cost of the sequence does not change if the order of two consecutive server searches is inverted.*

Proof. Let $p(x, y)$ be the set of nodes in the path from node x to its ancestor y in a split tree. Let $|p(x, y)|$ be the number of arcs in $p(x, y)$. Let $search(s', s)$ and $search(t', t)$ be two consecutive server searches for server s' (resp. t') in $ST(s)$ (resp. $ST(t)$). If $p(t', t) \bigcap p(s', s) = \emptyset$, then the two server searches do not affect each other and their position can be exchanged. Let us assume $p(t', t) \bigcap p(s', s) = p \neq \emptyset$ and without loss of generality let $t \in p(s', s)$ and $search(s', s)$ precedes $search(t', t)$. Then $search(s', s)$ costs $|p(s', s)|$ and $search(t', t)$ costs $1 + |p(t', t) - p|$, because of the compression of path from s' to s in $ST(s)$ and of path p in $ST(t)$. Let us now exchange the position of the two server searches. Now $search(t', t)$ costs $|p(t', t)|$ and $search(s', s)$ costs $1 + |p(s', s) - p|$, because of the compression of path from t' to t in $ST(t)$ and of path p in $ST(s)$. In both cases the total cost of the two server searches is the same.

Lemma 5. *Let σ'' be a sequence of operations in split trees, where all splits are at beginning. We say a server search(s', s) in σ'' is of height $h(s)$, where $h(s)$ is the height of s in $ST_0(s_0)$, assigning height 0 to s_0. Let h be the height of the highest server in $ST_0(s_0)$. Let σ''' be a permutation of σ'', obtained through exchanges of adjacent server searches, where all server searches of height k precedes all server searches of height $k - 1$, for $k = h, h - 1, ..., 1$. Then σ'' and σ''' have the same cost.*

Proof. We reorder σ'' exchanging consecutive server searches. For lemma 4 each exchange does not change the total cost.

We now show how to build a sequence ρ of operations for the set union problem that is equivalent to σ'''. We can write $\sigma''' = \sigma*, \sigma_h, \sigma_{h-1}, ..., \sigma_0$, where $\sigma*$ is the initial sub-sequence of *splits* and σ_k denotes the sub-sequences of *server searches* of height k, for $k = h, h - 1, ..., 0$. We start ρ with a sequence of *make set*, each corresponding to a *split* in $\sigma*$. Then we add to ρ a *find* for each *server search* in σ_h. Then for each server s' at height $h - 1$ and satisfying the condition that s' is the parent of s'' in $ST(s_0)$ we add to ρ operation $union(s'', s')$. Now, for each $k = h - 1, h - 2, ..., 1$ we repeat the above process of adding to ρ a *find* operation for each *server search* in σ_k and a *union* for each server at height $k - 1$ satisfying the above condition. Finally we add to ρ a *find* for each *server search* in σ_0.

Note that since the sequence σ''' has been reordered according to server heights, each *server search*(s', s) is executed when s satisfies the hypothesis of lemma 2. Hence it is $ST(s) = T_{s_0}(s)$ and the cost of *server search*(s', s) can be analyzed in $ST(s_0)$.

Let $p_{CT}(s', s) = \langle s' = x_1, x_2, \ldots, x_r = s \rangle$ be the path connecting s' to its ancestor s in $CT(s)$. Let $p_{ST}(t', t) = \langle t' = y_1, y_2, \ldots, y_r = t \rangle$ be the path connecting t to its descendant t' in $ST(s_0)$. We say $p_{CT}(s', s)$ and $p_{ST}(t', t)$ are isomorphic if elements x_i corresponds to server y_i for $i = 1, 2, \ldots, r$.

Lemma 6. *Let* server-search(s', s) *belong to* σ_k *($k = h, h-1, \ldots, 0$) and* find(s') *be the corresponding operation in* ρ*. Then* find(s') *is executed in a compressed tree* $CT(s)$*, which has the same structure of* $T_{s_0}(s)$*, and after its execution* $CT(s)$ *has the same structure of* $T_{s_0}(s)$ *after the execution of* server-search(s', s)*.*

Proof. Lemma is trivially true for server searches in σ_h, since $CT(s)$ and $T_{S_0}(s)$ are made up only by s.

Let us now assume, by induction, that lemma is true for all $k = h - 1, h - 2, \ldots, j$. Let us consider *unions* in ρ following the *finds* corresponding to *server searches* in σ_j. The execution of each of these *union* links an element of the set union problem corresponding to a server s of height $j - 1$ to the sets of the set union problem corresponding to servers s' children of s in $ST(s_0)$. The new $CT(s)$ is made up by the compressed trees $CT(s')$ and the arcs (s', s). Then $CT(s)$ has the same structure of $T_{s_0}(s)$ (see figure 4).

We now have to show that after the execution of *server-search*(s', s) belonging to σ_{j-1} and the corresponding execution of *find*(s') $CT(s)$ has the same structure of $T_{s_0}(s)$.

Since the execution of *server-search*(s', s) in $T_{s_0}(s)$ follows a path $p_{ST}(s', s)$ and the corresponding execution of *find*(s') follows a path $p_{CT}(s', s)$ in $CT(s)$ and $p_{ST}(s', s)$ and $p_{CT}(s', s)$ are isomorphic, due to the fact that $CT(s)$ and $T_{s_0}(s)$ have the same structure before the execution of the operation, then their executions compresses the two paths in an isomorphic way and we have the thesis.

Theorem 1. *Let* $C(m, n)$ *be the cost in terms of number of messages of a sequence of* m *requests over a DRT* starting with one empty server and with* n *servers at the end. We have:*

$$C(m, n) = O\left(m \log_{(1+m/n)} n\right).$$

Proof. We always have $m > n$, because of the result in section 2.1.

From lemma 6 we have that *server-search*(s', s) and the corresponding *find*(s') have the same cost. Let C_s be the cost of the $n - 1$ *splits* that have produced the n servers. Let C_m be the cost of the n *make-sets*, and C_l be the cost of all the *unions*, which are at most $n - 1$. It is $C_s = O(C_m + C_l)$, hence:

$$C(m, n) = O\left(m \log_{(1+m/n)} n\right).$$

Since in DRT* there is a relation between m and n (see section 2.1), namely $n \leq \frac{m}{A}$, then we have:

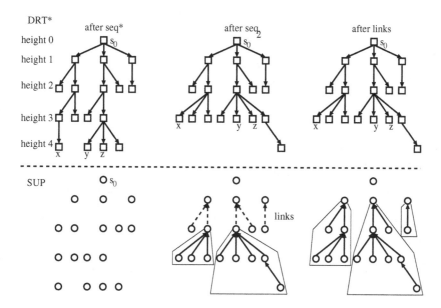

Fig. 4. The evolution of $ST(s_0)$ in the DRT* and the set of compressed trees in the set union problem (SUP) during the server searches in theorem 1.

Corollary 1. *Let $C(m,n)$ the cost in terms of number of messages of a sequence of m requests over a DRT* starting with one empty server and with n servers at the end. We have:*

$$C(m,n) = O\left(m \log_{(1+A)} n\right).$$

Please note that for $A = 10^3$ we have $\log_{(1+A)} n \leq 4$ for $n \leq 10^{12}$ servers. We therefore can assume to have an amortized constant cost in real SDDSs.

4   Extension to the Multi-dimensional Case

In the multi-dimensional case we use as indexing structure a distributed version of k-d tree called *lazy k-d tree*, introduced in [10] and extensively analyzed in [11, 12], with index on clients and servers. The local tree is also a lazy k-d tree.

Therefore for the multi-dimensional case we modify the search process of lazy k-d trees as in the case of DRT*. More precisely, with reference to the figure 1, when a request generates a chain of address error, the pertinent server builds up the correction tree C and sends it within the LTC messages to each server in the chain. In this case C is a connected portion of the overall k-d tree. It contains the whole path from the node associated to s_0 to the one associated to s_k. A server simply adjusts its local tree adding the unknown portion of the tree. The analysis of previous section exactly applies to the multi-dimensional case.

5 Conclusions

We have introduced and analyzed a variant, called DRT*, of the addressing method for SDDSs used in DRT [7]. Our variant, DRT*, has a very good behavior in the amortized case, close to the optimality.

The method is also extendible to the multi-dimensional case, applying the same variation to the lazy k-d tree [10,12].

In particular for a real SDDS (made up by hundreds or thousands of servers) we can assume to have an almost constant amortized cost for the insert and search operations.

To prove the result we used a structural analogy between DRT* and compressed trees used in the set union problem [13,15]. A deeper analysis of this analogy might suggest other protocols, possibly more efficient, for the management of distributed data.

In the k-dimensional case only worst case analysis was previously considered and the almost constant cost for the general k-dimensional case appears to be very promising in the light of well known difficulties in proving optimal worst case bounds for such a case.

References

1. F. Barillari, E. Nardelli, M. Pepe: Fully Dinamic Distribuited Search Trees Can Be Balanced in $O(\log^2 N)$ Time, Technical Report 146, Dipartimento di Matematica Pura ed Applicata, Universita' di L'Aquila, July 1997, accepted for publication on the *Journal of Parallel and Distributed Computation*.
2. Y. Breitbart, R. Vingralek: Addressing and Balancing Issues in Distributed B+-Trees, *1st Workshop on Distributed Data and Structures (WDAS'98)*, 1998.
3. Chorochronos: A Research Network for Spatiotemporal Database Systems. *SIGMOD Record* 28(3): 12-21 (1999).
4. A.Di Pasquale, E. Nardelli: Balanced and Distributed Search Trees, *Workshop on Distributed Data and Structures (WDAS'99)*, Princeton, NJ, May 1999.
5. A.Di Pasquale, E. Nardelli: Design and analysis of distributed searching of k-dimensional data with almost constant costs, Tech.Rep. 00/14, Dept. of Pure and Applied Mathematics, Univ. of L'Aquila, May 2000.
6. B.A. Galler, M.J. Fisher, An improved equivalence algorithm, *Commun. ACM* 7, 5(1964), 301-303.
7. B. Kröll, P. Widmayer: Distributing a search tree among a growing number of processor, in *ACM SIGMOD Int. Conf. on Management of Data*, pp 265-276 Minneapolis, MN, 1994.
8. W. Litwin, M.A. Neimat, D.A. Schneider: LH* - Linear hashing for distributed files, *ACM SIGMOD Int. Conf. on Management of Data*, Washington, D. C., 1993.
9. W. Litwin, M.A. Neimat, D.A. Schneider: RP* - A family of order-preserving scalable distributed data structure, in *20th Conf. on Very Large Data Bases*, Santiago, Chile, 1994.
10. E. Nardelli: Distribuited k-d trees, in *XVI Int. Conf. of the Chilean Computer Science Society (SCCC'96)*, Valdivia, Chile, November 1996.
11. E.Nardelli, F.Barillari and M.Pepe, Design issues in distributed searching of multi-dimensional data, *3rd International Symposium on Programming and Systems (ISPS'97)*, Algiers, Algeria, April 1997.

12. E. Nardelli, F.Barillari, M. Pepe: Distributed Searching of Multi-Dimensional Data: a Performance Evaluation Study, *Journal of Parallel and Distributed Computation*, 49, 1998.

13. R.E. Tarjan, Efficiency of a good but non linear set union algorithm, *J. Assoc. Comput. Mach.*, 22(1975), pp. 215-225.

14. T.Tzouramanis, M.Vassilakopoulos, Y.Manolopoulos: Processing of Spatio-Temporal Queries in Image Databases. ADBIS 1999, pp.85-97.

15. J. Van Leeuwen, R.E. Tarjan, Worst-case analysis of set union algorithms, *J. Assoc. Comput. Mach.*, 31(1984), pp. 245-281.

X²QL: An eXtensible XML Query Language Supporting User-Defined Foreign Functions

Norihide Shinagawa[1], Hiroyuki Kitagawa[2], and Yoshiharu Ishikawa[2]

[1] Doctoral Program in Engineering, University of Tsukuba
[2] Institute of Information Sciences and Electronics, University of Tsukuba
1-1-1 Tennohdai, Tsukuba, Ibaraki 305-8573, Japan
{siena,kitagawa,ishikawa}@is.tsukuba.ac.jp
http://www.dblab.is.tsukuba.ac.jp/kde/

Abstract. With the recent and rapid advance of the Internet, management of structured documents such as XML documents and their databases has become more and more important. A number of query languages for XML documents have been proposed up to the present. Some of them enable tag-based powerful document structure manipulation. However, their contents processing capability is very limited. Here, the contents processing implies the similarity-based selection, ranking, summary generation, topic extraction, and so on, as well as simple string-based pattern matching. In this paper, we propose an extensible XML query language X²QL, which features inclusion of user-defined foreign functions to process document contents in the context of XML-QL-based document structure manipulation. This feature makes it possible to integrate application-oriented high-level contents processing facilities into querying documents. We also describe an implementation of an X²QL query processing systemon top of XSLT processors.

1 Introduction

With the recent and rapid advance of the Internet, management of structured documents such as XML documents and their databases has become more and more important [1]-[10]. A number of query languages for XML documents have been proposed up to the present [3]-[8].

XML-QL [3] and XQL [4] are well-known XML query languages. Although Lorel [5], UnQL [6], StruQL [7], and YATL [8] are proposed as query languages for semistructured data, XML documents are their potential targets. They allow the user to describe queries in a declarative manner. Especially, XML-QL and many query languages for semistructured data enable tag-based powerful document structure manipulation such as restructuring element hierarchies and joins. However, they are very weak in document contents processing.

Here, the document contents processing implies the similarity-based selection, ranking, summary generation, topic extraction, and so on [11]-[14]. Some of the aforementioned query languages have certain kinds of string-based pattern matching facilities. However, they are not enough to perform, for instance, summary generation.

Requirements for document contents processing vary depending on applications, target document types, and target element types. For example, several techniques have

J. Štuller et al. (Eds.): ADBIS-DASFAA 2000, LNCS 1884, pp. 251–264, 2000.

been proposed for summary generation [11]. Even in similarity-based search, measures proposed so far have their own strong and weak points [12]. Thus, it is very difficult to provide a complete set of contents processing facilities in advance to cope with the variety of requirements. A promising approach to this difficulty is to make a query language extensible to adopt user-defined contents processing functions.

In this paper, we propose an extensible XML query language X^2QL, which features inclusion of user-defined foreign functions to process document contents in the context of XML-QL-based document structure manipulation. XML-QL is the most well-known XML query language featuring tag-based powerful document structure manipulation. This is the reason we have designed X^2QL taking XML-QL as a starting basis. Foreign functions are given as external programs written in programming languages. By including appropriate user-defined foreign functions, each user can extend the processing power of X^2QL. This extensibility makes it possible to integrate application-oriented high-level contents processing facilities into querying documents. We also describe an implementation of an X^2QL query processing system on top of XSLT [15]-[16] processors.

The remaining part of this paper is organized as follows. In Section 2, we show some examples of queries, in which inclusion of document contents processing is beneficial. Section 3 gives a brief overview of XML-QL. Section 4 explains the main constructs of X^2QL, and shows its query examples. Section 5 gives an overview of XSLT. Section 6 describes implementation of the X^2QL query processing system on top of XSLT processors. Section 7 summarizes related work. Finally, we conclude this paper in Section 8.

2   Motivating Examples

In this section, we show two examples of XML queries, in which inclusion of document contents processing is beneficial. These query examples are specified in X^2QL in Section 4.

Suppose that an XML document including newspaper articles is given, in which each article consists of its publication date, headline, and news body. Its DTD is given as follows.

```
<!-- DTD of the input document -->
<!ELEMENT Document  Article+>
<!ELEMENT Article   (Date,Headline,Body)>
<!ELEMENT Body        Paragraph+>
<!ELEMENT Date        (Year,Month,Day)>
<!ELEMENT Year        #PCDATA>
<!ELEMENT Month       #PCDATA>
<!ELEMENT Day         #PCDATA>
<!ELEMENT Headline    #PCDATA>
<!ELEMENT Paragraph #PCDATA>
```

Example 1 We generate a new XML document in which articles published after 1999 are selected and grouped by the publication dates, and their summaries are added. The DTD of the output document is shown below. This query requires both the document structure manipulation to select `Article` elements published after 1999 and group them by the Date values and the document contents processing to generate summaries of `Article` elements.

```
<!-- DTD of the output document -->
<!ELEMENT Document   DateGroup+>
<!ELEMENT DateGroup Article+>
<!ATTLIST DateGroup Date CDATA #REQUIRED>
<!ELEMENT Article   (Date,Headline,Summary,Body)>
<!ELEMENT Summary   Paragraph+>
<!-- Body, Date, Year, Month, Day, Headline, and
     Paragraph elements are the same as above. -->
```

Example 2 We give a set of keywords and get the top N articles related to the keywords. The rank of each `Article` element is determined by the similarity with the keywords. The similarity measure is given by the contents processing function.

3   XML-QL

As mentioned in Section 1, X^2QL is based on XML-QL [3]. In this section, we give a simplified overview of XML-QL.

3.1   XML-QL Query

The basic syntax of an XML-QL query as follows.

```
where      patterns [in source] [,patterns [in source]]*[,predicate]*
[order-by keys of output [descending]]
construct construction of each output
```

For example, given the sample XML document in Section 2, the query to generate a new XML document in which articles published after 1999 are selected and grouped by the publication dates can be specified as shown below. This query corresponds to Example 1 except for the summary generation.

```
where      <Document></> content_as $x
construct <Document>
  where      <Article>
                <Date> <Year> $y </> </> content_as $d
             </> element_as $a in $x,  $y >= 1999
    order-by  $d
    construct <DateGroup ID=DateID($d) Date=$d> $a </>
             </>
```

Where clause: This specifies the element patterns, predicates, and variable bindings. Element patterns are given by XML-like forms. Each variable is bound to either an element, the content of an element, an element name, an attribute name, or an attribute value. The expression `element_as $x` binds the variable $x to the preceding element, and the expression `content_as $x` binds $x to the content of the preceding element.

In the above example, $x is bound to the content of a Document element in the first where clause. Variables $a, $d, and $y are bound to an Article element, the content of a Date element in the Article element, and the content of a Year element in the Date element, respectively, in the second where clause. Moreover, the Year value must be greater than or equal to 1999.

Construct clause: This clause specifies how to construct an output element for each set of bound variables. The query result is a sequence of output elements. As shown in this example, the where· · ·construct clauses may be nested.

Each output element can be given its ID attribute value by a Skolem function. The Skolem function gives one-to-one mapping from a set of arguments to an ID attribute value. In the query result, elements which have the same element name, parent node, and ID value are grouped into a single element. This feature can be utilized for grouping elements.

The above query returns a Document element which contains the result of the subquery. The subquery returns a sequence of DateGroup elements. Each DateGroup element has a one-to-one correspondence to a Date value, and contains Article elements of the day. The Date value is given by $d, and each Article element is given by $a.

Order-by clause: This clause specifies the ordering of output elements. They are sorted by the sort key. In the above query, the output elements are sorted in the ascending order of the value of $d, namely the Date value.

3.2 Function Definition

In XML-QL, canned queries can be defined as functions as follows.

```
function function-name( argument-list )
    XML-QL query
end
```

Namely, each function is a query which can include unbound variables given in function arguments. The return value of a function is the result of the query.

4 X^{2}QL: An eXtensible XML Query Language

The syntax of X^{2}QL is similar to that of XML-QL. However, X^{2}QL can incorporate user-defined foreign functions. The implementation of foreign functions is given as external programs. First, we give the syntax of X^{2}QL in Subsection 4.1. Then, we explain foreign functions in Subsection 4.2. In Subsection 4.3, we show how example queries in Section 2 are specified in X^{2}QL.

4.1 Overall Syntax

As aforementioned, the syntax of X^2QL is based on XML-QL as follows.

```
where      patterns [in source][,patterns [in source]]*[,predicate]*
[rank-by   keys of input  top number]
[order-by  keys of output [descending]]
construct  construction of each output
```

The where, order-by, and construct clauses are same as in XML-QL, except that they can contain foreign function calls as explained in Subsection 4.2.

The extension here is the rank-by clause. This clause is used to specify at most the top *number* sets of variable bindings are selected based on the value of the *keys of input*. This selection is performed before the construct clause is executed, and the order of output elements is not affected by this clause. In the document contents processing, it is often necessary to rank target elements by some similarity or importance measure derived by the foreign function and to select the top N elements based on their ranks. To facilitate such processing, we have included the rank-by clause as an extension.

4.2 Foreign Functions

As explained in Subsection 3.2, functions defined in XML-QL are just canned queries. In X^2QL, users can define foreign functions whose implementation is given as external programs. In the current version of X^2QL, we assume that they are written in Java.

Foreign functions are classified into *general functions* and *methods*. A method is associated with a specific element type. Therefore, methods of the same name can be defined for different element types. When a foreign function is called, the element type of the target element is checked, then an appropriate method is invoked depending on the target element. Functions other than methods are general functions.

Let us consider foreign functions required for the examples in Section 2. For Example 1, we need a method (named abstract()) associated with the Article element type to summarize each Article element and to return a Summary element. The method generates a summary of an Article element considering the target dependent property such that terms appeared in its Headline element are important.

For Example 2, we need a function to measure the similarity between the given keywords and an element content. Here, let us define it as a general function, z say sim_cosine(), that calculates similarities based on the traditional cosine measure [13]. By applying the function to an Article element, its similarity value is returned. [1]

In our environment, foreign functions are defined as follows.

```
function  type function-name( argument-list )
defined-by "URI of the implementation"

function  type element-type-name.method-name( argument-list )
defined-by "URI of the implementation"

argument-list ::= type argument-name [, type argument-name]*
```

---

[1] Similarity measures often need document-dependent global factors (e.g. idf). The implementations of foreign functions are responsible to calculating them in their first invocation.

In the definition of a foreign function, the data types of arguments and return values are specified. The data types `number`, `string`, `element`, and `content` are allowed. Variables bound by `element_as` and `content_as` are associated with element and content, respectively.

The definitions of `abstract()` and `sim_cosine()` are given as follows.

```
function  element Article.abstract()
defined-by "http://fqdn/path/pkg.article#abstract"

function  number sim_cosine( content )
defined-by "http://fqdn/path/common.vecspace#cosine"
```

As mentioned before, the implementations of foreign functions are written as Java programs. In Java mapping, data types `number`, `string`, `element`, and `content` correspond to `Number`, `String`, `Element`, and `Content` interfaces in the package provided for X^{2}QL. When a method is to be implemented, a Java class is created and the implementation is given as its method. When a method is invoked for an element, the element is added as the first argument `self` in the argument list of the Java function. For example, the Java implementation for the method `abstract()` is given as below. The query processor checks the element type of the element bound to `self` before the method invocation.

```
// a class located at http://fqdn/path/
package pkg;
class Article { Element abstract(Element self) { ... } }
```

4.3   Query Specification Examples

The query specification for Examples 1 and 2 in Section 2 are given as follows.

```
where       <Document> $x </>
construct <Document>
   where       <Article>
                  <Date> <Year> $y </> </> content_as $d
                  <Headline></> element_as $h
                  <Body></>      element_as $b
               </> element_as $a in $x,   $y >= 1999
   order-by    $d
   construct <DateGroup ID=DateID($d) Date=$d>
                  <Article> <Date> $d </>
                    $h $a.abstract() $b
                  </>
               </>
            </>
                        Query Specification 1

where       <Document> $x </>
construct <Document>
   where    <Article> </> element_as $a in $x
```

```
rank-by    sim_cosine($a, keywords)
top        N
construct $a
        </>
```
Query Specification 2

In Query Specification 1, the method `abstract()` associated with the `Article` element type is used. The query returns a `Document` which is a sequence of `DateGroup` elements. The `DateGroup` elements are sorted by the `Date` values. Each `DateGroup` element groups `Article` elements with the same `Date` value. A `Summary` element is created by `abstract()` and inserted between the `Headline` and `Body` elements.

In Query Specification 2, a general function `sim_cosine()` is used. It gives the similarity of an `Article` element with respect to the given eywords. With the use of the `rank-by` clause, only the top N `Article` elements are contained in the result. They appear in the same order as in the source document.

5 XSLT

XSLT is an XML transformation language for XSL (XML stylesheet language) and a recommendation of W3C [15]. Today, several XSLT processors are available, and their use has become popular in the context of XML document processing. We have developed an X^2QL query processing system on top of an XSLT processor. The rationale here is three-fold. First, the approach contributes to rapid development of the prototype of an X^2QL query processing system. Second, an implementation on top of XSLT processors assures certain level of portability. Third, X^2QL can work as a front end to XSLT processors. As shown below, XSLT specifications are low-level and procedural, and they are difficult for novice users. With X^2QL, we can specify document manipulation more declaratively.

We give a simplified overview of XSLT in this section, and explain the query processing scheme on top of XSLT processors in Section 6.

5.1 Template Rules

A transformation expressed in XSLT is an XML document, called a *stylesheet*, whose root element is `xsl:stylesheet` containing a set of *template rules*. We explain template rules by describing how document manipulation by the following X^2QL query is expressed in XSLT. This query extracts `Item` elements whose `Number` element values are less than 100. Its result is a `Document` element consisting of the `Item` elements sorted by the `Number` value.

```
where      <Document></> content_as $d
construct <Document>
   where      <Item> <Number> $n </> </> element_as $i in $d,
              $n < 100
   order-by   $n
   construct $i
          </>
```

A template rule corresponding to the query is as follows.

```
<xsl:template match="/Document">
  <xsl:variable name="d" select="."/>
  <Document>
    <xsl:for-each select="Item/Number[ . < 100 ]">
      <xsl:sort     select="."/>
      <xsl:variable name="n" select="."/>
      <xsl:for-each select="..">
        <xsl:variable name="i" select="."/>
        <xsl:copy-of  select="$i"/>
      </xsl:for-each>
    </xsl:for-each>
  </Document>
</xsl:template>
```

Element whose tags are in the namespace xsl are called *instructions*. A template rule is represented as a nested structure of instructions. Each XML document is modeled as a tree whose nodes are elements, attributes, texts (#PCDATA), and so on. Each instruction in the body of a template rule is applied to the nodes selected by a path expression called *location path* [16] (for example, "/Document", ".", and "Item/Number[.<100]"). The selected nodes and their set are called *context nodes* and *context node list*, respectively.

Location paths may be relative or absolute. Relative location paths are evaluated based on the current context node. Location paths which appear in this paper are as follows: (1) "." selects the current context node itself, (2) ".." selects the parent node, (3) a/b selects the child b nodes of a, (4) a/@b selects the attribute b nodes of a, and (5) a[x] selects a nodes which satisfy the condition x. The condition x is given by location paths and predicates combined by and/or. Note that these are abbreviated notations, and more sophisticated location paths can be specified. We omit explanation for those notations. In following, we briefly explain the major instructions. Then, we give interpretation of the above template rule.

xsl:template A template rule is an element whose tag is this instruction. The match attribute specifies a location path to identify the target nodes to which the rule applies. When an element matches the location path of a template rule, the content of the rule, which is a sequence of instructions, is instantiated as the output.

xsl:variable This instruction is used to bind a variable. The variable name is given by the name attribute, and its value is given as the content of the element or the location path specified in the select attribute. In XSLT, the value of a variable is denoted by its name with a prefix "$".

xsl:for-each This instruction is used to select the context nodes specified by the select attribute, and to construct the output for each context node in a similar way to xsl:template.

xsl:sort This instruction is used to sort the context nodes. It must occur first in an xsl:for-each element.

xsl:copy-of This instruction is used to copy a node set selected by the select attribute.

`xsl:if` This instruction is used for conditional processing. When the condition given by the `test` attribute is true, the content is instantiated.

When the template rule given at the beginning of this subsection is applied to a `Document` element in a source XML document, a `Document` element is created as an output. It contains the result generated by other instructions in the template rule. The first `xsl:for-each` instruction selects `Number` elements whose values are less than 100, and the `xsl:sort` instruction sorts them. Then, the second `xsl:for-each` instruction selects the parent `Item` element of the current `Number` element, and the `xsl:copy-of` instruction copies the current `Item` element. The result document is what the X^2QL query specifies.

5.2   Extension Functions

The XSLT specification mentions the use of *extension functions* [15]. Essentially, they are external programs written in programming languages. However, the availability and the usage of extension functions depend on the underlying XSLT processor, because their details are left to the implementation.

In this study, we use LotusXSL [17], which is an XSLT processor developed by IBM alphaWorks. Extension functions in LotusXSL are defined by `lxslt:component` elements as follows.

```
<lxslt:component prefix="namespace"
           functions="list of the extension functions">
  <lxslt:script lang="javaclass" src="URI"/>
</lxslt:component>
```

Example: Suppose we define an extension function `head()` in the namespace `my-space`. It is implemented as a method of `MyHead` class in Java. It returns the head part of the given string whose length is less than or equal to the specified length.

```
<lxslt:component prefix="my-space" functions="head">
  <lxslt:script lang="javaclass" src="MyHead"/>
</lxslt:component>
```

In template rules, we can call extension functions, for example,

```
<xsl:value-of select="my-space:head( string( . ), 10 )"/>.
```

6   Query Processing on XSLT Processors

Query processing in our prototype system is shown in Figure 1. The translator translates each X^2QL query into XSLT template rules in stylesheets. Then, the XSLT processor executes the query by interpreting the stylesheets.

The current implementation has the following restrictions.

- The query does not include joins of multiple documents.
- No regular path expressions containing closures of tag names are used.
- No subblocks[2] are used.
- No elements with IDs specified by skolem functions are nested.

---

[2] A subblock is an XML-QL subquery enclosed '{' and '}', and is used for outer joins.

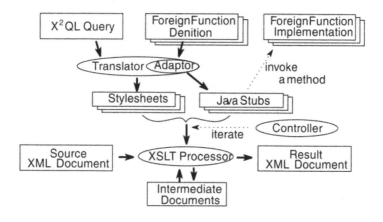

Fig. 1. Query Processing Scheme

6.1 Query Translation

First, we describe the translation of queries without `rank-by` and `order-by` clauses. In this case, a query is translated into a stylesheet with a corresponding template rule.

Basic Translation Basic constructs in `where` and `construct` clauses in X^2QL are translated into their counterparts in XSLT as illustrated in Subsection 5.1. Basically, template rules are generated along the element structure specified in `construct` clauses, because template rules describe the output document structure. Namely, the tags used in the outermost construction enclose the others. Element hierarchy patterns given in `where` clauses are expressed as location paths, and variables are bound as occasion demands.

Variable binding is done with `xsl:for-each` and `xsl:variable` instructions. Generally, in template rules, some auxiliary variables are introduced in addition to ones specified in the given query. They are used to simplify the location path derivation, and to keep values depending on the current context node list.

The order of variable bindings primarily coincides with the order in which they are used in the output construction in the query. When it gives the same order to multiple variables, their usage in Skolem functions and sorting keys is taken in consideration.

Grouping by Skolem Functions The return value of the Skolem function has a one-to-one correspondence to the set of values given in arguments. Based on this, a grouping specifyied using the Skolem function is translated as shown below.

Here, `Article` elements are grouped by the `Date` values. First, an `Article` element is selected. Its `Date` value is bound to the variable `$d`. The `xsl:if` instruction says that, if it is the first `Article` element having a `Data` value, the `DateGroup` element, collecting `Article` elements sharing the same `Date` value, is the output. If this condition is not met, no `DateGroup` element is created. Thus, a grouping of `Article` elements by the `Date` values is attained.

```
<!-- a given query fragment -->
...
where      <Article> <Date> $d </> </> element_as $a
construct <DateGroup ID=DateID($d)> $a </>
                           (a) Query Fragment
...

<!-- the template rule to group Articles -->
...
<xsl:variable name="x" select="."/>
<xsl:for-each match="Article">
  <xsl:variable name="d" select="Date"/>
  <!-- grouping by using Skolem function: apply to
       only the first Article with each Date value -->
  <xsl:variable name="pos" select="position()" />
  <xsl:if test="count( ( $x/Article[ position() < pos ] )
                              [ Date = $d ] ) = 0">
    <DateGroup>
      <!-- select the Articless with same Date value -->
      <xsl:for-each select="$x/Article[ Date = $d ]">
        <xsl:copy-of select="."/>
      </xsl:for-each>
    </DateGroup>
  </xsl:if>
</xsl:for-each>
...                        (b) Translation Result
```

6.2   Mapping of Foreign Functions

Foreign functions in X^2QL are mapped to extension functions. As mentioned before, implementation of extension functions depends on the underlying XSLT processor. In this study, we concentrate on the implementation on LotusXSL to make our discussion concentrate. The implementation of foreign functions of X^2QL are written in Java.

The definition of each foreign function is processed before the stylesheet generation. This is done by the adaptor module inside the translator. Implementation of the adaptor module depends on the underlying XSLT processor.

The LotusXSL adaptor module refers to the foreign function definitions and generates stub classes in Java. A stub class is created for each element type associated with method[3]. A stub class has stub methods which work as extension functions in LotusXSL. Foreign function calls in X^2QL queries are translated into calls for appropriate stub methods. When a certain stub method is called, the stub method translates the argument type in LotusXSL into the Java type according to the Java mapping for the X^2QL, and calls the implementation of the corresponding foreign function. (See Figure 2.) The type of the return value is translated in the reverse direction. We have also developed a class loader to load the implementation of foreign functions through the network, and the Java Reflection API is used to manipulate classes and methods dynamically.

---

[3] In the current implementation, general functions are treated as if they were methods associated with a dummy class.

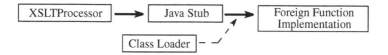

Fig. 2. Mechanism of a Method Invocation

6.3 Translation of Rank-by and Order-by Clauses

Generally, queries with `rank-by` and `order-by` clauses are translated into two and three stylesheets, respectively. They are interpreted in the XSLT processor one by one, and the controller in Figure 1 controls the interpretation.

Queries having only `order-by` clauses are processed in the following two steps, and a stylesheet is associated with each step.

1. Construct the output as explained above. The difference is that the sort key values are added to elements to be sorted.
2. Sort the target elements, and remove the added sort key values.

Queries having `rank-by` clauses are processed in three steps. They are translated into three stylesheets, each with a template rule. Here, we show how Query 2 in Section 4 is translated. Tthe first stylesheet is shown below. Other two stylesheets are omitted.

The template rule in the first stylesheet generates an `x2ql:order` element for each `Article` element. It has `rank` and `pos` attributes. The `rank` attribute gives the similarity of the `Article` element calculated by the foreign function `sim_cosine()`. The `pos` attribute has the relative position of the `Article` element. It has the `Article` element as its sub-element. Moreover, we generate an `x2ql:sort` element which contains the `x2ql:order` elements. It is used in the second and third steps.

```
<!-- first template rule -->
<xsl:template match="/Document">
  <Document>
    <x2ql:sort>
      <xsl:for-each select="Article">
        <xsl:variable name="a" select="." />
        <xsl:variable name="p" select="position()" />
        <x2ql:order rank="{sim_cosine( $a )}" pos="{$p}" >
          <xsl:copy-of select="$a" />
        </x2ql:order>
      </xsl:for-each>
    </x2ql:sort>
  </Document>
</xsl:template>
```

The second template rule selects the `x2ql:order` elements, and sort them by the `rank` value. Then, we output the first N `x2ql:order` elements.

The last template rule sorts the remaining N `x2ql:order` elements by the `pos` value, and remove unnecessary elements.

7 Related Work

Several languages have been proposed for manipulating XML documents. XSLT [15] is a transformation language, and XQL [4] is proposed as an extension of XPath [16], which is a location path language used in XSLT. XQL is very weak in document structure manipulation. XSLT features tag-based powerful document structure manipulation, but it requires low-level and procedural description.

XML-QL [3] is a query language for XML documents, and it is used as a basis of X^2QL. In the current version of XML-QL, user-defined functions are just canned queries. The proposal mentions the possible use of user-defined predicates as a future research issue. However, their scope, role, syntax, and semantics are not specified. Foreign functions in X^2QL can represent user-defined predicates. Moreover, they can be used for a wide range of applications, and can return elements and contents.

YATL is a rule-oriented language for YAT semistructured data model [8]. YATL has a powerful structure manipulation capability, and the authors mention the use of foreign functions. However, YATL is not dedicated to XML document processing, and their usage of foreign functions is limited to string-based pattern matching.

Lorel [5] is a query language for OEM, a graph-based semistructured data model. Lorel can be regarded as an extension of OQL [18]. Its data restructuring capability is very limited. UnQL [6] is a query language for a semistructured data model similar to OEM. UnQL has a powerful data restructuring capability. However, the use of foreign functions is not considerd.

8 Conclusion

Some XML query languages provide tag-based powerful document structure manipulation. However, they are generally weak in document contents processing such as similarity-based selection, ranking, summary generation, topic extraction. Requirements for document contents processing vary depending on application context, and it is very difficult to provide the complete set of contents processing facilities.

In this paper, we have proposed X^2QL (eXtensible XML Query Language), which features inclusion of user-defined foreign functions (external programs) to process document contents in the context of XML-QL-based document structure manipulation. We have also explained the implementation of the X^2QL query processing system on top of XSLT processors. We have been developing the prototype system as a command line Java application.

The future work includes relaxation of the restriction on X^2QL queries mentiond in Section 6. Another important research issue is the development of an X^2QL query processing system without the use of an XSLT processor. Inheritance of methods associated with element types and other object-oriented extension are also interesting future research topics.

Acknowledgment. This research was supported in part by the Grant-in-Aid for Scientific Research from the Ministry of Education, Science, Sports and Culture, Japan.

References

1. R. Sacks-Davis, T. Arnold-Moore, and J. Zobel. Database Systems for Structured Documents, *International Symposium on ADTI '94*, pp.272-283, Nara, 1994.
2. World Wide Web Consortium, http://www.w3.org/.
3. A. Deutsch, M. Fernandez, D. Florescu, A. Levy, and D. Suciu. A Query Language for XML, *Proceedings of the Eighth International World Wide Web Conference (WWW8)*, Computer Networks, Vol. 31, No. 11-16, pp. 1155-1169, 1999.
4. J. Robie, J. Lapp, and D. Schach. XML Query Language (XQL), *The Query Languages Workshop (QL'98)*, http://www12.w3.org/TandS/QL/QL98/pp/xql.html, 1998.
5. S. Abiteboul, D. Quass, J. McHugh, J. Widom, and J. Wiener. The Lorel Query Language for Semistructured Data, *International Journal on Digital Libraries*, Vol. 1, No. 1, pp. 68-88, 1997.
6. P. Buneman, S. B. Davidson, G. G. Hillebrand, and D. Suciu. A Query Language and Optimization Techniques for Unstructured Data, *Proceedings of ACM-SIGMOD '96*, pp. 506-516, Motreal, 1996.
7. M. F. Fernandez, D. Florescu, J. Kang, A. Y. Levy, and D. Suciu. Catching the Boat with Strudel: Experiences with a Web-site Management System, *Proceedings of ACM-SIGMOD '98*, pp. 414-425, Seattle, 1998.
8. S. Cluet, C. Delobel, J. Simeon, and K. Smaga. Your Mediators Need Data Convention!, *Proceedings of ACM-SIGMOD '98*, pp. 414-425, Seattle, 1998.
9. D. Konopnicki, and O. Shmuel. W3QL: Query System for the World Wide Web, *Proceedings of Twenty-First Conference on VLDB*, pp. 54-65, Zurich, 1995.
10. A. Mendelzon, G. Mihaila, and T. Milo. Querying the World Wide Web, *International Journal on Digital Libraries*, Vol. 1, No. 1, pp. 54-67, 1997.
11. I. Mani, and M. T. Maybury (eds.). *Advances in Automatic Text Summarization*, MIT Press, 1999.
12. J. Zobel, and A. Moffat. Exploring the Similarity Space, *ACM SIGIR Forum*, Vol. 32 No. 1, pp. 18-34, 1998.
13. G. Salton. *Automatic Text Processing: The Transformation, Analysis, and Retrieval of Information by Computer*, Addison-Wesley, 1989.
14. H. A. Hearst. Subtopic Structuring for Full-Length Document Access, *Proceedings of ACM-SIGIR '93*, pp. 59-68, Pittsburg, 1993.
15. J. Clark (ed.). *XSL Transformations (XSLT) Version 1.0*, http://www.w3.org/TR/xslt, 1999.
16. J. Clark, and S. DeRose. *XML Path Language (XPath) Version 1.0*, http://www.w3.org/TR/WD-xpath, 1999.
17. IBM alphaWorks, LotusXSL, http://www.alphaWorks.ibm.com/tech/LotusXSL.
18. R. G. G. Cattell, D. K. Barry, M. Berler, J. Eastman, D. Jordan, C. Russell, O. Schadow, T. Stanienda, and F. Velez (eds.). *The Object Data Standard: ODMG 3.0*, Morgan Kaufmann Publishers, 2000.

Decision Committee Learning
with Dynamic Integration of Classifiers

Alexey Tsymbal

Department of Computer Science and Information Systems,
University of Jyväskylä, P.O.Box 35, FIN-40351 Jyväskylä, Finland
alexey@cs.jyu.fi

Abstract. Decision committee learning has demonstrated spectacular success in reducing classification error from learned classifiers. These techniques develop a classifier in the form of a committee of subsidiary classifiers. The combination of outputs is usually performed by majority vote. Voting, however, has a shortcoming. It is unable to take into account local expertise. When a new instance is difficult to classify, then the average classifier will give a wrong prediction, and the majority vote will more probably result in a wrong prediction. Instead of voting, dynamic integration of classifiers can be used, which is based on the assumption that each committee member is best inside certain subareas of the whole feature space. In this paper, the proposed dynamic integration technique is evaluated with AdaBoost and Bagging, the decision committee approaches which have received extensive attention recently. The comparison results show that boosting and bagging have often significantly better accuracy with dynamic integration of classifiers than with simple voting.

1   Introduction

Currently electronic data repositories are growing quickly and contain huge amount of data from commercial, scientific, and other domain areas. The capabilities for collecting and storing all kinds of data totally exceed the development in abilities to analyze, summarize, and extract knowledge from this data. Data mining is the process of finding previously unknown and potentially interesting patterns and relations in large databases [8].

A typical data mining task is to predict an unknown value of some attribute of a new instance when the values of the other attributes of the new instance are known and a collection of instances with known values of all the attributes is given. The collection of the instances with the known attribute values is treated as a training set for a learning algorithm that derives a logical expression, a concept description, or a classifier, that is then used to predict the unknown value of the attribute for the new instance [1].

Decision committee learning has demonstrated spectacular success in reducing classification error from learned classifiers [2,4,9,18,19,25]. These techniques develop

J. Štuller et al. (Eds.): ADBIS-DASFAA 2000, LNCS 1884, pp. 265–278, 2000.

a classifier in the form of a committee of subsidiary classifiers. The committee members are applied to a classification task and their individual outputs combined to create a single classification from the committee as a whole. This combination of outputs is usually performed by majority vote. Decision committee learning can be especially recommended for learning tasks where there is no prior opportunity to evaluate the relative effectiveness of alternative approaches, there is no a priori knowledge available about the domain, and the primary goal of learning is to develop a classifier with the lowest possible error [25].

Two decision committee learning approaches, boosting [18,19] and bagging [4], have received extensive attention recently. They repeatedly build different classifiers using a base learning algorithm, such as a decision tree generator, by changing the distribution of the training set. Bagging learns the constituent classifiers from bootstrap samples drawn from the training set. Boosting learns the constituent classifiers sequentially. In boosting, the weights of training examples used for creating each classifier are modified based on the performance of the previous classifiers in such a way as to make the generation of the next classifier concentrate on the training examples that are misclassified by the previous classifiers. Both boosting and bagging are generic techniques that can be employed with any base learning algorithm [25].

The voting technique used to combine the outputs of committee members in bagging and boosting, however, has an important shortcoming. It is unable to take into account local expertise. When a new instance is difficult to classify, then the average classifier will give a wrong prediction, and the majority vote will more probably result in a wrong prediction. The problem may consist in discarding base classifiers (by assigning small weights) that are highly accurate in a restricted region of the instance space because this accuracy is swamped by their inaccuracy everywhere else. It may also consist in the use of classifiers that are accurate in most of the space but still unnecessarily confuse the whole classification committee in some regions of the space.

Instead of voting, dynamic integration of classifiers [15] can be used to overcome this problem. Dynamic integration of classifiers is based on the assumption that each committee member is best inside certain subareas of the whole feature space. The dynamic meta-classification framework consists of two levels [15]. The first level contains base classifiers, while the second level contains a combining algorithm that predicts the local classification errors for each of the base classifiers. In the training phase the information about the local errors of the base classifiers for each training instance is collected. This information is later used together with the initial training set as meta-level knowledge to estimate the local classification errors of the base classifiers for a new instance.

In this paper, an application of the technique for dynamic integration of classifiers to classifiers generated with decision committee learning is investigated. In chapter 2, AdaBoost and Bagging, the decision committee learning algorithms, which have received extensive attention recently, are reviewed. In chapter 3, the technique for dynamic selection of classifiers is considered. In chapter 4, results of experiments with the AdaBoost and Bagging algorithms are presented, and chapter 5 concludes with a brief summary and further research topics.

2   Bagging and Boosting for Decision Committee Learning

Two decision committee learning approaches, boosting [18] and bagging [4], have received extensive attention recently. Both boosting and bagging operate by selectively resampling from the training data to generate derived training sets to which the base learner is applied. They are generic techniques that can be employed with any learning algorithm [25].

Given an integer T as the committee size, both bagging and boosting need approximately T times as long as their base learning algorithm does for learning a single classifier. A major difference between bagging and boosting is that the latter adaptively changes the distribution of the training set based on the performance of previously created classifiers and uses a function of the performance of a classifier as the weight for voting, while the former stochastically changes the distribution of the training set and uses equal weight voting [25]. In general, bagging is more consistent, increasing the error of the base learner less frequently than does boosting. However, boosting has greater average effect, leading to substantially larger error reductions than bagging on average. Boosting tends to reduce both the bias and variance terms of error while bagging tends to reduce the variance term only [2]. Another notable feature of both boosting and bagging is that, on average, error keeps reducing as committee size is increased, but that the marginal error reduction associated with each additional committee member tends to decrease. Each additional member, on average, has less impact on a committee's prediction error than anyone of its predecessors [25].

The Bagging algorithm (**B**ootstrap **agg**regating) [4] votes classifiers generated by different bootstrap samples (replicates). A bootstrap sample is generated by uniformly sampling m instances from the training set with replacement. T bootstrap samples B_1, B_2, ..., B_T are generated and a classifier $C*$ is built from C_1, C_2, ..., C_T whose output is the class predicted most often by its base classifiers, with ties broken arbitrarily. For a given bootstrap sample, an instance in the training set has probability $1-(1-1/m)^m$ of being selected at least once in the m times instances are randomly selected from the training set. For large m, this is about $1-1/e=63.2\%$, which means that each bootstrap sample contains only about 63.2% unique instances from the training set. This perturbation causes different classifiers to be built if the inducer is unstable (e.g., neural networks, decision trees) [2] and the performance can improve if the induced classifiers are good and not correlated. However, bagging may slightly degrade the performance of stable algorithms (e.g., k-nearest neighbor) because effectively smaller training sets are used for training each classifier [4].

Boosting was introduced by Schapire [19] as a method for boosting the performance of a "weak" learning algorithm. In theory, boosting can be used to significantly reduce the error of any "weak" learning algorithm that consistently generates classifiers which need only be a little bit better than random guessing. This is a shift in mind set for the learning-system designer: instead of trying to design a learning algorithm that is accurate over the entire space, we can instead focus on finding weak learning algorithms that only need to be better than random [18].

The AdaBoost algorithm (**Ada**ptive **Boost**ing) was introduced by Freund&Schapire [9] as an improvement of the initial boosting algorithm [19]. AdaBoost changes the weights of the training instances provided as input to each inducer based on classifiers that were previously built. The goal is to force the inducer to minimize expected error over different input distributions [2]. Given an integer T specifying the number of trials, T weighted training sets $S_1, S_2, ..., S_T$ are generated in sequence and T classifiers $C_1, C_2, ..., C_T$ are built. A final classifier C^* is formed using a weighted voting scheme: the weight of each classifier depends on its performance on the training set used to build it. Let the proportion of misclassified instances at some trial be e, then the training set is reweighted so that these instances get boosted by a factor of $1/(2e)$, thus causing the total weight of the misclassified instances after the reweighting to be half the original training set weight. Similarly, the correctly classified instances will have a total weight equal to half the original weight, and thus no normalization is required.

The AdaBoost algorithm requires a weak learning algorithm whose error is bounded by a constant strictly less than ½. In practice, the inducers we use provide no such guarantee. The original algorithm aborted when the error bound was breached [19], but this case is fairly frequent for some multiclass problems [2]. In this paper, a bootstrap sample from the original data S is generated in such case, and the boosting continues up to a limit of 25 such samples at a given trial, as proposed in [2]. The same is done when the error is equal to zero at some trial. Some implementations of AdaBoost use boosting by resampling because the inducers used were unable to support weighted instances [2]. In this work, boosting by reweighting is implemented with the C4.5 decision tree learning algorithm [17], which is a more direct implementation of the theory. Some evidence exists that reweighting works better in practice [2].

3 Dynamic Integration of Decision Committees

In this chapter, integration of multiple classifiers, and particularly the dynamic one is discussed and a variation of stacked generalization, which uses a distance metric to locally estimate the errors of base classifiers, is considered.

The integration of multiple classifiers has been under active research in machine learning and neural networks, and different approaches have been considered [7]. The challenge of integration is to decide which classifier to rely on or how to combine classifications produced by several classifiers. In general the integration of an ensemble of classifiers has been shown to yield higher accuracy than the most accurate component classifier alone in different real-world tasks.

Recently, two main approaches to integration have been used: first, *combination* of the classifications produced by the base classifiers, and, second, *selection* of the best classifier from the committee. The most popular and simplest method of combining classifiers is voting (also called majority voting and Select All Majority, SAM) [2]. The classifications produced by the base classifiers are handled as equally weighted votes for those particular classifications and the classification with most votes is selected as the final classification. More sophisticated classification algorithms that use combination of classifiers include the stacking (stacked generalization) architecture [26], the SCANN method that is based on the correspondence analysis and the nearest neighbor procedure [14], combining the minimal nearest neighbor classifiers within the stacked generalization framework [20], and different versions of resampling (as boosting, bagging, and cross-validated resampling) that use one learning algorithm to train different classifiers on subsamples of the training set and then voting to combine the classifications of those classifiers [4,18]. Two effective classifiers' combination strategies based on stacked generalization (called an arbiter and combiner) were analyzed in [5] showing experimentally that the hierarchical combination approach based on the use of the subsets of the dataset is able to sustain the same level of accuracy as a global classifier trained on the entire data set.

One of the most popular and simplest selection approaches is CVM (Cross-Validation Majority) [10], which estimates the accuracy of each base classifier using cross-validation and selects a classifier with the highest accuracy. More sophisticated selection approaches use estimates of the local accuracy of the base classifiers by considering errors made in similar instances [13] or the meta-level classifiers ("referees"), which predict the correctness of the base classifiers for a new instance [12].

Classifier selection methods can also be divided into two subsets: *static* and *dynamic* methods. A static method proposes one "best" method for the whole data space (as for example CVM), while a dynamic method takes into account characteristics of a new instance to be classified.

There are still many open questions even with the most widely used architectures like stacked generalization, as which base classifiers should be used, what attributes should be used at the meta-level training, and what combining classifier should be used. Different combining algorithms have been used by various researchers, as simple voting in bagging [4], ID3 for combining nearest neighbor classifiers [20], and the nearest neighbor classification in the space of correspondence analysis results (not directly on the predictions) [14].

Common solutions of the classification problem are based on the assumption that the entire space of features for a particular domain area consists of null-entropy areas, in other words, that instances of one class are not uniformly distributed, but concentrated inside some subareas. In fact, the accuracy of a model depends on many factors as the size and shape of decision boundaries, the number of null-entropy areas (problem-depended factors), the completeness and cleanness of the training set (sample-depended factors) and certainly, on the individual peculiarities of the learning algorithm (algorithm-depended factors). Instances misclassified by a model are not uniformly distributed and the whole space can be regarded to consist of a set of null-entropy areas with categories "the classifier gives correct classification" and "the classifier gives incorrect classification". The dynamic approach to the integration of multiple classifiers attempts to create a meta-model according to this vision. This meta-model is then used to predict the errors of the base classifiers in new instances [15].

A dynamic integration technique that uses the estimation of the local accuracy of the base classifiers by analyzing the accuracy in near-by instances was elaborated [15]. Instead of training a meta-level classifier that will derive the final classification using the classifications of the base classifiers as in stacked generalization, it is proposed to train a meta-level classifier that will estimate the errors of the base classifiers for each new instance and then use these errors to derive the final classification. The goal is to use each base classifier just in that subarea for which it is the most reliable one. The dynamic approach to the integration of multiple classifiers attempts to create a meta-model about the subareas correctly classified by the corresponding base classifiers. This approach is closely related to that considered by Koppel, and Argamon-Engelson [12]. The main difference between these two approaches is in the combining algorithm. The C4.5 decision tree induction algorithm was used to predict the errors of the base classifiers [17], but in the considered dynamic integration technique, the weighted nearest neighbor prediction (WNN) is used [6], which simplifies the learning phase of the composite classifier. It is enough to calculate the performance matrix for the base classifiers during the learning phase. In the application phase, nearest neighbors of a new instance among the training instances are found out and the corresponding base classifiers' performances are used to calculate the estimated classifiers' performance for each base classifier. This is done by summing up the corresponding performance values of a classifier using weights that depend on the distances between a new instance and its nearest neighbors.

Thus the dynamic integration approach contains two phases. In the learning phase (procedure *learning_phase* in Fig. 1), the training set $\mathbf{T}$ is partitioned into v folds. The cross-validation technique is used to estimate the errors of the base classifiers $E_j(\mathbf{x}^*)$ on the training set and the meta-level training set $\mathbf{T}^*$ is formed. It contains the attributes of the training instances $\mathbf{x}_i$ and the estimates of the errors of the base classifiers on those instances $E_j(\mathbf{x}^*)$. Several cross-validation runs can be used in order to obtain more accurate estimates of the base classifiers' errors. Then each estimated error will be equal to the number of times that an instance was incorrectly predicted by the classifier when it appeared as a test example in a cross-validation run. The learning phase finishes with training the base classifiers C_j on the whole training set.

In the application phase, the combining classifier (either the function *DS_application_phase* or the function *DV_application_phase* in Fig. 1) is used to predict the performance of each base classifier for a new instance. Two different functions implementing the application phase were considered [15]. The first function DS implements Dynamic Selection. In the DS application phase the classification error E_j^* is predicted for each base classifier C_j using the WNN procedure and a classifier with the smallest error (with the least global error in the case of ties) is selected to make the final classification. The second function DV implements Dynamic Voting. In the DV application phase each base classifier C_j receives a weight W_j that depends on the local classifier's performance and the final classification is conducted by voting classifier predictions $C_j(\mathbf{x})$ with their weights W_j.

Previously an application of the dynamic classifier integration in medical diagnostics was considered in [21-23]. A number of experiments comparing the dynamic integration with such widely used integration approaches as CVM, and weighted voting were also conducted [15,16,23,24]. The comparison results show that the dynamic integration technique outperforms often weighted voting and CVM. In this paper, the goal is to apply the dynamic classifier integration to decision committee learning, combining the generated classifiers in a more sophisticated manner than voting.

```
T component classifier training set
T_i i-th fold of the training set
T* meta-level training set for the combining algorithm
x attributes of an instance
c(x) classification of the instance with attributes x
C set of component classifiers
C_j j-th component classifier
C_j(x) prediction produced by C_j on instance x
E_j(x) estimation of error of C_j on instance x
E*_j(x) prediction of error of C_j on instance x
m number of component classifiers
W vector of weights for component classifiers
nn number of near-by instances for error prediction
W_NNi weight of i-th near-by instance
```

procedure *learning_phase*(**T,C**)

      begin {fills in the meta-level training set **T***}

          partition **T** into v folds

          loop for $\mathbf{T}_i \subset \mathbf{T}$, $i = 1,...,v$

             loop for j **from** 1 **to** m train(C_j, **T-T_i**)

             loop for $\mathbf{x} \in \mathbf{T}_i$

                loop for j **from** 1 **to** m

                   compare $C_j(\mathbf{x})$ with $c(\mathbf{x})$ and derive $E_j(\mathbf{x})$

               collect $(\mathbf{x}, E_1(\mathbf{x}), ..., E_m(\mathbf{x}))$ into **T***

             loop for j **from** 1 **to** m train(C_j, **T**)

      end

function *DS_application_phase*(**T***,**C,x**) **returns** class of **x**

      begin

          loop for j **from** 1 **to** m

$$E_j^* \leftarrow \frac{1}{nn}\sum_{i=1}^{nn} W_{NN_i} \cdot E_j(\mathbf{x}_{NN_i}) \quad \{\text{WNN estimation}\}$$

$$l \leftarrow \arg\min_j E_j^* \quad \{\text{number of cl-er with min. } E_j^*\}$$

          {with the least global error in the case of ties}

          return $C_j(\mathbf{x})$

      end

function *DV_application_phase*(**T***,**C,x**) **returns** class of **x**

      begin

          loop for j **from** 1 **to** m

$$W_j \leftarrow 1 - \frac{1}{nn}\sum_{i=1}^{nn} W_{NN_i} \cdot E_j(\mathbf{x}_{NN_i}) \quad \{\text{WNN estimation}\}$$

          return Weighted_Voting(**W**, $C_1(\mathbf{x}), ..., C_m(\mathbf{x})$)

      end

Fig. 1. The algorithm for dynamic integration of classifiers [15]

4   Experiments

In this chapter, experiments with the use of the dynamic classifier integration algorithm to combine classifiers generated with AdaBoost and Bagging decision committee learning approaches are presented. First, the experimental setting is described, and then, results of the experiments are presented. The experiments are conducted on nine datasets taken from the UCI machine learning repository [3]. Previously the dynamic classifier integration was experimentally evaluated in [15]. Here a similar experimental environment is used, extended with the Bagging and AdaBoost algorithms to generate decision committees described in chapter 2.

The main characteristics of the nine datasets are presented in Table 1. The table includes the name of the dataset, the number of instances included in the dataset, the number of different classes of instances, and the numbers of different kind of features included in the instances.

Table 1. Characteristics of the datasets

Dataset	Instances	Classes	Features	
			Discrete	Continuous
Breast	286	2	9	0
Diabetes	768	2	0	8
Glass	214	6	0	9
Heart	270	2	8	5
Iris	150	3	0	4
Liver	345	2	0	6
MONK-1	432	2	6	0
MONK-2	432	2	6	0
MONK-3	432	2	6	0

For each dataset 30 test runs are made. In each run the dataset is first split into the training set and the test set by random sampling. Each time 30 percent of the instances of the data set are first randomly picked up to the test set. The rest 70 percent of the instances are then passed to the learning algorithm where the accuracy history of the committee classifiers on the initial training set is collected for later use in the dynamic integration. Cross-validation is not used here as described in chapter 3 for the case of classifiers built with different learning algorithms. Instead, the committee classifiers are simply applied to each instance of the initial training set, and their accuracy is collected into the performance matrix. The committee classifiers themselves are learnt using the C4.5 decision tree algorithm with pruning [17].

In the estimation of the classification errors of the committee classifiers for a new instance, the collected classification information about classification errors for seven nearest neighbors of the new instance is used. The selection of the number of nearest neighbors has been discussed in [15]. Based on the comparisons between different distance functions for dynamic integration presented in [16] it was decided to use the Heterogeneous Euclidean-Overlap Metric, which produced good test results. The test environment was implemented within the MLC++ framework (the machine learning library in C++) [11]. In the experiments, committee size equal to 5 is set in Bagging and AdaBoost (exactly 5 classifiers are generated and integrated both in Bagging and AdaBoost).

Table 2. Accuracy values for Bagging and AdaBoost decision committees integrated with different approaches

DB	Decision committee: C4.5 trees with pruning, accuracy											
	min	aver	max	agree	cover	B	DS	DV	DVS	DS'	DV'	DVS'
Breast	0.643	0.702	0.760	0.465	0.883	0.727	0.713	0.729	0.719	0.705	0.727	0.715
	0.541	0.636	0.724	0.252	0.928	0.691	0.689	0.693	0.701	0.680	0.692	0.696
Diabetes	0.679	0.711	0.739	0.430	0.924	0.741	0.713	0.741	0.728	0.709	0.741	0.732
	0.649	0.686	0.729	0.343	0.946	0.725	0.682	0.725	0.715	0.686	0.726	0.708
Glass	0.550	0.624	0.698	0.319	0.867	0.674	0.692	0.685	0.695	0.651	0.674	0.667
	0.529	0.603	0.681	0.228	0.903	0.685	0.640	0.684	0.671	0.630	0.683	0.667
Heart	0.670	0.734	0.796	0.445	0.936	0.781	0.743	0.781	0.765	0.750	0.781	0.762
	0.601	0.690	0.774	0.290	0.956	0.760	0.726	0.760	0.740	0.732	0.760	0.735
Iris	0.909	0.933	0.959	0.890	0.975	0.934	0.933	0.934	0.936	0.941	0.934	0.938
	0.896	0.931	0.961	0.865	0.975	0.940	0.938	0.940	0.937	0.939	0.940	0.935
Liver	0.551	0.608	0.665	0.241	0.897	0.653	0.618	0.656	0.626	0.620	0.654	0.629
	0.537	0.600	0.660	0.200	0.921	0.640	0.594	0.640	0.610	0.606	0.640	0.623
MONK-1	0.741	0.847	0.940	0.550	1.000	0.922	0.992	0.928	0.987	0.991	0.927	0.985
	0.779	0.864	0.928	0.575	0.996	0.943	0.959	0.943	0.966	0.957	0.943	0.966
MONK-2	0.495	0.546	0.595	0.216	0.858	0.559	0.546	0.557	0.550	0.545	0.559	0.554
	0.475	0.537	0.597	0.185	0.926	0.513	0.593	0.516	0.574	0.590	0.516	0.570
MONK-3	0.981	0.993	1.000	0.981	1.000	0.998	1.000	0.998	1.000	1.000	0.998	1.000
	0.960	0.962	0.963	0.959	0.964	0.960	0.964	0.964	0.964	0.964	0.964	0.964
Average	0.691	0.744	0.795	0.504	0.927	0.777	0.772	0.779	0.778	0.768	0.777	0.776
	0.663	0.723	0.780	0.433	0.946	0.762	0.754	0.763	0.764	0.754	0.763	0.763

Table 2 presents accuracy values for Bagging and AdaBoost decision committees integrated with different approaches. The first five columns include the average of the minimum accuracies of the committee classifiers (min), the average of the average accuracies of the committee classifiers (aver), the average of the maximum accuracies of the committee classifiers (max), the average percentage of test instances where all the committee classifiers managed to produce the right classification (agree), and the average amount of test instances where at least one committee classifier during each run managed to produce the right classification (cover). The seven next columns of the right-hand side of Table 2 include the accuracies for different types of integration of the committee classifiers. All the above columns are averaged over the 30 test runs.

In vertical direction the main body of the table is divided into groups of two rows each corresponding to one dataset. The first row contains accuracies received with the Bagging decision committee learning, and the second row contains accuracies received with the AdaBoost algorithm. The last group in the table shows corresponding accuracies averaged over all the datasets.

The integration types considered in Table 2, correspondingly, include: B – usual Bagging (unweighted voting, the first row) or AdaBoost (weighted voting, the second row), DS – Dynamic Selection, DV – Dynamic Voting, and DVS – Dynamic Voting with Selection. DS and DV integration were considered in chapter 3. Previous experiments with these two integration strategies [15] have shown that the accuracies of the strategies usually differ significantly; however, it depends on the dataset, what a strategy is preferable. In this paper, a combination of these strategies is considered, DVS – Dynamic Voting with Selection. According to this strategy, first, the local errors for the committee classifiers are estimated as usually. Then, the classifiers with high local errors are discarded (the classifiers with local errors that fall into the upper half of the error range of the committee). After, locally weighted voting (DV) is applied as usually to the restricted set of classifiers. One could guess that this integration strategy should be more stable than the other two.

In these experiments, strategies that use simple unweighted nearest neighbor classification for estimation of the local errors of committee classifiers are also considered. They are denoted as DS', DV', and DVS' correspondingly. Usually, in the DS, DV, and DVS application phases, nearest neighbors of a new instance among the training instances are found out and the corresponding base classifiers' errors are used to calculate the estimated classification error for each base classifier. This is done by summing up the corresponding errors of a classifier using weights that depend on the distances between a new instance and its nearest neighbors. DS', DV', and DVS' do not take into account the distances to the nearest neighbors, treating all nearest neighbors as equally weighted. The last three strategies are significantly less computationally expensive. The experiments are conducted to check whether they provide competitive accuracy.

From Table 2 one can see that on each considered dataset at least some dynamic integration strategy works better than classical Bagging or AdaBoost. For example, on the MONK-2 dataset, Dynamic Selection (DS) from AdaBoost classifiers gives 0.593 accuracy on average, while the classical AdaBoost with weighted voting gives only 0.513. Dynamic integration strategies DV and DVS are also better on average than Bagging and AdaBoost. DV and DVS are generally better than DS in these experiments. As one could guess, DVS works quite stable on the considered datasets. Sometimes, it overcomes even both DS and DV, as on the Breast and MONK-1 datasets (with AdaBoost), and the Glass dataset (with Bagging). DVS is slightly better on average than both DS and DV.

The integration with weighted error prediction (DS, DV, and DVS) is generally better than the integration with unweighted error prediction (DS', DV', and DVS'). However, there is usually no big difference in accuracies between those two types of integration, while the second one requires much less time. Sometimes (on the Liver and Iris datasets), the second strategy is even better.

A number of recent investigations of decision committees have analysed error performance in terms of *bias* and *variance* [25]. The squared *bias* is a measure of the contribution to error of the central tendency or most frequent classification of the learner when trained on different training data. The *variance* is a measure of the contribution to error of deviations from the central tendency.

The bias/variance analysis is useful in focusing attention on two significant factors that govern the accuracy of classifiers learned by a learning system. If a learning system when provided different training data develops classifiers that differ in their predictions, then the extent of such variations provides a lower limit on the average error of those classifiers when applied to any subsequent set of test data.

However, preventing such variance between the classifiers will not guarantee the elimination of prediction error. This error is also governed by both the degree to which the correct classifier for an object can differ from that for other objects with identical descriptions (irreducible error) and the accuracy of the learning bias.

A number of different formulations of bias and variance have been proposed in the field of classification learning [4, 25]. Two bias/variance related metrics are used in this research. *Contribution of bias to error* is that portion of the total error across the distribution of test sets that is due to errors committed by the central tendency of the learning algorithm. This is the proportion of classifications that are both incorrect and equal to the central tendency. The central tendency is the most frequent classification for an object. *Contribution of variance to error* is that portion of the total error across the distribution of test sets that is due to errors that are deviations from the central tendency of the learning algorithm. This is the proportion of classifications that are both incorrect and not equal to the central tendency. These two terms must sum to total error.

These metrics are used to evaluate the extent to which variations in the classifiers formed from one training set to another affect the error of the learning algorithm. High contribution of bias to error indicates high error resulting from the learning bias whereas high contribution of variance to error indicates high error resulting from the algorithm's responsiveness to variations between training sets [25]. These two definitions have the desirable properties that: (1) bias is a direct measure of the contribution of the central tendency to total error, (2) variance is a direct measure of the contribution to error of deviations from the central tendency, and (3) the two terms (bias and variance) sum to total error [25].

The bias/variance analysis was conducted as a different set of experiments. The same test setting was used, but values for the metrics were estimated by ten runs of three-fold cross-validation to provide equal number of tests (10) for each instance. In each three-fold cross-validation, the data were randomly divided into three subsets. Each case in each subset is classified once by a classifier learned by the algorithm under evaluation from the other two subsets. Thus, each case is classified once for each three-fold cross-validation, and hence ten times in all.

Table 3 presents preliminary bias/variance analysis' results for Bagging and AdaBoost decision committees integrated with different approaches. The table columns include bias/variance estimations for classical Bagging and AdaBoost (Bagging and Boosting), and for these decision committee learning approaches integrated with Dynamic Selection (Bagg.+DS, and Boost.+DS) and Dynamic Voting (Bagg.+DV, and Boost.+DV). All the above columns are averaged over the 10 test runs.

In vertical direction the main body of the table is divided into groups of two rows each corresponding to one dataset. The first row contains estimation of the bias contribution to error, and the second row contains corresponding estimation of the variance contribution to error. The last group in the table shows corresponding error constituents (bias and variance) averaged over all the datasets.

The results presented in the table confirm the common opinion that AdaBoost is on-the-whole more effective at reducing bias that is bagging, but bagging is more effective than AdaBoost at reducing variance. This holds true also for AdaBoost and bagging with dynamic integration. One could see from the table that when applicable, the dynamic integration (and especially the dynamic selection) tries to reduce the bias constituent of the error. One good example of this effect is the Monk-1 dataset, where the bias constituent of error is equal to 0.000 for Bagging, and to 0.001 for Boosting! One could conclude that when the dynamic integration is profitable, then the error reduction takes place mostly due to the reduction of the bias constituent of error.

Table 3. Bias/variance analysis for Bagging and AdaBoost decision committees integrated with different approaches

DB	Bias/variance contribution to error					
	Bagging	Bagg.+DS	Bagg.+DV	Boosting	Boost.+DS	Boost.+DV
Breast	0.228	0.188	0.223	0.225	0.218	0.225
	0.056	0.103	0.061	0.103	0.112	0.103
Diabetes	0.189	0.182	0.189	0.191	0.191	0.191
	0.071	0.108	0.072	0.089	0.132	0.089
Glass	0.261	0.227	0.246	0.188	0.194	0.190
	0.084	0.130	0.082	0.127	0.161	0.124
Heart	0.147	0.145	0.147	0.163	0.147	0.163
	0.086	0.110	0.086	0.089	0.140	0.089
Iris	0.051	0.051	0.051	0.044	0.045	0.044
	0.009	0.012	0.009	0.009	0.011	0.009
Liver	0.240	0.239	0.230	0.242	0.239	0.242
	0.114	0.135	0.118	0.117	0.140	0.117
MONK-1	0.036	0.000	0.025	0.003	0.001	0.007
	0.077	0.026	0.081	0.067	0.044	0.067
MONK-2	0.303	0.342	0.305	0.374	0.313	0.374
	0.142	0.135	0.141	0.118	0.131	0.118
Average	0.182	0.172	0.177	0.179	0.169	0.180
	0.080	0.095	0.081	0.090	0.109	0.090

5   Conclusion

Decision committee learning has demonstrated spectacular success in reducing classification error from learned classifiers. These techniques develop a classifier in the form of a committee of subsidiary classifiers. The combination of classifier outputs is usually performed by majority vote. Voting, however, has an important shortcoming, that it does not take into account local expertise.

In this paper a technique for dynamic integration of classifiers was proposed for the use instead of voting to integrate classifiers generated with decision committee learning. The technique for dynamic integration of classifiers is based on the assumption that each committee member is best inside certain subareas of the whole feature space. The considered algorithm for dynamic integration of classifiers is a new variation of stacked generalization, which uses a distance metric to locally estimate the errors of committee classifiers.

The proposed dynamic integration technique was evaluated with AdaBoost and Bagging, the decision committee approaches which have received extensive attention recently, on nine datasets from the UCI machine learning repository. The results achieved are promising and show that boosting and bagging have often significantly better accuracy with dynamic integration of classifiers than with simple voting. Commonly this holds true on the datasets for which dynamic integration is preferable to static integration (voting or cross-validated selection) as it was shown by previous experiments. Preliminary bias/variance analysis of the proposed techniques was made.

Further experiments can be conducted to make deeper analysis of combining the dynamic integration of classifiers with different approaches to decision committee learning. Decision committees with different committee sizes can be analyzed. The dependency between the committee size and the accuracy of dynamic integration can be investigated. Another potentially interesting topic for further research is the bias-variance analysis of various decision committees integrated with the dynamic approaches.

Acknowledgments: This research is partly supported by the COMAS Graduate School of the University of Jyväskylä. I would like to thank the UCI machine learning repository of databases, domain theories and data generators for the datasets, and the machine learning library in C++ for the source code used in this study. I am grateful to the anonymous referees for their valuable comments and constructive criticism.

References

1. Aivazyan, S.A.: Applied Statistics: Classification and Dimension Reduction. Finance and Statistics, Moscow (1989).
2. Bauer, E., Kohavi, R.: An Empirical Comparison of Voting Classification Algorithms: Bagging, Boosting, and Variants. Machine Learning, Vol.36 (1999) 105-139.
3. Blake, C.L., Merz, C.J.: UCI Repository of Machine Learning Databases [http://www.ics.uci.edu/ ~mlearn/ MLRepository.html]. Dep-t of Information and CS, Un-ty of California, Irvine CA (1998).
4. Breiman, L.: Bagging Predictors. Machine Learning, Vol. 24 (1996) 123-140.
5. Chan, P., Stolfo, S.: On the Accuracy of Meta-Learning for Scalable Data Mining. Intelligent Information Systems, Vol. 8 (1997) 5-28.
6. Cost, S., Salzberg, S.: A Weighted Nearest Neighbor Algorithm for Learning with Symbolic Features. Machine Learning, Vol. 10, No. 1 (1993) 57-78.

7. Dietterich, T.G.: Machine Learning Research: Four Current Directions. AI Magazine, Vol. 18, No. 4 (1997) 97-136.
8. Fayyad, U., Piatetsky-Shapiro, G., Smyth, P., Uthurusamy, R.: Advances in Knowledge Discovery and Data Mining. AAAI/ MIT Press (1997).
9. Freund, Y., Schapire, R.E.: A Decision-Theoretic Generalization of On-Line Learning and an Application to Boosting. In: Proc. 2nd European Conf. on Computational Learning Theory, Springer-Verlag (1995) 23-37.
10. Kohavi, R.: A Study of Cross-Validation and Bootstrap for Accuracy Estimation and Model Selection. In: C. Mellish (ed.), Proceedings of IJCAI'95, Morgan Kaufmann (1995).
11. Kohavi, R., Sommerfield, D., Dougherty, J.: Data Mining Using MLC++: A Machine Learning Library in C++. Tools with Artificial Intelligence, IEEE CS Press (1996) 234-245.
12. Koppel, M., Engelson, S.P.: Integrating Multiple Classifiers by Finding their Areas of Expertise. In: AAAI-96 Workshop On Integrating Multiple Learning Models (1996) 53-58.
13. Merz, C.: Dynamical Selection of Learning Algorithms. In: D.Fisher, H.-J.Lenz (eds.), Learning from Data, Artificial Intelligence and Statistics, Springer-Verlag, NY (1996).
14. Merz, C.J.: Combining Classifiers Using Correspondence Analysis. In: M.I.Jordan, M.J.Kearns, S.A.Solla (eds.), Advances in Neural Information Processing Systems 10, MIT Press (1998).
15. Puuronen, S., Terziyan, V., Tsymbal, A.: A Dynamic Integration Algorithm for an Ensemble of Classifiers. In: Z.W. Ras, A. Skowron (eds.), Foundations of Intelligent Systems: ISMIS'99, Lecture Notes in AI, Vol. 1609, Springer-Verlag, Warsaw (1999) 592-600.
16. Puuronen, S., Tsymbal, A., Terziyan, V.: Distance Functions in Dynamic Integration of Data Mining Techniques. In: B.V. Dasarathy (ed.), Data Mining and Knowledge Discovery: Theory, Tools and Technology II, Proceedings of SPIE, Vol. 4057, USA (2000) 22-32.
17. Quinlan, J.R.: C4.5 Programs for Machine Learning. Morgan Kaufmann, San Mateo, CA (1993).
18. Schapire, R.E.: A Brief Introduction to Boosting. In: Proc. 16th Int. Joint Conf. on Artificial Intelligence (1999).
19. Schapire, R.E.: The Strength of Weak Learnability. Machine Learning, Vol. 5, No. 2 (1990) 197-227.
20. Skalak, D.B.: Combining Nearest Neighbor Classifiers. Ph.D. Thesis, Dept. of Computer Science, University of Massachusetts, Amherst, MA (1997).
21. Skrypnik, I., Terziyan, V., Puuronen, S., Tsymbal, A.: Learning Feature Selection for Medical Databases. In: Proc. 12th IEEE Symp. on Computer-Based Medical Systems CBMS'99, IEEE CS Press, Stamford, CT (1999) 53-58.
22. Terziyan, V., Tsymbal, A., Puuronen, S.: The Decision Support System for Telemedicine Based on Multiple Expertise. Int. J. of Medical Informatics, Vol. 49, No. 2 (1998) 217-229.
23. Tsymbal, A., Puuronen, S., Terziyan, V.: Advanced Dynamic Selection of Diagnostic Methods. In: Proceedings 11th IEEE Symp. on Computer-Based Medical Systems CBMS'98, IEEE CS Press, Lubbock, Texas, June (1998) 50-54.
24. Tsymbal, A., Puuronen, S., Terziyan, V.: Arbiter Meta-Learning with Dynamic Selection of Classifiers and its Experimental Investigation. In: J.Eder, I.Rozman, T.Welzer (eds.), Advances in Databases and Information Systems: 3rd East European Conference ADBIS'99, LNCS, Vol. 1691, Springer-Verlag, Maribor (1999) 205-217.
25. Webb, G.I.: MultiBoosting: A Technique for Combining Boosting and Wagging. Machine Learning (2000) in press.
26. Wolpert, D.: Stacked Generalization. Neural Networks, Vol. 5 (1992) 241-259.

Multiversion Linear Quadtree
for Spatio-Temporal Data *

Theodoros Tzouramanis, Michael Vassilakopoulos, and Yannis Manolopoulos

Data Engineering Lab
Department of Informatics, Aristotle University
54006 Thessaloniki, Greece
theo@delab.csd.auth.gr, mvass@computer.org, manolopo@csd.auth.gr

Abstract. Research in spatio-temporal databases has largely focused on extensions of access methods for the proper handling of time changing spatial information. In this paper, we present the Multiversion Linear Quadtree (MVLQ), a spatio-temporal access method based on Multiversion B-trees (MVBT) [2], embedding ideas from Linear Region Quadtrees [4]. More specifically, instead of storing independent numerical data having a different transaction-time each, for every consecutive image we store a group of codewords that share the same transaction-time, whereas each codeword represents a spatial subregion. Thus, the new structure may be used as an index mechanism for storing and accessing evolving raster images. We also conducted a thorough experimentation using sequences of real and synthetic raster images. In particular, we examined the time performance of temporal window queries, and provide results for a variety of parameter settings.

1 Introduction

Spatial Databases (SDBs) represent, store and manipulate spatial data, such as points, lines, surfaces, volumes and hyper-volumes in multi-dimensional space. Numerous applications require efficient retrieval of spatial objects: geographical information systems (GIS), image and multimedia databases, urban planning, computer-aided design (CAD), rule indexing in expert database systems, etc. The traditional indexing methods are not suitable to store spatial data because of their inability to implement a total ordering of objects in space and preserve proximity, at the same time. References [5,10] are extensive surveys with detailed methodology and algorithms of a plethora of techniques for spatial data.

On the other hand, *Temporal Databases* (TDBs) support the maintenance of time-varying data and specialized queries on them. Conventional databases are not suitable to handle continuously changing data, since they can store only one version of data, the one applicable at *present time*. Therefore, whenever a piece of data is not valid any longer, it is either deleted or updated, at the physical level.

---

* Research performed under the European Union's TMR Chorochronos project, contract number ERBFMRX-CT96-0056 (DG12-BDCN).

J. Štuller et al. (Eds.): ADBIS-DASFAA 2000, LNCS 1884, pp. 279–292, 2001.

Two concepts of time are usually considered in TDBs, *valid* and *transaction time*. According to [6], valid time is the time during which a fact is true in the real world. Transaction time is the time during which a piece of data is recorded in a relation. Each of these two notions of time is comprised by a *start time point* and an *end time point* or, equivalently, an *interval* [*StartTime, EndTime*) and has specific properties associated with it. A TDB handling valid time only is called *valid* or *historical*. When it handles transaction time only, it is then called *transaction* or *rollback*. When handling both of these notions of time at once it is called *bi-temporal*. A number of access methods for temporal data have been proposed up to now. Some of these methods achieve acceptable performance in real-life applications [12].

Until recently the fields of temporal and spatial databases remained two separate worlds. However, modern applications (GIS, time-sequence analysis and forecasting, animation etc.) demand the efficient manipulation of spatial information that change over time. *Spatio-temporal Databases* (STDBs) are spatial databases in which data objects may change their spatial locations and/or their shapes at different time intervals. In these databases, special implementation techniques should be developed for efficient storage and access of spatial objects, their geometric representations and their time-varying characteristics. Reference [1] is an excellent survey on the advances made during the last years, in spatio-temporal database research.

The fundamental objective of the proposed study is to present an efficient spatio-temporal access method (STAM) for storing and accessing evolving raster images (regional data). Efficiency is considered in terms of space requirements and time performance during query processing. The new indexing structure that is based on transaction time is called *Multiversion Linear Quadtree* (MVLQ).

The motivation for devising this new spatio-temporal access method is the Multiversion B-tree (MVBT) [2], however the proposed method differs for a number of reasons. Instead of storing independent numerical data having a different transaction-time each, for every consecutive image MVLQ stores a group of codewords that share the same transaction-time, whereas each codeword represents a spatial subregion. As a consequence, the algorithms of insertion, deletion and update processes in MVLQ are significantly different from the corresponding algorithms in MVBT. This is due to fact that after a batch operation with many insertions, deletes and updates of data records at a specific transaction-time, we may have significant different policies in node splitting and merging.

MVLQ has analogous functionality to another significantly different structure proposed by the authors, Overlapping Linear Quadtrees (OLQs) [14,15,17]. Both structures have the same origin, Linear Region Quadtree (LRQ) [4]. However, MVLQ stores the codewords present in LRQs in a modified MVBT, while OLQs apply the technique of overlapping in a sequence of LRQs. The purpose of this article is to present the MVLQ along with an initial experimental study of the time performance of temporal window queries, and provide results for a variety of parameter settings. We conducted a thorough experimentation using sequences of real and synthetic raster images. A comparison with OLQs is a research activity in progress.

The rest of the paper is organized as follows. Section 2 provides a description of the new structure. Section 3 discusses query processing in MVLQ. Section 4 presents experimental results regarding space requirements and query performance. Finally, Section 5 concludes the paper introducing, also, ideas for further research.

2   The New Structure

2.1   Framework and Assumptions

In our discussion of STDBs we assume that a sequence of evolving raster images is stored in the database. Each of these images is represented as a $2^n \times 2^n$ array of pixels ordered by rows, where n is a positive integer. If the pixel colors are black and white only, the image is said to be a *binary* one, where 1 stands for black and 0 for white color. Each image has a unique timestamp[1] T_i, where $i=1$, 2, ..., N, and N is the total number of images. This temporal attribute expresses transaction time.

A transaction time STAM implicitly associates a time interval to each record representing a spatial object. When a new record is inserted at time T_1, this time interval is set equal to $[T_1, *)$ [2]. A "real world" deletion at time point T_2 is implemented as a *logical* deletion by changing the *EndTime* timestamp of the time interval from * to T_2.

2.2   Quadtrees and Linear Quadtrees for Regional Data

The *region Quadtree* is based on the successive decomposition of two-dimensional binary raster images into four quadrants of $2^{n-1} \times 2^{n-1}$ pixels. If a part of an image is not covered entirely by black or white, it is recursively subdivided into four subquadrants, until each subquadblock is entirely unicolor. An example of binary raster image arrays of pixels and their corresponding region Quadtrees appears in Fig. 1.

The region Quadtree is a main memory structure. However, the represented image may be very large and its Quadtree can not be stored in main memory. In such a case, information about the leaves that correspond to black quadblocks of the image array, can be inserted into a B$^+$-tree producing, thus, a pointerless version of the Quadtree. The latter method is called *Linear region Quadtree* (*Linear Quadtree* in the sequel, [4,10]).

Each black Quadtree node is represented by a pair of numbers (C, L). The first number C is termed *a locational code* and denotes the correct path to this node, traversing the Quadtree from its root till the appropriate leaf. Each one of the n digits of C can be 0,1,2 or 3 corresponding to quadrants NW, NE, SW and

---

[1] "A timestamp is a time value associated with some object, e.g. an attribute value or a tuple" [6]

[2] The symbol '*' refers to *now* which is a special value in TDBs. Its usage means that the respective object will be valid until some time point far in the future, that is not known beforehand.

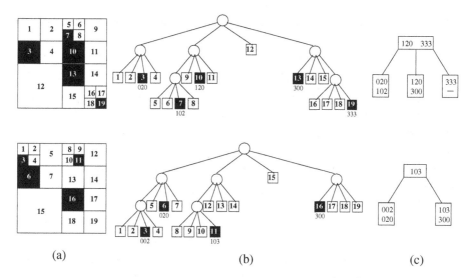

Fig. 1. Two similar binary $2^3 \times 2^3$ raster images (left) and their corresponding region Quadtrees (middle) and Linear region Quadtrees (right).

SE, respectively. The second number L of the pair is the Quadtree level where the node is located.

This linear representation of the Quadtree nodes, is called FD (Fixed length - Depth) linear implementation. The interested reader can find two other linear implementations in the literature: FL (Fixed Length) and VL (Variable Length) (see [11] for details). For reasons that are explained in [14], the choice of the linear representation for the black Quadtree nodes was the FD (Fixed length - Depth) implementation. The right part of Fig. 1 presents two different Linear Quadtrees that can be obtained from the corresponding Quadtrees in the middle of the same figure. For simplicity, only the FD locational codes (*quadcodes* in the sequel) of the black nodes appear in the Linear Quadtrees, whereas the levels of the nodes are not shown.

2.3   Multiversion Linear Quadtree

If a sequence of N images has to be stored in a Linear Quadtree, each image labeled with a unique timestamp T_i (for $i=1, 2, ..., N$), then updates will overwrite old versions and only the last inserted image will be retained. In applications where spatial queries refer to the past, all the successive versions of the structure need to be accessible. MVLQ converts the ephemeral Linear Quadtree to a *persistent data structure* [3], where past states are also maintained.

MVLQ couples time intervals with spatial objects in each node. Data records residing in leaves contain records of the form $< (C, L), T >$ where (C, L) is the FD code of a black node of the region Quadtree and T represents the time interval when this black node appears in the image sequence. Nonleaf nodes contain entries of the form $< C', T', Ptr >$, where Ptr is a pointer to a descendent node,

C' is the smallest C recorded in that descendent node and T' is the time interval that expresses the lifespan of the latter node.

In each MVLQ node, we added a new field, called "$StartTime$", to hold the time instant when it was created. This field is used during the modification processes and will be examined further, later. Moreover, in each leaf we added one more extra field called "$EndTime$", to register the transaction time when a specific leaf changes and becomes historical. The structure of the MVLQ is accompanied by two additional main memory sub-structures:

- the *root* table*: it is built on top of MVLQ. MVLQ hosts a number of version trees and has a number of roots in such a way that each root stands for a time/version interval $T''=[T_i, T_j)$, where $i, j \in \{1, 2, ..., N\}$ and $i < j$. Each record in the root* table represents a root of MVLQ and obeys the form $< T'', Ptr' >$, where T'' is the lifespan of that root and Ptr' is a pointer to its physical disk address.
- the *Depth First-expression* (DF-expression, [7]) of the last inserted image: its usage is to keep track of all the black quadblocks of the last inserted image, and to be able to know at no I/O cost, the black quadrants that are identical between this image and the one that will appear next. Thus, given a new image, we do know beforehand which exactly are the FD code insertions, deletions and updates. The DF-expression is a compacted array that represents an image in the preorder traversal of its Quadtree.

As we claimed earlier the basis for the new access method is the MVBT. However, its algorithms of insertion, deletion and update processes are significantly different from the corresponding algorithms in the MVBT.

Insertion
If during a quadcode insertion, at time point T_i, the target leaf is already full, a *node overflow* occurs. Depending on the StartTime field of the leaf, the structural change may be triggered in two ways.

- If $StartTime=T_i$ then *a key split* occurs and the leaf splits. Assuming that b is the node capacity, after the key split the first $\lceil b/2 \rceil$ entries of the original node are kept in this node and the rest are moved to a new leaf.
- Otherwise, if $StartTime < T_i$, a copy of the original leaf must first be allocated, since it is not acceptable to change past states of the spatio-temporal structure. In this case, we remove all non-present (past) versions of quadcodes from the copy node. This operation is called *version split* [2] and the number of present versions of quadcodes after the version split must be in the range from $(1+e)d$ to $(k-e)d$, where k is a constant integer, $d=b/k$ and $e > 0$. If a version split leads to less than $(1+e)d$ quadcodes, then a merge is attempted with a sibling or a copy of that sibling containing only its present versions of quadcodes (the choice depends on the StartTime field of the sibling). If a version split leads to more than $(k-e)d$ quadcodes in a node, then a key split is performed.

Deletion

Given a "real world" deletion of a quadcode at time point T_j, its implementation depends on the StartTime field of the corresponding leaf.

- If $StartTime=T_j$ then the appropriate entry of the form $< C, L, T >$ is removed from the leaf. After this *physical* deletion, the leaf is checked whether it holds enough entries. If the number of entries is above d, then the deletion is completed. If the latter number is below that threshold, then the *node underflow* is handled as in the classical B$^+$-tree, with one difference that if a sibling exists (preferably the right one) then we have to check its StartTime field before proceeding to a merge or a key redistribution.
- Otherwise, if $StartTime < T_j$ then the quadcode deletion is handled as a *logical* deletion, by updating the temporal information T of the appropriate entry from $T=[T_i, *)$ to $T=[T_i, T_j)$, where T_i is the insertion time of that quadcode. If an entry is logically deleted in a leaf with exactly d present quadcode versions, then a *version underflow* [2] occurs that causes a version split of the node, copying the present versions of its quadcodes into a new node. Evidently, the number of present versions of quadcodes after the version split is below $(1+e)d$ and a merge is attempted with a sibling or a copy of that sibling.

Update

Updating (i.e. changing the value of the level L of) an FD code leaf entry at time point T_j is implemented by (i) the logical deletion of the entry and (ii) the insertion of a new version of that entry; this new version of the entry has the same quadcode C but a new level value L'.

Example

Consider the two consecutive images (with respect to their timestamps $T_1=1$ and $T_2=2$) on the left of Fig. 1. The MVLQ structure after the insertion of the first image is given in Fig. 2a. At the MVLQ leaves, the level L of each quadcode should also be stored but for simplicity only the FD-locational codes appear. The structure consists of three nodes: a root R and two leaves A and B. The node capacity b equals 4 and the parameters k, d and e equal 2, 2 and 0.5, respectively. The second version of the structure is constructed based on the first one, by inserting the FD code $< 002, 0 >$ (in the form $< C, L >$), the deletion of $< 102, 0 >$, the insertion of $< 103, 0 >$ and the deletion of FD codes $< 120, 1 >$ and $< 333, 0 >$.

Figure 2b shows the intermediate result of the insertion of FD code $< 002, 0 >$, the deletion of $< 102, 0 >$ and the insertion of FD code $< 103, 0 >$. When we attempt to insert the quadcode 103 in the leaf A of Fig. 2b, the leaf overflows and a new leaf C is created after a version split. All present versions of quadcodes of leaf A are copied into leaf C and the parent R is updated for the structural change. Leaf C holds now more than $(k-e)d=3$ entries and a key split is performed producing a new leaf D. Again, the parent R is updated.

The final status of MVLQ after the insertion of the second image is illustrated in Fig. 2c. The quadcode 120 is deleted from leaf D of Fig. 2b and a node underflow occurs (the number of entries is above d), which is resolved by merging

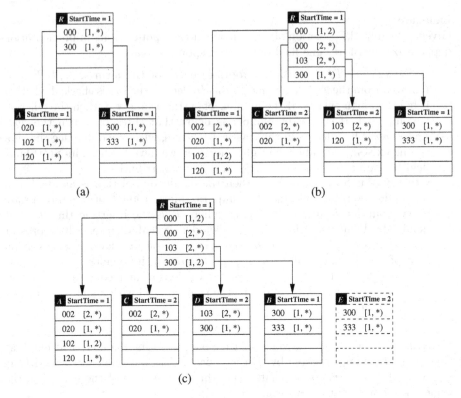

Fig. 2. (a) The MVLQ structure after the insertion of the first image, (b) a preliminary result during the insertion of the second image, and (c) the final result after the insertion of the second image.

this node with its right sibling B or a copy of it, containing only its present versions of quadcodes. After finding out that the StartTime field of leaf B is smaller than T_2, a version split on that leaf is performed, which is followed by a merge of the new (but temporary) leaf E and leaf D, in leaf D. The process terminates after the physical deletion of quadcode 333 from leaf D. The final number of entries in leaf D equals d. Both versions of MVLQ (Fig. 2a and Fig. 2c) have the same root R, although in general, more than one roots may exist.

Generally, we face the insertion of a new image in two stages. The first stage is to sort the quadcodes of the new image and compare this sequence against the set of quadcodes of the last inserted image, using the binary table of its DF-expression. Thus, there is no I/O cost for black quadrants that are identical between the two successive images. During the next stage we use of the root* table to locate the root that corresponds to the last inserted image. Then, following ideas of the approach of [8], we build the new tree version by performing all the quadcode insertions, updates and deletions in a batched manner, instead of performing them one at a time. (We did not follow this approach in the example of Fig. 2 for simplicity reasons). It is obvious that after a batch operation with insertions, deletions and updates at a specific time point, we may have conceptual node splittings and mergings. Thus, a specific leaf may split in more than two nodes and in a similar manner, more than two sibling leaves may merge during FD code deletions.

3 Spatio-Temporal Window Query Processing

The MVLQ structure is based on transaction time and is an extension of MVBT and Linear Quadtree for spatio-temporal data. It supports all the well-known spatial queries for quadtree-based spatial databases (spatial joins, nearest neighbor queries, similarity and spatial selection queries, etc.) without taking into account the notion of time. However, the major feature of the new STAM, is that it can efficiently handle all the special types of spatio-temporal window queries for quadtree-based databases, described in detail in [15,17].

Window queries have a primary importance since they are the basis of a number of operations that can be executed in a STDB. Given a $k \times k$ window and a sequence of N binary images stored in a STDB, each one associated with an unique timestamp T_i (where i=1, 2, ..., N), we considered the satisfaction of the following queries by the use of MVLQ:

- The Strict Containment Window Query
- The Border Intersect Window Query
- The General Border Intersect Window Query
- The Cover Window Query
- The Fuzzy Cover Window Query

Definitions and algorithms for the processing of the above queries were described in [15,17] and can be applied to MVLQ with slight modifications. For brevity, the description of these modifications is not included in this report.

In order to improve spatio-temporal query processing on raster images, we added four "horizontal" pointers in every MVLQ leaf. The use of these pointers was first introduced in [13] and later it was adapted to spatiotemporal data in [14]. This way there is no need to top-down traverse consecutive tree instances to search for the history of a specific FD code and excessive page accesses are avoided. The names of these pointers are: B-pointer, BC-pointer, F-pointer and FC-pointer. Their roles and functions are described in [14].

Alternative naive approaches for answering the above spatio-temporal queries are easy to devise. The respective algorithms would perform a suitable range search for every MVLQ version that corresponds to the given time interval as if each one of them was separately stored in an LRQ, starting from the respective MVLQ roots. These alternative approaches would not take into account the horizontal pointers resulting in significantly worse I/O performance.

4   Experiments

4.1   Preliminaries

The MVLQ structure was implemented in C++ and all the experiments were performed by using the following parameter values. Assuming that the page size is 1K, the size of a time interval is 8 bytes, the size of an FD locational code as well as the size of a pointer are 4 bytes each, and the size of the level of an FD code is 1 byte, we conclude that the internal nodes of the MVLQ can accommodate 60 $< C', T', Ptr >$ entries, whereas leaves contain 75 records of the format $< (C, L), T >$. For a given node capacity b, it is useful for the time complexity to choose a large d, whereas k should be as small as possible [2]. To guarantee a good space utilization it is also useful to choose a large e. It has been proved that the maximum value of e is equal to $e=1-1/d$, whereas for the parameter k, the following inequality should hold [2]:

$$k \geq 2 + 3e - \frac{1}{d} \tag{1}$$

Thus, for a leaf (internal) node capacity equal to $b=75$ ($b'=60$), the values used in experimentation for the above parameters were: $d=15$ ($d'=12$), $k=5$, and $e=0.933$ ($e'=0.916$).

The evolving images were synthetic and real raster binary images of sizes: 512×512 and 1024×1024 pixels. For the experiments with synthetic (real) images, the number of evolving images was $N=2$ ($N=26$). The size of the DF-expression, for a 512×512 image is 85.3 Kbytes, whereas for a 1024×1024 image it is 341.3 Kbytes in the worst case. Therefore, in any case it is small enough to be stored in main memory. For every insertion of a new image (for converting it from raster to linear FD representation) in the MVLQ, we used the algorithm OPTIMAL_BUILD described in [10].

We performed an extensive experimentation with respect to the storage performance. For brevity, we do not include any such results. However, the interested reader may find additional details and results in [16].

4.2   Query Processing

Each sophisticated algorithm for the five spatio-temporal window queries was executed several times for different window sizes and in a random window position every time. Besides, the respective naive algorithms were executed by performing independent searches through multiple MVLQ roots. In each run, we kept track of the average number of disk reads needed to perform the query per time point. For a more effective comparison of the two different algorithmic approaches, we excluded from the measurement the number of disk reads spent for the very first image of the sequence of the N images. The reason is that both algorithms would perform the same range search in the corresponding tree instance, starting from its root and, thus, accessing the same number of disk pages. We are interested only in the I/O cost profit we can succeed by the use of the horizontal pointers.

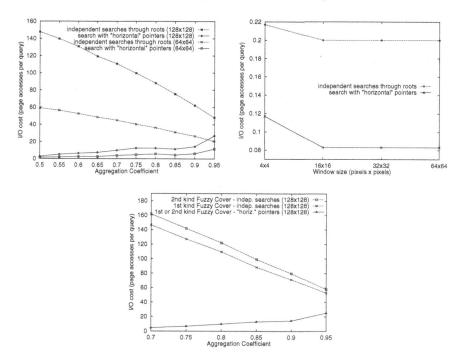

Fig. 3. The I/O efficiency of the Strict Containment (upper left) of the Cover (upper right) and Fuzzy Cover Window Query (lower middle).

Experiments with Synthetic Data Sets

Every experiment was repeated 10 times using a pair of similar images. In the beginning, the first image was created with a specific black/white analogy and an aggregation coefficient $agg()$ that was increased at various amounts. The quantity $agg()$ has been defined in [9] and expresses the coherence of regions of homogeneous colors in an image. Starting from a random image and using the algorithm presented in [9], an image with exactly the same black/white analogy and higher aggregation (more realistic, including larger regions covered entirely by black or white) can be created. After the insertion of the first image, the second image was created by randomly changing the color of a given percentage (2%) of the pixels of the first image. Finally, the FD codes of that image were compared with those of the previous image and inserted in the MVLQ. Note that the random changing of single pixels is an extreme method of producing evolving images and the results derived by this policy should be seen as very pessimistic. In practice, much higher performance gains are expected. Windows of sizes ranging from 4×4 to 128×128 pixels were queried 10 times each against the structure produced. Thus, every algorithm was executed 10×10 times.

The performance of the sophisticated and the naive algorithms is illustrated in Fig. 3. The upper left (upper right) part shows the I/O cost of the Strict

Containment (Cover) Window Query as a function of the aggregation coefficient (of the window size) for 50% black images (70% black images and aggregation coefficient equal to 0.7). The lower middle part shows the I/O cost of the Fuzzy Cover Window Query for 80% threshold and 70% black images, as a function of the aggregation coefficient. The linear decrease of the I/O cost for the naive algorithms of the Strict and Fuzzy Cover Window Queries is explained by the fact that images with larger aggregation form larger and solid black spatial regions ("islands") and thus the corresponding Linear Quadtree holds less number of FD codes. An interesting remark is that the use of horizontal pointers leads to a remarkably high and stable I/O performance for all the spatio-temporal window queries examined.

Experiments with Real Data Sets

In the sequel, we provide the results of some experiments based on real raster images, which were meteorological views of California, and may be acquired via anonymous FTP from `ftp://s2k-ftp.cs.berkeley.edu/pub/sequoia/bench-mark/raster/`. These images correspond to three different categories of spectral channels: visible, reflected infrared, and emitted (thermal) infrared. Originally, each 8-bit image pixel represented a value in a scale of 256 tones of gray. We transformed each image to a binary one, by choosing a threshold accordingly, so as to achieve a black analogy ranging between 20% and 80%. The total number of evolving binary images was $N=26$ in every channel, and, therefore, the time point values varied from $T_1=1$ to $T_N=26$.

Figure 4 depicts three successive images of the visible spectrum. Table 1 shows that from the comparison of the 26 consecutive images of the visible spectral channel, the average percentage of pixels changing value from each image to the following one is from 12.5% to 21.2%, depending on the average percentage of the black/white analogy. Thus, many differences appear from image to image (Fig. 4 confirms also this fact) and it could be argued that the specific images are not the most suitable data to test the performance of MVLQ and the results produced should be seen as very pessimistic.

It is self-evident that the larger the image difference in percentage of pixels, the worse the query time performance of the sophisticated algorithmic approa-

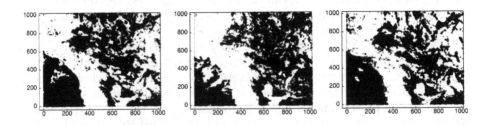

Fig. 4. Three successive 60% black images.

Table 1. Values of different parameters came up from the experimentation with the 26 consecutive images of the visible spectral channel.

	Average values in $N{=}26$ images			
Black analogy	20%	40%	60%	80%
Difference	16.22%	21.22%	18.77%	12.49%
Aggr. coefficient	89.70%	92.38%	95.55%	98.18%

ches. However, the query performance results we obtained with these real images were encouraging in such a worst case environment.

Windows of sizes ranging from 4×4 to 256×256 pixels were queried 50 times each against the structure produced. It is important to highlight that we are only interested in the I/O cost profit we achieve by the use of horizontal pointers for the images 2 to 26.

The upper left (upper right) part of Fig. 5 depicts the time performance of the Strict Containment (Fuzzy Cover) Window Query as a function of black analogy (and threshold 80%), for two different window sizes. The lower middle part presents a general performance comparison of the I/O cost of the sophisticated algorithms for the four different window queries and window size 128×128. Again, a general remark from the diagrams, is that the use of horizontal pointers leads to significantly higher I/O efficiency for all the spatio-temporal window queries examined.

5   Conclusions

In the present paper, we proposed a new spatio-temporal structure: Multi-Version Linear Quadtree. This access method is based on transaction time and can be used as an index mechanism for consecutive raster images. Five efficient algorithms for processing temporal window queries were also adapted to an image database organized with MVLQ. It was demonstrated that this structure can be used in spatio-temporal databases to support query processing of evolving images. More specifically, we studied algorithms for processing the following spatio-temporal queries: Strict Containment, Border Intersect, General Border Intersect, Cover and Fuzzy Cover Window Queries. Besides, we presented experiments performed for studying the I/O efficiency of these algorithms. The latter experiments were based on real and synthetic sequences of evolving images. In general, our experiments showed clearly that, thanks to the "horizontal" pointers in the MVNQ leaves, our algorithms are very efficient in terms of disk activity.

In the future, we plan to compare the space and time performance of MVLQ to those of OLQs. We also plan to develop algorithms for other new spatio-temporal queries that take advantage of MVLQ, OLQs and other Quadtree-based STAMs and study their behavior. Moreover, we plan to investigate the possibility of analyzing the performance of such algorithms. Also, it is considered important

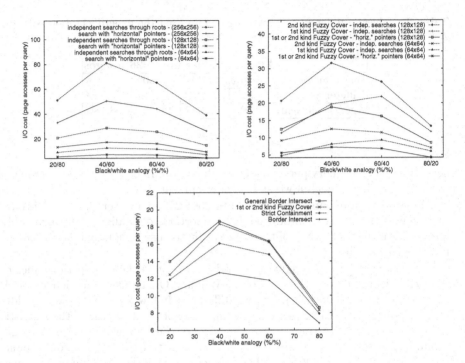

Fig. 5. The I/O efficiency of the Strict Containment (upper left), the Fuzzy Cover Window Query (upper right) and performance comparison of four different window queries (lower middle) as a function of the black/white analogy of the evolving images.

to examine the performance of MVLQ and OLQs in the context of various spatio-temporal operations, such as spatio-temporal joins, as well as spatio-temporal nearest neighbor queries [18].

Acknowledgments We would like to thank Prof. Bernhard Seeger of the University of Marburg for kindly providing the MVBT code.

References

1. T. Abraham and J.F. Roddick: Survey of Spatio-Temporal Databases, *Geoinformatica*, Vol.3, No.1, pp.61-99, 1999.
2. B. Becker, S. Gschwind, T. Ohler, B. Seeger and P. Widmayer: An Asymptotically Optimal Multiversion B-tree, *The VLDB Journal*, Vol.5, No.4, pp.264-275, 1996.
3. J.R. Driscoll, N. Sarnak, D.D. Sleator, and R.E. Tarjan: Making Data Structures Persistent, *Journal of Computer and System Sciences*, Vol.38, pp.86-124, 1989.
4. I. Gargantini: An Effective Way to Represent Quadtrees, *Communications of the ACM*, Vol.25, No.12, pp.905-910, 1982.
5. V. Gaede and O. Guenther: Multidimensional Access Methods, *ACM Computer Surveys*, Vol.30, No.2, pp.123-169, 1998.

6. C.S. Jensen et al.: A Consensus Glossary of Temporal Database Concepts, *ACM SIGMOD Record*, Vol.23, No.1, pp.52-64, 1994.

7. E. Kawaguchi and T. Endo: On a Method of Binary Picture Representation and its Application to Data Compression, *IEEE Transactions on Pattern Analysis and Machine Intelligence*, Vol.2, No.1, pp.27-35, 1980.

8. S.D. Lang and J.R. Driscoll: Improving the Differential File Technique via Batch Operations for Tree Structured File Organizations, *Proceedings IEEE International Conference on Data Engineering (ICDE'86)*, Los Angeles, CA, 1986.

9. Y. Manolopoulos, E. Nardelli, G. Proietti and M. Vassilakopoulos: On the Generation of Aggregated Random Spatial Regions, *Proceedings 4th International Conference on Information and Knowledge Management (CIKM'95)*, pp.318-325, Washington DC, 1995.

10. H. Samet: *The Design and Analysis of Spatial Data Structures*, Addison-Wesley, Reading MA, 1990.

11. H. Samet: *Applications of Spatial Data Structures*, Addison-Wesley, Reading MA, 1990.

12. B. Saltzberg and V. Tsotras: A Comparison of Access Methods for Time Evolving Data, *ACM Computing Surveys*, Vol.31, No.2, pp.158-221, 1999.

13. T. Tzouramanis, Y. Manolopoulos and N. Lorentzos: Overlapping B^+-trees: an Implementation of a Temporal Access Method', *Data and Knowledge Engineering*, Vol.29, No.3, pp.381-404, 1999.

14. T. Tzouramanis, M.Vassilakopoulos and Y. Manolopoulos: Overlapping Linear Quadtrees: a Spatio-temporal Access Method, *Proceedings 6th ACM Symposium on Advances in Geographic Information Systems (ACM-GIS'98)*, pp.1-7, Bethesda MD, November 1998.

15. T. Tzouramanis, M. Vassilakopoulos and Y. Manolopoulos: Processing of Spatio-Temporal Queries in Image Databases, *Proceedings 3rd East-European Conference on Advances in Databases and Information Systems (ADBIS'99)*, pp. 85-97, Maribor, September 1999.

16. T. Tzouramanis, M. Vassilakopoulos and Y. Manolopoulos: Multiversion Linear Quadtree for Spatio-Temporal Data, Technical Report, Data Engineering Lab, Department of Informatics, Aristotle University of Thessaloniki. Address for downloading: http://delab.csd.auth.gr/~theo/TechnicalReports

17. T. Tzouramanis, M. Vassilakopoulos and Y. Manolopoulos: Overlapping Linear Quadtrees and Window Query Processing in Spatio-Temporal Databases, submitted.

18. Y. Theodoridis, T. Sellis, A. Papadopoulos and Y. Manolopoulos: Specifications for Efficient Indexing in Spatiotemporal Databases, *Proceedings of the 7th Conference on Statistical and Scientific Database Management Systems (SSDBM'98)*, pp.123-132, Capri, Italy, 1998.

On the Analysis of On-Line Database Reorganization*

Vlad I.S. Wietrzyk, Mehmet A. Orgun**, and Vijay Varadharajan

School of Computing and Information Technology
University of Western Sydney - Nepean
P.O BOX 10 Kingswood, NSW 2747 Australia
vlad@cit.nepean.uws.edu.au

Abstract. We consider the problem of on-line database reorganization. The types of reorganization that we discuss are restoration of clustering, purging of old data, creation of a backup copy, compaction, and construction of indexes. The contributions of this paper are both of theoretical and of experimental nature.

Keywords: On-line Reorganization, Dynamic Clustering, Statistical Profile of Access Patterns, Object Database Systems, Performance Analysis, Buffering.

1 Introduction

The goal of dynamic reorganization is to arrive at an optimal data layout based on observed access patterns. To accomplish this, the reorganizer must solve three problems. First, it needs to keep track of the history of previous events. Second, it must find a layout that would deliver near-optimal performance for the observed access patterns, assuming that past is a good predictor of future access patterns. Third, it must analyze the difference between the current layout and the desired layout and if necessary, issue I/O requests to correct the difference.

The clustering algorithms presented so far in the literature aim at determining a good initial placement of an object, but none of them take into account *dynamic evolution.*

To summarize, the new aspects of our approach to on-line reorganization of the database include the following research contributions. The novel approach to incremental on-line maintenance of good clustering which employs the maintainance of the minimum spanning tree of a dynamic object graph under the presence of concurrent additions and deletions of data objects. We designed and implemented the Large Complex Object Manager (LCOM) on top of the VERSANT disk manager, for managing variable-size storage clusters. During

---

* Research supported by the **Versant Technology Corporation** and **Intel Corporation**

** Department of Computing Macquarie University - Sydney NSW 2109, Australia

J. Štuller et al. (Eds.): ADBIS-DASFAA 2000, LNCS 1884, pp. 293–306, 2000.

operation our system is incrementally saving all work already done while maintaining consistency after system crashes.

The rest of this paper is organized as follows. Related work on on-line reorganization of the DBMS is discussed in section 2. Section 3 introduces the VERSANT DBMS, the storage system used in our experiments and the way statistical profile of user application software is captured by the mechanism that, actively interface an Object Database Management System to application programs. Section 4 describes new algorithms designed for minimizing object access time under the presence of concurrent additions and delitions of objects. The application of reliable memory for the purpose of enhancing reliability and performance is demonstrated in section 5. In this section we also discuss concurrency control and recoverability under the operation of the reliable memory and its possible effect on the state-of-the-art recovery schemes (e.g. ARIES [11]). In section 6 we discuss the question of *optimal cluster size*. Section 7 presents preliminary experiments and results. Section 8 concludes the paper with a summary and a short discussion of future research.

2   Related Works

Though there has been much work in the area of on-line reorganization in recent years [12], [13], [14], [15], there has been hardly any work that considers on-line incremental cluster modification under concurrent additions and delitions of data. Perhaps [14] is one of the few, research papers that discusses an approach for on-line index modification. In [14] records are moved from one location to another location one at a time. All references and the record move are encapsulated in a database transaction. However this technique is too slow for massive reorganization of DBMS, because changes to the secondary index pages are performed immediately which would necessitate a disk I/O for each index leaf page that is not in the buffer at the time of the access. In [16], an on-line algorithm for the reorganization of key sequenced files is presented.

Some researchers propose a cost model to evaluate the benefit and cost of reclustering. A fully dynamic reclustering scheme will reduce the access time, and hence the overhead imposed on the system by reorganization could offset the benefit. Our estimation of reorganization cost is based on copy-and-reclaim method [4]. Reorganizing clusters of objects saved on physical pages is justified only if reclustering overhead - (T_{reorg}) together with the time taken to write all pages back to the disk - (T_{clus}) is smaller than the summary time of present accesses to the related pages residing in the scattered form - (T_{scat}) [5].

$$T_{reorg} + T_{clus} < T_{scat}$$

Before reclustering, costs and benefits must be precisely estimated. However, to collect the whole set of statistics for every object, especially during the whole object life may prove to be very expensive and quite unrealistic.

3   The VERSANT Storage System

We use the VERSANT database management system developed at *Versant Object Technology Corporation, California* as the database in our experiments [10]. VERSANT is a fourth-generation DBMS combining the direct modeling of complex graph-structured data with the power of today's leading object programming languages. VERSANT has certain unique features which are relevant to our experiments, but our results should apply to more conventional databases as well [3].

3.1   Monitoring Objects

Statistical profile of user application software is captured by the mechanism, which actively interfaces an Object Database Management System to application programs. The database monitor mechanism observes which and how values of attributes of database objects change as a function of time. By means of Versant SQL we can specify the derived or stored associated attribute.

4   Dynamic Algorithms Designed for Automatic Database Reorganization

In this section we present the algorithm without the details of logging and recovery.

Database accesses in an Object DBMS are very complex due to the rich variety of type constructors provided. Additionally ODBMS often use navigation-like access among object hierarchy, therefore inter-object references often generate random disk access if the entire database does not fit in main memory. Dynamical hierarchical clustering, where records remain clustered in a hierarchical order after numerous insertions and deletions, has generated very little publicity, and remains an unsolved problem.

4.1   Reorganization Strategy Offered by Commercial Object Database Systems

Usually placement of objects on disk depends on control information given by the database administrator describing the placement of objects. Often physical placement of object on disk is bounded to schema information. Strictly speaking, the placement strategy that has been implemented in existing commercial systems aims at determining a good initial placement of an object, but does not take into account dynamic evolution.

4.2   Frequency of Access and Reachibility Index in an OODB

Our method does not assume any prior knowledge of user queries and their frequencies, except that the object graph structure is available in main memory.

The clustering problem is closely related to the partitioning problem in which a hypergraph is to be partitioned into several disjunct subgraphs. For more information on hypergraphs see [1].

We used the cost analysis in order to derive automatically an optimal object placement graph. The naive approach, which consists in building all the possible subgraphs and computing their cost functions on-line and then selecting optimal, is not tractable. Such a combinatorial structure is exponential with respect to the number of edges covered by the subgraphs related to the particular methods.

Instead we used a minimum spanning tree, computed dynamically from augmented object graph. We make use of a *path-method* (*pm*) which is a mechanism to retrieve information relevant to one class, in an object-oriented database (OODB), that is not stored with that class but with some other class. For more information on *path-method* see [30]. Our algorithm uses numerical *reacheability index* between pairs of classes as a guide for the traversal of an object graph.

Our method is greatly improved by assigning a *reachibility index* value from the range $[0, 1]$ to each edge in the object graph. The sum of the weights - (D_i) on the n outgoing connections of a node (class) conforms to the following constraint: $\sum_{i=1}^{n} D_i = 0.5 * n$. From this formula's sum value, each connection is assigned a weight from the interval $[0, 1]$, reflecting its relative frequency of traversal. We combined *frequency of access* with *reachibility index*. The *reacheability index* of a connection from a class c_{alpha} to a class c_{beta} is a measure of its significance according to the frequency of traversing this connection relative to all connections involving class c_{alpha}. To express it in a different way; *reacheability index* characterizes the strength of the connection between two classes. The *reacheability index* values are assigned relevant to the frequencies of use of the connections accumulated during the operation of the database.

The importance of a path is measured by the *Access Relevance Index* $ARI(P)$. To compute various *access relevance* values we utilized approach used in [30].

Table 1 The meaning of various coefficients.

Definition 1. *The Access relevance* $AR(c_\alpha, c_\beta)$ *from a node* c_α *to a node* c_β *is a number describing the strength of the strongest path between those two nodes, including into account all the paths from* c_α *to* c_β.

We can describe formally, that if a single path $P(c_\alpha, c_\beta) = c_\alpha(=c_{i_1})$, c_{i_2}, $c_{i_3}, \ldots, c_{i_k}$ $(= c_t)$ connects two nodes c_{alpha}, c_{beta}, then the access relevance index of P is computed by applying the following formula:

$$ARI(P) = \prod_{1 \leq r < k} \left[D(c_{i_r}, c_{i_{r+1}}) \right]$$

The *access relevance* of this pair of nodes, if there are m paths $P_1, \ldots, P_m$ from c_α to c_β, is expressed by the following formula:

$$AR(c_\alpha, c_\beta = max_{j=1}^{m} ARI(P_j)$$

$$= max_{j=1}^{m} \prod_{(c_{i_r}, c_{i_{r+1}}) \in P_j} \left[D(c_{i_r}, c_{i_{r+1}}) \right]$$

Table 1. The meaning of various coefficients.

P	path.
c_x	(x)-node of the object graph.
ARI	access relevance index.
$ARI(P)$	the access relevance index
	of a path P.
D	an access weight of a connection
	in the OODB, where $0 \leq D \leq 1$.
AR	the access relevance–a number
	reflecting the strength
	of the strongest
	path between two nodes.
D_F	weighting function expressing
	the strength of connection
	between two nodes.
trb_{c_x}	attribute of the class (node) c_x.

By definition $AR(c_\alpha, c_\alpha) = 1$. To derive a path with the highest product of *reacheability indices* of all its edges, we have to maximize the $PRODUCT$ weighting function.

In what follows, we assume that, using an efficient algorithm, access relevances-(AR) for OODB are already computed and stored. We shall also assume that all edge weights are nonnegative. (If not, we can add a positive value to each edge weight to give an equivalent problem with all edge weights nonnegative.)

4.3   The Algorithm for Maintaining Minimum Spanning Trees in Dynamic Graphs

The basic idea of our dynamic clustering method is to maintain a *minimum spanning tree*, derived from weighted object graph subjected to objects insertions, deletions and updates. In case of frequent changes of user's access patterns our technique based on *reachibility index* values continuously reflect those changes in the augmented object graph.

Now, we will present our first design of the clustering algorithm as follows: a clustering algorithm takes as input a random sequence of nodes of a configuration Directed Acyclic Graph (DAG), and generates a clustering sequence of nodes. Our approach is to generate and cluster a minimum spanning tree of the nodes of a given object graph configuration.

Our strategy for clustering objects is mainly based on the estimated inter-object communication volume represented by the weight between pairs of objects. In order to keep all clusters within a reasonable size, we impose a limit on cluster size: P_{max}, which is a page size. When the total size of objects of P_x and P_y is less than P_{max}; $\{P_x + P_y \leq P_{max}\}$, they can be clustered together by moving objects from P_y to P_x. The result of this clustering process is a set of pages $P_1, P_2, \ldots$, each of which is a set of o_i objects, $\{1 \leq o_i \leq N\}$, and the size of each page, P_i, satisfies the condition $\{1 \leq P - i \leq P_{max}\}$.

Let N be the number of objects in the object net of application software system; w_{v_1,v_2} is the weight representing totality of references between objects v_1 and v_2.

In order to minimize intercluster connectivity and maximize concurrency, the objective function can be expressed as follows:

$$IR = min \left\{ \sum_{i}^{N-1} \sum_{j}^{N} \sum_{k}^{P} w_{v_1,v_2} \; \lambda_{ik} (1 - \lambda_{jk}) \right\}$$

where:

$$\lambda_{ik} = \begin{cases} 1 & \text{if object is clustered on page } k \\ 0 & \text{otherwise} \end{cases}$$

$$\{(1 \leq i \leq N - 1) \; and \; (1 \leq k \leq P)\}$$

In the description of the first algorithm the following notations are used, see also [3]. The edges of G are stored in the list E, i.e., $E(i)$ is the pair of the end vertices of the $i - th$ edge. The list W contains the edge weights: $W(i)$ is the weight of the $i - th$ edge. ET is the set of edges of the current forest T, p is the number of its components, E_1 is the set of minimum-weight edges for the current forest T. In order to improve the performance of the construction of the minimum-weight edge sets, the following scratchpad, auxiliary work lists are used: $COMP(j)$ is the index of the component of the current forest which contains the vertex j; $MWE(i)$ is the index of the minimum-weight edge for the $i - th$ component of the growing forest; $MW(i)$ is the weight of the edge $MWE(i)$.

Algorithm Cluster Object Net

Input: Weighted, undirected graph G
with n vertices and edge list E
Output: Clustering Mapping
{Compute MST (Min. Weight Span. Tree)}
{

1. *Initialization step: Set $ET \leftarrow \emptyset$,*
   $COMP(i) \leftarrow i$, $MW(i) \leftarrow \infty$ for $i = 1$,
   $2, \ldots, n. p \leftarrow n$.
   //Operations $2 - 8$ gradually build-
   //up the set E_1 of minimum-
   //weight edges for the forest T.
2. *$k \leftarrow 1$.*
3. *Let $E(k) = uv; i \leftarrow COMP(u)$,*
   $j \leftarrow COMP(v)$.
4. *If $i \neq j$ then go to step 5,*
   otherwise go to step 7.

5. *If $w(uv) = W(k) < MW(j)$ then*
   $$MW(j) \leftarrow w(uv),\ MWE(j) = k.$$
6. *If $w(uv) = W(k) < MW(i)$ then*
   $$MW(i) \leftarrow w(uv),\ MWE(i) = k.$$
7. *If $k = |EG|$ then go to step 8,*
   otherwise $k \leftarrow k + 1$
   and go to step 3.
   //Immediately before the
   //execution of step 8, the first p
   //entries of MWE contain the
   //indices of edges from the
   //minimum-weight set for T
8. *Examine the first p elements of MWE*
   and create the set E_1 of the minimum-
   weight edges for the forest T.
9. *$ET \leftarrow ET \cup E_1$.*
   //This is the edge set
   //for the "new" forest T'
10. *Using the depth-first search, extract*
    the connected components of the
    "new" forest $T' = T' \cup E_1$.
    //The list $COMP$ and the value
    //of p are updated
11. *IF $p = 1$ then terminate*
    //ET is the edge set of the
    //minimum spanning tree
    otherwise go to step 2.
    RETURN $M_{ST} = \{ET\}$

}

The algorithm constructs a minimum spanning tree in time $\theta(|EG|\ log_2|G|)$ [2]. At the first iteration it handles the spanning forest of a graph G consisting of $n = |G|$ single-vertex components. Each iteration acts as follows. First, it constructs a set M of minimum-weight edges for a forest T produced before this iteration.

This can be done during a single scan of the set EG. Let e be the edge to be examined next: if e induces a cycle in M, then e is discarded. Otherwise, edge e is chosen and the new forest will be $M \in \{e\}$. Then using the depth-first search it extracts the connected components of the graph $T' = T + M$, which is a forest. This forest is passed to the next iteration; clearly, T' has fewer components than T. The algorithm will recourse on subgraphs that are not necessarily connected. When the input graph G is not connected, a spanning tree does not exist and we generalize the notion of a minimum spanning tree to that of a minimum spanning forest (MSF) [6].

We now describe a simple fully dynamic minimum spanning tree algorithm (DMST), see also [7]. DMST is an appropriate implementation of a partially dynamic data structure, which is itself a combination of the linking and cutting trees introduced by Tarjan and Sleator in [8], methodology of Italiano et. al., in [7] and our MST algorithm. During its operations, DMST maintains two data structures. It stores all the edges of graph G in a priority queue Q according to their cost and it also maintains the minimum spanning tree T of the graph G as a linking and cutting tree [8].

In case when a new edge e is inserted into object graph G, DMST updates T and Q in time $\theta(\log n)$. In case when an edge e is deleted from graph G and it is a non-tree edge, DMST does nothing else - it only deletes e from Q in $\theta(\log n)$ time. In case when tree edge is deleted from Q, DMST calls minimum spanning tree (MST) algorithm on the edges in Q. As a result of those operations DMST requires $\theta(\log n)$ time plus the running time of MST in case of a tree edge deletion. The expensive case happens with *probability* n/m, if the edge to be deleted is chosen uniformly at random from object graph G, resulting in an average running time of $\theta\{\log n + (n/m) \times (m + n \log^2 n)\} = \theta\{n + (n \log n)^2/m\}$ for DMST algorithm.

The above analysis suggests that running time of DMST will decrease as the graph density increases - this actually coincides with the results of our experiments.

5 Application of Reliable Memory for Databases

Safe RAM allows systems that support reliable updates, such as databse and transaction processing systems, to perform more efficiently. Significant improvement in response time can always be realized, and a throughput improvement can be realized by limiting disk access due to the use of the safe RAM [17]. We make use of an area of main memory, maintained by the operating system, that buffers file system data [18]. Our design uses a memory interface to reliable memory with virtual memory protection to protect against wild stores to dirty, commited buffers–this approach was suggested in [19]. In our design we used reliable memory to store the log. Keeping the log in reliable memory removes all synchronous disk writes from the critical path of a transaction [17]. This technique decreases transaction commit time and can help to reduce lock contention with the resulting benefit of increased concurrency [20]. By storing important system information in the stable memory we can help to improve recovery time. We did achieve reduction of time needed to scan the log to find the last checkpoint by storing a pointer in reliable mamory. In our experiments we used the reliable memory to store the database buffer cache. Theoretically this makes all buffer cache changes permanent without writing to disk. Similar to the force-at-commit policy, this eliminates the need for checkpoints and a redo log in recovering system crashes—partial redo [21], [22]. In summary reliable memory also allows state-of-the-art recovery schemes (e.g. ARIES family of protocols [11] to become much more simpler. Since, for example, the need for fuzzy checkpoints is reduced because transactions can commit faster.

We also present a new solution to an old, yet very important problem known as the "on-line object placement problem", which can be stated more precisely as the problem of choosing a disk page to hold a newly allocated object. To the best of our knowledge, the database literature contains no studies of object allocation with the objective to optimize storage utilization and placement performance, with the exception of excellent treatment of the subject in [29]. Since our approach provides for incremental on-line clustering which allows also concurrent updates to data, the object allocation problem is solved by our clustering algorithm as described in section 4 above.

5.1 Buffer Policies

In the *shared disks scheme*, each site broadcasts its updates to other sites. However, a broadcast is required only if the transaction updates one or more pages.

Table 2 summarizes the parameters of our system.

Table 2. The parameters of our system.

p_{bdcst}	the probability that transaction requires
	a broadcast.
D_P	number of database partitions.
p_{u_i}	probability of update for pages
	of partition i.
T	number of pages accessed per transaction.
ψ_i	probability of accessing
	i_{th} partition.

The probability that transaction requires a broadcast, p_{bdcst} is given by:

$$p_{bdcst} = 1 - \prod_{i=1}^{D_P} (1 - p_{ui})^{T\psi i}$$

In our experiments we validated our analysis of buffer models and integrated system models for the response times using the Distributed Database VERSANT.

In our experiments we used the reliable memory to store the database buffer cache. Theoretically this makes all buffer cache changes permanent without writing to disk. Similar to the force-at-commit policy, this eliminates the need for checkpoints and a redo log in recovering system crashes–partial redo [21], [22]. According to [23], the redo log is still necessary in recovering from media failures–global redo; however, redundant disk storage makes this scenario less probable. Because redundant undo log records can be purged after a transaction commits, removing the redo log has a result that no log records need be written if memory has enough capacity to contain the undo records for all current transactions in progress [24], [25]. Also, according to [24], storing the databse buffer cache in reliable memory allows the system to begin operation after a crash with the contents of a warm cache, see also [26], [27], [28].

To integrate buffer management with the recovery model, we guarantee that a modified segment is flushed to the database only after the log records associated with those modifications have been written. Outside of that constraint, the buffer manager is free to use any appropriate buffer replacement policy.

In summary reliable memory also allows state-of-the-art recovery schemes (e.g. ARIES family of protocols [11] to become much more simpler. For example, the need for fuzzy checkpoints is reduced because transactions can commit faster.

6   Variable-Size Storage Clusters

Related issue to the *"on-line object placement problem"* is the question of *optimal cluster size*. Our experimental system operates under the assumption that the exchange granularity between disk and main memory is the logical cluster. To group as many objects as possibly, we select those objects which were already stored on disk and group some of the created objects with them. In that way objects already existing on disk are reclustered, which effectively reorganizes ODBMS on-line.

7   Preliminary Experimental Study

The clustering algorithm has been implemented in our experimental system.

We would like to emphasize that at this stage of our research efforts the study limits itself to exploring the feasibility of the techniques we have proposed. In order to test our method for on-line reorganization (specifically, for restoration of clustering), we conducted a series of object clustering experiments. While performing experiments we considered only the time that the algorithms used in recomputing a new solution after each update; we did not measure the time necessary for initializing the data structures and for loading the initial object graph.

For our experiments we used a Pentium Pro 200 MHz based workstation supported by Intel-initiated PCI-ISA bus system, with 128 MB main memory and two disk drives: one 3.2 AT/S gigabyte holding the software - VERSANT ODMS Release 5.0 and 6.4 AT/S gigabyte accommodating the database. Both disk drives model Quantum FireballTM ST. We have adapted hypermodel benchmark [9] to test our clustering algorithms.

We present in this section only a few experimental results concerning our experiences with the hypermodel benchmark. We found that the size of workstation buffer pool has no effect on the performance of the sequential scan query and the

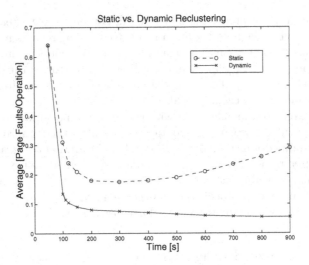

Fig. 1. Static vs. Dynamic Reclustering

results are not included. Fig. 1 depicts a comparison between the average miss rates as a function of time in case where dynamic, on-line reclustering was active and operational and where it was not. Reductions in the average miss rate were generally noticed in case when DMST algorithm was active. A decreased miss rate was expected for those user processes that utilized the part of the database after it has been reclustered. Indeed this effect was observed in the miss rate results of our benchmark runs. Fig. 2 shows relationships between the number

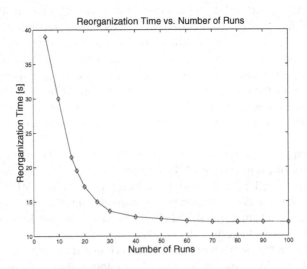

Fig. 2. Reorganization Time vs. Number of Runs

of reorganizations and the average duration of those reorganizations. With the number of reorganizations increasing during a run, the time interval between them decreases.

This is due to the fact that as the frequency of reorganizations increases during a particular run, the statistics that are gathered to support clustering cover a smaller part of the database, since it makes references to the smaller number of objects. This analysis is also supported by looking at Fig. 2, showing that reorganization duration decreases as the number of reorganizations during a particular run increases. We can deduce (from Fig. 2 that this behavior will increase with concurrency, since user transactions do not need to wait as long to gain access to the necessary database locks.

8   Conclusion and Future Work

We believe that a wide class of applications such as CAM and $CASE$ systems can greatly benefit form an on-line dynamic reorganization via clustering since they normally use low number of competing concurrent transactions.

Since we want to keep main operational data structures in main memory, it is essential to be able to reconstruct them after system failure – we do this by the integration of an area of main memory—the reliable memory into a database system.This has also a positive effect in substantially reducing I/O traffic, which improves the overall performance of the DBMS. Our tests show that mapping reliable memory into the database memory space does not substantially hurt reliability. Our main objective of incremental on–line reorganization is to change a part of the database without affecting on-going transactions for very long. To perform reorganization more efficiently, the ways to group to be reorganized are examined. Our methodology has advantages over many other proposed or cited approaches because it does not require any beforehand knowledge of the query frequencies, nor does it trigger a reclustering process based on trace analysis.

We demonstrated that on-line reclustering is possible, but more research is required to demonstrate its suitability in many practical situations, especially in the presence of greater degrees of concurrently operating transactions.

For our purposes, the value of this experimental work is the comparison of the relative performance of the new algorithms under a range of different operational scenarios. In that sense, the results are used to demonstrate practical feasibility of the proposed approach.

Acknowledgments. Also we would like to acknowledge *Intel Corporation* for making their tools available for our experiments.

Microsoft, Windows and Windows NT are trademarks of *Microsoft Corporation. VERSANT* is a trademark of *Versant Technology Corporation. Intel* and *Pentium* are trademarks of *Intel Corporation.*

References

1. T. Eiter and G. Gottlob.: Identifying the minimal transversals of a hypergraph and related problems. SIAM Journal on Computing, 24(6):1278 – 1304, Dec. 1995.
2. V. Wietrzyk, Mehmet A. Orgun.: A Foundation for High Performance Object Database Systems. In Databases for the Millennium 2000 in proceedings of the 9th International Conference on Management of Data, Hyderabad, December, 1998.
3. V. Wietrzyk, M. A. Orgun.: VERSANT Architecture: Supporting High-Performance Object Databases. International Database Engineering and Applications Symposium, IDEAS98, Cardiff, U.K., July 1998, IEEE Computer Society Press, Los Alamitos, Calif., 1998.
4. Batory, D. S.: Optimal File Designs and Reorganization Points. ACM Trans. On Database Systems, Vol.7, 1982.
5. J.B. Cheng, A.R. Hurson.: Effective Clustering of Complex Objects in Object-Oriented Databases. ACM SIGMOD Conference, 1991.
6. P. N. Klein, R. E. Tarjan.: A randomized linear-time algorithm for finding minimum spanning trees. In Proceedings of the 26th Annual ACM Symposium on Theory of Computing. Montreal, Que., Canada. May 23-25). ACM, New York, p. 9-15, 1994.
7. D. Alberts, G. Cattaneo, G. F. Italiano.: An empirical study of dynamic graph algorithms. Proc. 7th ACM-SIAM Symp. on Discrete Algorithms (1996).
8. R. E. Tarjan and D. D. Sleator.: A data structure for dynamic trees. J. Comp. Sys. Sci., 1983.
9. T. L. Anderson, A.J. Berre, M. Mallison et al.: The Hypermodel Benchmark in Bancilhon, Thanos, Tsichritzis (Eds.): Advances in Database Technology - EDBT'90, LNCS 416, 1990.
10. VERSANT System Manual.: VERSANT Release 5.0, February 1997.
11. C. Mohan, D. Haderle, B. Lindsay, H. Pirahesh et al.: ARIES: A Transaction Recovery Method Supporting Fine-Granularity Locking and Partial Rollbacks Using Write-Ahead Logging. ACM Transactions on Database Systems, 17(1):94-162, March 1992.
12. C. Mohan, I. Narang.: Algorithms for creating indexes for very large tables without quiescing updates In Proceedings ACM SIGMOD Intl Conf Management of Data, pages pp 361 - 370, June 1992
13. E. Omiecinski.: Concurrent file conversion between b+ tree and linear hash files. Information Systems. 14(5) pp 371 - 383, 1989
14. B. Salzberg, A. Dimock.: Principles of transaction-based on-line reorganization In Proceedings 18th Intl Conf Very Large Databases, pages pp 511 - 520, San Mateo, CA, Aug 1992 Morgan Kaufmann Publishers
15. G. Weikum, P. Zabback, P. Scheuermann.: Dynamic file allocation in disk arrayes In ACM SIGMOD International Conference on Management of Data, pages pp 406 - 415, 1991
16. G. S. Smith.: Online reorganization of key-sequenced tables and files Tandem System Review, 6(2), pp 52-59, Oct 1990.
17. G. Copeland, T. Keller, R. Krishnamurthy, M. Smith.: The Case for Safe RAM In Proceedings 15th Intl Conf Very Large Databases, pages pp 327 - 335, Amsterdam, The Netherlands, Aug 1989 Morgan Kaufmann Publishers
18. P. M. Chen, W. T. Ng, S. Chandra, Ch. M. Aycock, G. Rajamani, D. Lowell.: The Rio File Cache: Surviving Operating System Crashes In Proceedings of the 1996 International Conference on Architectural Support for Programming Languages and Operating systems (ASPLOS), pages pp 74 - 83, October 1996.

19. M. Sullivan, M. Stonebraker.: Using write protected data structures to improve software fault tolerance in highly available database management systems In Proceedings of the 1991 International Conference on Very Large Data Bases (VLDB), pages pp 171 - 180, September 1991.
20. D. J. DeWitt, R. H. Katz, F. F. Olken, L. D. Shapiro, M. R. Stonebraker, D. Wood.: Implementation Techniques for Main Memory database Systems In Proceedings of the 1984 ACM SIGMOD International Conference on Management of Data, pages pp 1 - 8, June 1984.
21. Theo Haerder, Andreas Reuter.: Principles of transaction-Oriented Database Recovery ACM Computing Surveys, 15(4):287–317, December 1983.
22. S. Akyurek, K. Salem.: management of partially safe buffers IEEE transactions on Computers, 44(3): 394–407, March 1995.
23. P. M. Chen, E. K. Lee, G. A. Gibson, R. H. Katz, D. A. Patterson.: RAID: High–Performance, Reliable Secondary Storage ACM Computing Surveys, 26(2): 145 – 188, June 1994.
24. Wee Teck NG, Ch. M. Aycock, G. Rajmani, P. M. Chen.: Comparing Disk and Memory's resistance to Operating system crashes International Symposium on Software reliability Engineering, 1996.
25. R. A. Agrawal, H. V. Jagadish.: Recovery Algorithms for database Machines with Nonvolatile main memory In Database Machines. Sixth international Workshop, IWDM'89 Proceedings., June 1989.
26. M. Sullivan, R. Chillarege.: A Comparison of Software Defects in Database Management Systems and Operating Systems In Proceedings of the 1992 international Symposium on Fault-Tolerant Computing, pages 475–484, July 1992.
27. K. Elhardt, R. Bayer.: A Database cache for High Performance and Fast restart in database Systems ACM Transactions on Database Systems, 9(4): 503–525, December 1984.
28. A. Bhide, D. Dias, N. Nagui Halim, B. Smith, F. Parr.: A Case for Fault-Tolerant Memory for Transaction Processing In Proceedings of the 1993 International symposium on Fault-Tolerant Computing, pages, pp: 451 – 460, June 1993.
29. M. L. McAuliffe, M. J. Carey, M. H. Solomon.: Towards Effective and Efficient Free Space Management In Proceedings of the 1996 ACM SIGMOD International Conference on Management of Data, pages pp 389 - 400, 1996.
30. A. Mehta, J. Geller, Y. Perl, E. J. Neuhold.: The OODB Path-Method Generator (PMG) Using Precomputed Access Relevance Proc. of the 2nd Int'l Conference on Information and Knowledge Management, Washington DC, 1993, pages pp:596–605.

Systematization of Approaches to Equality–Generating Constraints

Aleksander Binemann–Zdanowicz

Institute of Computer Science
Brandenburg University of Technology at Cottbus, Germany
abineman@informatik.tu-cottbus.de

Abstract The aim of this paper is to propose a uniform terminology for functional dependencies and their counterparts for n–ary relationship types. A variety of existing approaches is presented and the differences between them are discussed. A sound and complete axiomatization is introduced that allows one to check the consistency of a cardinality constraint specification and to derive new constraints from existing ones. The advantage of our system of rules is its applicability to the whole variety of existing approaches in this area. Our deductive system is non–redundant.

1 Introduction

In the last three decades, many approaches to specifying valid and not valid functional dependencies (FD's) in the relational model have been presented by various authors. The original approach to FD's (see [Arm74]) allows to infer valid FD's from already known ones, but using only this approach turned out to be insufficient to make any statements about whether a specific functional dependency is definitely not valid. Due to this fact, many authors presented their own propositions of defining a counterpart to FD's, e.g. Doležal, Janas, Paredaens, Thalheim. These approaches seem to be apparently different and independent of each other. Our aim is to present a systematization and clarification of the results that have been published in this field so far and to propose a uniform approach to handling FD's and their counterparts.

Motivation. The concept of FD's is commonly known (the reader may refer to [Ull88], [MaR92], [Tha91], [HeS95], [Tha00]). A functional dependency $X \to Y$ specifies that if two tuples from a relation are equal on the attributes from X then they are also equal on Y. FD's are used to ensure the consistency of a database, hence they are an important kind of static integrity constraints in the relational database theory. A sound and complete axiomatization of FD's was given in [Arm74] and similarly in [Tha85], [Tha91], [HeS95] and [Kle98]. An important part of the process of obtaining a cardinality constraint specification for a given relationship type is to determine which FD's follow from the already specified ones and which FD's are not valid. If we deal only with FD's and their axiomatization, we can only assume that every functional dependency that cannot

J. Štuller et al. (Eds.): ADBIS-DASFAA 2000, LNCS 1884, pp. 307–314, 2000.

be derived from existing ones is not valid (closed–world–assumption). Unfortunately, this assumption is not valid in the case of FD's. We cannot be sure that a functional dependency is not valid if it just cannot be derived from the already specified ones, because there may be incomplete knowledge on the application. We can have dependencies which are valid in any relation (instance of the relation schema), dependencies which are invalid in any relation and dependencies about which we currently do not know which of the first two categories they belong to.

The closed–world–assumption makes it impossible to distinguish between the last two categories. Therefore, we need to define a counterpart of FD's and provide a sound and complete system of rules in order to be able to derive *all* valid FD's and to check the consistency of a cardinality constraint specification.

Moreover, if the validity of some FD's cannot be determined with the set of already specified constraints (i.e. if our specification is incomplete), the designer has to decide whether some yet unspecified functional dependency is valid or not. In order to support this process, we need a complete and sound axiomatization of FD's and their counterpart.

Considering the variety of approaches to the problem of specifying FD's and negated FD's, it is necessary to develop a unified, clear approach which would allow to use results provided by various authors, support the database designer in obtaining constraints from an example database, help the database designer derive new cardinality constraints from already specified ones and support the database designer in completing an incomplete set of cardinality constraints (see [Dol99], [Kle98]).

Integrity Constraints in the Relational Model. We are going to use the relational notions. A *simple relation schema* $R = (attr(R), \underline{D}, dom)$ is a triple consisting of a finite set of attributes $attr(R) = \{B_1, B_2, ..., B_n\}$, a finite set of domains $\underline{D}$ and a mapping $dom : attr(R) \to \underline{D}$ which associates each attribute with a domain from $\underline{D}$. A *relation schema* (R, Σ) consists of a simple relation schema R and of a set Σ of local cardinality constraints. For our purpose we will consider Σ as a set of static integrity constraints: FD's and their counterparts (functional independencies or antifunctional constraints, as explained below). For a given set of attributes $X \subseteq attr(R)$, we define a *tuple t* on X as a function assigning a value from $dom(A)$ to each $A \in X$. A finite set R^c of tuples on R is a valid *instance (relation)* of the relational schema (R, Σ) iff Σ is satisfied by R^c. The set of all possible tuples on R is denoted as $Dom(R)$. The set of all valid instances of a relational schema (R, Σ) is denoted by $SAT(R, \Sigma)$. A set Σ of cardinality constraints[1] is satisfied by a relation R^c, iff every single constraint from Σ is satisfied by R^c. More formally, $R^c \vDash \Sigma \iff \left(\forall \alpha \in \Sigma : R^c \vDash \alpha \right)$.

Definition 1. *Assume* $X, Y \subseteq attr(R)$. *A functional dependency* $(X \to Y)$ *is satisfied by a relation* R^c, *iff* $\forall t_1, t_2 \in R^c : \left(t_1[X] = t_2[X] \implies t_1[Y] = t_2[Y] \right)$. *We say that a functional dependency is valid in a family of relations*

---
[1] In this paper we consider only Σ consisting of FD's and their counterpart.

$M \subseteq 2^{Dom(R)}$ *iff for every relation* $R^c \in M$ *this functional dependency is satisfied by* R^c. *A functional independency (FI)* $X \not\to Y$ *is valid in* $M \subseteq 2^{Dom(R)}$ *iff the functional dependency* $X \to Y$ *is not valid in* M. *In other words, a functional independency* $X \not\to Y$ *is valid in* M, *iff* $\exists R^c \in M : \exists t, t' \in R^c :$ $\left(t[X] = t'[X] \wedge t[Y] \neq t'[Y] \right)$. *An* antifunctional constraint $X \not\!\!\not\to Y$ *is valid in* $M \subseteq 2^{Dom(R)}$, *iff* $\forall R^c \in M : \exists t, t' \in R^c : \left(t[X] = t'[X] \wedge t[Y] \neq t'[Y] \right)$.

Example. Consider a simple relation schema R with $attr(R) = \{A, B, C, D\}$. Let us have a look at the following three relation instances over R (assume that different symbols denote different values):

R^c	A	B	C	D
	a	b	c_1	d_1
	a	b	c_1	d_2
	a'	b'	c_2	d_3

$R^{c'}$	A	B	C	D
	a	b	c_3	d_4
	a	b'	c_3	d_5
	a'	b	c_2	d_6

$R^{c''}$	A	B	C	D
	a	b	c_1	d_7
	a	b'	c_2	d_8
	a'	b''	c_3	d_7
	a'	b'''	c_4	d_8

It is easy to see that the the functional dependency $A \to B$ is satisfied by the relation R^c. It is also valid in the family of relations $\{R^c\}$, but it is not valid in $\{R^c, R^{c'}\}$ nor in $\{R^c, R^{c''}\}$. On the other hand, the functional independency $A \not\to BC$ is valid in the families of relations $\{R^c, R^{c'}\}$ and $\{R^c, R^{c'}, R^{c''}\}$, but it is not valid in the family $\{R^c\}$. We can also see that the antifunctional constraint $A \not\!\!\not\to BC$ is valid in $\{R^{c'}\}$ and in $\{R^{c'}, R^{c''}\}$, but it is not valid in the family $\{R^c, R^{c'}\}$.

Observation *The approach presented above can be adapted to the Higher–Order Entity–Relationship Model (HERM, see [Tha00]). Dependencies between component types of a specific relationship type in a HERM schema (functional cardinality constraints and negated functional cardinality constraints), can be viewed as FD's and functional independencies, respectively.*

2   Comparing Approaches to Definition of Constraints

2.1   Kinds of Constraints

Functional Independencies. Functional independencies (FI's) were introduced in [Jan89] and similarly in [Bel95] as a counterpart to FD's. They correspond with our definition of antifunctional constraints. Janas defined FI's as explicitly violated FD's (strong semantics), i.e. a relation R^c satisfies a functional independency $X \not\to Y$ iff $\exists t, t' \in R^c : t[X] = t'[X] \wedge t[Y] \neq t'[Y]$ holds.[2] A definition of FI's was also proposed independently in [Bel95]. It turned out to be equivalent to the one presented by Janas.

Excluded Functional Dependencies. As introduced in [Tha85], [Tha91], an EFD $X \not\to Y$ is valid in a family of relations $M \subseteq 2^{Dom(R)}$, iff the functional dependency $X \to Y$ is not valid in M, i.e. $M \vDash X \not\to Y \Longleftrightarrow M \nvDash X \to Y \Longleftrightarrow$

---

[2] In his definition, Janas deals with constraints that work with incomplete data. For our purpose, we do not consider incomplete information.

$\exists R^c \in M : R^c \nvDash X \to Y$. This definition differs from the one included in [Jan89] or [Bel95]. It corresponds with our definition of FI's presented at the beginning of this paper. The EFD's are constraints whose validity is defined for a family of relations, like $SAT(R, \Sigma)$. They can be handled as semantic constraints on data.

Corollary 1. *Assume conflict–free[3] Σ consisting only of FD's and EFD's, i.e. $\Sigma = \Sigma_{FD} \cup \Sigma_{EFD}$. Then for $M \subseteq SAT(R, \Sigma_{FD})$ the statement $M \vDash \Sigma_{EFD}$ is valid.*

Afunctional Dependencies. Afunctional dependencies [Par89] are a stronger kind of constraints (in comparison with the approaches discussed above) and are used for horizontal decomposition. A set of tuples $S^c \subseteq R^c$ is called X–complete iff all the tuples belonging to S^c have different X–values from those belonging to $R^c \setminus S^c$. More formally, S^c is X–complete, iff $\forall t \in S^c : \forall t' \in R^c \setminus S^c : t[X] \neq t'[X]$ holds. The afunctional dependency $X \nrightarrow\hspace{-0.5em}\rightarrow Y$ holds in the relation schema (R, Σ) iff for every instance R^c of (R, Σ) and for every nonempty X–complete subset $S^c \subseteq R^c$ the functional dependency $X \to Y$ does not hold.

N–Cardinalities. In [McA98] an alternative approach to specifying negated FD's was proposed. An N–cardinality $X \rightrightarrows Y$ indicates that the maximum possible number of tuples with the same X–value and different Y–values is un-bounded. An N–cardinality is said to be *realized* in a relation R^c when for any tuple $t \in R^c$ an unbounded number of tuples with the same X–value as t, but different Y–values, can be added into R^c without violating any other functional dependency or N–cardinality. This definition implies that the domain must be infinite (if it were finite, then the number of different tuples we can add would also be finite). So N–cardinalities are domain–dependent constraints and not proper dependencies.[4] However, this concept of is closer[5] to what we intuitively understand as negated FD's than the concepts presented in [Jan89], [Bel95]. On the other hand, this way of defining them does not necessarily seem to be the most suitable one for the database designer.

Doležal proposes in an analogous way in [Dol99] N–cardinalities for specifying negated FD's. It can be easily seen that it suffices when the expanded relation only does not violate any functional dependency from Σ, as adding tuples into R^c itself cannot violate any N–cardinality.

Proposition 1. *If a functional independency $X \nrightarrow Y$ is satisfied by a relation $R^c \in SAT(R, \Sigma)$ (according to [Jan89]), then the corresponding N–cardinality $X \rightrightarrows Y$ is realized by R^c.*[6]

---

[3] The conflict–freeness means: $\nexists X, Y \subseteq attr(R) : \Sigma \vDash X \to Y \wedge \Sigma \vDash X \nrightarrow Y$.

[4] Even if the definition required adding just one tuple, it would enforce the domain infiniteness, as one can add an unbounded number of tuples into a relation (without violating any constraint from Σ) iff one can add just one tuple into it.

[5] An N–cardinality can be realized in a relation in which the corresponding functional dependency is not violated.

[6] The proofs of theorems in this paper can be found in [Bin00], unless otherwise noted.

Proposition 2. *A relation $R^c \in SAT(R, \Sigma)$ realizes N–cardinality $X \rightrightarrows Y$ (according to [Dol99]), iff the corresponding excluded functional dependency $X \not\rightarrow Y$ is valid in $SAT(R, \Sigma)$.*

Propositional Dependencies. In [Tha91] propositional dependencies and the *dependency propositional logic* were introduced. Propositional dependencies can be understood as a representation of *generalized functional dependencies* [Tha91]. For instance, $A \rightarrow B \vee C$ means that if two tuples are equal on A then they are equal on B or on C. Thus, propositional dependencies are two–tuple dependencies and generalized functional (in)dependencies.

Observation *The implication problem for propositional dependencies can be solved on the basis of the Boolean interpretation, since the generalized functional dependencies are equivalent to positive Boolean dependencies (see [Tha91]).*

2.2 Existing Axiomatizations

Functional Independencies. Janas introduced in [Jan89] the following axiom system for inferring all FD's and FI's from given ones:

$$FD1: \ Y \subseteq X \Longrightarrow X \rightarrow Y \qquad FD2: \frac{X \rightarrow Y}{XZ \rightarrow YZ} \qquad\qquad FD3: \ \frac{X \rightarrow Y, Y \rightarrow Z}{X \rightarrow Z}$$

$$FI1: \ \frac{X \not\rightarrow Y}{X \not\rightarrow YZ} \qquad\qquad FI2: \frac{XZ \not\rightarrow YZ}{XZ \not\rightarrow Y} \qquad\qquad FI4: \ \frac{X \rightarrow Y, X \not\rightarrow Z}{Y \not\rightarrow Z}.$$

He proved the soundness of this axiom system. However, his axiomatization is not complete, as the correct rule $X \not\rightarrow Z \wedge Y \rightarrow Z \Longrightarrow X \not\rightarrow Y$ cannot be derived from it. In [Bel95] a following sound and complete axiomatization of FD's and FI's was introduced. It consists of the rules $FD1$, $FD3$, $FI4$ and of the rules $\quad FI1': \frac{XVW \not\rightarrow YW}{X \not\rightarrow Y}, \qquad FD2': \frac{X \rightarrow Y}{X \rightarrow XY}, \qquad FI4': \frac{Y \rightarrow Z, X \not\rightarrow Z}{X \not\rightarrow Y}.$

From an example relation R^c, valid and not valid FD's are derived, and, using the system of rules, further ones are derived. In other words, an example relation R^c brings the information about the set of constraints Σ. Next, using the axiomatization, the closure Σ^+ is computed. So, according to Bell's approach, the family of all valid relation instances $SAT(R, \Sigma)$ is determined on the basis of the example relation (because the set Σ is determined by this example relation).

Afunctional Dependencies. In [Par89] the following axiomatization for afunctional dependencies and FD's was introduced, which is sound and complete [Par89]: it consists of the rules $FD1$, $FD2'$, $FD3$ and of the following three rules: $FA1: \frac{X \rightarrow Y, X \not\hspace{-2pt}\not\rightarrow Z}{Y \not\hspace{-2pt}\not\rightarrow Z}$, $FA2: \frac{Y \rightarrow Z, X \not\hspace{-2pt}\not\rightarrow Z}{X \not\hspace{-2pt}\not\rightarrow Y}$, $A1: \frac{XV \not\hspace{-2pt}\not\rightarrow YW, W \subseteq V}{X \not\hspace{-2pt}\not\rightarrow Y}$.

N–Cardinalities. McAllister proposed in [McA98] an axiomatization for FD's and N–cardinalities. He showed its soundness and completeness. However, due to the fact that his system of rules is equivalent to the one included in [Dol99], we are not going to discuss it separately. Doležal proposed in [Dol99] the following system of rules for deriving FD's and N–cardinalities from existing ones:

$$EXP_{1L}: \frac{X \to Y}{XZ \to Y} \qquad RED_{1R}: \frac{X \to YZ}{X \to Y} \qquad EXP_{NR}: \frac{X \rightrightarrows Y}{X \rightrightarrows YZ} \qquad RED_{NL}: \frac{XY \rightrightarrows Z}{X \rightrightarrows Z}$$

$$CMOVE_1: \frac{XY \to Z, X \to Y}{X \to YZ} \qquad CEXP_{NL}: \frac{X \rightrightarrows Y, X \to Z}{XZ \rightrightarrows Y} \qquad CRED_{NR}: \frac{X \rightrightarrows YZ, XY \to Z}{X \rightrightarrows Y}.$$

This system is sound [Dol99]. It is not really complete, as the trivial axiom $\forall X \subseteq attr(R) : X \to X$ is missing (it cannot be derived, either). However, this system is complete if we add the axiom $X \to X$ into it (the completeness proof in [DoD99] works if we add this axiom). The system of rules in [Dol99] (enhanced by the axiom $X \to X$) is equivalent to the one proposed in [McA98]. The proof of soundness and completeness in [DoD99] is claimed to be deeper than the one in [McA98]. However, it does not have any advantages in comparison with the typical method of proving soundness and completeness of a Hilbert–type calculus. It is remarkable that the approach from [Dol99], [McA98] differs from the one presented in [Jan89], [Bel95] in terms of how an N–cardinality (or functional independency, respectively) is satisfied by a relation, e.g. by an empty relation.

Excluded Functional Dependencies. In [Tha91] the following sound and complete system of rules was proposed for FD's combined with EFD's:

Axiom: $\forall X \subseteq attr(R) : X \to X$ FDEFD1: $\frac{X \to Y, Y \to Z}{XVW \to ZW}$

FDEFD2: $\frac{X \to Y, XVW \not\to ZW}{Y \not\to Z}$ FDEFD3: $\frac{Y \to Z, XVW \not\to ZW}{X \not\to Y}$

3   Axiomatizations of Equality–Generating Constraints

3.1   Axiomatic Systems

Assume $X, Y, Z \subseteq attr(R)$. Let $\mathbb{A}$ be the following axiomatization of FD's and FI's: R0 (axiom): $X \subseteq Y \Longrightarrow Y \to X$,   R1: $\frac{X \to Y, Y \to Z}{WXV \to ZV}$,

R2: $\frac{XZ \not\to YZ}{XZ \not\to Y}$ R3: $\frac{X \to Y, X \not\to Z}{Y \not\to Z}$ R4: $\frac{X \not\to Z, Y \to Z}{X \not\to Y}$

The axiom $R0$ together with the rule $R1$ are a sound and complete axiomatization for FD's (they are equivalent to the Armstrong's axioms). The rules $R2$ and $R3$ were included in [Jan89]. The rule $R4$ was added by Bell in [Bel95].

This axiomatization does not differ very much from the earlier ones. However, it is important to know where the differences between all approaches are.

Corollary 2. *The system $\mathbb{A}$ is a sound and complete axiomatizations of both FD's combined with FI's and FD's combined with antifunctional constraints.*

Theorem 1. *The axiomatization $\mathbb{A}$ is sound and complete.*

The soundness of this axiom system for FD's combined with FI's can be proven as in [Dol99] (for N–cardinalities[7]) and [Tha85] (for EFD's); the proof of

---

[7] As mentioned above, the N–cardinalities are not real dependencies, so the proof applies actually to N–cardinalities understood just as one special sort of static integrity constraints.

the completeness is analogous to the one in [Tha85] and to the proof in [DoD99] (provided we assume that the trivial functional dependency $X \to X$ is implicit for every $X \subseteq attr(R)$). For FD's and antifunctional constraints, the proof of soundness and completeness is analogous to the one in Bell's work.

Corollary 3. *The axiomatization $\mathbb{A}$ can be applied to functional cardinality constraints and to negated functional cardinality constraints in the HERM model. It is also sound and complete in this case.*

Proposition 3. *The axiomatization $\mathbb{A}$ is non–redundant.*

Theorem 2. *The axiomatization $\mathbb{A}$ for FD's and FI's is equivalent to the axiomatizations presented in [Bel95], [Dol99], [McA98], [Par89] and [Tha91].*

3.2   Incremental Process of Completing a Constraint Specification

Having a set Σ of FD's and FI's, we can use our system of rules to derive the closure Σ^+.[8] But it can happen that the closure does not contain all valid/not valid FD's, i.e. it is incomplete.[9] As our aim is a complete specification, we have to decide about the validity of the rest of FD's, i.e. which FD's might be added. According to [DoD99] and [Kle98], we may add stepwise a new functional dependency $X \to Y$ *or* N–cardinality $X \rightrightarrows Y$ into Σ and the enhanced specification will still be consistent, thus performing specification as shown in Fig. 1.

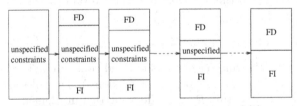

Figure 1. Incremental constraints acquisition.   **Figure 2.**

Another problem is making the decision about each unspecified functional dependency. According to [Kle98], unspecified constraints are estimated and weighted by heuristic rules in respect of possible validity *before* the dialog with the designer occurs. These rules use the knowledge implicitly contained in an example database: from the data stored in it, dependencies between attributes (e.g. whether one of them is a sum of the others) and plausibilities of the validity of yet unspecified FD's are derived, see Fig. 2.

---

[8] It applies also to functional cardinality constraints and negated functional cardinality constraints.

[9] Here the word "complete" means that the specification contains the whole information about all valid and invalid FD's.

4   Conclusion

This paper proposes a terminology systematization for FD's and their counterparts: FI's and antifunctional constraints. On one hand, FI's defined in this paper are a properly formulated negation of FD's. On the other hand, antifunctional constraints defined hereare very useful for obtaining information about valid FD's from an example database. The FD's combined with the FI's defined here can be easily adapted to the Higher–Order Entity–Relationship Model. Another advantage of this work is the consideration of different variants of deductive systems proposed by various authors. Our deductive system is non–redundant. It is sound and complete for FD's combined with FI's /antifunctional constraints and it is equivalent to all other sound and complete axiomatizations presented above.

References

Arm74. W. W. Armstrong: *Dependency structure of database relationships*, Proceedings IFIP, North Holland, Amsterdam, 1974, p. 580-583

Bel95. S. Bell: *The expanded implication problem of data dependencies*, Technical Report LS-8-16, Computer Science Department, University of Dortmund, 1995

Bin00. A. Binemann–Zdanowicz: *Systematization of Approaches to Equality–Generating Constraints*, Computer Science Report 02–2000, Brandenburg University of Technology, Institute of Computer Science, Cottbus, 2000

Dol99. T. Doležal: *Cardinality constraints for n–ary relationship types*, ADBIS '99, Maribor, 1999

DoD99. T. Doležal: *Cardinality constraints and associative data model*, Doctoral thesis, Charles University Prague, 1999

HeS95. A. Heuer, G. Saake: *Datenbanken, Konzepte und Sprachen* (in German), International Thomson Publishing Group, 1995

Jan89. J. M. Janas: *Covers for functional independencies*, MFDBS 89, LNCS 364, p.294-268, Visegrád, 1989

Kle98. M. Klettke: *Akquisition von Integritätsbedingungen in Datenbanken*, Infix Publishers, Sankt Augustin, 1998

MaR92. H. Mannila, K.–J. Räihä: *The Design of Relational Databases*, Addison–Wesley, Reading, 1992

McA98. A. McAllister: *Complete rules for n–ary relationship cardinality constraints*, Data & Knowledge Engineering 27 (1998) 255–288

Par89. J. Paredaens, P. De Bra, M. Gyssens, D. Van Gucht: *The Structure of the Relational Database Model*, Springer, Berlin, 1989

RAD97. M. Albrecht, M. Altus, E. Buchholz, H. Cyriaks, A. Düsterhöft, J. Lewerenz, H. Mehlan, M. Steeg, K.–D. Schewe, B. Thalheim: *Rapid Application and Database Development - Project Report*, internal report, Brandenburg University of Technology at Cottbus, Cottbus, 1997

Tha85. B. Thalheim: *Abhängigkeiten in Relationen*, habilitation thesis, Technical University of Dresden, 1985

Tha91. B. Thalheim: *Dependencies in Relational Databases*, Teubner, Leipzig, 1991

Tha00. B. Thalheim: *Entity–Relationship Modeling - Foundations of Database Technology*, Springer, Berlin, 2000

Ull88. J. D. Ullman: *Principles of Database and Knowledge–Base Systems*, Computer Science Press, Rockville, 1988

Efficient Region Query Processing by Optimal Page Ordering

Dae-Soo Cho and Bong-Hee Hong

Department of Computer Engineering, Pusan National University
Chang-Jun-Dong, Kum-Jung-Gu, Pusan, South Korea
{dsjo, bhhong}@hyowon.cc.pusan.ac.kr

Abstract. A number of algorithms of clustering spatial data for reducing the number of disk seeks required to process spatial queries have been developed. One of the algorithms is the scheme of page ordering, which is concerned with the order of pages in one-dimensional storage for storing two-dimensional spatial data. The space filling curves, especially the Hilbert curves, have been so far used to impose an order on all of pages. Page ordering based on the space filling curves, however, does not take into account the uneven distribution of spatial objects and the types of spatial queries. We will develop a cost model to define the page ordering problem based on performance measurement and then find out the method of page ordering for efficiently processing region queries in static databases. The experimental results will show that the newly proposed ordering method achieves better clustering than older methods.

1 Introduction

An efficient spatial query processing can be achieved by reducing the cost of disk accesses, because the cost is the main factor on the performance of query processing. The scheme of the clustering of spatial objects can play an important role in decreasing the cost of disk access. The clustering can be defined to associate spatially adjacent objects to the physically same page (or consecutive pages) on the disk or to impose a linear ordering on a set of pages (or objects) to a one-dimensional disk.

In this paper, we develop a cost model for optimal page ordering which minimizes the number of disk seeks for answering a range query, which is one of the frequently used spatial queries. Little work has been done to impose a linear ordering on pages. The goal of page ordering is that all of pages, which are close to each other in the data space, should be stored adjacently in a linear order. We assume that all pages are arranged on disk in a purely linear fashion. In this type of a disk, therefore, no rotational delay exists. We also assume pages are created by the conventional file manager and a number of adjacent pages on a disk can be fetched with a single read request (called set-oriented I/O in [15]).

The main motivation for this work is to uncover the limitation of the previous ordering method based on Hilbert values. In the previous works [5, 7, 9, 10], the space filling curves were only used to impose an order on all of the pages (or objects) and it was argued that the order based on Hilbert values was the best. The manifest limitation of the Hilbert ordering method is that the order is imposed on pages without

J. Štuller et al. (Eds.): ADBIS-DASFAA 2000, LNCS 1884, pp. 315–322, 2000.

considering the distribution of spatial data. The spatial proximity between pages is explicitly expressed in the fixed order on Hilbert curves. To overcome the limitation of the Hilbert ordering method, we propose a new page ordering method in which the distribution of spatial data as well as the types of spatial queries are considered.

In the next Section, we propose the cost model of page ordering and define the page ordering problem. In Section 3, we shortly present the implementation of an algorithm to solve the problem and discuss the results of the experiments. Finally, we draw conclusions in Section 4.

2 Page Ordering

First, we introduce several notations and functions in developing a cost model for defining the problem of page ordering. Let $DS = [0,1) \times [0,1)$ be the data space of unit square in which all geometric objects are defined. Without loss of generality, we consider a two-dimensional space. Let r be the region which is a sub-space of DS of rectangular shape. Let $RS = \{$all valid region $r\}$ be a region set. The function $Area\_of$ can be defined as a generalized area function to calculate the area of an arbitrarily shaped sub-space. The region-area function $f_a : RS \rightarrow R$ (R is the set of real numbers) is a specialized area function such that $f_a(r) = Area\_of(r)$ for $r \in RS$. Let q be a region query. The region query q is a region of constant size with q_x as its width and q_y as its height. Let $Q = \{$all valid $q\}$, $Q \subset RS$ be a query set. In this paper, we assume a query region to be a rectangular shape which has the same width and height. We also assume that all of the centers of query regions are uniformly distributed.

Let $P = \{p_1, p_2, .., p_k\}$ be a page set, and $OP = (op_1, op_2, .., op_k)$, $op_k \in P$ be an ordered page set of P. The ordered set is denoted by parentheses rather than braces. All of the pages are stored sequentially on disk according to the order listed in OP. For example, op_i and op_{i+1} are sequentially stored on disk, for op_i, $op_{i+1} \in OP$, $1 \leq i \leq k-1$. The page-region function $f_r : P \rightarrow RS$ is a function such that $f_r(p_i) = r_i$, where r_i is a minimal region enclosing all of the spatial objects in p_i.

Let $I(r)$ be an inflated region of r by $q_x/2$ and $q_y/2$. $I(r)$ is a clipped region against DS. The domain of $I(r_i)$ is the set of center points of all region queries which intersect with r_i. $I(r_i)$ is characterized as follows.

$$Area\_of\,(\,I(r_i)\,) = probability(\,query\ q\ retrieves\ page\ p_i) \tag{1}$$

Eq.1 proposed in [2, 11] formulates the probability that the execution of a query q makes an access to a page p_i. It means that a region query of which the center point is inside $I(r_i)$ retrieves a page p_i. [2, 11] also propose the function of performance measurement $PM(P, Q)$ based on Eq.1. For a page set P and a query set Q, the expected number of page accesses needed to perform a query q is defined by PM, and is given by

$$PM(P,Q) = \sum_{i=1}^{k} probability(query\ q\ retrieves\ page\ op_i) = \sum_{i=1}^{k} f_a(I(f_r(p_i))) \tag{2}$$

The purpose of [2, 11] is to generate a page set for a given data set to reduce the cost of page accesses, whereas that of this paper is to generate an ordered page set for a given page set to reduce the number of seeks. In this paper, we propose the function of performance measurement $PM(OP, Q)$ based on Eq.2 for optimal page ordering to reduce the cost of disk access. $PM(OP, Q)$ is defined as the number of seeks, rather than the number of page accesses, and is given by

$$PM(OP,Q) = \sum_{i=1}^{k} probability(query\ q\ retrieves\ page\ op_i) \tag{3}$$

$$-\sum_{i=1}^{k-1} probability(query\ q\ retrieves\ both\ pages\ of\ op_i\ and\ op_{i+1})$$

Lemma 1 For an ordered page set OP and a query set Q, the expected number of disk seeks, $PM(OP, Q)$ is given by

$$PM(OP,Q) = \sum_{i=1}^{k} f_a(I(r_i)) - \sum_{i=1}^{k-1} f_a(I(r_i) \cap I(r_{i+1})) \tag{4}$$

Proof:
We will just sketch the main steps of the proof. Let $N(k)$ be the expected number of seeks for the ordered page set $OP = (op_1, op_2, .., op_k)$ and the page set Q. We show that

$$N(k) = \sum_{i=1}^{k} f_a(I(r_i)) - \sum_{i=1}^{k-1} f_a(I(r_i) \cap I(r_{i+1})) \tag{5}$$

For $OP = (op_1, op_2, .., op_k, op_{k+1})$, $N(k+1)$ is the sum of $N(k)$ and the additional expected number of seeks by op_{k+1}. $I(r_{k+1})$ of r_{k+1} derived from $f_r(op_{k+1})$ can be divided into two parts.
Part I: $I(r_k) \cap I(r_{k+1})$ that is the intersected region of $I(r_{k+1})$ and $I(r_k)$.
If the center point of q is inside *Part I*, two pages, op_k and op_{k+1}, should be accessed. In this case, no more additional disk seeks for $N(k+1)$ from the viewpoint of $N(k)$ are required because op_k and op_{k+1} are stored sequentially on disk.
Part II: $(I(r_{k+1})-I(r_k))$ that is the rest space of $I(r_{k+1})$.
If the center point is inside *Part II*, the access of op_k is not required any more. This means that reading op_{k+1} requires one additional disk seek.
Therefore, $N(k+1)$ is the sum of $N(k)$ and the probability that processing q requires an access to op_{k+1} and does not require any access to op_k. We get

$$N(k+1) = N(k) + Area\_of\,(I(r_{k+1}) - I(r_k)) \tag{6}$$

$$= \sum_{i=1}^{k} f_a(I(r_i)) - \sum_{i=1}^{k-1} f_a(I(r_i) \cap I(r_{i+1})) + f_a(I(r_{k+1})) - f_a(I(r_k) \cap I(r_{k+1}))$$

$$= \sum_{i=1}^{k+1} f_a(I(r_i)) - \sum_{i=1}^{k} f_a(I(r_i) \cap I(r_{i+1}))$$

We then proceed as before to conclude that Eq. 5 is true. ∎
We are now able to define the page ordering problem based on $PM(OP, Q)$ and show that the problem is equivalent to the traveling salesman problem.

Definition 1. Page Ordering Problem (POP)
Given a page set P and a query set Q, POP is to determine an ordered page set OP for which $PM(OP, Q)$ is minimal.

Because the value of $\Sigma f_a(I(r_i))$ is independent of page order, determining an ordered page set OP for which $PM(OP, Q)$ is minimal is equivalent to determining an ordered page set OP for which $\Sigma f_a(I(r_i) \cap I(r_j))$ is maximal. We conclude that POP is very similar to the well-known minimum weighted Hamiltonian path problem without specifying the starting point and the terminating point. And it is known in [14] that a minimum weighted Hamiltonian path problem can be treated as a standard Traveling Salesman Problem (TSP).

Lemma 2 POP is equivalent to TSP for a weighted graph $G = (V, E, w)$ such that
$$V = P \cup \{v_0\},$$
where $P = \{p_1, p_2, .., p_k\}$ is a set of pages and v_0 is an artificial vertex to solve the minimum weighted Hamiltonian path problem by TSP,
$$E = \{(p_i, p_j) \mid p_i, p_j \in P, i \neq j\} \cup \{(p_i, v_0) \mid p_i \in P\},$$
and
$$w: E \to R.$$
Edge weights are computed as follows:
1. For edge $e = (p_i, p_j) \in P^2$, $w((p_i, p_j)) = 1 - f_a(I(r_i) \cap I(r_j))$.[1]
2. For edge $e = (p_i, v_0) \in P \times \{v_0\}$, $w((p_i, v_0)) = 0$.

Proof:
The Graph G is Hamiltonian, because G is a complete and weighted graph. Let $C = \{(v_0, op_1), (op_1, op_2), ..,(op_{k-1}, op_k), (op_k, v_0)\}$, $op_i \in P$ be a minimum weighted Hamiltonian cycle in G. By removing two edges incident with the vertex v_0 from C, we can get a minimum weighted Hamiltonian path L in G from op_1 to op_k. Now we can easily get a solution of POP from a solution of the corresponding TSP by interpreting a minimum weighted Hamiltonian path L as an ordered page set $OP = (op_1, op_2, .., op_k)$. From the viewpoint of constructing a corresponding weighted graph, it is obvious that the solution of POP is identical with that of TSP. ∎

3 Experimental Evaluation

To solve the NP-hard problem of TSP, we implement a heuristic based on the Simulated Annealing (SA) method which is one of the probabilistic hill climbing algorithms. Because TSP is NP-hard, exhaustive exploration of all the states is impractical.

All possible Hamiltonian cycles in a weighted graph G can be defined by the state spaces of SA. Each state corresponds to a Hamiltonian cycle, and the cost associated

---

[1] The weight of an edge is computed as the total area of data space minus the area of $f_a(I(r_i) \cap I(r_j))$ to convert a maximization problem into a minimization problem.

with each state is calculated as the sum of edge weights in a cycle. The goal of the traditional symmetric *TSP* is to find a state with a globally minimal cost.

The main advantage of *SA* is that only part of all the states is explored to find a global minimum. This algorithm has been very successful in practice to solve combinatorial optimization problems of various application domains[6, 8, 13].

There are some parameters of *SA* which are dependent upon implementation. Because the performance of *SA* has been greatly affected by the value of those parameters, they must be carefully selected. For our implementation, they have been chosen as follows:

1. Initial temperature T_0: The initial temperature is chosen to be twice the cost of the initial state. The factor 2 is chosen based on the experience in [8].
2. Freezing criterion: This criterion is a combination of two verification tests; the first is the temperature is below 0.001, the other is the cost of the last state has to be the same for three consecutive stages.
3. Equilibrium criterion: We set the number of repetition to 500*n. The constant n is the cardinality of a page set P in *POP*.
4. Temperature decrement factor α: The temperature decrement factor is set to 0.9.
5. Initial state s_0: We generate an initial state based on an approximation algorithm (Approx-TSP-Tour) proposed in [3].
6. Local search heuristics for choosing a next state from the current state: A next state is chosen by simple local search heuristics such as non-crossing paths and nearest neighbors(see [14]).

3.1 Experimental Testbed

We investigated the performance of our page ordering method based on the above proposed cost model, and compare it with that based on Hilbert values. Our test data is based on polygonal data from Sequoia 2000 benchmark. We use two test data sets: a data set DS-A consists of 1,022 pages with 17,048 spatial objects whereas a data set DS-B consists of 3,490 pages with 65,157 spatial objects. We select five different sizes of query regions. For each size, 10,000 region queries are randomly generated, and each query has at least one result page. Each region query of a different size covers 0.25%, 1.00%, 4.00%, 9.00%, and 16.0% of the data space.

There are two types of the test query sets. One is the simple query sets which are composed of 10,000 queries of the same size. Each simple query set Q is denoted by adding the size of queries it contains as a suffix. A simple query set $Q0.25$, for example, is composed of region queries of which size covers 0.25% of the data space. The other is the mixed query sets, which are composed of 10,000 queries of different size. A mixed query set consists of 6000 queries in one major simple query set and each 1000 queries in four other simple query sets. Each mixed query set MQ is denoted by adding the size of major queries it contains as a suffix.

We have generated five optimal ordered page sets, OP($Q0.25$), OP($Q1.00$), OP($Q4.00$), OP($Q9.00$), and OP($Q16.0$) for each test query set Q and an ordered page set OP(H) based on Hilbert values. OP($Q0.25$) means the ordered page set for which the performance measurement for the query set $Q0.25$ is minimal.

3.2 Experimental Results

We have evaluated the performance of various ordered page sets. For a given query, we have computed the number of seeks, rather than the number of page accesses. It was expected that for a query set Q, the ordered page set for which the performance measurement for this query set is minimal shows the best performance over any other ordered page sets. To save the space, we discussed the performance comparison of the data set DS-A. This is because the experimental results of the data set DS-B were very similar to those of this data set.

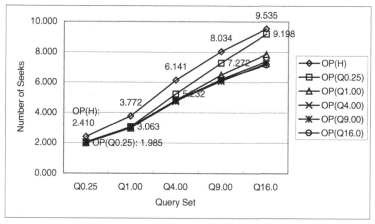

(a) The number of seeks per query for each query set

	OP(Q0.25)	OP(Q1.00)	OP(Q4.00)	OP(Q9.00)	OP(Q16.0)
Q0.25	**17.62%**	17.33%	16.23%	14.91%	15.16%
Q1.00	18.79%	**21.02%**	19.97%	19.22%	19.13%
Q4.00	14.81%	21.55%	**22.78%**	22.18%	21.49%
Q9.00	9.49%	19.23%	22.75%	**24.21%**	23.36%
Q16.0	3.53%	17.67%	22.56%	24.06%	**24.95%**

(b) Relative improvement of the optimal ordered page sets over *OP(H)*

Fig. 1. Experimental results for the simple query sets with the data set DS-A

Figure 1 shows the result of performance evaluation carried out for simple query sets and the data space DS-A. Because the number of seeks varies as the query size increases, this number has been normalized by the total number of queries. Figure 1 (a) depicts the normalized number of seeks which is defined to be the number of seeks per query, and Figure 1 (b) shows the relative improvement of five optimal ordered page sets over *OP(H)*. As the query size increases, the optimal ordered page set shows better performance over *OP(H)*. Furthermore, an ordered page set which is optimal for a specific query set shows better performance than *OP(H)* for other query sets.

The optimal page ordering method proposed in this paper is based on performance measurement for a given query set Q, which is composed of queries of the same size.

In most of spatial databases, however, region queries of various size are used. For a mixed query set MQ, we evaluate the performance of the optimal ordered page set, which is optimal for simple query set Q.

If the ratio of the number of queries for each size to the number of total queries is known in advance, we can expect the number of seeks per query for the mixed query set by using the result of Figure 1 (a). For example, the expected number of seeks per query for $OP(H)$ and $OP(Q0.25)$ with the mixed query set $MQ0.25$, which is composed of 6000 queries in the query set $Q0.25$ and each 1000 queries in four other simple query sets, is calculated as follows:

☐ The expected number of seeks per query for $OP(H)$: (6000*2.410 + 1000*3.771 + 1000*6.141 + 1000*8.034 + 1000*9.534) / 10000 = 4.1940

☐ The expected number of seeks per query for $OP(Q0.25)$: (6000*1.985 + 1000*3.063 + 1000*5.232 + 1000*7.272 + 1000*9.198) / 10000 = 3.6675

With the same way, we can calculate the expected number of seeks for all the ordered page sets and all the mixed query sets. The experimental results are very similar to expected results. Table 1 shows the relative improvement of the optimal ordered page set over $OP(H)$.

Table 1. Experimental results for the mixed query sets with the data set DS-A: Relative improvement of the optimal ordered page set over $OP(H)$

	OP(Q0.25)	OP(Q1.00)	OP(Q4.00)	OP(Q9.00)	OP(Q16.0)
MQ0.25	12.41%	18.31%	20.06%	19.89%	**20.07%**
MQ1.00	13.52%	19.40%	**20.85%**	20.73%	20.81%
MQ4.00	12.48%	20.07%	**22.06%**	**22.06%**	21.72%
MQ9.00	10.03%	19.25%	22.44%	**23.63%**	23.14%
MQ16.0	6.22%	18.07%	22.18%	23.35%	**24.04%**

As a result of evaluating the number of seeks per query for the mixed query sets, we would like to point out the following statements. First, the optimal ordered page sets always do better than $OP(H)$ regardless of the type of the mixed query sets. The best one for each of the mixed queries, performs about 20% better than $OP(H)$. Second, the above mentioned experimental results with simple query sets is very similar to the experimental results for the mixed query sets. This means that we can also generate an optimal ordered page set for the mixed query sets.

4 Summary

The main contributions of this paper are as follows: We defined the page ordering problem in static spatial databases, and uncovered the drawbacks of the previous methods based on Hilbert values. To determine the optimality of a certain page order, we developed a new cost model of page ordering as a formula for performance measurement. We implemented a heuristic based on the existing Simulated Annealing method to solve the optimization problem which is NP-hard, and investigated the performance of our page ordering method based on the cost model. The experimental results showed that the newly proposed optimal page order outperforms the fixed order of pages based on Hilbert curves. Future work will explore the issues of page ordering for different types of spatial queries.

References

1. Thomas Brinkhoff, and Hans-Peter Kriegel, "The Impact of Global Clustering on Spatial Database Systems", pp168-179, VLDB, 1994
2. Lukas Bachmann, Bernd-Uwe Pagel, and Hans-Werner Six, "Optimizing Spatial Data Structures For Static Data", pp247-258, IGIS, 1994
3. Thomas H. Cormen, Charles E. Leiserson, and Ronald L. Rivest, "Introduction to algorithms", McGraw-Hill Company, 1989
4. Cisbert Dröge, and Hans-Jörg Schek, "Query-Adaptive Data Space Partitioning using Variable-Size Storage Clusters", pp337-356, SSD, 1993
5. Christos Faloutsos, and Shari Roseman, "Fractanls for Secondary Key Retrieval", pp247-252, PODS, 1989
6. Kien A. Hua, Sheau-Dong Lang, and Wen K. Lee, "A Decomposition-Based Simulated Annealing Technique for Data Clustering", pp117-128, PODS, 1994
7. Andreas Hutflesz, Hans-Werner Siz, and Peter Widmayer, "Globally Order Preserving Multidimensional Linear Hashing", pp572-579, ICDE, 1988
8. Y. E. Ioannidis, and Eugene Wong, "Query optimization by simulated annealing", pp9-11, SIGMOD, 1987
9. H. V. Jagadish, "Linear Clustering of Objects with Multiple Attributes", pp332-342, SIGMOD, 1990
10. H. V. Jagadish, Laks V. S. Lakshmanan, and Divesh Srivastava, "Snakes and Sandwiches: Optimal Clustering Strategies for a Data Warehouse", pp37-48, SIGMOD, 1999
11. Ibrahim Kamel, and Christos Faloutsos, "On Packing R-trees, Information & Knowledge Management", pp490-499, CIKM, 1993,
12. Ibrahim Kamel, and Christos Faloutsos, "Hilbert R-tree: An improved R-tree using fractals", pp500-509, VLDB, 1994
13. Bernd-Uwe Pagel, Hans-Werner Six, and Mario Winter, "Window Query-Optimal Clustering of Spatial Objects", pp86-94, PODS, 1995
14. G. Reinelt, "The Traveling Salesman Problem", Springer Verlag, 1994.
15. Gerhard Weikum, "Set-Oriented Disk Access to Large Complex Objects", pp426-433, ICDE, 1989

On Deploying and Executing Data-Intensive Code on SMart Autonomous Storage (SmAS) Disks*

V.V. Dimakopoulos, A. Kinalis, E. Pitoura, and I. Tsoulos

Computer Science Department, University of Ioannina,
GR 45110 Ioannina, Greece
{dimako, pitoura}@cs.uoi.gr

Abstract. There is an increasing demand for storage capacity and storage throughput, driven largely by new data types such as video data and satellite images as well as by the growing use of the Internet and the web that generate and transmit rapidly evolving datasets. Thus, there is a need for storage architectures that scale the processing power with the growing size of the datasets. In this paper, we present the SMAS system that employs network attached disks with processing capabilities. In the SMAS system, users can deploy and execute code at the disk. Application code is written in a stream-based language that enforces code security and bounds the code's memory requirements. The SMAS operating system at the disk provides basic support for process scheduling and memory management. We present an initial implementation of the system and report performance results that validate our approach for data-intensive applications.

1 Introduction

There is an increasing demand for storage capacity and storage throughput. This demand is driven largely by new data types such as video data and satellite images as well as the growing use of the Internet and the web that generate and transmit rapidly evolving datasets, take for example the huge amount of data produced by e-commerce transactions [8,6]. Furthermore, there is growing interest in data mining applications that efficiently analyze large datasets for decision support. Thus, there is a need for storage architectures that scale the processing power with the growing size of the datasets.

Recent disks embed powerful ASIC designs in order to deliver their high bandwidth; such chips are capable of doing considerable processing (for instance, see how complex the SCSI protocol is [2]). In addition, current disks have caches in the order of MB (for example, Seagate's Cheetah has up to 16 MB of cache). This suggests that data can be processed locally at the disk. Such disks are called active [1,9] or intelligent [7] disks. The idea of data processing at the disk

---

* Work supported in part by the Hellenic General Secretariat of Research and Technology through grant PENED–99/495.

J. Štuller et al. (Eds.): ADBIS-DASFAA 2000, LNCS 1884, pp. 323–330, 2000.

is not a new one. Early proposals include the IBM 360 I/O processors and the specialized database servers of the 80's [4]. What makes active disk architectures attractive today is that current technology is such that sufficient processing power and memory can be economically embedded in disks. Active disks have been proposed as a cheap replacement to expensive disks; they communicate with the host processor through the local bus (typically SCSI or Fiber Channel). It is envisioned that they will be able to relieve the host processor by acquiring and executing part of the application very close to the data. Such architectures are capable of handling large datasets, since the number of processors scale with the number of disks. In addition, they can effectively reduce the amount of data transfered from the disk to the host processor.

At the same time, distributed file systems are used increasingly nowadays. A good reason is the huge databases maintained by various companies [14]. Thus, a distributed storage architecture is needed to provide efficient and scalable access to data. Such an architecture is provided by NASD [5] coupled with their object-oriented file system for network attached storage.

Active disks have been mainly envisioned as attachments to the local bus of a server [12]. This would however require expensive server architectures especially if one also considers the resources required for supporting multiple interconnected active disks. Furthermore, it is essential, from a practical point of view, to investigate devices that do not require alterations to a given infrastructure. To this end, a smart disk should use part of its processing capabilities to support a simple TCP/IP stack and attach itself on a local network. Apart from the obvious cost reductions, this approach has the additional advantage of true distributed processing, without the bottleneck of a front-end processor, since in a multiple active disk arrangement [12] disks can only communicate with clients through the server processor's connection to the network.

In this paper, we present the SMart Autonomous Storage (SMAS) system. SMAS devices are autonomous (i.e. network-ready) disks but they also have significant processing capabilities like active disks. A SMAS device could possibly include interface support for SCSI or FiberChannel local buses, so as to be attached on a local bus if desired. SMAS disks reduce the communication overhead of transmitting large volumes of data over the network by executing data-intensive applications at the disk. In addition, they release the host processor by undertaking part of the computation.

Our focus is on building a running system. We consider the actual constraints placed on the application programs to be run on the disk and the necessary operating system support for executing them. Portions of the application programs to be executed at the disk, called *filters*, are written in a special-purpose language that ensures code safety, sets bounds on the filter's memory requirements and provides a stream-based interface. Operating system support at the disk is kept at a minimum and includes filter scheduling and memory management. We have tested our initial implementation of SMAS and compare its performance with NFS. The results are encouraging since the measured performance is close to the expected ideal speed-up.

The remainder of this paper is organized as follows. In Section 2, we introduce the SMAS architecture, while in Section 3, we report on the implementation of SMAS. In Section 4, we present related work. Section 5 concludes the paper.

2   The SmAS Architecture

SMAS disks are network-attached disks with processing power. In order for the disk to be employed seamlessly in an existing network, all standard operations are supported (`open()`, `read()`, `write()`, `lseek()` etc.); a SMAS disk can easily replace a conventional NFS server.

The application code consists of two portions: the client-side part, executed at the client, and the SMAS-side part, executed at the smart disk. The latter is called *filter*, and is written in a special-purpose, C-like language. In general, filters are expected to implement processing that reduces the volume of data to be transfered from the disk to the client. For example, instead of transferring the whole file at the client side and performing an SQL-Select there, a filter may perform an SQL-Select locally and thus communicate only the selected data to the application. Filters are cross-compiled at the host disk. Clients can then register the executable code at the client's side. They can then be downloaded (registered) to the smart disk. The client programs invoke filters through a specific series of function calls. The filter code is executed at the disk. Basic minimum operating system support is required at the disk for efficiently executing the filters.

Filter Characteristics. Filters are programs that are executed at the disk. Special requirements imposed on filters include the following: (a) Since disk memory is limited, each filter program should use only a pre-specified portion of this memory. Furthermore, a filter should not dynamically allocate or free memory. (b) Filters should not be allowed to directly read from or write to the disk, to avoid any disk corruption.

We have adopted a stream-based interface for filters similar to the one proposed in disklets [12,1]. A filter, upon registration, specifies its exact memory requirements. A filter reads from an input stream and writes to an output stream, both of which are controlled by the disk's OS.

Writing and Registering Application Code. Filters are written in a special-purpose language, quite similar to C. This language enforces filters to declare all the variables that they need as global variables, allowing thus for statically calculating their exact memory requirements. Two functions are then expected to be defined: a `filter_init()` function and a `filter_body()` function. The former is used to possibly initialize the filter's global variables. `filter_body()` is the function that implements the core filter processing and has two parameters: an `input_buffer` and an `output_buffer`. Both functions have no local variables; the only variables they can use are the global ones, if any. In addition, they are not allowed to perform any function calls.

A filter is cross-compiled at the client's side. The compiled code can be registered at the smart disk by using a `smass_addfilter()` call, which results in downloading the executable code of the filter at the disk. Filters thus registered are placed in a filter library.

The client-side part of the application selects the required filter with a `smas_usefilter()` call; this call identifies the filter to be used and causes the execution of the respective `filter_init()` function at the smart disk. After that, the client has access to the relevant remote data, one entry at a time, by continuously calling `smas_nextrecord()`. A call to `smas_nextrecord()` will ship the next filtered record to the client-side part. What actually happens is that `smas_nextrecord()` reads a record from the disk and then invokes the `filter_body()` function, with the read record as a parameter (`input_buffer`). The filter's function, in turn, decides whether the record meets the criteria, and if so it notifies `smas_nextrecord()` by returning a value of `Send`. `smas_nextrecord()` then sends whatever the filter has placed in its `output_buffer` to the client. If `filter_body()` returns a value of `NoSend`, `smas_nextrecord()` does not ship anything to the client, loads the next record from the file and invokes the filter again. This is useful when more than one records of the file must be processed before returning control to the client (e.g., computing the maximum value). Fig. 1 provides an example of writing and invoking a filter.

```
/* Define the record structure for easy handling */
typedef struct{ int key; char data[96]; } recstruct;

/* Nothing useful here */
filter_init() {}

/* The filter's body – pass only records with key > 10 */
filter_body(recstruct *in, void *out, int *outbytes) {
    if (in->key <= 10) /* Compare to 10 */
        return (NoSend);
    out = (void *) in; *outbytes = sizeof(recstruct);
    return (Send);
}
```

(a) writing a filter

```
/* Register a filter */
smas_addfilter(SQL_SELECT);

/* Open remote file */
fd = smas_open("zeus.cs.uoi.gr:/pub/testfile", O_RDONLY);
/* Specify the file and filter to use */
smas_usefilter(fd, SQL_SELECT);

/* Now get and process all selected records */
while ( (output = smas_nextrecord(fd)) != EndOfFile )
    process(output);
```

(b) invoking a filter

Fig. 1. Writing and invoking the SQL_SELECT filter.

Disk-side Support. The SMAS operating system (SMAS OS) should be as thin as possible in order to minimize execution overheads and memory costs. Consequently, its functionality should be kept down to a minimum. The only offered services must be networking, process (filter) management, and memory management. Full networking functionality is necessary for attaching the disk to an existing network. Such functionality should be considered rather common place and inexpensive (consider for example the network-ready CD-ROM server by Axis [3]).

A limited form of process management will be required in order to schedule the filter execution. Such a need arises when multiple clients are connected to the disk. Process management should be simple and efficient. However, as discussed in [1], simple strategies like run-to-completion could ultimately limit the disk's performance. In our case, the fact that filters are pre-compiled and embedded in the disk's library allows for accurate estimations of their running times and, consequently, for more informed scheduling strategies, like shortest-job-first [11].

Finally, memory management is probably the most important service since disk's memory is usually its most limited resource. However, memory management is highly simplified due to the filter-based processing: the memory requirements of the filters are known apriori and are satisfied as soon as a filter starts execution. There is no memory swap or process switching. Thus, since the filter cannot allocate dynamically any more memory, it is a simple (and quick) matter to free the allocated memory as soon as the filter completes its execution. We use a first-fit method to allocate memory.

3   Implementation

We have emulated a SMAS device using an old Pentium-based PC, running at 166 Mhz, with 32Mbyte of memory and with a minimized version of Linux as its operating system. The hardware components are analogous to that found inside a present-day disk only much more economical. The SMAS system software (SMASOS) is running as a Linux daemon and awaits at a particular port for a client connection. Communication is handled by the standard `socket` library. At startup, SMASOS acquires a 16Mbyte memory chunk and uses it for implementing its own memory management.

The special-purpose language in which filters are written is an enriched subset of C. We have implemented a compiler for this language, that converts the filter code to standard C code which is then cross-compiled at the client side. Currently, the produced code is in the Linux shared library format which is directly down-loadable to the SMAS disk at run time. To verify the validity of our approach as well as reveal any inefficiencies in the implementation, we have experimented with a number of applications.

Although simple, a particularly illuminating application is the SQL-Select filter shown in Fig. 1. The client utilizes the SQL-Select filter in order to obtain and process relevant records from a file stored at the smart disk. The filtering is done locally at the disk, which returns only the appropriate records to the application, minimizing thus network communication.

```
/* Open the remote file - NFS mounted */
fd = open("/mnt/zeus/pub/testfile", O_RDONLY);

/* Get, filter and process records */
while ( read(fd, buffer, 100) != 0 )
    /* Filter at our (client) side */
    if ( checkcondition(buffer) )
        process(buffer);
```

Fig. 2. Sample application: Traditional NFS approach

We then executed the same application by NFS-mounting the file (Fig. 2) and compared the total running times. If T_{SMASS} and T_{NFS} are the corresponding running times of the two approaches, the observed speedup is defined as T_{NFS}/T_{SMASS} and is plotted in Fig. 3, for various record sizes.

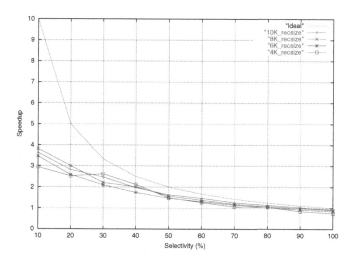

Fig. 3. Speedup with respect to traditional NFS handling

Let s be the *selectivity factor*, that is the probability that a data record is selected by the SQL-Select filter. If a file contains N records then the SMAS code will only deliver sN of them to the application. We generated files that would result in prescribed values for the selectivity factor s (between 10% and 100%). Fig. 3 shows clearly that the SMAS version is able to deliver superior performance, especially for smaller selectivity values. This fact should actually be expected because of the reduced network communication.

The results in Fig. 3 were obtained for file sizes in the area of 100MBytes. In order to determine the socket messaging overheads we experimented with various record sizes. It can be seen from the figure that the performance did not exhibit a wide variance; however, the smaller the record size the smaller the observed speedup. This is due to the headers inserted by the socket library to a message; these extra bytes account for a smaller percentage as the message size grows, thus improving performance.

Assuming that the communication / computation (processing) time ratio per record is greater than one, computation (processing) time, then the total running time should be dominated by the total communication time. Since the SMAS version only communicates a portion s of the total data, while the NFS-mounted file approach communicates all of it to the client, it is expected that (ideally) a speedup of the order of $1/s$ should be observed.

Fig 3 however shows that despite the improvements over NFS, the performance of the SMAS application is actually well below the ideal. This is largely due to the fact that NFS is highly optimized, utilizing prefetching and caching techniques which in effect pipelines computation and communication to a high degree. We are currently optimizing SMASOS and investigate data prefetching techniques. We are confident that performance will move much closer to the ideal. It is also in our future plans to provide kernel support for SMAS in Linux, which will improve performance significantly.

4   Related Work

A stream-based programming model for disklets (i.e., disk-resident code) is presented in [12,1]. Their active disks are attached to the local bus of the host processor. The disklet programming model is similar to ours. They justify their design decisions by providing a detailed simulation of active disks. In contrast, our focus is on building an actual system which introduces practical restrictions. In [12,13], an evaluation of the disklet model is provided against two alternative architectures: shared memory multiprocessors (SMPs) and workstation clusters. For most of the applications tested, active disks and clusters significantly outperformed the SMP architecture. The IDISKs (Intelligent disks) architecture proposed in [7] is based on replacing the nodes in a shared-nothing cluster server with intelligent disks that is disks capable of local processing. The main difference in the IDISKs architecture is that the disks are directly connected with each other via switches thus exhibiting much higher bandwidth disk-to-disk communication. The architecture closest to SMAS is the active disks of [9]. The authors of [9] concentrate on developing a number of applications to validate the active disks approach. Their analytical and experimental results promise linear speed-ups in disk arrays of hundreds of active disks for certain data-intensive applications. Instead, the alternative of directly attaching a number of traditional SCSI disks to the local bus of a single server machine caused the server CPU or the interconnect bandwidth to saturate even when a small number of disks (less that ten) was attached. Besides research on active disk, there is some recent interest in shipping application code to the data sources [10]. Application code is in the form of bytecodes. Using bytecodes is not a feasible approach in our case since the limited resources of the disk do not allow for a java execution machine.

5 Summary

In this paper, we introduced the SMAS network attached disk architecture. As compared to a classical file server, an autonomous network-attached device offers significant advantages. First of all, the cost is much smaller, so that one could purchase a number of smart disks for the price of a mid-sized server. Second, SMAS devices have dedicated processing on the disk that provides for efficient distributed processing. A server on the other hand is a general purpose machine that has to deal with many other things apart from file processing. Third, by shipping computation at the disk, network traffic is reduced, since only the relevant data are tranferred to the clients. The results of an initial implementation of SMAS are encouraging and justify our design decisions.

References

1. A. Acharya, M. Uysal, and J. Saltz. Active disks: programming model, algorithms and evaluation. In *ASPLOS '98, 8th Conf. on Archit. Support for Programming Languages and Operationg Systems*, pages 212–217, San Jose, California, Oct. 1998.
2. ANSI. Information systems - small computer system interface-2 (scsi-2). Technical report, ANSI X3.131-1994, 1994.
3. Axis Communications. Cd-rom servers, white paper. Technical report, 1996.
4. D. J. DeWitt and P. Hawthorn. A performance evaluation of database machine architectures. In *VLDB '81*, September 1981.
5. G. Gibson, D. Nagle, K. Amiri, F. Chang, E. Feinberg, H. Gobioff, C. Lee, B. Ozceri, E. Riedel, D. Rochberg, and J. Zelenka. File server scaling with network-attached secure disks. In *Sigmetrics '97*, Seattle, Washington, June 1997.
6. J. Gray. What happens when processors are infinitely fast and storage is free? In *5th Workshop on I/O in Parallel and Distributed Systems*, November 1997.
7. K. Keeton, D. A. Patterson, and J. M. Hellerstein. A case for intelligent disks (idisks). *SIGMOD Record*, 27(3):42–52, July 1998.
8. George Lawton. Storage technology takes central state. *IEEE Computer*, 32(11), November 1999.
9. E. Riedel, G. Gibson, and C. Faloutsos. Active storage for large-scale data mining and multimedia. In *VLDB '98*, pages 62–73, New York, USA, August 1998.
10. M. Rodriguez and N. Roussopoulos. Automatic deployment of application-specific metadata and code in mocha. In *7th Conference on Extending Database Technology (EDBT)*, March 2000.
11. A. S. Tanenbaum and A. S. Woodhull. *Operating Systems: Design and Implementation. 2nd ed.* Prentice Hall, 1997.
12. M. Uysal, A. Acharya, and J. Saltz. An evaluation of architectural alternatives for rapidly growing datasets: active disks, clusters, smps. Technical report, Dept. of Computer Science, University of California, Santa Barbara, Technical Report TRCS98-27, October 1998.
13. M. Uysal, A. Acharya, and J. Saltz. Evaluation of active disks for decision support databases. In *HPCA*, 2000.
14. R. Winter and K. Auerbach. The big time: the 1998 vldb survey. *Database Programming and design*, 11(8), August 1998.

An Efficient Storage Manager

Dimitris G. Kapopoulos, Michael Hatzopoulos, and Panagiotis Stamatopoulos

Department of Informatics, University of Athens,
Panepistimiopolis, Ilisia 157 84, Greece
{dkapo, mike, takis}@di.uoa.gr

Abstract. When dealing with large quantities of clauses, the use of persistent knowledge is inevitable, and indexing methods are essential to answer queries efficiently. We introduce PerKMan, a storage manager that uses G-trees and aims at efficient manipulation of large amount of persistent knowledge. PerKMan may be connected to Prolog systems that offer an external C language interface. As well as the fact that the storage manager allows different arguments of a predicate to share a common index dimension in a novel manner, it indexes rules and facts in the same manner. PerKMan handles compound terms efficiently and its data structures adapt their shape to large dynamic volumes of clauses, no matter what their distribution. The storage manager achieves fast clause retrieval and reasonable use of disk space.

1   Introduction

Efficient management of persistent knowledge in deductive database systems requires the adoption of effective indexing schemes in order to save disk accesses, whilst maintaining reasonable use of available space. *Deductive database systems* incorporate the functionality of both logic programming and database systems. As referred to [6], they have four major architectures: *logic programming systems enhanced with database functionality* (NU-Prolog [11]), *database access from Prolog* (BERMUDA [6], TERMdb [1]), *relational database systems enhanced with inferential capabilities* (Business System 12 [4]), and *systems from scratch* (SICStus [9], CORAL [10], Aditi [13], Glue-Nail [2], XSB [12], ECL^{i}PS^e [3]).

In *multidimensional data structures*, all attributes are treated in the same way and no distinction exists between primary and secondary keys. This seems to be suitable in a knowledge base environment, where queries are not predictable and clauses may be used in a variety of input/output combinations.

The *G-tree* [8] is an adaptable multidimensional structure that combines the features of B-trees and grid files. It divides the data space into a grid of variable size partitions and adapts its shape to high dynamic data spaces and to non-uniformly distributed data. Only non-empty partitions are stored in a B-tree-like organization. The G-tree uses a variable-length partition numbering scheme. Each partition is assigned a unique binary string of 0's and 1's. In [8], the G-tree arithmetic, algorithms for update and search operations and the advantages of the G-tree over similar data structures are examined. The G^r_tree [7] combines the features of metric spaces and G-trees. It considers every data space as a metric space through the use of the Euclidean norm and an algorithm that transforms strings to unsigned long integers.

J. Štuller et al. (Eds.): ADBIS-DASFAA 2000, LNCS 1884, pp. 331–338, 2000.

Although the G^r_tree requires distance computations and has the overhead of a small amount of storage space, due to the introduction of active regions inside the partitions of the data space, it reduces the accesses of partial match and range queries.

This work introduces PerKMan, a new storage manager that uses G^r_trees, makes database access from Prolog and aims at efficient manipulation of large amount of persistent knowledge. The rest of the paper is organized as follows: Section 2 deals with the use of user-defined domains. Section 3 explains the data structures of the storage manager. Section 4 gives experimental results and shows that PerKMan achieves fast clause retrieval and good utilization of disk space. Section 5 concludes this work with a summary and a future research issue.

2   User-Defined Domains

PerKMan provides persistent storage of any size of knowledge and may be connected to Prolog systems that offer an external C language interface. The arguments of each permanent predicate belong to predefined domains and this cannot be changed at run time. From the Prolog point of view, the definition and manipulation of knowledge may be achieved through appropriate built-in predicates that have to be defined, using the external C language interface, in terms of the functions provided by PerKMan.

User-Defined (or *custom*) *Domains (UDDs)* are built up from simple (*sdomain*) or complex (*cdomain*) domains. Domains are created with cr_dom/2. Its syntax is

cr_dom(*cdomain, domain* {; *domain*})

domain = *cdomain* |*sdomain* |⟨*functor*⟩ (*domain* {, *domain*}) |*udom*.

The universal domain *udom* incorporates any structure including lists. A basic unit *sdomain* is one of the types atom, integer and real.

Apart from storing the data as an unsorted sequence of clauses (heap organization), PerKMan supports the G^r_tree to store and retrieve clauses. A predicate definition is added to a knowledge base with cr_pred/3. Its syntax is

cr_pred(*predicate*, ((*argument, domain*, y |n) {, (*argument, domain*, y |n)})).

The value y (n) means the participation (or not) of the argument in the index.

UDDs are distinguished between Non-Recursive Domains (NRD) and Recursive Domains (RD). PerKMan does not employ RDs in indices due to their unpredictable number of elements. The following program udd_ex is an example of UDDs.

```
?- cr_dom(q,a(z,c)).
?- cr_dom(z,d(atom) ; e(integer)).
?- cr_dom(c,f(s,t) ; w(integer)).
?- cr_dom(s,s(integer)).
?- cr_dom(t,l(atom) ; v(atom)).
?- cr_pred(pr, ((name, q, y)), b(300)).
?- ins_c(pr(a(d(atm1),f(s(9),v(atm2))))).
```

A knowledge base is queried through PerKMan either with set-oriented or clause-oriented operations. Clauses retrieval can be transparent if a permanent predicate p(X,..) is defined as p(X,..):-sel_c(p(X,..)). The predicates sel_c/1 and ins_c/1 selects and inserts clauses in a clause-oriented mode respectively.

PerKMan flattens UDDs in order to handle them efficiently. *Domain Trees (DTs)* of UDDs include functors and sub-terms and assists understanding. Figure 1 shows the DT of q. We use dashed lines for disjunction and continuous for conjunction.

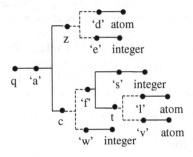

Fig. 1. The tree of the user-defined domain q.

DTs are unbalanced AND/OR-trees. *sdomains* reside on the leaf nodes of DTs and the way we traverse them gives the form of the clauses. Possible paths are constructed by successive replacements of UDDs. Because the hierarchical structure of *cdomains* is flattened, they can be organized into G^r_trees. As an example, we decompose the UDD q. The symbols + and · denote disjunction and conjunction respectively.

q=z.c=(atom+integer)·(integer·(atom+atom)+integer)

= atom·integer·atom+atom·integer·atom+atom·integer+

integer·integer·atom+integer·integer·atom+integer·integer

The six components of the last equation span the space of the alternative expressions and each one represents the ordered leaf nodes of a possible path.

For the storage of clauses involving UDDs, we use a *Path Identity (PI)* prefix that declares the correspondence between arguments and used terms. In other words, *PI* is the path of the DT that corresponds to the selected terms. Its use is necessitated by the existence of disjunctions between sub-terms. We use the depth-first method to traverse a DT. If there are alternatives, we select a node according to a number that declares its position among the other nodes of the disjunction. The storage of a clause includes its *PI* and the used terms. Only the arguments that participate in indices are involved in *PIs*. The length of *PIs* is limited, for RDs are not included in indices.

We examine the *PI* of the clause of the program udd_ex. The first choice occurs at node z. The d(atom) is chosen and thus 1 is the first element of *PI*. Next, at node c, we select the f(s,t), and so the second element of *PI* is 1. The last decision concerns node t, and the selection of v(atom) corresponds to number 2. We have, $PI = 1,1,2$.

3   Data Structures

The data structures that PerKMan uses to organize persistent knowledge form four areas: User-Defined Domains (UDDA), Predicate Declarations (PDA), Index (IA) and Clauses (CA) area. The first two are loaded into main memory when a knowledge base is opened, whilst the other two remain on disk. Figure 2 shows the above areas.

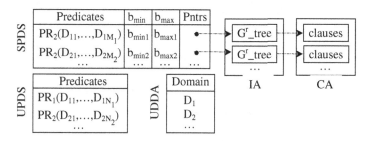

Fig. 2. Data structures of PerKMan.

3.1   Predicate Declarations Area

It includes in two segments the predicate declarations as they are provided by the users (UPDS) and subsequently converted by the system (SPDS).

UPDS: This contains for each persistent predicate, its name and arity, the domains of its arguments and the participation of each argument in the index.

SPDS: For the persistent predicates it contains their names, arity, domains, the number of bits of the largest and the smallest partition (b_{min}, b_{max}) and addresses in IA.

If at least one UDD with *cdomain* has been declared in the index of a predicate PR_i, then the predicate arity and domains in SPDS are different from the ones in UPDS. In general, it is $N_i{\neq}M_i$. In SPDS, the predicate dimensions are related to *sdomains*. When a clause is inserted, each of its arguments corresponds to the first non-occupied dimension of the index that has the same domain type.

3.2   Index Area

The IA is composed of G^r_trees and is used for the fast retrieval of clauses. Each G^r_tree corresponds to one predicate. A G^r_tree dimension can be shared by two or more predicate arguments that belong to different paths. These arguments have to be of the same type, e.g., the argument with domain atom of the first path of the UDD q and the argument with the same domain type of the second path can share an index dimension with data type atom. Thus, the required dimensions to index the q have types integer, integer, atom and atom. Consequently, the pr is declared in SPDS as

    pr(integer,integer,atom,atom).

If some index dimensions are left without arguments, they take a default value from their domain. If the number of paths in the DT of a UDD is n, k are the different *sdomain* types in it and l_{ij} is the number of *i*-domains in the *j*-path, $1 \leq i \leq k$, then the number of required G^r_tree dimensions to index a UDD is

$$\sum_{i=1}^{k} \max_{j=1,..,n} l_{ij} \qquad (1)$$

We examine the insertion of the clause of the udd_ex. The first argument (atom) corresponds to the third dimension, which has the same type. Likewise, the second argument corresponds to the first dimension and the last argument to the fourth. The second dimension takes the default value that is not necessary to be stored in the CA due to the existence of *PIs*. The clause is stored as '1,1,2 (atm1,9,atm2)'.

The retrieval procedure is analogous to the insertion one, e.g., the goal

```
?- pr(a(e(X),f(s(8),l(atm3)))).
```

triggers a search for clauses with *PI* = 2,1,1 and data (_,8,atm3). When a query does not have an explicit functor declaration, it is replaced with the set of goals that corresponds to the paths of the DT, e.g., the query

```
?- pr(a(X,w(7))).
```

is analyzed into the pr(a(d(Y),w(7)) and pr(a(e(Y),w(7)). The first corresponds to clauses with *PI* = 1,2 and data (_,7), whilst the second to clauses with *PI* = 2,2 and data (_,7). Answers that have the form X=d(atm4) or X=e(9).

Indexing the head of rules is achieved by inserting them into the G'_trees. In order to do that, PerKMan relates the declaration of variables in rules head to the lower values of their domains. For integer and real numbers, 'lower' means the minimum value that the variable could have, e.g., for integer it is -2147483647. For atoms, the 'lower' is NULL. Lower values are reserved by the manager and cannot be regarded as data. For example, to retrieve rules with head gp(X,Y) the index is searched for the partition where the entry gp(NULL,-2147483647) belongs (X stands for atoms and Y for integers). The clauses block of this partition is accessed and rules like the gp(X,Y):-sp(_,X,Y),Y<10 are found where they exist. Rules in secondary storage are interpreted after their retrieval; that is, no compilation is needed at run time. Non-ground facts are treated as rules, e.g., the gp(_,20) is indexed as gp(NULL,20). The lower values of *cdomains* are constructed from the lower values of the *sdomains* that reside in the leaf nodes of their DT.

In each recursive step of a rule application, PerKMan retrieves the first block that includes at least one matching clause. The first matching clause is used for the next step. Backtracking uses the second matching clause from the buffer and so on until all the matching clauses are exhausted. Then, a second matching block comes into main memory. We do not support the presentation of answers according to the insertion order of clauses in order to avoid additional cost.

3.3   Clauses Area

CA includes the clauses of all persistent predicates. Each block in it is composed of a header, a Clause Allocation Table (CAT), the clause declarations and the free space.

The header includes control information, the amount of free space, the number of clauses in the block (*NBC*) and one pointer that connects blocks in case of overflow. A block may overflow when its clauses have their arguments that participate in the index identical. This means that the block cannot be split. This may occur when the index includes only attributes that do not identify its predicate, or there are many rules with variables in the same indexing arguments. The size of a clause cannot be larger than the size of its block. A CAT contains *NBC*+1 pointers. The first *NBC* pointers indicate the beginning of clauses whereas the last one indicates the end of the last clause. The use of CAT is necessary due to the variable length of clauses.

4   Experimental Results

In this Section we provide experimental results on the performance of PerKMan and compare them to the corresponding performance of ECL^iPS^e.

ECL^iPS^e is a Prolog-based system, whose aim is to provide a platform for integrating various extensions of logic programming. One of these extensions is the persistent storage of clauses through the DataBase (DB) and the Knowledge Base (KB) module [3]. The BANG file [5], a variant of the BD-tree, is used in both modules to index on the attributes that the user indicates. The DB module does not manipulate rules and non-ground facts, and attributes of type term cannot be included in the index. The KB module supports the persistent storage of any clause. The KB version is less efficient than the DB version and the second should be preferred when possible. None of the modules supports the coexistence of DB and KB relations.

The statistics of ECL^iPS^e inform us about the size of the page buffer area for the DB handling, the pages of the relations that are currently in buffers, the real I/O and buffer access. This allows a comparison between the access efficiency of ECL^iPS^e and PerKMan, on the base of disk reads. We present experiments with four dimensions, all included in the index and attribute size of 4 bytes. We used 8 Kbytes page size because this is the default for the BANG file in ECL^iPS^e. The data followed the normal distribution with mean value 0 and variation $5*10^6$. We chose to present our experiments with data following the normal distribution because as well as the fact that this distribution is common in real world measurements, it approximates many other distributions well. We used non-duplicate facts. Their range was $[10^5, 2*10^6]$ and the step of increment 10^5. Similar experiments with other distributions showed that results depend very slightly upon the nature of the distribution from which the data is drawn. Our implementation was made in C and the performance comparison on a SUN Ultra 5/10 under SunOS 5.6.

Figure 4 shows the total insertion time in minutes versus the number of facts. We repeated the insertion procedure three times in a dedicated machine. We present the average insertion times. The insertion time of PerKMan is linear and becomes lower than the one of ECL^iPS^e in a volume of $2*10^6$ facts.

Figure 5 shows the space requirements of the two systems in Mbytes compared with the number of facts. We present the total storage space, as ECL^iPS^e does not inform us about the storage space of index and data separately. As shown in this figure, PerKMan needs much smaller storage space than ECL^iPS^e to organize its data.

The following results correspond to the average disk block accesses using 100 queries of the same type. The queries are taken uniformly from the insertion file. That is, the constant values of a partial match query over a file of NC clauses were taken from the places $j*\lfloor NC/100 \rfloor$, $1 \leq j \leq 100$, of the insertion file.

Figure 6 shows that the two systems need the same number of disk accesses for exact match queries. Figures 7, 8 and 9 concern partial match queries with one, two and three variables, respectively. They show that the disk accesses required by PerKMan are fewer than the ones required by ECL^iPS^e. For PerKMan there are two curves that represent the number of accesses to find the first and all matching facts. ECL^iPS^e statistics give us the same number of accesses for both cases. In some steps of these figures we observe some decrements in the number of disk accesses, despite the corresponding increment in the number of data. This is justified by the fact that

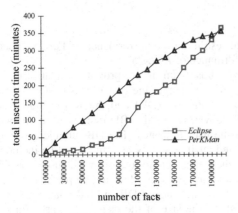

Fig. 3. Total insertion time.

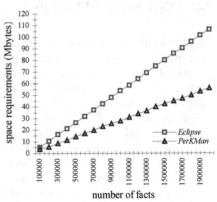

Fig. 4. Space requirements.

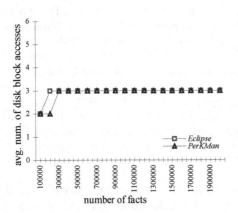

Fig. 5. Average number of accesses per exact match query.

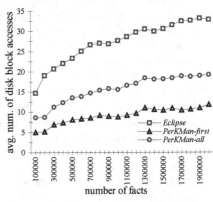

Fig. 6. Average number of accesses per partial match query of one variable.

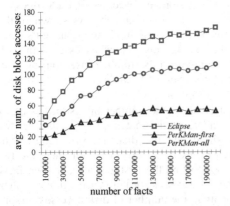

Fig. 7. Average number of accesses per partial match query of two variables.

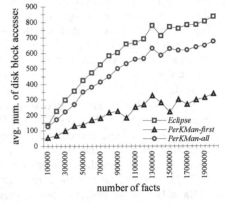

Fig. 8. Average number of accesses per partial match query of three variables.

queries were taken uniformly from the insertion file and, consequently, the queried facts were not the same for all steps.

5   Summary

The increasing need for large knowledge bases and efficient handling of ad hoc queries implies the adoption of effective data structures. We presented PerKMan, a storage manager that may be connected to Prolog systems that offer an external C language interface. PerKMan handles facts and rules uniformly and allows different arguments of a predicate to share an index dimension in a novel manner. It indexes compound terms efficiently and its data structures are not only independent of the data distribution, but also adapts well to dynamic large volumes of clauses. From the performance of PerKMan, we believe that it achieves its design motivation, which is to handle efficiently large quantities of persistent knowledge.

Planned research work includes sophisticated methods that relate rules to data on a scheme that is based on the distribution of query types.

References

1. Cruickshank, G.: Persistent Storage Interface for Prolog – TERMdb, System Documentation. Draft Revision:1.5, Cray Systems (1994)
2. Derr, M.A., Morishita, S., Phipps, G.: The Glue-Nail Deductive Database System: Design, Implementation, and Evaluation. The VLDB Journal, vol.3, no.2 (1994) 123-160
3. ECL^{i}PS^e 3.7: Knowledge Base User Manual. ECRC GmbH (1998)
4. Van Emde Boas, G., Van Emde Boas, P.: Storing and evaluating Horn-clause rules in a relational database. IBM J Res.Develop. vol. 30, no. 1 (1986) 80-92
5. Freeston, M.: The BANG file: a new kind of grid file. Proc. of ACM, SIGMOD Conf. (1987) 260-269
6. Ioannidis, Y.E., Tsangaris, M.: The Design, Implementation, and Performance Evaluation of BERMUDA. IEEE Trans. on Knowledge and Data Eng., vol. 6, no. 1 (1994) 38-56
7. Kapopoulos D.G., Hatzopoulos, M.: The G^r_Tree: The Use of Active Regions in G-Trees. In: J.Eder, I. Rozman and T. Welzer (eds.): Advances in Databases and Information Systems. Lecture Notes in Computer Science, vol. 1691. Springer-Verlag, (1999) 141-155
8. Kumar, A.: G-Tree: A New Data Structure for Organizing Multidimensional Data. IEEE, Trans. on Knowledge and Data Eng., vol. 6, no. 2 (1994) 341-347
9. Nilsson, H., Ellemtel, A.: The External Storage Facility in SICStus Prolog. R:91:13, Swedish Institute of Computer Science (1995)
10. Ramakrishnan, R., Srivastava, D., Sudarshan, S., Seshadri, P.: The CORAL Deductive System. The VLDB Journal, vol.3, no.2 (1994) 161-210
11. Ramamohanarao, K., Shepherd, J., Balbin, I., Port, G., Naish, L., Thom, J., Zobel, J., Dart, P.: The NU-Prolog deductive database system. In: Gray, P.M.D., Lucas, R.J. (eds.): Prolog and Databases. West Sussex, Ellis Horwood limited (1988) 212-250
12. Sagonas, K., Swift, T., Warren, D.S.: XSB as an Efficient Deductive Database Engine. Proc. of ACM SIGMOD Conf. (1994) 442-453
13. Vaghani, J., Ramamohanarao, K., Kemp, D.B., Somogyi, Z., Stuckey, P.J., Leask T.S., Harland, J.: The Aditi Deductive Database System. The VLDB Journal, vol.3, no.2 (1994) 245-288

A Timeout-Based Mobile Transaction Commitment Protocol

Vijay Kumar*

Computer Science Telecommunications
University of Missouri-Kansas City
Kansas City, MO 64110, U.S.A.
kumar@cstp.umkc.edu
Phone: (816) 235 2366. FAX: (816) 235 5159.

Abstract. We investigate transaction commit in Mobile Database Systems (MDS) and develop a commitment protocol based on "timeout" approach. Timeout approach is universally used to reach a decision as a last option in all message oriented systems. With this approach we have minimized the use of wireless message cost in commiting transactions.

1 Introduction

Mobile Database Systems (MDS) offers a connectivity mode, which we refer to as *mobile connectivity*. Two parameters define *mobile connectivity*, (a) geographical (spatial) mobility of the processing node and (b) wireless channel for communication among nodes. Spatial mobility allows a processing unit (mobile unit, e.g., a laptop), to roam around in the space even when it is processing data or actively communicating with other nodes. The wireless channel provides communication capability, which is not subjected to spatial and temporal constraints. Due to some practical limitations (hardware characteristics, channel capacity, etc.), the extent of their freedom may be affected, however, they do not alter the definition of *mobile connectivity*. Thus, *The mobile connectivity between two nodes exists if they are continuously connected through wireless channel, and can utilize the channel without being subjected to spatial and temporal constraints.*

2 Mobile Database System (MDS)

The architecture of our MDS is shown in Figure 1. We have added Database Servers (DBS) to incorporate database processing capability without affecting any aspect of the generic mobile network [1]. The entire platform is comparable to a distributed multidatabase systems.

We make the following assumptions about the functionality of DBSs and *MUs*: (a) A DBS is an independent data processing node on the wired network,

* This research was supported by a grant from National Science Foundation under grant number IRI-9979453.

J. Štuller et al. (Eds.): ADBIS-DASFAA 2000, LNCS 1884, pp. 339–345, 2000.

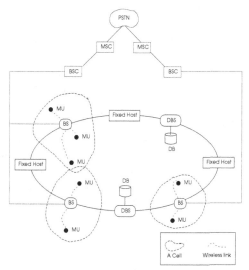

Fig. 1. A general architecture of MDS

(b) A DBS provides full database services and it communicates with *MUs* only through *BS*, (c) Transactions may originate at a DBS or they may come to DBS from *MUs* through *BSs*, (d) Each *MU* caches some portion of the database and has some database functionality, and (e) A *MU* can go into a doze mode anytime during the execution of its transaction.

We present a commit protocol for MDS where (a) Transaction commitment uses least number of messages, (b) Every processing unit (*MU* and DBS) has more or less independent decision making capability, and (c) The commit protocol is *non blocking* [3].

3   Mobile Transaction and System Components

In this section we first define a number of essential components and present assumptions for developing our algorithms.

Definition 1. *A Mobile Transaction* $T_i = \{e_i1, \ e_i2 \ ... \ e_in\}$, *where each* e_ij *is an "execution fragment" [2]. Henceforth, we drop the second subscript of* e_ij *and add only when it is necessary.*

Although $e_i's$ of T_i are semantically related, each can commit independently leading to the commit of the T_i. It is also possible to "rectify" individual $e_i's$ if T_i could not be committed. We identify the following components of MDS: (a) **Home Mobile Unit (H-MU):** A *H-MU* is the MU where T_i originates or is requested, (b) **Home Cell:** The cell where *H-MU* of T_i initially registered, and (c) **Home Base Station (H-BS):** A *H-BS* of a *MU* is the *BS* where the *MU* initially registers.

3.1   Transaction Processing Scenarios

In MDS (a) T_i originates at *H-MU* and entirely completes its execution there. The *H-MU* does not move during the execution of T_i, (b) T_i originates at *H-MU* and entirely completes its execution there, (c) a *MU* does not receive any transaction which originates at a different *MU* or at a DBS, and (d) A T_i originates at *H-MU* and cannot be executed entirely at this node so it is sent to *H-BS* of the *MU*. If necessary, *H-BS* fragments T_i, identifies a set DBSs and sends $e_i's$ and to relevant DBSs and possibly to *H-MU* for execution. At the end of the commit, the result is sent to *H-MU* through *H-BS* to be delivered to the user who initiated T_i.

We identify *BS* to serve as a coordinator. In Figure 2a *BS1* is statically identified as the coordinator and it remains the coordinator even if *MU*, which is processing an e_i moves to cell $C2$. In Figure 2b the role of coordinator is changed from *BS1* to *BS2* when *MU* moved to $C2$.

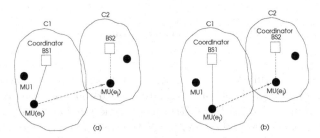

Fig. 2. Change of coordinator due to mobility

Definition 2. *A commit set of a T_i is a set of DBS and H-MU, which take part in the processing and commit of T_i. A DBS is identified as a static member and the MU is a mobile member of a commit set.*

When a *MU* moves to another cell, then during registration it informs the *BS* (next possible coordinator) about its last coordinator and sends other relevant information (Figure 2b).

3.2   Characteristics of Our Protocol

We have used the "timeout" approach in our protocol for declaring and accepting a decision from a processing unit (*BS* and *MU*). A "timeout" is a duration within which an operation is said or assumed to be completed. In distributed database systems the use of timeout is necessary for developing "non-blocking" transaction commit protocol [3]. It is well known that finding the most appropriate value of a timeout is not always easy but, we can safely assume that it can be precisely defined if a large number of system characteristics are taken into consideration [3].

3.3   Types of Timeout

We define two types of timeout: (a) *Execution Timeout* (E_t) and (b) *Update Shipping Timeout* (S_t).

Execution timeout E_t: A timeout value within which a node of a commit set completes the execution of e_i. It is an upper bound of the time a DBS or a *MU* requires to execute e_i. Thus, the coordinator assumes that a *MU* or a DBS will finish its e_i in E_t. The value of E_t may depend on the size of e_i and the characteristics of the processing unit. We identify *MU* timeout by *Et(MU)* and DBS timeout by *Et(DBS)*. The relationship between these two timeouts is *Et(MU) = Et(DBS)* + Δ. The Δ accounts for the characteristics such as poor in resources, disconnected state, availability of wireless channel, etc. The value of a timeout for a *MU* depends on its characteristics, thus, $Et(MU_i)$ may not be equal to $Et(MU_j)$, $(i \neq j)$. It is possible that a *MU* may take less time than its E_t to commit its e_i.

Shipping timeout S_t: Defines the upper bound of the data shipping time from *MU* to DBS. In E_t, the cached copy of the data is updated at the *MU*. To maintain the global consistency all data updates done by an *MU* must be shipped and installed at the database at DBS. Thus, at the end of E_t the coordinator expects the updates to be shipped to the correct DBS and logged there within S_t.

3.4   Transaction Roll-Back and Abort

If a *MU* fails to commit its e_i, then it is rolled back. To remove the effect of a committed e_i from the local cache, we propose the concept of "rectifying" transaction. Figure 3 illustrates the relationship among E_t, S_t, abort, and rectification. After S_t an *MU* can make data items available to other transactions. This means that after S_t an e_i can only be rectified.

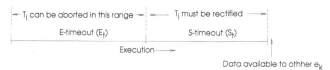

Fig. 3. Relationship between E_t and S_t, abort, and rectification

4   TCOT: Transaction Commit on Timeout Protocol

We refer to our protocol as "TCOT" in this paper. Unlike 2PC or 3PC [3], TCOT instead of sending enquiry or vote messages sits, tight and let things happen. Thus every members waits for the timeout to expire and then takes necessary action.

A coordinator can decide not to commit a T_i (a) before the expiration of $ct(MU)$, or (b) after the expiration of $ct(MU)$, or (c) after it has received updates from all members of the commit set. In case (a) the coordinator will force a rollback (abort) of T_i, but in case (b) and (c) it will force a rectification.

When T_i arrives at $H\text{-}MU$, then it may or may not be processed at $H\text{-}MU$ entirely or partially in which case it will be into execution fragment. A T_i can be fragmented at the $H\text{-}MU$ or at the $H\text{-}BS$. We investigate the performance of both options. However, for explaining TCOT we assume that T_i is fragmented at $H\text{-}BS$.

We assume that there is no failure of any kind and list the necessary steps of our protocol.

4.1 Steps of TCOT with No Handoff and No Failure

- T_i arrives at $H\text{-}MU$. $H\text{-}MU$ extracts its e_i from T_i, computes its E_t, and sends $T_i - e_i$ to the coordinator along with E_t of e_i.
- The coordinator splits $T_i - e_i$ into e_j's ($i \neq j$) and assigns them to a subset of DBSs. The assignment of e_i and e_j's creates the commit set of T_i. The coordinator, then composes a message for each e_i, which we refer to as *assignment* and sends it to each member along with their fragment (Figure 4).
- The coordinator sends *assignments* to all members of the commit set through which each member knows its E_t, identity of other members of the commit set, and the identity of the current coordinator.

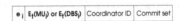

Fig. 4. Assignment from the coordinator to an MU

- The member of the commit set of T_i begins processing their fragments.
- $H\text{-}MU$ updates its cache copy of the database and executes its e_i in $Et(MU)$. Similarly, DBSs processes its e_i. A DBS does not ship updates to the coordinator but sends a "commit message" at the end of $Et(DBS)$. This does not mean that T_i is committed.
- The $H\text{-}MU$ ships its updates to the coordinator within S_t. The coordinator forwards the updates from $H\text{-}MU$ to the right DBS, which are logged there.
- At the end of S_t, $H\text{-}MU$ makes data items available to other T_i's.
- End of commit of T_i.

4.2 Steps of TCOT with No Handoff and with Failure

In the above case we assumed no failure of any kind. Every member of the commit set was free to execute and complete its e_i within the assigned timeouts. In the following scenario, we introduce failure of a fragment.

- A T_i arrives at *H-MU*. *H-MU* extracts its e_i from T_i, computes its E_t, and sends $T_i - e_i$ to the coordinator along with $E - T$ of e_i.
- The coordinator splits $T_i - e_i$ into e_j's and assigns them to a subset of DBSs.
- The coordinator waits until *Et(DBS)* has expired. If a DBS cannot commit its fragments for any reason, then it sends an abort message to the coordinator within *Et(DBS)*. As soon as the coordinator receives an abort message from any DBS, it sends abort to all members of the commit set, except the members who sent abort messages to the coordinator.
- If a DBS successfully finishes its *Et(DBS)*, then it sends a commit message to the coordinator.
- If the coordinator does not receive any abort message from any DBS, then it waits until S_t of *H-MU* has expired. If the coordinator does not receive the updates from *H-MU* by the end of S_t, then it aborts T_i and sends abort message to all members of the commit set. Some members have to undo their $e_i's$ and some have to rectify their e_i's.
- If the *H-MU* receives an abort message from the coordinator before the end of *Et(MU)*, then it aborts its e_i. If it receives the abort message after *Et(MU)* has expired, then it rectifies its e_i.
- If *H-MU* decides to abort its e_i for some reason, then it sends an abort message to the coordinator within *Et(MU)*. If *H-MU* realizes that it cannot process and commit its e_i within *Et(MU)*, then either (a) it sends an abort message to the coordinator, or (b) increases its *Et(MU)* value and sends it to the coordinator. The coordinator has two options: (a) accept the new timeout for this *MU* and delay the declaration of commit of T_i, or (b) abort T_i. Similarly, if a DBS decides that it cannot commit its e_i in *Et(DBS)*, then it also uses the above two options.
- If the coordinator decides to abort, then it sends an abort message to the commit set.
- When the coordinator receives an abort message from any member of the commit set, it notifies all other members about T_i's abort and every member aborts their e_i's. Some *MU*s might have committed their e_is, in which case they rectify.
- If the coordinator has received updates from *H-MU*, then it declares commit of T_i.

4.3   Steps of TCOT with Handoff and Failure

We do not repeat the common steps of other scenario. We begin from the point where *H-MU* and other members of the commit set have their fragments. We describe the case where coordinator changes dynamically.

- *H-MU* migrates, say from cell C1 to cell C2. Suppose there is a change in the coordinator. During the registration process *H-MU* sends to the new *BS* the *assignment* it received from the initial coordinator. The new coordinator learns the identity of the initial coordinator and about the commit set from the *assignment*. The new coordinator informs all members of the commit set about the change in the coordinator. It prepares a new *assignment* and sends it to all members of the commit set. ¿From this point onward other steps are identical to the failure case.

5 Proof of Correctness

We want to establish that a commit decision of a coordinator is "correct", that is, the decision to commit is unanimous. Let us assume that the coordinator decides to commit T_i when at least one member of the commit set is undecided. This is possible only if the coordinator declares commit before the expiration of either S_t or $Et(DBS)$. This, however, will be the violation of the protocol, which will not happen. Further, suppose that a member of the commit set failed and could not recover before the S_t expired or the commit message is not received by the coordinator. In this situation the coordinator will not receive updates from at least one member of the commit set and will abort T_i.

Since our algorithm is based on timeout, it is not possible that at any stage the coordinator will enter into an infinite wait. We, therefore, establish that a commit decision is correct and the wait is bounded. □

6 Conclusion

We have used timeout approach to develop a transaction commit protocol for MDS. In our approach instead of communicating with mobile units to know their progress in processing transactions (as in 2PC), we set a timeout for the completion of the assigned task. If a processing unit was unable to process its fragment within the timeout, then it has an option of asking for more time or abort the operation. This required only one message in committing a transaction.

References

1. M. H. Dunham and A. Helal, Mobile Computing and Databases: Anything New? *SIGMOD Record*, December 1995, Vol 24, No. 4, pp. 5-9.
2. V. Kumar and M. Dunham, Defining Location Data Dependency, Transaction Mobility and Commitment, Technical Report 98-cse-1, Southern Methodist University, Feb. 98.
3. Bernstein, P. A., Hadzilacos, V., and Goodman, N. Concurrency Control and Recovery in Database Systems. Addison-Wesley, 1987.

Flexible Integration of Optimistic and Pessimistic Concurrency Control in Mobile Environments*

Kaleem A. Momin and K. Vidyasankar

Department of Computer Science
Memorial University of Newfoundland
St. John's, Newfoundland, Canada, A1B 3X5
(momin, vidya)@cs.mun.ca

Abstract. Limited execution capability, weak connections with the fixed network, frequent disconnections, and mobility dictate naturally an optimistic mode for transaction execution at mobile hosts (MH): the relevant computation is performed at MHs with cached data to provide quick response to the user, but the execution is validated against concurrent transactions and ACID properties maintained at the fixed network. Some of the proposals in the literature to reduce the likelihood of invalidation and thus increase the meaningfulness of computation at MH are: (i) If the validation fails, the transaction could be re-executed and accepted even when the results differ from the original ones but within certain limits; (ii) Validation/re-execution idea can be extended to several intermediate stages and the computation at MH adjusted with respect to changes in the database state at the fixed network. In this paper, we strengthen the computation at MH further by facilitating partial guarantee against invalidation. This is accomplished by switching the computation to a pessimistic mode. Varying degrees of pessimism are provided. They balance the guarantee against its effect on other transactions' executions.

Keywords: Mobile computing, Transaction processing, Concurrency control, Re-execution, Pessimistic mode.

1   Introduction

The architecture of a general mobile database system [1,2,4,9] consists of a static backbone network called the *fixed network*, a *wireless network*, *mobile hosts* and *mobile support stations*. A host that can move freely while retaining its network connection through the wireless network is a *mobile host* (MH). A *mobile support station* (MSS) is a host that is connected to the static network through wired communication links, and augmented with a wireless interface for MHs to interact with the static network. Each MSS's wireless interface has a geographical

---

*   This research is supported in part by the Natural Sciences and Engineering Research Council of Canada Individual Research Grant OGP0003182.

J. Štuller et al. (Eds.): ADBIS-DASFAA 2000, LNCS 1884, pp. 346–353, 2000.

coverage area called a *logical cell*. At any moment, an MH can only be in one cell and directly communicate with only one MSS. Wireless networks are more expensive, offer less bandwidth, and are less reliable than wired networks [9]. An MH may be connected to different networks, at different times, with varying degrees of bandwidth and reliability. The weakest connection, of course, is disconnection. Disconnection here implies a voluntary disconnection and not a failure.

Mobility, low bandwidth and frequent disconnections pose new problems in the processing of transactions on the MHs. The model advocated in the literature [8] is keeping the required data locally in a cache and executing the transactions in MH, and delegating the task of committing the transactions to the MSS. If the transaction aborts, then the cache can be updated and the transaction re-executed in the MH. In this approach, we are moving the expensive part of the transaction processing (for example, concurrency control) to the static portion of the network, where communication is an order of magnitude cheaper. Then, the primary purpose of transaction execution at the MHs is to minimize the response time to users [8].

The above model suggests naturally an optimistic scheme of execution. Optimistic concurrency control [5] necessitates validation of the transaction steps, that were executed at MH, at MSS with respect to the current data values and other transactions validated thus far. If the cached values had not changed in the fixed network, then validation will be successful. If the values did change, then the transaction has to be aborted. For this case, Gray et al. [3] have proposed re-execution of the transaction at MSS, instead of simply aborting the transaction. The transactions (or steps) executed in the cached data in MHs are referred to as *tentative transactions*, and they are re-executed on the MSS as *base transactions*. As long as the results of the re-execution at MSS satisfy certain *acceptance criteria* the execution is considered successful [3]. If the acceptance criteria are not met, then the user is consulted for possible abort or reconciliation.

In [6], we proposed *to extend the re-execution idea to various intermediate stages of execution of a transaction* at MH. At every stage (for example, at reconnection points), *all the steps* which have been executed at MH thus far are validated, and, if the validation fails, re-executed at MSS, and the results are checked against the acceptance criteria. Thus the transaction execution at MH is *adjusted* to the database state in the MSS. We also argued that validation need not be done with respect to the entire read set of the transaction, but with respect to only relevant data which may be a subset of the read set. This further increases the possibility of successful validation. Despite frequent validations and re-executions along the way, transactions could still be aborted when they come for commitment. That is, the MH's computation is not guaranteed to commit in spite of frequent adjustments. If at some stage at least some guarantee can be given, the utility of the computation at MH can be enhanced.

In this paper, we aim to provide such guarantee. It is obvious that providing any guarantee involves some kind of 'locking' or pessimistic approach; and this will restrict or delay other (conflicting) transactions' executions. These effects are significant in mobile environments since MHs (holding locks) may be disconnected from the fixed network for long, unpredictable, durations. We accommodate this problem in two ways: (i) varying degrees of pessimism are allowed and (ii) a timeout period is associated with each pessimistic access. Several factors may determine both the degree of pessimism and the duration of the timeouts. The degrees of pessimism are those introduced in [10]; here they are tailored to the mobile environment. They reflect conflict-level integration of optimistic and pessimistic concurrency control. The timeout period is the estimated time interval within which the transaction is expected to commit. If the commitment does not occur (for example, the MH does not reconnect) within that period, then the pessimistic access is switched to optimistic one.

We describe the features of the integrated concurrency control method in section 2, and the new model for transaction execution in mobile environments in section 3. Section 4 concludes the paper.

2   Integrated Concurrency Control Method

Two transactions are said to be *conflicting* if the write set of one intersects with either the read set (RW-conflict), or the write set (WW-conflict) of the other. The main concern of the concurrency control mechanism is to correctly process conflicting transactions. The *capability structure* described below not only achieves this but also provides the MH's user with the flexibility of switching the transaction execution between optimistic and pessimistic modes at any stage.

A transaction that wants to read (write) a data item must first obtain a *read (write) capability* (permit to access) for that data item. The capabilities may have *priority* or *no_priority* with respect to conflicts. Priorities provide pessimistic access to data items and no_priorities optimistic access. Therefore, we have (i) two types of read capabilities, P_RW and NP_RW indicating priority or no_priority with respect to RW-conflicts, and (ii) four types of write capabilities, (P_RW P_WW), (P_RW NP_WW), (NP_RW P_WW), (NP_RW NP_WW), for the two options for the two types of conflicts. Priority with respect to a conflict facilitates automatic validation with respect to that conflict in the validation phase. That is, a P_RW read capability for data item x guarantees that at the time of validation no other transaction would have modified the value of x. A (P_RW NP_WW) write capability for x implies guarantee and hence no waiting against concurrent transactions reading x, but no guarantee and therefore waiting until concurrent transactions writing x finish commitment (or abort). A (NP_RW P_WW) write capability for x implies waiting until all transactions with P_RW read capability for x finish but no waiting against transactions writing x. The (P_RW P_WW) and (NP_RW NP_WW) write capabilities are to be interpreted similarly.

The capabilities are granted according to the compatibility matrix given in the Figure 1. The conditional 'Y', 'Y^1', represents concurrent write capabilities with priorities allowed by the application. The number of such capabilities may be decided by MSS based on the maximum number of transactions holding the writes on x, the user, or the time at which the request is made. When concurrent write capabilities with priorities are not allowed, 'Y^1' is replaced by 'N'. We note that an NP_RW read capability for x can be issued to T_i irrespective of any other transaction T_j holding any capability for x. That is, data item x can be allowed access in both modes P_RW and NP_RW by different transactions at the same time.

		READS		WRITES			
		P_RW	NP_RW	P_RW P_WW	NP_RW P_WW	P_RW NP_WW	NP_RW NP_WW
R E A D S	P_RW	Y	Y	N	Y	N	Y
	NP_RW	Y	Y	Y	Y	Y	Y
W R I T E S	P_RW P_WW	N	Y	Y^1	Y^1	Y	Y
	NP_RW P_WW	Y	Y	Y^1	Y^1	Y	Y
	P_RW NP_WW	N	Y	Y	Y	Y	Y
	NP_RW NP_WW	Y	Y	Y	Y	Y	Y

Fig. 1. Compatibility Matrix

The transaction processing in an MH can be considered to consist of five (not necessarily distinct) phases:

1. **Request and acquisition of capabilities:** A transaction must acquire the respective read or write capabilities before performing the operations. *If a request for a capability cannot be granted right away, the respective optimistic read and write capabilities are granted as default* and the transaction allowed to proceed in an optimistic fashion. The capabilities are acquired based on the rules in the compatibility matrix. (We note from the compatibility matrix that (i) the optimistic capabilities, read in NP_RW mode and write in (NP_RW, NP_WW) mode, can always be granted, and (ii) whether a nonoptimistic capability can be granted or not does not depend on optimistic capabilities currently issued for the same data items to other transactions.) Some of the capabilities may get revoked due to timeout periods or commitment of other transactions. These capabilities are re-obtained and steps re-executed.
2. **Execution:** Each MH is provided with a *private workspace* on the MSS. All the MH's tentative transaction writes are done first in this private work space, and only after successful final validation they are done in the data-

base itself. The private workspace also holds relevant information about the transaction's execution.

3. **Final validation:** The final validation is different from the intermediate validations during the transaction execution in our model. Final validation can be thought of as conversion of the capabilities into pessimistic capabilities, that is, read (shared) and write (exclusive) locks. This is the "locking" phase.

4. **Write phase:** Writes are transferred from the private workspace to the database after successful final validation.

5. **Release of capabilities:** All the capabilities held by the transaction are released simultaneously after the write phase or the abortion of the transaction. This is the "unlocking" phase.

3   Transaction Execution Model

The transactions submitted by the user on the MH may be either *interactive* or *non-interactive*. A non-interactive transaction is submitted as a single request message by the user, whereas an interactive transaction is submitted as multiple request messages or *steps*. Each step may consist of one single operation (e.g., read/write) or a group of operations. For simplicity of exposition, we assume the submission of a single interactive transaction to the MH in the following. We also assume, in this paper, that the MH remains in the same cell during the execution of the transaction.

By default, the transactions are granted no_priority capabilities in MH. Specific pessimistic capabilities are requested during reconnection with MSS. The MSS issues the capabilities to MH's transactions based on the capability structure described above. Some capabilities may be granted right away. Some others may be issued only in subsequent reconnections. Timeout periods are introduced for capabilities with priorities to safeguard against the 'number of disconnections' and 'periods of disconnections'. Once the timeout period expires, the MSS can revoke the capability. Timeout periods could be based on the application, the time at which the priorities are made, or some tariffs (user may be charged according to the timeout period). The MSS keeps track of the data items read (written), capabilities held, transaction steps executed so far, etc., both for recovery purposes and management of capabilities while MH is disconnected.

The following is a brief description of the mobile transaction processing algorithm. A more detailed version appears in [7].

The MSS maintains a workspace with the following information for each MH: requested capabilities set, granted capabilities set, revoked capabilities set, base steps, and affected steps (steps affected due to revoked capabilities). In addition to this, the MSS also keeps the process image containing the current values of the program counter, registers and variables of the program under execution. The MSS also maintains, for each data item, the capabilities given to different transactions.

In addition to the process image, the MH maintains the following information: granted capabilities set, requested capabilities set, requested cache, capabilities not required by the transaction any longer (due to irrelevant data read), base steps (executed so far by the transaction as well as in the current period of disconnection), and deleted steps (due to irrelevant data read).

3.1   Disconnection

1. a) Just before disconnecting from the MSS, the MH caches the data required to execute transactions in disconnected mode. The granted capabilities on data items for the transaction are maintained both on the MH and the MSS.

    b) While being disconnected, the MH
       - executes the (tentative) steps of the transactions.
       - stores the requested data items (along with capability requests) to be cached at the time of next reconnection.
       - creates the respective base steps with an acceptance criteria and stores them.
       - before every step, deletes any previous operations or steps which become irrelevant. These are logged on the MH so as to revoke the respective capabilities held by the transaction on the MSS.
       - if the transaction is executed to completion in the disconnected mode, records this fact.

2. a) When the MH disconnects from the MSS, the MSS stores the requested capabilities set, granted capabilities set, base steps, and current process image of the transaction in the workspace of the MH. The first three sets will be empty at the beginning of a transaction.

    b) While the MH remains disconnected, the MSS
       - tries to obtain the read and write capabilities for the transaction which were not granted at the time of last reconnection, indicated by a non-empty requested capability set.
       - keeps track of capabilities that were granted but later revoked in the revoked capability set along with the affected steps.

3.2   Reconnection

1. When the MH connects to the MSS:
    a) The MH sends the requested capabilities set, requested data items, capabilities and steps not required any more, new steps executed in the last disconnection period, the process image, along with any input parameters to the MSS and waits for the validation and, if necessary, re-execution of the base steps on the MSS.
    b) If the transaction execution can continue, then it accepts from the MSS the process image after the transaction steps were re-executed on the MSS, cache updates (correction of data items on cache), updated set of granted capabilities for the transaction and new data to continue execution of the transaction in disconnected mode.

2. When the MSS is contacted by the MH:
   a) The MSS accepts the requested capabilities set, requested data items, capabilities and steps no longer needed by the transaction, base steps of tentative steps executed so far, the process image, any input parameters given by the user on the MH, and acceptance criteria, if any, and updates requested capabilities, revoked capabilities, granted capabilities, base steps, affected steps accordingly.
   b) The MSS checks the revoked capability set. If it is not empty, the affected steps are re-executed and if the acceptance criteria are not satisfied then it aborts the transaction or consults the user for possible reconciliation, e.g., for new acceptance criteria. If the requested capabilities cannot be granted in the reconnection period, the transaction is allowed default (optimistic) read and write capabilities. If the revoked capability set is empty or re-execution results are acceptable, the transaction execution can continue. If the transaction execution is complete, then the final validation is done.

3.3   Final Validation, Write Phase, and Release of Capabilities

Each transaction on completion of its execution must be validated. Here the validation is different from the intermediate validations during the transaction execution. The final validation can be thought of as conversion of capabilities into 'read' (shared) and 'write locks' (exclusive locks).

We assume that the final validation phase, write phase and release of capabilities are all done in the critical section. The validation procedure is as follows:

1. Validation of read capabilities for data item x involves the following:
   a) if capability held is in P_RW mode, validation is automatic.
   b) if capability is in NP_RW mode, wait until no other transaction holds a write in P_RW modes; while waiting, the capability may be revoked, as stated below.
2. Validation of write capability for data item x involves the following:
   a) if capability is in (P_RW P_WW) mode, validation is automatic.
   b) if capability is in (P_RW NP_WW) mode, wait until no other transaction holds a write capability on x in P_WW mode.
   c) if capability is in (NP_RW P_WW) mode, wait until no other transaction has read capability on x in P_RW mode.
   d) if capability is in (NP_RW NP_WW) mode, wait until no other transaction has read capability in P_RW mode or write capability in P_RW or P_WW mode.

If all capabilities have been validated, that is, all 'locks' are obtained by T_i: (i) Do the write phase. That is, the values written by the transaction are transferred from its private workspace to its database; (ii) Invalidate the NP_RW mode read capabilities held by other transactions on the data items that were modified by T_i; (iii) Commit the transaction; and (iv) Release all the capabilities (locks).

The point at which all the locks are obtained is the 'lock point', and the lock point order is the effective serialization order of transactions. This follows from the basic two phase locking protocol which ensures serializability. Deadlocks may occur when transactions are waiting for priority capabilities or locks held by the others to be released. We can use timeout mechanism to handle deadlocks also. The timeout periods, for this purpose, can be either always fixed or based on the number of data items accessed by the transaction, the number of capabilities held by the transaction, etc.

4   Conclusion

In this paper, we have presented a flexible concurrency control scheme integrating optimistic and pessimistic approaches to access the data items based on RW- and WW-conflicts for mobile environments. Issues relating to providing (partial) guarantees, like capability granting, revoking, timeout period management, etc., can be delegated completely to the MSS. The MH's role could be restricted to simply requesting "some" guarantees of the execution thus far. In fact, even this task could be given to the MSS, keeping the capability mechanism completely transparent from the MH. Thus, our proposal can be implemented with very little overhead on the MH, adhering to the philosophy that the primary goal of transaction execution at MH is to provide quick response to the user, and the other aspects of transaction processing are to be done in the MSS.

References

1. R. Alonso and H. F. Korth 1993. Database System Issues in Nomadic Computing, SIGMOD 5:388-392.
2. D. Barbara and T. Imielinski 1994. Sleepers and Workaholics: Caching Strategies in Mobile Environments, SIGMOD 5:1-12.
3. J. Gray, P. Helland, P. O'Neil and D. Shasha 1996. The Dangers of Replication and a Solution, Proc. SIGMOD, 173-182.
4. H. Koch, L. Krombholz and O. Theel 1993. A Brief Introduction into the World of 'Mobile Computing', Tech. Report, University of Darmstadt, THD-BS-1993-03.
5. H. T. Kung and J. T. Robinson 1981. On Optimistic Methods for Concurrency Control, ACM TODS, 6(2):213-226.
6. K. A. Momin and K. Vidyasankar 1998. A Model for Transaction Execution in Mobile Environments, Proc. Intl. Conf. on Information Technology, India, 162-167.
7. K. A. Momin 1999. A Transaction Execution Model for Mobile Computing Environments, Master's Thesis, Memorial University of Newfoundland, Canada.
8. V. R. Narasayya 1993. Distributed Transactions in a Mobile Computing System, Technical Report, University of Washington.
9. E. Pitoura and G. Samaras 1998. Data Management for Mobile Computing, Kluwer Academic Publishers.
10. K. Vidyasankar and V. V. Raghavan 1985. Highly Flexible Integration of the Locking and the Optimistic Approaches of Concurrency Control, Proc. 9th COMPSAC, 489-494.

An Analysis of Alternative Methods for Storing Semistructured Data in Relations*

Igor Nekrestyanov, Boris Novikov, and Ekaterina Pavlova

University of St. Petersburg, Russia
{igor,katya}@meta.math.spbu.ru, borisnov@acm.org

Abstract. Although the major source of semistructured data is WWW and therefore the representation of data cannot be controlled by any single site, in many cases the data are replicated and stored locally in a database to support sophisticated query processing.
To date a number of approaches to store data in relations were proposed. In this paper we present an analysis of alternative mapping schemes.

1 Introduction

In recent years there has been an increased interest in managing semistructured data. One of most popular data models for semistructured data is OEM [1], that is based on labeled directed graphs.

The XML is emerging as standard to exchange semistructured data. To retrieve data from semistructured sources a number of novel query languages for semistructured data and XML were proposed [2].

There are several possible approaches to store semi-structured data and to execute queries against them:

Special-purpose DBMS Such systems are particularly tailored to store and retrieve semistructured data, using specially designed structures and indices [8,10] and particular query optimization techniques [9,7]. Examples are Strudel, Lore [1].

OODBMS In this approach, the rich data modeling capabilities of object-oriented database systems are exploited. Processing of SGML documents using OODBMS was discussed in [3]. The conclusion was that this is feasible with some extensions to OO query languages.

RDBMS In this approach semistructured data are mapped into tables of a relational scheme and queries in a semistructured query language are translated into SQL queries [14,4].

It is still unclear which way will find wide-spread acceptance. While special-purpose approach will clearly work it is going to take a long time before such systems will mature. The downside of using semi-structured techniques is that this

---

* This work was supported in part by RFBR (grant 98-01-00436) and INTAS (grant OPEN-97-11109).

J. Štuller et al. (Eds.): ADBIS-DASFAA 2000, LNCS 1884, pp. 354–361, 2000.

approach turns it back on 20 years work invested in relational and object-oriented database technology. Therefore, usage of relational [14,6], object-oriented [3,13] and object-relational [15] databases for storage of semistructured data recently attracted attention.

In this work we focus on relational model. A number of methods to store semistructured data in relations were discussed [4,6,14]. The crucial decision here is to select relational scheme to represent semistructured data.

One approach is to use basic, universal mapping schemes of generic directed labeled graph to relations [6]. Alternative is to use schemes which are tailored for semistructured data instance. The scheme extraction as cost-optimization problem was discussed in [4]. It is also possible to type semistructured data [16, 11] and store objects of each type in separate table.

In the frame of this work we evaluate several techniques to store semistructured data in relations. We show that for some access patterns the approaches based on scheme extraction are preferable than universal graph mappings. We also compare several algorithms in terms of quality of extracted scheme.

Rest of the paper is organized as follows: we briefly review methods in the next section and further discuss them in section 3; section 4 contains results of our experiments; we describe related works in section 5 and conclude.

2   Mapping Schemes

2.1   Universal Mapping Schemes

Universal mapping schemes are schemes which can be used to store generic labeled directed graph, i. e. they are applicable to storage of any semistructured data. We will consider only several representatives of universal schemes [6]:

Edge All data are stored in single table of triples (*source*, *label*, *target*) describing edges of the graph.

Attribute A separate table for each existing *label* is created. Table consists of pairs of (*source*, *target*) form describing edges.

Wide According to this approach all data are represented by single table whose columns correspond to all labels found in the graph. Conceptually, this table corresponds to result of an outer join of all *Attribute* tables.

2.2   Extracted Schemes

Extracted schemes are schemes which are tailored for specific semistructured data instance. Note, that such scheme may not cover all data. However, it is always lossless: parts of the semistructured data that do not fit the scheme are stored in an "overflow" graph that is stored as table of triples (*source*, *label*, *target*) describing graph edges. In this work we consider following approaches:

STORED The technique for generation of relational storage mappings given semistructured data instance was proposed in [4]. Effectiveness of mapping is determined by several competing goals. These goals are modeled as cost-optimization problem. Considered storage-cost function take into account such parameters as number of tables, disk space, number of nulls, etc.

The problem of computing an optimal storage mapping is *NP-hard* in size of *data*. Therefore, authors consider heuristics, starting from frequent tree patterns in the data discovered by adopted version of WL's data mining algorithm [16]. To reduce complexity only relatively often used paths are considered during data mining step.

Jump An algorithm for deriving approximate type hierarchy from semistructured data was proposed in [11]. Proposed technique is based on the relative importance of some attributes in a larger set that is measured by *Jump* function. Given a set of labels S it is defined as follows

$$Jump(S) = \frac{|\{o : attributes(o) = S\}|}{|\{o : attributes(o) \supseteq S\}|}$$

where *attributes(o)* is a set of labels on the outgoing edges at object *o*.

Datalog Approximate typing of semistructured data using Datalog was described in [12]. Typing is in the form of a monadic datalog program with each intensional predicate defining separate type.

The minimal perfect typing is performed using greatest fixpoint semantics of monadic datalog programs. Adopted k-clustering algorithm is used to collapse 'similar' types. The clustering is based on weighted symmetric difference between the bodies of their rule definitions.

Note, that *Jump* and *Datalog* do not produce relational scheme explicitly. Straightforward solution is to store objects of the same type in the same table.

3   Comparative Analysis

3.1   Comparison of Schema Generation Methods

Comparison (see table 3.1 for summary) is based on following criteria:

Support for Cycles This is essential for real-world data. Indeed, OEM graph of many Web-documents is cyclic.

Support for Multiple Outgoing Edges with Same Label Multiple edges with same label conceptually are represented by set-valued attributes which are not directly supported by relational databases. Solution is either use several attributes in relation or use nested relation.

Unnesting Objects with similar deep structure are unnested: only values of their leaves need to be stored in relations.

Computational Complexity In this case complexity usually depends on size of *data n* that might be very big.

STORED expects that cycles are cut in some arbitrary, but systematic way. This is not only affects resulted scheme but also causes new untyped references

Table 1. Methods comparison

Criteria	STORED	Jump	Datalog
Cycles in the Data	no	yes	yes
Multiple Outgoing Edges with Dame Label	both	nested tables	nested tables
Unnesting	yes	no	no
Computational Complexity[1]	$O(c^m)$	$O(n^2)$	$O(n^2)$

to be introduced. Note that untyped references cannot be handled in relational systems without proliferation of joins — for each possible reference type [14].

Usage of only nested relations for representation of multiple outgoing edges with label seems to be not so serious limitation because usage of data clustering techniques significantly decreases expenses of extra join.

3.2 Query Optimization

Access Patterns The performance of a data structures depends heavily on access patterns used to process these data, and data representation is always defined with certain access pattern types in mind. Of course, the access patterns may depend on logical structure of dataset.

For any query the amount of extracted data is restricted in two ways: conditions on attribute values, or selection predicates, or logical location of data, or paths. For example, in SQL query the selection predicate is placed in WHERE clause, while path is specified in FROM clause.

An important feature of query languages for semistructured data is that complex path expressions may be included into any part of a query, specifying navigation through the graph. The mapping of such path expressions to any relational representation contains several join operations and therefore may significantly slow down the evaluation of a query.

Completely different type of access pattern can be found for such data sets as, for example, DBLP bibliography collection, which is used as a common test data set for research in semistructured data. In this, relatively large dataset, the graph representing data in semistructured model, is essentially a tree with 3 levels. A typical meaningful query should restrict the result, using predicates on attribute values, rather than complex path expressions.

Obviously, the performance of any particular relational representation depends on which of access patterns dominates in typical queries.

Universal vs Derived from Data Approaches In general, it should be expected that any universal representation is less efficient than one based on derived data structure. Further, we expect that *Edge* representation might be more efficient than *Wide* representation for queries where navigation dominates. We verify these hypotheses in our performance experiments.

Although other research reports *Edge* representation as relatively efficient (e.g. for bulk loads and reconstruction of the whole graph as a document) [6],

Table 2. Dataset's summary information

	DBLP	DBLP-small	Shakespeare	CyclicDataset
Real-world	yes	yes	yes	no
Have cycles?	no	no	no	yes
Number of edges	1900k	90k	330k	30k
Maximum path length	3	3	7	—

it cannot be efficient for more complex or more selective queries, because both navigation and predicate checking require several joins of this table to itself to be performed.

The *Attribute* approach was reported as best [6]. However we feel it may be efficient for navigation but not conditions on attribute values. The reason is that the while size of joined tables is significantly less than in *Edge* representation, but the number of joins is the same.

The *Wide* approach seems especially suitable for selection based on attribute values. The advantage of this representation is that attribute columns may be indexed to ensure very efficient query evaluation by relational engine. The disadvantages are large number of NULL values and huge size of the table.

Deriving scheme from the data allows to reduce the number of NULLs as well as overall size of database. Most likely, the best results can be achieved if both approaches are combined — regular parts of the data are stored according to derived scheme and universal mapping is used for "overflow" (that is, exceptions).

4   Experiments

4.1   Test Datasets

DBLP[2] This is the collection of XML-like files with bibliography data. Data is quite irregular: some entries have multiple author's. optional url's, etc.

DBLP-small This is the subset of DBLP in which the numbers of *conf's* and *journal's* entries were limited by 3000. These two kinds of entities are dominating in the DBLP dataset and this cause other kinds of entities to be considered as random irregularity.

Shakespeare[3] This is the set of plays of Shakespeare marked up in XML. Note, that it has deepest tree structure among considered datasets.

CyclicDataset This is synthetic dataset that has cycles in the data. Usage of synthetic data is attractive for our purposes because we are able to measure the effect of various perturbations of the data on the extracted scheme.

4.2   Scheme Quality

We measure scheme quality in terms of number of generated tables, coverage, number of null values, overall size and scheme generation time. Results of experiments for two datasets are summarized in the table 4.2. For other datasets

Table 3. Experimental results for DBLP and DBLP-small

	DBLP			DBLP-small		
	STORED	Jump	Datalog	STORED	Jump	Datalog
Number of tables	4	18	40	7	12	25
Coverage	90%	91%	70%	90%	88%	72%
Number of Nulls	70k	196k	65k	10k	19,5k	14k
Overall size (Mb)	67	72	69	3,2	3,5	3,4
Schema generation time	24 h	8 min	40 min	90 min	2 min	15 min

the situation is essentially the same with two notes: all methods perform worse on *CyclicDataset* and scheme extraction with STORED for *Shakespeare* dataset took more than 60 hours.

While STORED is specially designed to solve scheme generation problem (unlike both other approaches) it has a number of weak sides. One of the most important is very high complexity of data-mining steps that forces exclusion of rarely used paths from the consideration. While this probably does not reduce coverage too much it does not look like a best idea. For example, for DBLP dataset this implies that only information about *conf* and *journal* entities will be stored in typed tables and other information will be in "overflow". However this information actually consists of fairly regular subsets, such as *books*, and is preserved by both other approaches.

Quality of results *Datalog* approach was not as good as we expected but this seems crucially depend on distance function used on the clustering stage.

It's interesting what simple *Jump* approach shows results comparable to results of much more sophisticated (and computationally expensive) STORED technique. However, we do not feel that this is absolutely best approach to use because it did not perform well in some cases.

4.3   Query Performance

The experiments with relational database engine included several steps. Most of these steps were measured for two datasets: DBLP and DBLP-small.

For each dataset, both *Edge* and *Wide* representations were created in the database. In addition, some of *derived* representations were created as projections of universal representations. Two sets of queries, parametrized with values in selection predicates, were used: simple queries, such as "list table of contents for particular journal issue", and more complex queries involving several joins. All queries return small amount of data (up to few hundreds of rows).

The first measured step was bulk load of data into database. The typical results are shown in the table 4.3. To improve performance, indices were always built after initial bulk load as a separate step. The time of full scan on these tables ranges from sub-second time for small dataset to 14 and 24 seconds for different representations of the full collection.

Table 4. Typical results of bulkloading experiments

Dataset	Mapping Scheme	Dataset size (Mb)	Load time	Table size (Mb)
DBLP-small	*Edge*	2.79	44 sec	5.8
DBLP	*Edge*	60.8	25 min	106
DBLP-small	*Wide*	4.51	77 sec	9.7
DBLP	*Wide*	110.3	39 min	181

Table 5. Typical query performance for DBLP dataset

Query	*Wide*	*Edge*	*Attribute*	*Derived*
Simple	1.4 – 2.9	5.2 – 19.8	2.7 – 10.1	0.5 – 1.1
Complex	15.9 – 27.3	5.7 – 23.6	4.1 – 16.8	10.3 – 21.8

The time needed for query evaluation varied dramatically depending on physical structure (indices and clustering of tables). Without additional tuning of physical structure, even simple queries took unacceptably long time for any of representations (see table 4.3). If indices for all columns are built, the *Wide* representation clearly outperforms *Edge* representation.

For complex queries, the performance is slightly better for *Edge* representations, due to smaller size of tables. The *Attribute* and *Derived* representations are better than *Edge* and *Wide*, respectively.

5   Related Work

Usage of several universal mapping schemes of XML data to relational databases was studied in [6]. Performance experiments analyzed the space requirements, the bulkloading times, the running time to reconstruct XML document, the running times of series of queries and update functions for each mapping scheme. Results show that an *Edge* approach is the best overall approach. Our work consider a more sophisticated scheme mappings which are derived from the data.

Virtues and limitation of relational model for processing queries over XML dataset conforming to a scheme were studied in [14]. Results show that it is possible to handle most of queries on XML documents using RDBMS, barring certain type of complex recursion. Authors suggest some extension to relational systems that will improve efficiency of handling XML queries. However, they assumed that all documents conform to some scheme (in form of DTD). Unlike them we consider the situation when nothing about the data is known a-priori.

The problems of dynamic exporting XML data from relational databases are addressed in [5]. Proposed approach is to use virtual XML views on relational data and to automatically rewrite queries on XML data into relational queries. This work is related because they consider evaluation of semistructured queries over relational database. However it is quite different from the focus of our work because it considers relational data with predefined scheme.

6 Conclusion

In this paper we analyzed and compared several different approaches of storing semistructured data in relational database.

The comparison of structure extraction methods shows that sophisticated and time-consuming methods often cannot produce much better structure that more straightforward ones.

Further, the performance of actual representation depends on the contents of data and access patterns. There is no representation which outperforms other for all datasets and/or all access patterns.

For relatively small datasets with path-oriented access, an *Edge* representations are probably best, but for large collections and queries with low selectivity more traditional representation based on derived types provide best performance.

References

1. S. Abiteboul, D. Quass, J. McHugh, J. Widom, and J. Wiener. The Lorel query language for semistructured data. *Journal on Digital Libraries*, 1:68–88, Apr. 1997.
2. A. Bonifati and S. Ceri. Comparative Analysis of Five XML Query Languages. *SIGMOD Record*, 29(1), Mar. 2000.
3. V. Christophides, S. Abiteboul, S. Cluet, and M. Scholl. From Structured Documents to Novel Query Facilities. In *Proc. of the SIGMOD'94*, 1994.
4. A. Deutsch, M. Fernandez, and D. Suciu. Storing semistructured data with STORED. In *Proc. of the ACM SIGMOD'99*, June 1999.
5. M. Fernandez, W.-C. Tan, and D. Suciu. SilkRoute: Trading between Relations and XML. Nov. 1999.
6. D. Florescu and D. Kossmann. A Performance Evaluation of Alternative Mapping Schemes for Storing XML Data in a Relational Database. In *Proc. of the VLDB'99*.
7. D. Florescu, A. Levy, I. Manolescu, and D. Suciu. Query Optimization in the Presence of Limited Access Patterns. In *Proc. of the ACM SIGMOD'99*, 1999.
8. R. Goldman and J. Widom. Approximate DataGuides. In *Proc. of the VLDB'97*.
9. J. McHugh and J. Widom. Query Optimization for XML. In *Proc. of the VLDB'99*, pages 315–326, Sept. 1999.
10. T. Milo and D. Suciu. Index Structures for Path Expressions. In *Proc. of the International Conference on Database Theory*, 1999.
11. S. Nesterov, S. Abiteboul, and R. Motwani. Inferring Structure in Semistructured Data. In *Proc. of the Workshop on Management of Semistructured data*, 1997.
12. S. Nesterov, S. Abiteboul, and R. Motwani. Extracting Schema from Semistructured data. In *Proc. of the ACM SIGMOD'98*, pages 295–306, 1998.
13. D.-Y. Seo, K.-M. Lee, and J.-Y. Lee. Discovery of Schema Information from the forest of Selectively Labeled Ordered Trees. In *Proc. of the Workshop on Management of Semistructured Data*, May 1997.
14. J. Shanmugasundaram, K. Tufte, C. Zhang, G. He, D. J. DeWitt, and J. F. Naughton. Relational Databases for Querying XML Documents: Limitations and Opportunities. In *Proc. of the VLDB'99*, pages 302–314, Sept. 1999.
15. T. Shimura, M. Yoshikawa, and S. Uemura. Storage and Retrieval of XML Documents using Object-Relational Databases. In *Proc. of the DEXA'99*, 1999.
16. K. Wang and H. Lui. Discovering Typical Structures of Documents: A Road Map Approach. In *Proc. of the SIGIR'98*, 1998.

Main-Memory Management in Temporal Object Database Systems

Kjetil Nørvåg

Department of Computer and Information Science
Norwegian University of Science and Technology
7491 Trondheim, Norway
noervaag@idi.ntnu.no

Abstract. In this paper, we describe main-memory management and the most important buffers in the Vagabond server, a transaction-time temporal object database system currently under development at the Norwegian University of Science and Technology. Special emphasis is given to fine granularity buffering of OID index entries and objects.

1 Introduction

In a transaction-time temporal object database system (TODB), every object update creates a new object version that has to be stored. In an object database system (ODB), an object is uniquely identified by a logical object identifier (OID), and an OID index (OIDX) is used to map from the OID to the physical location of an object. The entries in the OIDX, the *object descriptors* (OD)s, contain administrative information, including information to do the mapping from logical OID to physical address. In a TODB, we use one OD for each object version, and the OD also contains the timestamp of the transaction that created the particular version.

An important difference between OIDX management in non-temporal and temporal ODBs, is that with only one version of an object (non-temporal), the OIDX needs only to be updated when an object is created. This can be done efficiently as an efficient append-only operation if a multiway tree index is used. However, in a TODB the OIDX has to be updated every time an object is updated: an object update creates a new object version, without deleting the previous version, and a new OD for the new object version has to be inserted into the OIDX. In order to reduce disk I/O, the most recently used *index pages* are kept in an *index page buffer*. OIDX pages will in general have low locality, and in order to increase the probability of finding a certain OD needed for a mapping from OID to physical address, it is also possible to keep the most recently used *index entries* (the ODs) in a separate *OD cache*, as is done in the Shore ODB [2]. With low locality on index pages, a separate OD cache utilizes memory better, space is not wasted on large pages where only small parts of them will be used. In non-temporal ODBs, an OD cache is only useful as a read buffer, because the OIDX update cost is low anyway (it is updated append-only). In a TODB, on

J. Štuller et al. (Eds.): ADBIS-DASFAA 2000, LNCS 1884, pp. 362–370, 2000.

the other hand, individual entries are to be inserted into the OIDX. In order to make it possible to do the installation of ODs into the OIDX asynchronously, we also store these new ODs in the OD cache. At commit time, the new ODs are written to the log, and are inserted lazily into the OIDX later. By doing it this way, we increase the probability of having more than one entry for each index page that is updated. This significantly reduces the OIDX update cost.

In this paper, we describe the main memory buffers to be used in Vagabond [4], a TODB currently under development at the Norwegian University of Science and Technology. Special emphasis is given to the OD cache, small object buffer, and the OIDX page buffers. The organization of the rest of the paper is as follows. In Sect. 2 we give an overview of related work. In Sect. 3 we give an overview of Vagabond. In Sect. 4, 5, and 6 we describe the OD cache, the small object buffer, OIDX and subobject index buffers. Finally, in Sect. 7, we conclude the paper.

2   Related Work

In the area of transaction-time temporal object database systems, we are only aware of one prototype, the POST/C++ temporal object store [7], which is based on the Texas persistent store. In POST/C++, objects are indexed with physical OIDs (addresses in a persistent memory space), and a new object is created to hold the previous version when an object is updated. To be able to access the historical versions, a separate B+-tree based history index is used. This index uses the OID of the current version object, concatenated with time, as the index key. There is no object buffering, and no index entry buffering. There have also been prototypes implemented on top of non-temporal ODBs, for example by Steiner and Norrie [6] which implemented a temporal ODB on top of O_2.

3   An Overview of Vagabond

In this section we provide a brief overview of the most important aspects of Vagabond in order to set the work reported in this paper into context. For more comprehensive overview and references, we refer to [4].

Server Architecture. A Vagabond server is an object server, and objects are the unit of transfer between the server and the clients. Vagabond is based on a peer-to-peer server architecture, similar to the Shore project [1]. All application programs (AP) in the system are connected to *one server* running. This server is the gateway to the database system, including remote servers.

Object Storage. Object storage in Vagabond is based on the log-only approach, in contrast to most current database systems where data is updated

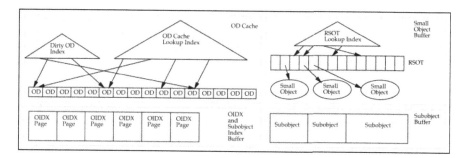

Fig. 1. Important memory buffers.

in-place (cf. the paper *Design issues in transaction-time temporal object database system* in this proceedings for more details about log-only storage).

In Vagabond, all objects smaller than a certain threshold , e.g. 64 KB, are written as one contiguous object. They are not segmented into pages as is done in other systems. However, objects larger than this threshold are segmented into *subobjects*, and a *large object index* is maintained for each large object. When a large object is updated, only the modified subobjects have to be written. The subobject threshold and the subobject size can be set independently for different object classes. This is useful because different object classes can have different object retrieval characteristics. To reduce the storage space and disk bandwidth, objects can be compressed before they are written. With the log-only approach, objects are written to a new location every time, so that *we only use as much disk space as the size of the current version written.*

Main Memory Buffers. We will in the following sections describe the most important main memory buffers in Vagabond, as illustrated in Fig. 1: 1) OD cache, 2) small object buffer, and 3) large granularity buffers (for subobjects, OIDX-, and subobject index pages).

4   Object Descriptor Cache

As described previously, an OD cache is used to reduce the OIDX access costs, and reduces lookup costs as well as index update costs. ODs retrieved from lookups in the OIDX are inserted into the OD cache when retrieved, and new ODs resulting from object updates are inserted into the OD cache. However, new ODs from new objects are not initially inserted into the OD cache, they are written directly to the OIDX.

Designing an efficient OD cache is not straightforward. The requirements and functionality of the OD cache require a careful design. The entries in the OD cache are of a fine granularity, which means that additional overhead data can have a larger impact on performance than it would have in a page buffer, where the additional overhead usually is very small compared to the buffered items themselves. We will now describe operations the OD cache has to support, study some aspects of the writeback of ODs to the OIDX, and then describe the architecture of the OD cache.

OD Cache Operations. The OD cache has to support the following operations:

- `lookup_current(OID)` Returns the OD of the current version of the object if the OD is in the OD cache.
- `lookup_most_recent(OID)` Returns the most recent OD that is resident in the OD cache.
- `lookup_at(OID,TIME)` Returns the OD of the object version valid at `TIME` if the OD is in the OD cache.
- `lookup_start(OID,TIME)` Returns the OD of the object version that has start time (commit time) `TIME` if the OD is in the OD cache.
- `lookup_end(OID,TIME)` Returns the OD of the object version that has an end time `TIME` if the OD is in the OD cache. The end time is equal to the start time of the next version of the object (or delete item if this was the last version before the object was deleted).
- `insert(OD)` Inserts OD into the OD cache. If this is a new current version of an object, set the end timestamp of the current version of the object if resident in the OD cache.
- `remove(OD)` Removes an OD from the OD cache.

In order to iterate through versions of an object, `lookup_at()` and subsequent `lookup_start()` operations can be used.

OD Cache-to-OIDX Writeback. Because of the size of each item in the OD cache, it is very important that when dirty[1] ODs are to be written back to the OIDX, this can be done in batch. In order to reduce the number of index pages that has to be read (installation read of OIDX pages) and written, dirty ODs are sorted so that ODs that belong to the same OIDX pages can be installed into the OIDX pages at the same time. In most cases, disk seek time will also be reduced by updating the OIDX from the list of sorted ODs. This is similar to general use of an elevator algorithm when writing back pages from a page buffer.

A complicating factor for the OD cache, is the potentially large number of entries that has to be sorted. This can be time consuming. To have a sorted list of ODs, two approaches can be used:

1. When all dirty ODs from the last dirty list have been written back to the OIDX, a new list is generated by creating an array with pointers to all

---

[1] Note that *dirty* in this context means *dirty with respect to the OIDX*, i.e., new or a modified ODs that have not yet been inserted into the OIDX. Persistent copies of the ODs have already been written together with the objects to the log.

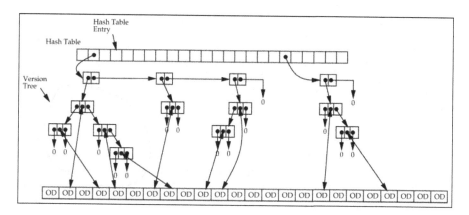

Fig. 2. The OD cache lookup index.

dirty ODs. This array is sorted, based on the OIDs, and then the ODs are asynchronously written back. The advantage with this approach, is that the extra space overhead is minimal. However, this approach has two important drawbacks:

a) ODs created after the array has been created and sorted, will have to wait until the next checkpoint interval, even if they belong to one of the OIDX pages that is retrieved and written when the array is processed.

b) The sorting of ODs can take several seconds of CPU time.

2. A *dirty OD index* with ordered elements, for example a binary tree, can be used. When a new OD is created, a pointer to the new OD is inserted into the index. During each checkpoint interval, the index is processed at least once. Because new entries are inserted immediately, we avoid the problem with the previous approach, where only ODs created during the previous checkpoint interval were available for the OD cache-to-OIDX writeback process. The disadvantage of this approach is a higher space overhead. For example, using a binary tree, two pointers are needed for each dirty OD. Note that a general priority queue is not sufficient for this index. The reason is that at some point in time, we have to be guaranteed that all entries inserted before a certain time (in this case, before the previous checkpoint interval), have been processed (in this case, before we can finish a new checkpoint).

We expect the space overhead of the dirty entry index to be compensated by increased writeback efficiency, and choose the dirty entry index approach.

OD Cache Architecture. It is possible to store *all* ODs, dirty as well as clean, in the index tree, and use the index tree as the access path for OD cache lookups as well. However, if that approach was used, we would have to scan through the whole index tree during each checkpoint interval. If most of the entries are clean, many CPU cycles will on average be needed in order to find the dirty ODs.

A better approach is to use one lookup index for all ODs in the OD cache, in addition to the dirty OD index. The lookup index is optimized for accesses to the OD of the most recent version of an object. The dirty entries are also indexed by this index, which means they are represented in both the dirty entry index and the lookup index. The reason for this is that without this redundancy, we would in many cases have to search both indexes when doing a lookup for a recent OD.

OD Cache Lookup Index. To understand the design of the OD cache index, it is important to remember that each update of an object creates a new OD. For each object, there will be one OD for each version, and more than one of these ODs can be in the OD cache at the same time. This means that even though the most frequent lookup operation is to retrieve the most recent OD of an object, it must be possible to store the other ODs in the OD cache as well, and it must be possible to retrieve these in an efficient way.

The index is based on a chained overflow hash table. The bucket to put an OD into, is chosen based on hashing the OID of the OD. In this way, all ODs of the same object (same OID) will be in the same bucket. The ODs of an object is inserted into a version tree, for example a binary tree, where time is used as the key. ODs with different OIDs can be hashed to the same bucket, and for each OID we have a separate version tree. The version trees are chained in a linear list. With an appropriate size of the hash table, the number of OIDs hashed to the same bucket should be low.

The architecture of the OD cache lookup index is illustrated in Fig. 2. Each entry in the hash table is a pointer to a list with pointers to the version trees. As can be observed, it would be possible to include the pointer to the next binary tree in the root of each version tree. In this way, we would avoid one pointer dereference. However, this is not done, because it could make some tree operations more complicated.

When choosing an appropriate version tree, the most important goals to achieve are 1) low insert cost, especially of a new current version OD, and 2) low lookup cost for the current version OD, which will be the most frequent operation. An ordinary binary tree is one possible solution. However, a problem with storing the ODs in a binary tree, is that if entries to be inserted into the tree have monotonically increasing key values, the result will be a linked list. Unfortunately, this is exactly the case when the inserts into the OD cache is ODs of new versions: The key value TIME is constantly increasing. One solution to this problem is to use a balanced tree, for example a splay-tree or a 2-3-tree. However, this increases the insert and space cost (it is possible to implement the splay tree with the same space cost as a binary tree, but this increases the access cost), and it is not certain that this approach will reduce the *average* access cost. Based on the knowledge of insert pattern and average number of versions, other heuristics can perform better, for example:

- When a new current version OD is inserted, its node is made the new root of the tree, and the current version of the tree is made the left subtree of this node. Non-current ODs are inserted into the tree following the binary tree insert algorithm. With this approach, search for the current version has a low cost.

- Another option is to keep a counter c which is increased for every insert of a new OD into the tree, and decreased for every delete from the tree (but always non-negative, i.e., if c is zero and we have a deletion, c will remain zero). If c reaches a certain threshold, the tree is reorganized and c is set to zero. Although a reorganizing approach in general is a bad idea, with higher cost than using a balanced tree, it can perform well in the OD cache if we assume that only a very few of the version trees have an insert rate that is high enough to result in reorganizations. The space overhead is low for this approach, as we only need an additional counter for each version tree.
- On average, it is even possible that a list could perform well. The problem with this approach, is the high worst case cost.[2]

OD Cache Replacement. The OD cache will only have empty slots during startup, before enough objects have been accessed to fill up the OD cache. After the cache has filled up, one of the ODs resident in the OD cache has to be discarded before a new OD can be inserted. Only non-dirty ODs (with respect to the OIDX) can be discarded, and the clock algorithm is used as an LRU approximation to decide which of the candidate ODs should be discarded. The number of dirty ODs in the OD cache should be kept relatively low, to reduce the cost when searching for a candidate OD for replacement.

5   Small Object Buffer

In Vagabond, small objects are stored and retrieved as separate entities, and an object buffer is the only reasonable choice.[3] Large objects have to be treated differently, because some of the subobject index pages and the subobjects of an object version might also be a part of other object versions. In this section aspects of the small object buffer are described, and in the next section buffering of large object subobject index pages and subobjects are described.

Modified Object Chain. For each active transaction, there is a *modified object chain*. This list contains the objects that have not yet been written to disk, but must be written before an commit operation can finish.

---

[2] Rastogi et al. used a linear list for versions of data items in the Dalí main memory storage manager [5]. However, in Dalí, versioning is only used to support transient versioning, and not to provide support for temporal data. Hence, the length of a version list will usually be short.

[3] In a temporal ODB using in-place updating for current object versions, a dual buffer consisting of a combined object and page buffer can be used. In that case, the object buffer part can be implemented like the small object buffer described here.

Small Object Buffer Architecture. For the objects in the small object buffer, a clock algorithm is used as an LRU approximation. The *resident small object table* (RSOT) is used to store administrative information on objects currently resident in the small object buffer. The access to the RSOT is through an index structure similar to the one used for lookups in the OD cache.

Although the information stored in the RSOT alternatively could be stored together with the ODs in the OD cache, the number of objects resident in memory is in general much smaller than the number of entries in the OD cache, making that approach less space efficient.

When an object is read into the buffer, its OD is removed from the OD cache, and reinserted into the OD cache when the object is discarded from the object buffer. Although this at first glance might seem to be inefficient, it simplifies the OD cache management considerably, and also has the benefit of removing interaction and synchronization between the OD cache and the small object buffer.

When a small object is retrieved, the memory location and the size of the object is inserted into the RSOT, together with the memory location and the size of the object. The reason for storing the object size in the RSOT entry, is that the object size in the OD is the size of the object while on disk. On disk the object might be compressed, and thus have a size different from the size when in main memory. Using the physical location field in the OD to store the main memory location of the object could be done to save space, but if that was done, we would have a problem when the object was discarded from the buffer. We would then have lost the log address, and the OD would have to be discarded as well. That would make it necessary to do a costly OIDX lookup the next time the object was to be accessed.

Note that when an object is updated, a new OD is created for the object. If both versions are to be stored in main memory, a new RSOT entry has to be created for the new version.

6   Large Granularity Buffers

The most frequently used subobjects and OIDX and subobject index pages, are buffered in the large granularity buffers. In Fig. 1, separate buffers are used for each of the categories, but it is possible to use a common buffer if desired. The large granularity buffers are similar to traditional disk page buffers, where an item is retrieved from disk to the buffer on demand.

7   Conclusions

In this paper, we have described the design of the main memory buffers to be used in Vagabond, and described in detail the management of fine granularity buffer items like OID index entries and small objects.

In order to make it easier for the system to adaptively change the size of the buffers with different access patterns and workload, we have also developed buffer models that can be used to decide the buffer sizes adaptively. Due to space constraints, we have not been able to include the model in this paper. However, the model and the validations are included in an extended version of this paper, available on the Web [3].

References

1. M. J. Carey et al. Shoring up persistent applications. In *Proceedings of the 1994 ACM SIGMOD Conference*, 1994.
2. M. L. McAuliffe. *Storage Management Methods for Object Database Systems*. PhD thesis, University of Wisconsin-Madison, 1997.
3. K. Nørvåg. Main-Memory Management in Temporal Object Database Systems,. Extended version of paper from *2000 ADBIS-DASFAA*, 2000. Available from http://www.idi.ntnu.no/IDT/grupper/DB-grp/tech_papers/.
4. K. Nørvåg. The Vagabond parallel temporal object-oriented database system: Versatile support for future applications. In *Proceedings of Norsk Informatikkonferanse 1999*, Trondheim, Norway, November 1999.
5. R. Rastogi, S. Seshadri, P. Bohannon, D. Leinbaugh, A. Silberschatz, and S. Sudarshan. Logical and physical versioning in main memory databases. In *Proceedings of the 23rd VLDB Conference*, 1997.
6. A. Steiner and M. C. Norrie. Implementing temporal databases in object-oriented systems. In *Proceedings of the 5th International Conference on Database Systems for Advanced Applications (DASFAA'97)*, 1997.
7. T. Suzuki and H. Kitagawa. Development and performance analysis of a temporal persistent object store POST/C++. In *Proceedings of the 7th Australasian Database Conference*, 1996.

Design Issues in Transaction-Time Temporal Object Database Systems

Kjetil Nørvåg

Department of Computer and Information Science
Norwegian University of Science and Technology
7491 Trondheim, Norway
noervaag@idi.ntnu.no

Abstract. In a transaction-time temporal object database system (ODB) an object update creates a new object version, but the old versions are still accessible. Each object version has an associated timestamp, and this versioning, related to time, is supported and maintained by the system. The system also provides support for querying the temporal data. The area of temporal ODBs is still immature, and there are many design issues that need to be solved. In this paper, we discuss some issues and possible solutions derived from the design of the Vagabond temporal ODB. This includes physical object storage, clustering of temporal objects, OID indexing, and language bindings in a temporal ODB.

1 Introduction

In a transaction-time temporal object database system (ODB), every object is associated with time, and an object can exist in several versions, each version being valid in a certain time interval. Every update creates a new object version. The new version is called the *current version*, while the previous versions are called *historical versions*. This versioning, related to time, is supported and maintained by the system. The system also provides support for querying the temporal data.

In a non-temporal ODB, space is allocated for an object when the object is created, and updates to the objects are done in-place. This implies that after an object update, the previous version of the object is not available. In an ODB, an object is uniquely identified by a logical object identifier (OID), and an OID index (OIDX) is used to map from the OID to the physical location of an object (Some systems use a physical OID, which means that the disk page of the object is given directly from the OID. However, in a temporal ODB, logical OIDs is the only reasonable alternative, because of objects being moved.) The entries in the OIDX, the *object descriptors* (ODs), contain administrative information, including information to do the mapping from logical OID to physical address. In a non-temporal ODB, the physical location of the new version is the same as the previous version, hence, the OIDX needs only to be updated when objects are created and when they are deleted. In a temporal ODB on the other hand, we have to either 1) write the new current version to a new location, or 2) copy the previous version to a new location before we update the current version in-place. In any case, we have to update the OIDX every time we update an object, and we use one OD for each object version.

J. Štuller et al. (Eds.): ADBIS-DASFAA 2000, LNCS 1884, pp. 371–378, 2000.

The area of temporal ODBs is still immature, and most of the work has been done on data models and query languages. However, designing and implementing a system is something completely different, and introduces new problems that have to be solved. In this paper, we discuss problems and possible solutions derived from the design of Vagabond, a temporal ODB currently under development at the Norwegian University of Science and Technology.

The organization of the rest of the paper is as follows. In Sect. 2 we give an overview of related work. In Sect. 3 we discuss object management issues, including object storage alternatives, OID indexing and temporal clustering and access patterns. In Sect. 4 we discuss issues related to object access and queries, including programming language bindings. In Sect. 5, we conclude the paper and outline issues for further research.

2   Related Work

Even though temporal databases have a long history, few full scale systems have been implemented. Common for most of these, is that they have only been tested on small amounts of data, which make the scalability of the systems questionable. In most of the application areas where temporal database systems are needed, scalability is an important issue, as the amount of data will be large. In the area of temporal object database systems, we are only aware of one prototype, the POST/C++ temporal object store [9], based on the Texas persistent store (see below). There have also been prototypes implemented on top of non-temporal ODBs, for example by Steiner and Norrie [8], which implemented a temporal ODB on top of O_2.

Vagabond is based on the same approach as log-structured file systems (LFS), which was introduced by Rosenblum and Ousterhout [6]. LFS has been used as the basis for two other object managers: the Texas persistent store [7], and as a part of the Grasshopper operating system[3]. Both object stores are page based, i.e., when an object has been modified, the whole page it resides on has to be written back, while Vagabond is object based.

3   Object Management Issues

In this section, we consider the physical management of objects, clustering aspects, and OID indexing.

3.1   Object Storage

A temporal database system can be implemented either through a *stratum* or an *integrated* approach. With the stratum approach, the database system is built on top of a non-temporal database system, and a layer converts temporal query language statements into conventional statements that are executed by the underlying system. Although this approach makes the introduction of temporal support into existing database systems easier, we do not see it as a long-term solution, because temporal query execution with this approach can be very costly.

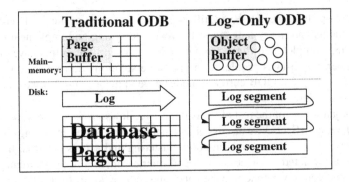

Fig. 1. In-place update page server vs. log-only object database system.

Using an integrated approach, there are several way to organize the storage of objects. We will now discuss two interesting alternatives, the *partitioned storage* approach using in-place updating, and the *log-only* approach.

Partitioned Storage. Storage of data in a temporal database system is not very different from storage of data in a traditional database system. However, because current data tend to be more frequently accessed than historical data, the database is often partitioned into a *current store* and a *history store*. The two stores can utilize different storage formats, and even reside on different storage media [1]. In this way, frequently accessed data is clustered together, stored on fast storage media, while historical versions can be stored on slower but cheaper storage media. In this way, the total storage cost is reduced, similar to the goal of general storage hierarchies.

One way to implement partitioned storage in a temporal ODB, is to store current version objects clustered together (similar to a non-temporal ODB), and write historical versions sequentially to an historical object store (for example a separate file). When an object is updated, the previous current version is copied to the history store before the new current version is update in-place. In order to be able to access the historical versions, a separate history index can be used. This index can be as simple as a B+-tree using the OID of the current version object, concatenated with time, as the index key. The leaf node entry is the OID of the current version of the object, the time interval where this version was valid, and the OID of the historical version. The location of the historical version is given through the OID in the leaf node. A variant of this approach has been used in the POST/C++ temporal object store [9].

Log-Only Storage. In most current database systems, data is updated in-place. In order to support recovery and increase performance, write ahead logging is used. This logging defers the in-place update, but sooner or later, the update has to be done. This often results in the writing of lots of small objects, creating a write bottleneck. To avoid this, another approach is to eliminate the database completely, and use a *log-only* approach, based on the same philosophy as log-structured file systems, which was introduced by Rosenblum and Ousterhout [6]. The log is written contiguously to the disk, in a no-overwrite way, in large blocks. This is done by writing many objects and index entries, possibly from many transactions, in one write operation. This gives good write performance, but possibly at the expense of read performance. Fig. 1 illustrates the most important differences between a traditional ODB, and a log-only ODB.

Using the log-only approach also gives new opportunities to improve performance. In order to reduce storage space and disk bandwidth, objects can be compressed before they are written. With the log-only approach, objects are written to a new location every time, so that *we only use as much disk space as the size of the current version written.* In a system employing in-place updating, it is difficult to benefit from object compression, because the compression ratio will be different from version to version, and it is difficult to know how much space to reserve. Another important advantage with the log-only approach is fast crash recovery. Only one pass through the log is necessary. This is very important in order to achieve high availability.

Logically, the log in a log-only system is an infinite length resource, but the physical disk size is, of course, not infinite. This problem is solved by dividing the disk into large, equal sized, physical segments. When one segment is full, writing is continued in the next available segment. As data is vacuumed, deleted or migrated to tertiary storage, old segments can be reused. Dead data, in a temporal ODB most often old index nodes, will leave behind partially filled segments, the data in these near empty segments can be collected and moved to a new segment. This process, which is called *cleaning*, makes the old segments available for reuse. By combining cleaning with reclustering, we can get well clustered segments. In a traditional system using in-place updating, keeping old versions of objects, which is required in a transaction time temporal database system, usually means that the previous version has to be copied to a new place before update. This doubles the write cost. With the log-only approach, this is not necessary. Keeping old versions comes for free, except for the extra disk space.

In a non-temporal ODB with in-place updating of objects, the OIDX needs only to be updated when objects are created, not when they are updated. In a log-only ODB, however, the OIDX needs to be updated on every object update. This might seem bad, and can indeed make it difficult to realize an efficient non-temporal ODB based on this technique. However, in the case of a *temporal* ODB, the OIDX needs to be updated on every object update also if using in-place updating, because either 1) the previous or 2) the new version must be written to a new place. Thus, when supporting temporal data management, the indexing cost is the same in these two approaches.

Previous log-only object database systems have been page server based. While this works well in many contexts, it is not ideal. By operating on page granularity, you get many of the disadvantages of traditional pager servers. For example, if clustering is bad, and only a small part of a page has been updated, it is still necessary to write back the whole page. With bad clustering, main memory buffer utilization will be bad as well. A page based log-only ODB also makes transaction management difficult. To avoid page level locking, you essentially need to have 1) a separate log anyway, or 2) use ad-hoc techniques to solve the problem. Both solutions are likely to hurt performance and increase complexity, and have convinced us that an object based log-only ODB is the way to go. One of the objections against operating on object granularity, has been that the read cost will be prohibitively high. We have recently shown that this is not necessarily true for a log-only temporal ODB, and that with the workload we expect to be typical for temporal ODBs, the log-only temporal ODB is highly competitive with the traditional approach [5]. This is the approach that will be used in the Vagabond temporal ODB. It is important to note that one of the main reasons why previous approaches to log-only systems have not been able to achieve significant speedup compared to traditional systems, is that they have not tried to benefit from the "free object versioning" feature. It should also be noted that some of the problems in previous no-overwrite database systems have been solved in the Vagabond system. For example, algorithms for steal/no-force buffer management, fuzzy checkpointing and fast commit have been developed.

3.2   Temporal Clustering and Access Patterns

The performance of page server based ODBs depend heavily on good clustering of objects, i.e., a high probability that more than one object on a disk page retrieved from the disk will be used in the near future, before the page is discarded from the buffer. A good clustering reduces the number of object pages that has to be read and written, and it also results in better buffer memory utilization. In practice, when different applications with different access patterns access the ODB, it is difficult to achieve good clustering. In a study by Tsangaris and Naughton [10], all practical clustering algorithms resulted in an average clustering less than 0.25. Although less of an issue when log-only storage is used (where we do not rely that much on clustering), writing related objects together increases the gain from prefetching and disk read ahead.

In non-temporal ODBs, clustering considers different objects, and we only try to predict cases like "when object O_i is accessed, it is also likely that object O_j will be accessed shortly after." However, it is likely that in a temporal ODB application, a good object clustering includes *historical* object versions as well as *current* object versions (after all, the reason for storing the historical object versions is that we want to access them later!). A good example that illustrates this is that in a traditional ODB without support for temporal objects, we would often simulate object versions by including timestamp as an user managed attribute in the objects, and store the objects in an object collection. With temporal support, the user will only see one object, but can access the different object versions. Thus, even if the object versions are historical versions, it is possible that some of these will be part of the hot set of object versions. As a result, possible access patterns in a temporal ODB also include cases like "if the current version of object O_i is accessed, it is also likely that all the historical versions of object O_i will be accessed in the near future" and "if the version of object O_i valid at time T_i is accessed, it is also likely that the version of object O_j valid at time T_i will be accessed in the near future." Many other access patterns exist, but this illustrates the increased complexity that is introduced in the clustering process. It also shows that partitioned storage makes clustering more difficult, there is no simple and efficient way to include historical objects in the clustering together with current objects. If log-only storage is employed, clustering of temporal objects is much easier, as it facilitates adaptive reclustering during segment cleaning.

In a traditional system, it is possible for the user or database administrator to define some clustering strategy for a database, for example by defining a clustering tree or using clustering hints. These approach can also be extended to temporal ODBs, but necessitates continuous reordering, because it is impossible to reserve space for all new versions that are created. We expect that even if these explicit clustering techniques extended with time can be used, adaptive reorganization will be even more important in future systems.

3.3   OID Indexing

In a temporal ODB, it is necessary to use logical OIDs, and an OIDX is needed to do the mapping from logical OID to physical location when retrieving an object. Such an index should have 1) support for temporal data, while still having index performance close to a non-temporal/one version database system for current version objects, 2) efficient object-relational operation, and 3) easy tertiary storage migration of partitions of the index. Achieving these goals with existing multiversion access methods, for example the TSB-tree or the R-tree, is difficult, and we have designed a new index structure that achieves these goals, the Vagabond Temporal OID Index (VTOIDX). The VTOIDX is described in more detail in [4].

4   Object Access and Queries

In non-temporal ODBMSs, ODMG's OQL or similar query languages can be used for ad-hoc queries. Similar to the way OQL is a superset of the part of standard SQL that deals with databases queries, it is possible to design a temporal OQL that is a superset of TSQL2. One such approach has been described by Fegaras and Elmasri [2]. However, one of the main advantages of ODBMSs is the avoidance of the language mismatch by providing computationally complete data manipulation languages with no mismatch between language and storage. In the ODMG standard, language bindings based on C++, Java and Smalltalk are described. Such language bindings are also needed for temporal ODBMSs. It should also be noted that in order to use methods in queries, these issues have to be resolved.

A general purpose programming language is only designed for current data. Integrating support for access of historical data into a programming language introduces a lot of interesting but difficult issues, including:

- Which object interface/signature to use when accessing an historical object version. The schema might have been changed since the historical version was created, so that the current interface to the class is different from the one previously used.
- Which method implementation to use when calling methods in historical objects. One straightforward approach is to use the implementation that was current at the same time as the actual object version was current. However, this is not necessarily what we want, if the reason for a new implementation of a method was a bug in the previous version. This problem can be solved by providing the necessary information at schema change time.
- How to integrate *time* into the syntax of the programming language.

In the rest of this section, we will discuss the integration of access to historical data into a general purpose programming language.

4.1 Temporal C++ Binding

In this section, we describe two approaches that extends the C++ language binding with support for access to historical data in a transaction-time ODBMS. The first approach is based on the language binding used in POST/C++ [9], while the second is to our knowledge new. The concepts of these approaches can also be employed for a Java language binding.

Explicit Object Version Access. The easiest way to integrate object version access into the programming language is to provide explicit access to the versions. This is the way it is done in POST/C++ [9]. Given an OID, the program can be given a pointer to an historical version valid at a particular time by calling a function `snapshot(OID,time)`. It is also possible to create iterators that can be used to navigate the versions of an object in chronological sequence.

This approach should be easy to use and understand, but if it should be possible to call a method in an historical object version that accesses other objects, the historical version must itself do the necessary operations in order to retrieve the objects valid at the same time as when the version was created.

The Explicit Snapshot Approach. A better and "cleaner" alternative than the one described above is to use explicit snapshots. Before calling a method in an historical version current at time `ts`, we set the snapshot time with a call to the function `set_snapshot(d_Timestamp ts)`. After the `set_snapshot()` function has been called, an access to a particular object will be to the object version current at time `ts`, *even though the reference is through a* `d_Ref`. A call to `set_current()` will set accesses back to normal, i.e., an access to a particular object will be to the current object version. Methods called in historical objects should in general be immutable, i.e., read-only methods. The advantage of this approach is that all object versions accessed will be object versions valid at the same time.

All access, creation, modification and deletion of persistent objects must be done within a transaction. In the ODMG C++ binding, transactions are implemented as objects of the class `d_Transaction`.

The `set_snapshot(d_Timestamp ts)` and `set_current()` functions are done in the scope of a certain transaction, so it is reasonable to extend the ordinary C++ transaction class with these methods, for example with a derived class based on `d_TTransaction`, which includes these functions as methods.

Each temporal object can be viewed as a collection of object versions. A collection interface should exist to make it possible to iterate through the object versions in a flexible way. This collection interface is also used when assigning a value to a `d_HRef` variable, i.e., assigning an object version to the `d_HRef`.

4.2 To Bind or Not to Bind?

We have now outlined how objects could be accessed through a standard language binding. It should be noted that the problems involved in this integration also can be an argument *against* doing this. It is possible that only allowing access to historical versions through a temporal query language is less error prone and more efficient than providing access through an explicit language binding. A more in-depth study of the language binding, and whether to have it at all, is interesting further work.

5   Conclusions

The area of temporal ODBs is still immature, and there are many design issues that need to be solved. In this paper, we have discussed problems and possible solutions derived from the design of Vagabond. These issues includes object storage, clustering of temporal objects, OID indexing, and language bindings.

We hope in the near future to have a prototype that can give a more final answer to the design choices, and what performance can be achieved in a system with real workloads. We also plan to study in more detail the aspects of access patterns and clustering of temporal objects.

References

1. I. Ahn and R. Snodgrass. Partitioned storage for temporal databases. *Information Systems*, 13(4), 1988.
2. L. Fegaras and R. Elmasri. A temporal object query language. In *Proceedings of the Fifth International Workshop on Temporal Representation and Reasoning*, 1998.
3. D. Hulse and A. Dearle. A log-structured persistent store. In *Proceedings of the 19th Australasian Computer Science Conference*, 1996.
4. K. Nørvåg. An efficient index structure for OID indexing in parallel temporal object-oriented database systems. Technical Report IDI 3/99, Norwegian University of Science and Technology, 1999.
5. K. Nørvåg. A performance evaluation of log-only temporal object database systems. Technical Report IDI 15/99, Norwegian University of Science and Technology, 1999.
6. M. Rosenblum and J. K. Ousterhout. The design and implementation of a log-structured file system. In *Proceedings of the Thirteenth ACM Symposium on Operating System Principles*, 1991.
7. V. Singhal, S. Kakkad, and P. Wilson. Texas: An efficient, portable persistent store. In *Proceedings of the Fifth International Workshop on Persistent Object Systems*, 1992.
8. A. Steiner and M. C. Norrie. Implementing temporal databases in object-oriented systems. In *Proceedings of the 5th International Conference on Database Systems for Advanced Applications (DASFAA'97)*, 1997.
9. T. Suzuki and H. Kitagawa. Development and performance analysis of a temporal persistent object store POST/C++. In *Proceedings of the 7th Australasian Database Conference*, 1996.
10. M. Tsangaris and J. Naughton. On the performance of object clustering techniques. In *Proceedings of SIGMOD'92*, 1992.

Mobile Transaction Management in Mobisnap*

Nuno Preguiça[1], Carlos Baquero[2], Francisco Moura[2], J. Legatheaux Martins[1],
Rui Oliveira[2], Henrique Domingos[1], J. Orlando Pereira[2], and Sérgio Duarte[1]

[1] Departamento de Informática, FCT, Universidade Nova de Lisboa,
Quinta da Torre, 2845 Monte da Caparica, Portugal,
{nmp,jalm,hj,smd}@di.fct.unl.pt
[2] Departamento de Informática, Universidade do Minho,
Largo do Paço, 4700 Braga, Portugal,
{cbm,fsm,rco,jop}@di.uminho.pt

Abstract. In this paper we describe a transaction management system designed to face the inherent characteristics of mobile environments. Mobile clients cache subsets of the database state and allow disconnected users to perform transactions independently. Transactions are specified as mobile transactional programs that are propagated and executed in the server, thus allowing the validation of transactions based on application-specific semantics. In the proposed model (as in others previously presented in literature) the final result of a transaction is only determined when the transaction is processed in the central server. Users may be notified of the results of their transactions using system support (even when they are no longer using the same application or even the same computer). Additionally, the system implements a reservation mechanism in order to guarantee the results of transactions performed in disconnected computers.

1 Introduction

Database systems designed for mobile computing must handle the inherent characteristics of those environments [10]. In particular, mobile applications have to face periods of disconnection that may arise due to economical factors, unavailable connectivity or application model. To allow mobile users to continue their work even during these periods, it is common to rely on optimistic replication techniques. In such approaches, shared data is replicated on mobile computers and users are allowed to continue their work while disconnected. Updates performed by disconnected users are logged and later propagated to servers. Several problems arise from such approaches: (1) updates performed by different disconnected users may conflict among them; (2) due to the previous problem, it is usually impossible to determine the result of an update in the mobile device; (3) mobile users may wish to perform operations over data that is not locally replicated. In this paper we present the Mobisnap [6] approach to tackle these problems in a relational database system.

---

* This work was supported in part by Praxis XXI

J. Štuller et al. (Eds.): ADBIS-DASFAA 2000, LNCS 1884, pp. 379–386, 2000.

The Mobisnap system is based on a central database server that holds the primary replica of all data items. Mobile clients replicate subsets of the database information and mobile users are allowed to update database information through the submission of "mobile transactions". These "mobile transactions" are specified in an extended subset of the PL/SQL language [8], allowing programmers to clearly state the intended semantics of each operation — pre-conditions, post-conditions and different alternatives may be defined for each transaction. The final result of a "mobile transaction" is only determined when the transaction is performed in the central database. The Mobisnap system provides linguistic and system support to allow mobile users to be notified of this final result (even when they are no longer using the same application or even the same computer).

"Mobile transactions" submitted while disconnected are tentatively applied to the local database state. The result of this local execution represents the expected final result of the transaction. However, concurrent updates performed by other users may lead to a different result when the transaction is performed in the master database. To alleviate this problem, we have designed a reservation mechanism that allows mobile clients to make reservations upon database information. Therefore, mobile clients are able to determine the result of mobile transactions that only depend on reserved information. This mechanism combines leasing [1] with an extension of, previously proposed, escrow techniques [5].

The remainder of this paper is organized as follows: Section 2 discusses the motivation and design principles; Section 3 describes the Mobisnap transactional model; Section 4 discusses related work and Section 5 concludes the paper with some final remarks.

2   Motivation and Design Principles

In this section we present the ideas that lead to the Mobisnap approach to mobile transaction processing. We illustrate the proposed mechanisms with a system intended to support salespeople. The system manages not only information about products but also the personal datebooks of sellers where product demonstrations can be scheduled by the salesperson or by the sales department. Although the presented database is very simplified, we believe that this example illustrates most of the proposed ideas. Furthermore, similar problems can be found in other applications designed for mobile environments. Details about the outlined mechanisms will be described in the next section.

2.1   Mobile Transactions should Be Conceptually Simple

In mobile computing, it is often necessary to rely on optimistic replication techniques to face disconnection: transactions are tentatively executed in mobile units and they are later validated and integrated in the master database. In Mobisnap, mobile transactions are defined in an imperative language based on PL/SQL [8], thus allowing programmers to specify the intended semantics for

```
-------------------------------- NEW ORDER -------------------------------
BEGIN
  SELECT price, stock INTO prd_price, prd_cnt FROM products WHERE name = 'BLUE THING';
  IF prd_price <= 10.00 AND prd_cnt >= 50 THEN
    -- update orders, current stock, ...
    NOTIFY( 'SMTP', 'sal-07@thingco.pt', 'Order completed ...');
    COMMIT;
  ENDIF;
  ROLLBACK;
ON ROLLBACK NOTIFY( 'SMS', '351927435456', 'Impossible order ...');
END;
-------------------------------- NEW DEMO --------------------------------
BEGIN
  SELECT count(*) INTO cnt FROM demo WHERE day='17-FEB-2000' AND hour=10;
  IF (cnt = 0) THEN
    -- update demos, send notification if appropriate, ...
    COMMIT;
  ENDIF;
  SELECT count(*) INTO cnt FROM demo WHERE day='18-FEB-2000' AND hour=9;
  IF (cnt = 0) THEN
    -- update demos, send notification if appropriate, ...
    COMMIT;
  END IF;
  ROLLBACK;
ON ROLLBACK NOTIFY( 'SMS', '351927435456', 'Impossible demo ... ');
END;
```

Fig. 1. Definition of two mobile transactions (declaration of variables is omitted).

each transaction, testing pre and post-conditions and defining possible alternatives. In the example of Figure 1 we present two mobile transactions. In the "new order" transaction the precise preconditions are tested — the customer orders some product if the price is less than a given maximum value and there are enough products in stock. There is no need that the values in the server are the same that have been seen in the mobile unit. In the "new demo" transaction two alternative schedules are checked for the request of a new demonstration. These mobile transactions are instantiated from predefined templates using the values selected by the users.

The result of a mobile transaction is completely and safely determined by the execution of the transaction program in the server. Instead of integrating mobile updates in the server relying on read/write and write/write conflicts to validate transactions, this approach allows the use of semantic information associated with the operations performed. Therefore, conflict detection and resolution can be specified in a precise and simple way in the code of the mobile transaction. The programmer can reason about the mobile transaction as a mobile program sent from the client to the server holding the primary copy and executing later on that server. We believe that this approach offers a conceptually simple model, allowing simple and powerful operation definition. We also believe that this model allows a high degree of concurrency and scalability since the asynchronous nature of the client/server interaction and the semantics of mobile transactions only require short lasting locks in the database (no "long transaction" processing is required).

2.2   Awareness Should Be a First-Class Citizen

The common client/server approach to transaction processing assumes that the user that issues a transaction is connected to the system when its execution is completed. Therefore, users can be immediately notified of the results of their transactions and may perform alternative actions if necessary — a typical example is the flight reservation system. The proposed mobile transaction model differs from this approach in a fundamental way: users may not be connected to the system when the results of their transactions are determined. Therefore, the propagation of transactions' results to the client machines is not sufficient (and it will be sometimes impossible due to the disconnection of those devices). The system should integrate a simple and clean mechanism that allows the active notification of users, to be used when it is appropriate, using the users preferred transport mechanisms – electronic mail, SMS/pager messages, ... (additionally, a pull-based mechanism should also be provided). In the examples of Figure 1 it is possible to observe the use of this mechanism in different situations and using alternative transports depending on the importance of the messages.

2.3   Guarantees Are Valuable

In the proposed mobile transaction model, as in others previously proposed in literature [11,4,2,9], the result of a transaction submitted in a mobile unit is only determined when the transaction is finally executed in the database server. However, the transaction is tentatively performed in the mobile unit to provide a hint of its final result. In some applications, the ability to provide a stronger hint about the results of transactions would be very valuable — for example, salespeople would like to immediately guarantee that they could meet customers orders. To this end, we have integrated a reservation mechanism in the Mobisnap system.

This reservation mechanism combines and extends ideas used previously in [5] (escrow techniques) and [1] (leases). We have defined four types of reservations:

Escrow It is used to divide a partitionable resource. For example, different subsets of the available instances of a given product can be reserved by different salesmen.
Slot It is used to reserve the right to insert a record with pre-defined values. For example, someone may want to reserve the right to schedule a meeting in a room in a defined period.
Value-change It is used to reserve the right to change some values in the database. For example, someone may reserve the right to change the description of some product.
Value-use It is used to reserve the right to perform transactions that use a given value for some fields. For example, a salesperson may reserve the right to sell some product for a given price, even if the price is updated.

Reservations held by mobile units are leased, i.e., limited in time, thus guaranteeing that the system will be able to use the reserved values after a limited period of time even if the mobile unit becomes permanently disconnected. However, while reservations are valid, the reserved values can not be used by any other transaction. Due to this reservation mechanism, the result of a transaction can be correctly established in the mobile unit if it only depends on reserved values (assuming that the mobile transaction can be propagated to the server before the expiration of involved reservations).

In the example presented in Figure 1, a salesman may request several reservations to be able to guarantee his decisions even while disconnected. These reservations would be granted during the period of his workday. First, he may request escrow and value-use reservations over some products to be able to guarantee orders — using both reservations he can guarantee not only that the product is available but also a given price. Second, he may request slot reservations to be able to schedule new demonstrations with the visited clients, without the danger of having multiple demonstrations scheduled for the same period of time (remember that the sales department may also schedule new demonstrations). In the next section we detail the outlined mechanism and describe the overall model for transaction processing in Mobisnap.

3   System Model

The Mobisnap system manages information structured according to the relational data model. Its architecture is based on the extended client-server model [3]. The server component is composed by a mostly connected server that holds the primary copy of all data items. The clients are devices that locally replicate a subset of the database state. They are allowed to continue their normal operation even while disconnected from the server. Clients can be mobile or stationary computers. In most situations the server will be a stationary computer but nothing prevents the server from being mobile, as long as the mostly connected assumption holds.

Clients maintain two copies of the replicated data: committed and tentative. The committed version contains data received directly from the server and it reflects a possibly outdated database state. The tentative version is based on the committed one and it reflects the execution of previously submitted mobile transactions in the client unit. While disconnected, applications may access both database versions. Applications should reflect the possible weak consistency of data to users, and they should use the tentative data version to present the expected data evolution.

When clients interact with the server to fetch data copies, they can also request data reservations. In the previous section we have already defined the different types of reservations that the Mobisnap system can handle. For each specific database, the database designer should specify the associated reservation script. This script specifies the data elements that can be reserved. For each data element, it defines the type of reservations available. In escrow reservations, it also defines the number of instances that can be reserved by each client. Finally, the reservation script specifies to whom and for how long can a reservation be granted. It should be noted that the efficiency of the reservation mechanism depends highly on the adequate definition of the above parameters for each specific system. It is also important that clients request the adequate reservations for their operation.

As usual, users manipulate the database information using applications that run on client units. These applications display data and provide operations to modify the database state through a graphical user interface. In consequence of each performed operation that modifies the database state, the application creates a mobile transaction instantiating a previously defined template with the values specified by the user. This mobile transaction program is submitted for evaluation.

If the client can communicate with the server, the mobile transaction is synchronously propagated to the server and the final result of its execution is returned to the application. If the client is disconnected, the mobile transaction is immediately executed in the client unit. The result of this execution can be one of the following:

Reservation commit. This result means that the mobile transaction code has executed successfully until a commit instruction and that all tests performed during its execution are backed up by granted reservations. This result guarantees that the transaction will commit when it is finally executed in the central server if it correctly tests all dependencies and if it is propagated to the server before the expiration of the involved reservations.

Tentative commit. This result means that the mobile transaction code has executed successfully until a commit instruction using the tentative database state. However, there is not enough reservations to guarantee that the transaction will commit when it is executed in the server.

Tentative abort. This result means that the mobile transaction code has executed until an abort instruction using the tentative database state.

Unknown. This result means that the currently cached data is not sufficient to evaluate the result of the transaction (e.g. a field or record that is referenced is not cached).

Mobile transactions are also stored by the system for later propagation to the server. By default, transactions that have been "tentatively aborted" are not uploaded. However, applications may request the propagation of all transactions. Transactions that have returned the result "reservation commit" are propagated to the server associated with references to the reservations used to guarantee them.

When the server receives a mobile transaction, it executes its transactional program. This execution may lead to the final commit or abort of the transaction. Besides propagating to users any messages defined in the mobile transaction, the server maintains a log recording the result of all executed transactions. Clients may access this log, if needed, to verify the result of any transaction. It should be noted that reserved values are not considered when transactions are processed (e.g. if for some product there are 10 instances in stock and some mobile client has reserved 4 instances, only 6 instances are available for usage by other transactions). Two exceptions exist. First, the reserved values used by a "reservation committed" transaction are used and consumed when it is executed in the server — this situation guarantees that the transaction will commit. Second, when a client synchronously submits a mobile transaction for execution, this transaction may consume any reservation held by that client.

4   Related Work

In this section we will briefly overview some of the previously proposed transaction management solutions designed for mobile environments.

In Oracle Lite [7], mobile units cache database snapshots. Transactions performed in mobile units are propagated as sets of modified values (write set/old write set values) that must be integrated in the master database. Validity of transactions is checked through conflict detection — write/write, uniqueness and delete conflicts are detected. Conflict resolution functions can be associated with different database tables (or table fields). This approach has some limitation in the use of semantic information to solve conflicts — semantic information associated with updates can not be used.

In Bayou [11], data is replicated in a group of servers that synchronize their state using epidemic techniques. Bayou updates include information to allow generic automatic conflict detection and resolution through dependency checks and merge procedures. In [2], mobile nodes may propose tentative update transactions. These transactions are propagated to base nodes, where they are reapplied to the object master copy. An acceptance rule can be specified to verify the validity of transaction execution. Invalid transactions are aborted and diagnostic messages are returned to the mobile nodes. In [9], for each transaction executed in a mobile unit, the read and write sets are stored. Additionally, each transaction must specify two functions: a conflict resolution and a cost function. These functions are used to serialize transactions in the server. The conflict resolution function is always executed in the server and it can capture not only the actions of client transactions but it can extend them to capture additional semantics on the server.

As in Mobisnap, the above approaches allow the use of semantic information associated with updates to detect and solve conflicts. However, they can not guarantee the result of updates in mobile units. To solve this problem, it has been proposed the use of escrow techniques — the idea is to divide the total number of available instances of an item among different sites and/or transactions. In [5] the authors use this idea to allow mobile units to independently guarantee the results of mobile transactions. The reservation mechanism proposed in this paper includes and extends these ideas. In [12] the authors generalize the usage of escrow techniques by exploiting object semantics. However, the proposed approach can be used only with some data types (e.g. stacks, sets) and it is more adequate to object oriented databases.

5 Final Remarks

In this paper, we have presented the Mobisnap mobile transaction management model. In this model, mobile transactions performed by applications are defined in a language based in PL/SQL. These "transaction programs" are propagated and executed in the server, thus allowing the validation of transaction execution based on application-specific semantics. As mobile users may not be connected to the system when the final result of a transaction is determined and therefore they can not immediately perform alternative actions if it aborts, these programs may contain a set of alternative actions to be executed depending on the database state. Moreover, our model provides explicit mechanisms to provide awareness information to mobile users.

One important aspect of our model is the reservation mechanism. It allows mobile units to guarantee, in some circumstances, that mobile transactions will commit. We propose the definition of several types of reservations. The interested reader can obtain more information about the Mobisnap project, including an extended version of this paper that includes the system design used to implement the proposed model, from [6].

References

1. Gray, C., Cheriton, D.: Leases: an efficient fault-tolerant mechanism for distributed file cache consistency. In *Proceedings of the 12th ACM Symposium on Operating Systems Principles*, 1989.
2. Gray, J., Helland, P., O'Neil, P., Shasha, D.: The dangers of replication and a solution. In *Proceedings of the ACM SIGMOD'96*, 1996.
3. Jing, J., Helal, A., Elmagarmid, A.: Client-server computing in mobile environments. ACM *Computing Surveys*, 1999.
4. Joseph, A., DeLespinasse, A., Tauber, J., Gifford, D., Kaashoek, M.: Rover: A Toolkit for Mobile Information Access. In *Proceedings of the 15th ACM Symposium on Operating Systems Principles*, 1995.
5. Krishnakumar, N., Jain, R.: Escrow techniques for mobile sales and inventory applications. *Wireless Networks*, 3, 1997.
6. http://gsd.di.uminho.pt/mobisnap
7. Oracle.: Oracle8i Lite replication Guide - release 4.0. 1999.
8. Oracle.: PL/SQL User's guide and reference - release 8.0. June 1997.
9. Phatak, S., Badrinath, B.: Multiversion reconciliation for mobile databases. In *Proceedings of ICDE'99*, 1999.
10. Satyanarayanan, M.: Fundamental Challenges in Mobile Computing. In *Proceedings of the 15th ACM Symposia on Principles of Distributed Computing*, 1996.
11. Terry, D., Theimer, M., Petersen, K., Demers, A., Spreitzer, M., Hauser, C.: Managing Update Conflicts in Bayou, a Weakly Connected Replicated Storage System. In *Proceedings of the 15th ACM Symposium on Operating Systems Principles*, 1995.
12. Walborn, G., Chrysanthis, P.: Supporting semantics-based transaction processing in mobile database systems. In *Proceedings of the 14th Symposium on Reliable Database Systems*, 1995.

How to Manage Evolution in OODB?

Dalila Tamzalit and Mourad Oussalah

IRIN, 2, rue de la Houssinière, BP 92208 44322 Nantes cedex 03, FRANCE
{Dalila.Tamzalit, Mourad.Oussalah}@irin.univ-nantes.fr

Abstract. We propose to face unpredicted requirements within OODB evolution problematic. We point to a designer having to cope with important and bulky OODB. We propose a simulation tool to help him to express new changes not directly on classes but on involved instances. The idea is to help him by proposing best ways of evolution, by provoking emergence of new adapted abstractions according to structural evolution of instances, and by analyzing these emergent abstractions by using metrics.

1 Introduction

Generally, a designer can choose among a great number of strategies to manage the evolution of engineering applications. Most of these strategies differ in the manner of managing evolution according to goals and needs, but they have a common point since they are defined to manage schemas and classes [6]. However, experience gained in OODB systems and applications [10] has brought to light that new needs appear more often during their manipulation, so during manipulating instances. We propose to cope with new or badly specified needs since they appear.

2 The Object Evolution: A State of the Art

In a general way, to prepare a system to evolve, it is necessary to be able to formulate changes in order to achieve the pursued goal, namely the model after evolution; to manage the impacts generated by these changes; to define the link between the starting model and the arrival one. OO defined systems and programming languages propose strategies and mechanisms to manage evolution. Experience gained in OODB design and development outlines, as well at design level as implementation one, lacks of actual evolutionary approaches. We propose to examine these strategies according to different viewpoints or *facets* of evolution:

2.1 The Three Facets of Evolution

Rather than classifying some evolutionary strategies according to some common but not exhaustive criteria, we propose a classification resting on own evolution's criteria. We consider that evolution of any OO system presents three facets:

J. Štuller et al. (Eds.): ADBIS-DASFAA 2000, LNCS 1884, pp. 387–394, 2000.

- **Type of evolution:** when needs are taken into account during the analysis and design phases, the evolutionary strategy is *preventive* or *anticipated*. When an evolutionary strategy can face new or badly specified needs, the evolution is said *curative* or *unanticipated*.
- **Object of Evolution:** the evolution can concern be the *product* (code, class, schema...) or the *process* (a part of reasoning, a development process of an application...).
- **Process of Evolution:** we distinguish two kinds of evolutionary processes: *development* and *emergence*. The development concerns classes and their impacts on corresponding sub-classes and instances. The emergence concerns instance evolution and their impacts on corresponding classes.

Each facet is represented by an axis. We obtain a three-dimension representation of the object evolution.

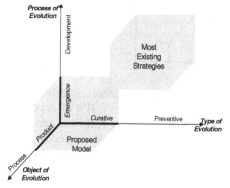

Fig. 1. Three facets of object evolution

In order to classify a strategy, we have just to answer these three questions:

1. *What kind of evolution this strategy propose (curative or preventive)?*
2. *What does it process on (product or process)?*
3. *What kind of evolutionary process does it allow (development or emergence)?*

2.2   Object Evolution Problematic under the Product Viewpoint

We restrict fig.1 to a two-dimension figure because we only consider the product. Fig.2 shows that most of OO evolutionary strategies (detailed in [9]) are preventives and allow development processes. We note that their principal lack is their inability to cope with unexpected or poorly specified needs and incomplete data. Moreover, instance evolution is always limited by class's one. Our model leads with this aspect, principally with the emergence.

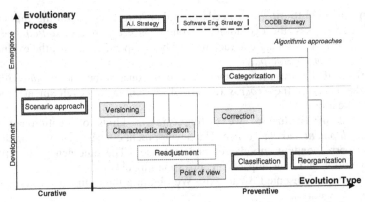

Fig. 2. Principal strategies according to the process and the type of evolution

3 The Model

Because instances are the object representatives of real entities, we consider them as full *individuals*. This leads de facto to make an analogy with living individuals, principally in their evolving and adapting feature according to their environment. We give a brief presentation of Artificial Evolution, since we use some of their principles and concepts (see [9]). Next, we present basic and advanced concepts of the model and its evolutionary processes:

3.1 Artificial Evolution

Even if they have been defined and are used in different scientific areas, Artificial Life [4] and Genetic Algorithms [3] toke their inspiration from biology in order to simulate evolutionary biological mechanisms. From evolutions and mutations, newly well adapted parts of information arise. We have been attracted by this principle. Artificial Life uses concepts of GTYPE and PTYPE (by analogy to *genotype* and *phenotype* of biology). They evolve by unceasingly interacting through *development* and *emergence* processes. Genetic Algorithms [3][5] inspire us in their mechanical operating and used operators.

3.2 Basic Concepts

- *Population and Genetic patrimony:* a group of classes representing various abstractions of the same entity forms a *population* (like members university population). All the attributes constitute its *Genetic Patrimony*.

- *Instance-PTYPE:* instances are the phenotype and represent real entities.

- *Class-GTYPE:* classes define instances features, their genetic code.

We present an example which will be taken again and unrolled all along the article :

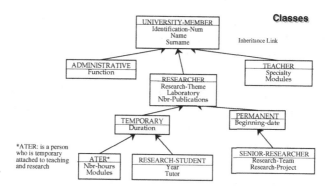

Fig. 3. Members of a university

3.3   Advanced Concepts

In a class, not every gene plays the same role or has the same prevalence. We consider that any class is entirely specified through three types of genotypes:

Fundamental Genotype FG: constituted of genes representing the minimal and fundamental semantics inherent to classes of a same population.

Inherited Genotype IG: properties inherited by a class from its super-class.

Specific Genotype SG: it consists of specific properties locally defined within a class.

Scheme: the scheme expresses in a simple and concise way, genes in the attributes and methods form. It has the same genetic structure as the represented entity. Each gene is represented by 0, 1 or #: 0 for absence of the gene, 1 for its presence and # for its indifference. The scheme is a simple and powerful means to model groups of individuals. We consider two kinds of schemes: the *permanent scheme*, associated with each specified class and having the same structure, and the *temporary scheme*, which is a selection unit of one or a group of entities (instances or classes).

3.4   Evolutionary Processes

An evolutionary process is triggered when a change, envisaged or not, appears in the model. The process must be able to detect this change, find entities implicated in the evolution and reflect this change adequately:

3.4.1   Phases

Each process is carried out in three phases: *extraction, exploration* and finally *exploitation:*

– *Extraction Phase:* extracts the object's genetic code within a temporary scheme.

– *Exploration phase:* explores all classes to locate adapted, even partially, ones. First it selects set of concerned populations, then it carries out the search in that set. *Selection is the operator used thanks to the calculation of the adaptation values Avs (section 0).*

– *Exploitation phase:* manages the impacts by development or emergence way. The *development process* represents the impact of class evolution on instances, while the *emergence processes* concern any emergence of new conceptual information, by way of impacts on classes. There are two possible outcomes: *local emergence* is related to the emergence of new information within existing class(es). The genetic code of the object has mutated and this can force mutation in its class; and the *global emergence* related to the emergence of a new conceptual entity.

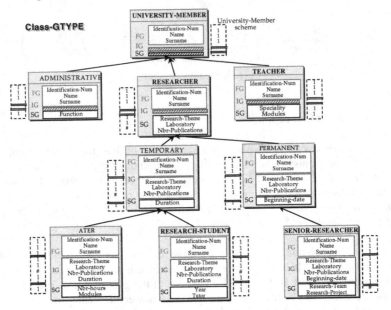

Fig. 4. the same example in our model

3.4.2 Object Operators

Basic operators are defined to handle instances and classes. This is a brief presentation (more details in [9]):

– *Selection:* is defined to determine, after structural evolution of an instance, which class holds part or all of its specification.

– *Crossing-over:* works on two entities via their scheme to interchange their genes to define a new group of genes. It constitutes the core of the emergence process (took from [8]). It amounts to granting a weight relating to parents for genes transmission to children. We add to that a significant constraint: a permanent scheme presents at most two significant blocks (after FG): IG's genes and SG' genes. When processing the crossing-over, these blocks must be respected. It is the constraint of *bocks of genes.* The crossing-over is guided by the block constraints in order to ensure a minimal coherence for emergent schemes.

– *Adaptation value Av:* calculate the semantic distance between the evolved object and classes. Denoting the evolved object's scheme by Sch_{obj} and the close class's scheme by Sch_{param}, the adaptive function is defined, using the operator $\wedge$

(and_logic): $Av\,(Sch_{param}) = \sum_{(i=1 \to n)} \{Sch_{obj}[i] \wedge Sch_{param}[i]\}/n$, where n is number of genes specified in the evolved object; i is the variable index from 1 to n, defining, at each stage, the position of two respective genes of the analyzed schemes.

- *Semantic Distance sd :* is the value which expresses the semantic proximity between an emergent scheme and one of its ancestor. It helps to choose the super-class of the new abstraction. We use the same adaptive function defined for the calculation of Avs.

3.4.3   Examples

We consider following instances evolving from their initial state and structure:

Genetic Patrimony	Instances become				
FG		O_1	O_2	O_3	O_4	O_5
	Identification-Num(1)	#3	#8	#4	#7	#1
	Name (2)	N1	N2	N3	N4	N5
	Surname (3)	P1	P2	P3	P4	P5
	Research-theme (4)	Automatic	-Mathematics	Object	Constraints	Object
	Laboratory (5)	L1	- L2	L3	L1	L5
	Nbr-Publications (6)		- 1	4	6	
	Specialty (7)					
	Modules (8)	+ Segmentation				DSI
	duration (9)				1	- 1
	Beginning-date (10)	01-10-2000		01-10-2000		01-09-2000
	Nbr-hours (11)					- 96
	Year (12)	- 1st	- 2nd	- 3rd		
	Tutor (13)	- Dupont	- Durant	- Dupond		
	Research-Team (14)	+ Vision		+ Object		
	Project-Team (15)					
	Rank	++ Professor				
	Position		++ Engineer			
	Responsibility			++ Supervisor		
	Responsible				++ Mr. X	

attribute : existing attribute	-attribute Lost attribute	+attribute : gained attribute	++attribute : new attribute

- Exploration phase: we calculate the Adaptation Value Av for each temporary scheme with each existing class:

Entity	Scheme (IG and SG)													AvO_1	AvO_2	AvO_3	AvO_4	AvO_5
Object O_1	1	1	#	#	1	0	1	0	0	0	1	#						
Object O_2	0	0	0	0	0	0	0	0	0	0	0	0						
Object O_3	1	1	1	0	0	0	1	#	0	0	1	#						
Object O_4	1	1	1	#	0	1	0	0	#	0	#	#						
Object O_5	1	1	#	#	1	0	1	0	0	0	#	#						
University-Member	0	0	0	0	0	0	0	0	0	0	0	0	0/5	0	0/5	0/4	0/4
Researcher	1	1	#	0	0	0	0	0	0	0	0	0	2/5	0	3/5	3/4	2/4
Teacher	0	0	0	1	1	0	0	0	0	0	0	0	1/5	0	0/5	0/4	1/4
Temporary	1	1	#	0	0	1	0	0	0	0	0	0	2/5	0	4/5	4/4	2/4
Permanent	1	1	1	0	0	0	1	0	0	0	0	0	3/5	0	4/5	3/4	3/4
Ater	1	1	#	0	1	1	0	1	0	0	0	0	3/5	0	3/5	4/4	3/4
Research-Student	1	1	#	0	0	1	0	0	1	1	0	0	2/5	0	3/5	4/4	2/4
Senior-Researcher	1	1	1	0	0	0	1	0	0	0	1	#	4/5	0	5/5	3/4	3/4

with :   IG   SG

Conclusions for each object: O_1 : partially adapted classes: Teacher, Ater, Research-Student and Senior-Researcher. They are candidates for crossing-over. *O_2 :* no adapted class. *O_3 :* one completely adapted class: Senior-Researcher. *O_4 :* three completely adapted classes: Temporary, Ater and Research-Student. *O_5 :* partially adapted classes: Teacher, Ater, Research-Student and Senior-Researcher. They are candidates for crossing-over

– Exploitation phase
  - O_1: *crossing-over* on Teacher, Ater and Senior-Researcher' schemes. Avp is an adaptation value which is pondered with the other Avs.

N°Population	Crossing-over
	O_1
	1
1 :	1
Teacher	#
Ater	#
Sr-Researcher	1
	0
	1
	O_1
	1
2 :	1
E1	#
E2	#
Sr-Researcher	1
	0
	1
	O_1
	1
3 :	1
E1	#
E3	#
E4	1
	0
	1

Scheme	Selected scheme
0	
	Absent gene from all schemes are ignored in the crossing-over since it has no significance

Crossing-over ends because we have two emergent schemes: E4 and E5.

– O_2: *global emergence by direct creation of the abstraction - place of insertion?* As a sub-class of University-Member because O_2 has only the FG which is common with all other classes.

  - O_3: *local emergence* of the new attribute 'Responsibility' in Senior-researcher class because it is the unique completely adapted class.
  - O_4: *global emergence by direct creation of the abstraction - place of insertion?* Three Avs are equal to 1. Among the three well-adapted classes, Temporary is the most eligible because it's the representative abstraction of the temporary subpopulation. But as it's an abstract class, O_4 represents another abstraction of temporary researchers. So, it provokes emergence of a new sub-class of temporary.
– O_5: *crossing-over* on the same population as O_1. Crossing-over steps are the same. The final step stops with the emergent scheme E5.

3.5 Discussion on Emergence

After the structural evolution of O_1, ..., O_2, the emergent processes permit to detect the kind of emergence, the abstractions concerned and also the location of changes and insertion of new classes (there are more details in [9]). But sometimes, we can just conclude that the emergent scheme is an abstraction of the permanent sub-population, but not it's precise location in this sub-population. We propose to enrich the emergence process in order to control it and to choose in a better way by using metrics.

4 Model of Metrics

We adopt for this the. We apply the GQM technique [1] in order to determine where metrics are useful in the emergence process. We take our inspiration from class context metrics [2]. We first distinguish the pertinent contexts for our model. As we want to analyze any emergent abstraction in an internal and external way, we identify two contexts for metrics:

Question	Sub-questions	Metric	Comments
Intra-Abstraction Context	the most *significant*	S=difference between scheme and instance	nearest scheme to instance
	the less *contradictory* ?	C_i= number of contradictions between attributes and attribute blocs	weaker =less contradictions
	the most *coherent*?	$C_h =\Sigma$simple attributes $+\Sigma$ attribute contradictions $+ \Sigma$ blocs $+ \Sigma$ blocs contradiction	weaker =less incoherence
Inter-Abstraction Context	*parents* ?	P_s = detection of super-class(s)	Sd
	Contradiction with *parents*?	$C_d=\Sigma$contradictory attributes$+\Sigma$contradictory blocs	weaker=less contradiction
	Coupling	$C_e = \Sigma$references towards and from other classes	weaker=minimal coupling
	Depth in hierarchy?	P_d = position inside the hierarchy	weaker=lessreorganization

Since we apply these metrics, we could better choose and apply emergence results.

5 Conclusion

The first objective of our research work is to allow a designer to attempt to apprehend and to anticipate the future changes and requirements of complex and bulky OODB applications. This is possible by simulating several evolution ways by expressing new requirements on instances. We have seen in fact that several ways of class evolution can emerge from structural instance evolution. In this paper, we propose metrics in order to analyze and control what emerge, how it can change class specifications and the possible impacts, according to two kinds of metrics: *intra-abstraction* and *inter-abstraction metrics*. Metrics are not systematically applied if the designer precise invariants to respect during evolution and emergence. All this is done in order to offer a simulation tool to help the designer for managing complex OODB applications.

Bibliography

[1] Basili, V.R., Weiss, D.,"A methodology for collecting valid software engineering data", IEEE TSE, Nov.1984 p728-738.
[2] Chidamber S.R Kemerer C.F"A Metrics Suite for OOD"IEEE TSE vol.20(6) 94, p.476-493.
[3] Goldberg D.E. "Algorithmes Génétiques", Edition Addison-Wesley, 1994
[4] Heudin J.C. "La Vie Artificielle", Edition Hermès, 1994.
[5] Holland J "Adaptation in Natural and Artificial Systems", University of Michigan Press, 75.
[6] Kim W. "Introduction to OODB", MIT Press, Cambridge Massachussetts, 1990.
[7] Napoli A. "Représentation à objets et raisonnement par classification en I.A", Thèse 1992.
[8] Syswerda G. "Uniform Crossover in Genetic Algorithms", ICGA, 1989, p.2-9.
[9] Tamzalit Oussalah"From Object Evolution to Object Emergence ACM CIKM'99 p.514-521
[10] Wei Li, J. Talburt "Empirically Analyzing OOSoftware Evolution" JOOP Sept 98, p.15-19

Author Index